6th Editi

Londe

Bus Hand

British Bus Publishing

Body codes used in the Bus Handbook series:

Type:

A	Articulated vehicle
B	Bus, either single-deck or double-deck
BC	Interurban - high-back seated bus
C	Coach
M	Minibus with design capacity of 16 seats or less
N	Low-floor bus (Niederflur), either single-deck or double-deck
O	Open-top bus (CO = convertible - PO = partial open-top)
S	Schoolbus configured with 3+2 seating

Seating capacity is then shown. For double-decks the upper deck quantity is followed by the lower deck.

Please note that seating capacities shown are generally those provided by the operator. It is common practice, however, for some vehicles to operate at different capacities when on certain duties.

Door position:-

C	Centre entrance/exit
D	Dual doorway.
F	Front entrance/exit
R	Rear entrance/exit (no distinction between doored and open)
T	Three or more access points

Equipment:-

T	Toilet	TV	Training vehicle.
M	Mail compartment	RV	Used as tow bus or engineers' vehicle.

Allocation:-

s	Ancillary vehicle
t	Training bus
u	out of service or strategic reserve; refurbishment or seasonal requirement
w	Vehicle is withdrawn and awaiting disposal.

e.g. - B32/28F is a double-deck bus with thirty-two seats upstairs, twenty-eight down and a front entrance/exit., N43D is a low-floor bus with two or more doorways.

Re-registrations:-

Where a vehicle has gained new index marks the details are listed at the end of each fleet showing the current mark, followed in sequence by those previously carried starting with the original mark.

Annual books are produced for the major groups:
The Stagecoach Bus Handbook
The First Bus Handbook
The Arriva Bus Handbook
The Go-Ahead Bus Handbook
The National Express Coach Handbook (bi-annual)

Regional books in the series:
The Scottish Bus Handbook
The Welsh Bus Handbook
The Ireland & Islands Bus Handbook
English Bus Handbook: Smaller Groups
English Bus Handbook: Notable Independents
English Bus Handbook: Coaches

Associated series:
The Hong Kong Bus Handbook
The Malta Bus Handbook
The Leyland Lynx Handbook
The Postbus Handbook
The Mailvan Handbook
The Toy & Model Bus Handbook - Volume 1 - Early Diecasts
The Fire Brigade Handbook (fleet list of each local authority fire brigade)
The Police Range Rover Handbook

Some earlier editions of these books are still available. Please contact the publisher on 01952 255669.

The London Bus Handbook

This sixth edition of the London Bus Handbook is dedicated to those operators that are contracted to Transport for London (TfL) for the provision of normal passenger services, rail replacement duties and other minor contracts. Also included are the providers of the major sightseeing tours.

During the course of a vehicle's life there are many occasions when, for a variety of reasons, it is considered desirable to move it from one depot to another, and from one fleet to another. The Bus Handbook series is concerned primarily with vehicles and features bus fleets, irrespective of the operator's disc that may be displayed.

Quality photographs for inclusion in the series are welcome, for which a fee is payable. Unfortunately the publishers cannot accept responsibility for any loss and they require that you show your name on each picture or slide. High-resolution digital images of six megapixels or higher are also welcome on CD or DVDs.

To keep the fleet information up to date we recommend the Key publication, Buses, published monthly, or for more detailed information, the PSV Circle monthly news sheets. The writer and publisher would be glad to hear from readers should any information be available which corrects or enhances that given in this publication.

Earlier editions of the London Bus Handbook are available from our website.

Series Editor: Bill Potter.
Principal Editor: Stuart Martin.

Acknowledgments:
We are grateful to the operating companies, Tom Johnson, Colin Lloyd, Andy Rigby for their assistance in the compilation of this book.
The cover photograph is by Tom Johnson; the frontispiece is by Richard Godfrey while the rear cover views are by Mark Lyons.

ISBN 9781904875567
Published by British Bus Publishing Ltd
16 St Margaret's Drive, Wellington, Telford, TF1 3PH
© British Bus Publishing Ltd, September 2013
e-mail: Orders@britishbuspublishing.co.uk
www.britishbuspublishing.co.uk

Contents

Commissioned by Transport for London (TfL) from Wrightbus, the first production examples of the New Bus for London (NBfL) have now entered service. Our cover shows TL13, LTZ1013, shortly after entering service with Metroline at their Holloway depot, while the frontispiece shows LT1 passing Hyde Park Corner while operating route 38.

Below is the latest integral single-deck from Wrightbus, the Streetlite, shown here as a wheel-forward (WF) model. Go-Ahead's WS2, LJ12CGG, is seen at Limes Farm. *Richard Godfrey*

ABELLIO

Abellio Group Ltd, 301 Camberwell New Road, London SE5 0TF

2401-2413			ADL Trident E400H		10.2m	ADL Enviro 400 4.4m		N37/24D		2011-12	
2401	WL	SN61DFL	2405	WL	SN61DFV	2408	WL	SN61DFZ	2411	WL	SN61DGO
2402	WL	SN61DFO	2406	WL	SN61DFX	2409	WL	SN61DGE	2412	WL	SN61DGU
2403	WL	SN61DFP	2407	WL	SN61DFY	2410	WL	SN61DGF	2413	WL	SN61DGV
2404	WL	SN61DFU									

2414-2443			ADL Trident E400H		10.2m	ADL Enviro 400 4.4m		N37/24D		2012	
2414	QB	SN61DGX	2422	QB	SN61CYC	2430	QB	SN61CYO	2437	QB	SN61CYX
2415	QB	SN61DGY	2423	QB	SN61CYE	2431	QB	SN61CYP	2438	QB	SN12AUE
2416	QB	SN61DGZ	2424	QB	SN61CYF	2432	QB	SN61CYS	2439	QB	SN12AUF
2417	QB	SN61DHA	2425	QB	SN61CYG	2433	QB	SN61CYT	2440	QB	SN12AUH
2418	QB	SN61CXX	2426	QB	SN61CYH	2434	QB	SN61CYU	2441	QB	SN12AUJ
2419	QB	SN61CXY	2427	QB	SN61CYJ	2435	QB	SN61CYV	2442	QB	SN12AUK
2420	QB	SN61CXZ	2428	QB	SN61CYK	2436	QB	SN61CYW	2443	QB	SN12AUL
2421	QB	SN61CYA	2429	QB	SN61CYL						

4001-4004			DAF DB250			Optare Spectra		N48/29F		1998	Reading Buses, 2011-12
4001	BF	S876BYJ	4002	BF	S877BYJ	4003	BF	S878BYJ	4004	BF	S881BYJ

8001-8004			ADL Dart 8.8m			ADL Mini Pointer		N29F		2006	
8001	BF	LJ56ONH	8002	BF	LJ56ONK	8003	BF	LJ56ONL	8004	BF	LJ56ONM

8013-8020			ADL Dart 8.8m			ADL Mini Pointer		N29F		2004	
8013	BC	BX54DLZ	8015	BC	BX54DMF	8017	BC	BX54DMU	8019	BC	BX54DMY
8014	BC	BX54DME	8016	BC	BX54DMO	8018	BC	BX54DMV	8020	BC	BX54DMZ

8024-8037			ADL Dart 8.8m			ADL Mini Pointer		N29F		2005	8033 Bennet, Kilwinning,' 12
8024	BC	BU05HDY	8027	BC	BU05HFB	8031	BC	BU05HFK	8036	BC	BU05HFW
8025	BC	BU05HEJ	8028	BC	BU05HFC	8033	TF	BU05HFN	8037	BC	BU05HFX
8026	BC	BU05HFA	8029	BC	BU05HFD	8035	BC	BU05HFV			

Abellio is a division of Nederlands Railways established to operate public transport contracts outside the Netherlands and currently has bases in several European countries, notably in the UK, Germany and the Czech Republic. The London and Surrey operations were acquired from National Express. Pictured in Parliament Square in June 2013 is a hybrid version of the Enviro 400, 2417, SN61DHA. *Richard Godfrey*

One of a pair of Alexander-Dennis Mini Pointer Darts acquired from Bluebird of Middleton, a district of Rochdale, is MX56HYR, now numbered 8116 with Abellio. It is seen in Twickenham Road, Isleworth, while operating route H20. *Mark Lyons*

8041-8062

						Dennis Dart SLF 8.8m			Plaxton Pointer MPD			N27F*	2000-01	*8058-62 are N29F
8041	WS	V301MDP	8045	u	V305MDP	8051	w	X311KRX	8058	TF	Y864KTF
8042	BF	V302MDP	8046	BF	V306MDP	8053	WL	X313KRX	8061	WS	X322KRX
8043	u	V303MDP	8047	BF	V307MDP	8054	BF	X314KRX	8062	WS	Y38YVV
8044	BC	V304MDP	8049	BF	V309MDP						

| 8064 | BF | RA51KVS | Dennis Dart SLF 8.8m | | | Plaxton Pointer MPD | | | N29F | 2002 |

8065-8074

						TransBus Dart 8.8m			TransBus Mini Pointer			N29F	2002	Wings Buses, 2004
8065	BC	SK02TZN	8068	BF	SK02TZR	8071	BF	SK02TZU	8073	BF	SK02TZW
8066	BF	SK02TZO	8069	BF	SK02TZS	8072	BF	SK02TZV	8074	BF	SK02TZX
8067	BF	SK02TZP	8070	BF	SK02TZT						

8086-8095

						TransBus Dart 8.8m			TransBus Mini Pointer			N29F	2003
8086	BF	KV03ZFM	8089	BF	KV03ZFR	8092	BF	KV03ZFU	8094	BF	KV03ZFX
8087	BF	KV03ZFN	8090	BF	KV03ZFS	8093	BF	KV03ZFW	8095	BF	KV03ZFY
8088	BF	KV03ZFP	8091	BF	KV03ZFT						

8101-8109

						ADL Dart 4 8.9m			ADL Enviro 200			N26F	2006-08
8101	TF	LJ56VSP	8104	TF	LJ56VSV	8106	TF	LJ56VSY	8108	BC	YX58DTY
8102	TF	LJ56VST	8105	TF	LJ56VSX	8107	BC	YX58DTV	8109	BC	YX58DTZ
8103	TF	LJ56VSU									

8110	TF	SN04EGD	TransBus Dart 8.8m	TransBus Mini Pointer	N23F	2004	Rotala, 2012
8111	TF	SN04EFJ	TransBus Dart 8.8m	TransBus Mini Pointer	N23F	2004	Rotala, 2012
8112	TF	DK04SUU	TransBus Dart 8.8m	TransBus Mini Pointer	N23F	2004	Rotala, 2012
8113	WS	KX06LYS	ADL Dart 8.8m	ADL Mini Pointer	N24F	2006	Jack, Edinburgh, 2012
8114	WS	KX06LYT	ADL Dart 8.8m	ADL Mini Pointer	N24F	2006	Jack, Edinburgh, 2012
8115	WS	KX56HCZ	ADL Dart 8.8m	ADL Mini Pointer	N24F	2006	Thames Travel, 2012
8116	TF	MX56HYR	ADL Dart 8.8m	ADL Mini Pointer	N23F	2006	Bluebird, Middleton, 2012
8117	TF	MX56HYS	ADL Dart 8.8m	ADL Mini Pointer	N23F	2006	Bluebird, Middleton, 2012

London Bus Handbook

The latest delivery of Enviro 200s comprises ten of the shortest model, the 8.9 metre version. Illustrating the full-height off-side door fitted to the latest version is 8118, YX13EHE, one of the type to be assembled at the Scarborough facility of ADL, more commonly known as Plaxtons. *Mark Lyons*

8118-8127

			ADL E20D 8.9m			ADL Enviro 200		N29F	2013		
8118	TF	YX13EHE	8121	TF	YX13EHH	8124	TF	YX13EHL	8126	TF	YX13EHN
8119	TF	YX13EHF	8122	TF	YX13EHJ	8125	TF	YX13EHM	8127	TF	YX13EHO
8120	TF	YX13EHG	8123	TF	YX13EHK						

8301-8318

			ADL Dart 10.2m			ADL Pointer		N27D	2004		
8301	WL	BX54DKA	8304	WL	BX54DKF	8307	WL	BX54DKL	8310	WL	BX54DKV
8302	WL	BX54DKD	8305	WL	BX54DKJ	8308	WL	BX54DKO	8318	WL	BX54DLU
8303	WL	BX54DKE	8306	WL	BX54DKK	8309	WL	BX54DKU			

8321-8329

			ADL Dart 4 9.4m			ADL Enviro 200		N24D	2010		
8321	WL	YX10EBA	8324	WL	YX10EBF	8326	WL	YX10EBJ	8328	WL	YX10EBL
8322	WL	YX10EBC	8325	WL	YX10EBG	8327	WL	YX10EBK	8329	WL	YX10EBM
8323	WL	YX10EBD									

8330-8342

			ADL Dart 4 9.4m			ADL Enviro 200		N24D	2011		
8330	WL	YX11AHA	8334	WL	YX11AHF	8337	WL	YX11AHK	8340	WL	YX11AHO
8331	WL	YX11AHC	8335	WL	YX11AHG	8338	WL	YX11AHL	8341	WL	YX11AHP
8332	WL	YX11AHD	8336	WL	YX11AHJ	8339	WL	YX11AHN	8342	WL	YX11AHU
8333	WL	YX11AHE									

8417	u	W435CRN	Dennis Dart SLF 10.3m	East Lancs EL2000	N30D	2000	Wings Buses, 2004
8418	u	W436CRN	Dennis Dart SLF 10.3m	East Lancs EL2000	N30D	2000	Wings Buses, 2004
8419	u	W437CRN	Dennis Dart SLF 10.3m	East Lancs EL2000	N30D	2000	Wings Buses, 2004

8434-8440

			Dennis Dart SLF 10.1m			Plaxton Pointer 2		N30D	2001		
8434	u	RX51FGG	8436	u	RX51FGK	8438	WS	RX51FGN	8440	QB	RX51FGP
8435	u	RX51FGJ	8437	QB	RX51FGM	8439	TF	RX51FGO			

8441-8452

			TransBus Dart 10.1m			TransBus Pointer		N35F	2002		
8441	BF	KM02HFP	8444	BF	KM02HFT	8447	TF	RD02BJK	8450	TF	RD02BJV
8442	BF	KM02HFR	8445	BF	KM02HFU	8448	TF	RD02BJO	8451	TF	RD02BJX
8443	BF	KM02HFS	8446	BF	KM02HFV	8449	TF	RD02BJU	8452	BF	RD02BJZ

Caetano Nimbus-bodied Dart 8490, KX03HZS, is seen on route 112 at Ealing Common. The bodywork was only ever constructed on the Dart chassis at Waterlooville in what was the UVG facility. *Dave Heath*

8460-8465
Dennis Dart SLF 10.5m   Caetano Nimbus   N29D   2001-02

8460	TF	RL02FOT	8462	TF	RL02FVM	8464	WS	RL02ZTB	8465	WS	RL02ZTC
8461	TF	RL02FOU	8463	WS	RL02FVN						

8466   WS   GM03TGM   TransBus Dart SLF 10.5m   Caetano Nimbus   N29D   2003

8467-8472
TransBus Dart SLF 10.5m   Caetano Nimbus   N29D   2004

8467	WS	HX04HTP	8469	WS	HX04HTU	8471	BC	HX04HTY	8472	BC	HX04HTZ
8468	WS	HX04HTT	8470	WS	HX04HTV						

8473-8477
ADL Dart 10.1m   ADL Pointer   N28D   2006

8473	BC	LF06YRJ	8475	BC	LF06YRL	8476	BC	LF06YRM	8477	BC	LF06YRN
8474	BC	LF06YRK									

8478-8487
Dennis Dart SLF 10.1m   Plaxton Pointer   N27D   2002   Armchair, Brentford

8478	TF	KP02PWV	8481	TF	KP02PVU	8484	TF	KM02HGE	8486	TF	KU52YKR
8479	TF	KP02PVE	8482	TF	KM02HGF	8485	TF	KU52YKO	8487	TF	KU52YKS
8480	TF	KP02PUK	8483	TF	KP02PUJ						

8488-8494
TransBus Dart 10.5m   Caetano Nimbus   N30D   2003   Ealing CT

8488	BC	KX03HZF	8490	WS	KX03HZS	8492	BC	KX03HZV	8494	BC	KX03HZZ
8489	WS	KX03HZR	8491	BC	KX03HZT	8493	BC	KX03HZY			

8495-8499
TransBus Dart 10.5m   Caetano Nimbus   N30D   2004   Burton, Haverhill, 2012

8495	BC	KX04HRD	8497	BC	KX04HRF	8498	BC	KX04HRG	8499	WS	KX04HRW
8496	BC	KX04HRE									

8501-8506
ADL Dart 4 10.2m   ADL Enviro 200   N29D   2006

8501	BC	LJ56ONN	8503	BC	LJ56ONP	8505	BC	LJ56ONS	8506	BC	LJ56ONT
8502	BC	LJ56ONO	8504	BC	LJ56ONR						

8507-8515
ADL Dart 4 10.2m   ADL Enviro 200   N29D   2008

8507	TF	LJ08CZP	8510	TF	LJ08CZT	8512	TF	LJ08CZV	8514	TF	LJ08CZY
8508	TF	LJ08CZR	8511	TF	LJ08CZU	8513	TF	LJ08CZX	8515	TF	LJ08CZZ
8509	TF	LJ08CZS									

8516-8528 — ADL Dart 4 10.2m / ADL Enviro 200 — N29D — 2009

8516	BC	YX59BYJ	8520	BC	YX59BYN	8523	BC	YX59BYR	8526	BC	YX59BYU
8517	BC	YX59BYK	8521	BC	YX59BYO	8524	BC	YX59BYS	8527	BC	YX59BYV
8518	BC	YX59BYL	8522	BC	YX59BYP	8525	BC	YX59BYT	8528	BC	YX59BYW
8519	BC	YX59BYM									

8529-8566 — ADL Dart 4 10.2m / ADL Enviro 200 — N29D — 2010-11

8529	TF	YX10FEF	8539	TF	YX10FEV	8549	TF	YX10FFL	8558	QB	YX11AEG
8530	TF	YX10FEG	8540	TF	YX10FFA	8550	TF	YX10FFM	8559	QB	YX11AEJ
8531	TF	YX10FEH	8541	TF	YX10FFB	8551	TF	YX10FFN	8560	QB	YX11AEK
8532	TF	YX10FEJ	8542	TF	YX10FFC	8552	QB	YX11AEA	8561	QB	YX11AEL
8533	TF	YX10FEK	8543	TF	YX10FFD	8553	QB	YX11AEB	8562	QB	YX11AEM
8534	TF	YX10FEM	8544	TF	YX10FFE	8554	QB	YX11AEC	8563	QB	YX11AEN
8535	TF	YX10FEO	8545	TF	YX10FFG	8555	QB	YX11AED	8564	QB	YX11AEO
8536	TF	YX10FEP	8546	TF	YX10FFH	8556	QB	YX11AEE	8565	QB	YX11AEP
8537	TF	YX10FET	8547	TF	YX10FFJ	8557	QB	YX11AEF	8566	QB	YX11AET
8538	TF	YX10FEU	8548	TF	YX10FFK						

8567-8575 — ADL Dart 4 10.2m / ADL Enviro 200 — N29D — 2011

8567	TF	YX11HPA	8570	TF	YX11HPF	8572	TF	YX61BXG	8574	TF	YX11HPN
8568	TF	YX11HPC	8571	TF	YX11HPJ	8573	TF	YX11HPL	8575	TF	YX11HOA
8569	TF	YX11HPE									

8577-8591 — ADL Dart 4 10.2m / ADL Enviro 200 — N29D — 2012

8577	TF	YX61GAA	8581	TF	YX61GBF	8585	WS	LX62DDE	8589	WS	LX62DVA
8578	TF	YX61GAO	8582	TF	YX61GBO	8586	WS	LX62DDO	8590	WS	LX62DVC
8579	TF	YX61GAU	8583	WS	LX62DAO	8587	WS	LX62DFE	8591	WS	LX62DVG
8580	TF	YX61GBE	8584	WS	LX62DBU	8588	WS	LX62DFO			

8726-8727

8726	BF	W606VGM	Dennis Dart SLF 10.7m	Plaxton Pointer 2	N32D	2000	TGM Logistics, 2012
8727	BF	W607VGM	Dennis Dart SLF 10.7m	Plaxton Pointer 2	N32D	2000	TGM Logistics, 2012

8743-8753 — Dennis Dart SLF 11m / Caetano Nimbus — N33D — 2003

8743	TF	RN52EYK	8746	TF	RN52FPC	8749	TF	RN52FVR	8752	TF	RN52FYO
8744	TF	RN52EYL	8747	TF	RN52FRD	8750	TF	RN52FVS	8753	TF	RN52FZA
8745	TF	RN52FPA	8748	TF	RN52FRF	8751	TF	RN52FXD			

8761-8774 — ADL Dart 11.6m / East Lancs Myllennium — N39F* — 2006-07 — *seating varies

8761	BF	LK55ACX	8765	BF	LK06BWD	8769	BF	LK56JKN	8772	BF	LK07CBF
8762	BF	LK55ADU	8766	BF	LK56JKE	8770	BF	LK56JKO	8773	BF	LK07CBV
8763	BF	LK55ADV	8767	BF	LK56JKF	8771	BF	LK56JKV	8774	BF	LK07CBX
8764	BF	LK06BWC	8768	BF	LK56JKJ						

Outside the Transport for London (TfL) area the livery applied is mostly white as shown by 8771, LK56JKV, at Hampton Court. This East Lancs Spryte-bodied Dart operates a tendered service for Surrey County Council. The batch was initially operated for Surrey by First. *Richard Godfrey*

A second view of one of the East Lancs Spryte-bodied Darts, this time showing the nearside. Production of this model at the Blackburn facility ceased following the acquisition of East Lancs by Optare. 8761, LK55ACX, is seen at Lyleham in Surrey. *Mark Lyons*

8775-8793

ADL Dart 4 10.8m — ADL Enviro 200 — N31D — 2011-12

8775	BC	YX61ELC	8780	BC	YX12DLJ	8785	BC	YX12DLV	8790	TF	YX12GHD
8776	BC	YX61ELH	8781	BC	YX12DLK	8786	BC	YX12DLY	8791	TF	YX12GHF
8777	BC	YX12DLD	8782	BC	YX12DLN	8787	BC	YX12DLZ	8792	TF	YX12GHG
8778	BC	YX12DLE	8783	BC	YX12DLO	8788	TF	YX12GHA	8793	TF	YX12GHH
8779	BC	YX12DLF	8784	BC	YX12DLU	8789	TF	YX12GHB			

8806-8817

ADL Dart 4 10.8m — ADL Enviro 200 — N31D — 2013

8806	TF	YX13EFM	8809	TF	YX13EFP	8812	TF	YX13EFT	8815	TF	YX13EFW
8807	TF	YX13EFN	8810	TF	YX13EFR	8813	TF	YX13EFU	8816	TF	YX13EFY
8808	TF	YX13EFO	8811	TF	YX13EFS	8814	TF	YX13EFV	8817	TF	YX13EFZ

8852	BF	YP02LCF	Optare Solo M850	Optare	N28F	2002

9001-9020

Volvo B7TL 10.6m — Wrightbus Eclipse Gemini — N45/24D — 2004

9001	WL	BX54DHJ	9006	WL	BX54DHO	9011	WL	BX54DJD	9016	WL	BX54DJO
9002	WL	BX54DHK	9007	WL	BX54DHP	9012	WL	BX54DJE	9017	WL	BX54DJU
9003	WL	BX54DHL	9008	WL	BX54DHV	9013	WL	BX54DJF	9018	WL	BX54DJV
9004	WL	BX54DHM	9009	WL	BX54DHY	9014	WL	BX54DJJ	9019	WL	BX54DJY
9005	WL	BX54DHN	9010	WL	BX54DHZ	9015	WL	BX54DJK	9020	WL	BX54DJZ

9021-9065

Volvo B7TL 10.6m — Wrightbus Eclipse Gemini — N45/24D — 2005

9021	BC	BX55XLS	9033	BC	BX55XMG	9044	WL	BX55XMV	9055	WL	BX55XNJ
9022	BC	BX55XLT	9034	WL	BX55XMH	9045	WL	LF55CZA	9056	WL	BX55XNK
9023	BC	BX55XLU	9035	WL	BX55XMJ	9046	WL	BX55XMW	9057	WL	BX55XNL
9024	BC	BX55XLV	9036	WL	BX55XMK	9047	WL	BX55XMZ	9058	WL	BX55XNM
9025	BC	BX55XLW	9037	WL	BX55XML	9048	WL	LF55CYZ	9059	WL	BX55XNN
9026	BC	BX55XLY	9038	WL	BX55XMM	9049	WL	LF55CYY	9060	WL	BX55XNO
9027	BC	BX55XLZ	9039	WL	BX55XMP	9050	WL	LF55CYX	9061	WL	BX55XNP
9028	BC	BX55XMA	9040	WL	BX55XMR	9051	WL	LF55CYW	9062	WL	BX55XNR
9029	BC	BX55XMB	9041	WL	BX55XMS	9052	WL	LF55CYV	9063	WL	BX55XNS
9030	BC	BX55XMC	9042	WL	BX55XMT	9053	WL	LF55CZB	9064	WL	BX55XNT
9031	BC	BX55XMD	9043	WL	BX55XMU	9054	WL	BX55XNG	9065	WL	BX55XNU
9032	BC	BX55XME									

The first Enviro 400 body was unveiled at the *Coach and Bus 2005 show*. This was also the first of the Trident 2 model chassis; the Trident 2 being the successor in the UK to the Trident (1) 2-axle model. From 2012 the name of the ADL chassis for the product was changed to the E40D or E40H for the hybrid version. 9530, SN12ABO, is shown. *Dave Heath*

9066-9073

Volvo B7TL 10.6m   Wrightbus Eclipse Gemini   N45/23D   2006

9066	BC	BX55XNV	9068	BC	BX55XNY	9070	WL	LF06YRC	9072	BC	LF06YRE
9067	BC	BX55XNW	9069	WL	BX55XNZ	9071	BC	LF06YRD	9073	BC	LF06YRG

9401-9427

ADL Trident 2 10.2m   ADL Enviro400   N41/26D   2007

9401	QB	LJ56VSZ	9408	QB	LJ56VTK	9415	QB	LJ56VTU	9422	QB	LJ56VUB
9402	QB	LJ56VTA	9409	QB	LJ56VTL	9416	QB	LJ56VTV	9423	QB	LJ56VUC
9403	QB	LJ56VTC	9410	QB	LJ56VTM	9417	QB	LJ56VTW	9424	QB	LJ56VUD
9404	QB	LJ56VTD	9411	QB	LJ56VTN	9418	QB	LJ56VTX	9425	QB	LJ56VUE
9405	QB	LJ56VTE	9412	QB	LJ56VTO	9419	QB	LJ56VTY	9426	QB	LJ56VUF
9406	QB	LJ56VTF	9413	QB	LJ56VTP	9420	QB	LJ56VTZ	9427	QB	LJ56VUG
9407	QB	LJ56VTG	9414	QB	LJ56VTT	9421	QB	LJ56VUA			

9428-9466

ADL Trident 2 10.2m   ADL Enviro400   N41/26D   2009

9428	WL	LJ09CAA	9438	WL	LJ09CBX	9448	WL	LJ09CCX	9458	WL	LJ09CDX
9429	WL	LJ09CAE	9439	WL	LJ09CBY	9449	WL	LJ09CCY	9459	WL	LJ09CDY
9430	WL	LJ09CAO	9440	WL	LJ09CCA	9450	WL	LJ09CCZ	9460	WL	LJ09CDZ
9431	WL	LJ09CAU	9441	WL	LJ09CCD	9451	WL	LJ09CDE	9461	WL	LJ09CEA
9432	WL	LJ09CAV	9442	WL	LJ09CCE	9452	WL	LJ09CDF	9462	WL	LJ09CEF
9433	WL	LJ09CAX	9443	WL	LJ09CCF	9453	WL	LJ09CDK	9463	WL	LJ09CEK
9434	WL	LJ09CBF	9444	WL	LJ09CCK	9454	WL	LJ09CDN	9464	WL	LJ09CEN
9435	WL	LJ09CBO	9445	WL	LJ09CCN	9455	WL	LJ09CDO	9465	WL	LJ09CEO
9436	WL	LJ09CBU	9446	WL	LJ09CCO	9456	WL	LJ09CDU	9466	WL	LJ09CEU
9437	WL	LJ09CBV	9447	WL	LJ09CCU	9457	WL	LJ09CDV			

9467-9504

ADL Trident 2 10.2m   ADL Enviro400   N41/26D   2009

9467	QB	LJ09OJZ	9477	QB	LJ09OKL	9487	QB	LJ09OKW	9496	QB	LJ09OLK
9468	QB	LJ09OKA	9478	QB	LJ09OKM	9488	QB	LJ09OKX	9497	QB	LJ09OLM
9469	QB	LJ09OKB	9479	QB	LJ09OKN	9489	QB	LJ09OKZ	9498	QB	LJ09OLN
9470	QB	LJ09OKC	9480	QB	LJ09OKO	9490	QB	LJ09OLA	9499	QB	LJ09OLO
9471	QB	LJ09OKD	9481	QB	LJ09OKP	9491	QB	LJ09OLB	9500	QB	LJ09OLP
9472	QB	LJ09OKE	9482	QB	LJ09OKR	9492	QB	LJ09OLC	9501	QB	LJ09OLR
9473	QB	LJ09OKF	9483	QB	LJ09OKS	9493	QB	LJ09OLE	9502	QB	LJ09OLT
9474	QB	LJ09OKG	9484	QB	LJ09OKT	9494	QB	LJ09OLG	9503	QB	LJ09OLU
9475	QB	LJ09OKH	9485	QB	LJ09OKU	9495	QB	LJ09OLH	9504	QB	LF59XDZ
9476	QB	LJ09OKK	9486	QB	LJ09OKV						

Inherited from National Express are four batches of the Trident (1) 2-axle model, all fitted with the ALX400 body designed by Alexanders team in Falkirk. From the 2001 delivery, 9769, YN51KWD, is shown on route 350 at Colnbrook. *Mark Lyons*

9505-9523

ADL Trident 2 10.2m   ADL Enviro 400   N41/26D   2009

9505	QB	SN59AVR	9510	QB	SN59AVX	9515	QB	SN59AWF	9520	QB	SN59AWO
9506	QB	SN59AVT	9511	QB	SN59AVY	9516	QB	SN59AWG	9521	QB	SN59AWP
9507	QB	SN59AVU	9512	QB	SN59AVZ	9517	QB	SN59AWH	9522	QB	SN59AWR
9508	QB	SN59AVV	9513	QB	SN59AWA	9518	QB	SN59AWJ	9523	QB	SN59AWU
9509	QB	SN59AVW	9514	QB	SN59AWC	9519	QB	SN59AWM			

9524-9558

ADL E40D 9.9m   ADL Enviro 400   N41/26D   2012

9524	QB	SN12AAV	9533	QB	SN12ABX	9542	QB	SN12ACZ	9551	QB	SN12AOY
9525	QB	SN12AAX	9534	QB	SN12ABZ	9543	QB	SN12ADO	9552	QB	SN12AOZ
9526	QB	SN12AAY	9535	QB	SN12ACF	9544	QB	SN12AUO	9553	QB	SN12APF
9527	QB	SN12AAZ	9536	QB	SN12ACJ	9545	QB	SN12AOS	9554	QB	SN12APK
9528	QB	SN12ABF	9537	QB	SN12ACO	9546	QB	SN12AOT	9555	QB	SN12APO
9529	QB	SN12ABK	9538	QB	SN12ACU	9547	QB	SN12AOU	9556	QB	SN12APU
9530	QB	SN12ABO	9539	QB	SN12ACV	9548	QB	SN12AOV	9557	QB	SN12APV
9531	QB	SN12ABU	9540	QB	SN12ACX	9549	QB	SN12AOW	9558	QB	SN12APX
9532	QB	SN12ABV	9541	QB	SN12ACY	9550	QB	SN12AOX			

9705-9729

Dennis Trident 9.9m   Alexander ALX400 4.4m   N45/20D   2000

9705	w	V305KGW	9715	BF	V315KGW	9725	BF	V325KGW	9729	w	V329KGW
9709	w	V309KGW									

9733-9772

Dennis Trident 9.9m   Alexander ALX400 4.4m   N43/19D   2001

9733	BF	Y133HWB	9744	WL	YN51KVA	9756	WL	YN51KVO	9766	WS	YN51KWA
9734	BF	Y134HWB	9747	WL	YN51KVD	9757	BC	YN51KVP	9767	WS	YN51KWB
9735	BF	Y235HWB	9750	QB	YN51KVG	9759	QB	YN51KVS	9768	WS	YN51KWC
9736	BF	Y36HWB	9751	QB	YN51KVH	9761	WL	YN51KVU	9769	WS	YN51KWD
9737	BF	Y37HWB	9752	BC	YN51KVJ	9763	WS	YN51KVW	9770	WS	YN51KWE
9739	WL	YN51KUU	9753	WL	YN51KVK	9764	WS	YN51KVX	9771	WS	YN51KWF
9741	WL	YN51KUW	9754	WL	YN51KVL	9765	WS	YN51KVZ	9772	WS	YN51KWG

9812-9829

TransBus Trident 9.9m   TransBus ALX400 4.4m   N43/19D   2002

9812	WL	LG52HWN	9817	QB	LG52XYM	9822	QB	LG52XYZ	9826	QB	LG52XYL
9813	QB	LG52XZB	9818	QB	LG52XYP	9823	QB	LG52XZA	9827	QB	LG52XZT
9814	QB	LB52URZ	9819	QB	LG52XYO	9824	QB	LG52XZS	9828	WL	LG52XYJ
9815	QB	LG52XWE	9820	QB	LG52XYN	9825	QB	LG52XZR	9829	WL	LG52XWD
9816	QB	LG52XYK	9821	QB	LG52XYY						

9830-9843 TransBus Trident 9.9m   TransBus ALX400   N43/19D 2003 Metroline, 2011

9830	WL	KN52NCE	9835	WL	KN52NDG	9838	WL	KN52NDZ	9841	WL	KN52NEU
9832	WL	KN52NDD	9836	WL	KN52NDJ	9839	WL	KN52NEJ	9842	WL	KN52NEY
9833	WL	KN52NDE	9837	WL	KN52NDY	9840	WL	KN52NEO	9843	WL	KN52NFA
9834	WL	KN52NDF									

Ancillary vehicles:

8723	QBt	W603UGM	Dennis Dart SLF 10.7m	Plaxton Pointer 2	N32D	2000	
8901	QBt	SN51SXK	Dennis Dart SLF 10.1m	Plaxton Pointer 2	N29D	2001	London United, 2010
8902	QBt	SN51SZF	Dennis Dart SLF 10.1m	Plaxton Pointer 2	N29D	2001	London United, 2010

Depots and allocations:

Battersea (Silverthorne Road) - QB

Dart	8440							
Enviro 200	8552	8553	8554	8555	8556	8557	8558	8559
	8560	8561	8562	8563	8564	8565	8566	
Trident	9751	9758	9813	9814	9815	9816	9817	9818
	9819	9820	9821	9822	9823	9824	9825	9826
	9827	9828	9829					
Enviro 400	9401	9402	9403	9404	9405	9406	9407	9408
	9409	9410	9411	9412	9413	9414	9415	9416
	9417	9418	9419	9420	9421	9422	9423	9424
	9425	9426	9427	9467	9468	9469	9470	9471
	9472	9473	9474					
	9475	9476	9477	9478	9479	9480	9481	9482
	9483	9484	9485	9486	9487	9488	9489	9490
	9491	9492	9493	9494	9495	9496	9497	9498
	9499	9500	9501	9502	9503	9504	9505	9506
	9507	9508	9509	9510	9511	9512	9513	9514
	9515	9516	9517	9518	9519	9520	9521	9522
	9523	9524	9525	9526	9527	9528	9529	9530
	9531	9532	9533	9534	9535	9536	9537	9538
	9539	9540	9541	9542	9543	9544	9545	9546
	9547	9548	9549	9550	9551	9552	9553	9554
	9555	9565	9557	9558				
Enviro 400 Hybrid	2414	2415	2416	2417	2418	2419	2420	2421
	2422	2423	2424	2425	2426	2427	2428	2429
	2430	2431	2432	2433	2434	2435	2436	2437
	2438	2439	2440	2441	2442	2443		

Beddington Cross (Beddington Lane) - BC

Dart	8013	8014	8015	8016	8017	8018	8019	8020
	8024	8025	8026	8027	8028	8029	8031	8035
	8036	8037	8044	8061	8062	8065	8471	8472
	8473	8474	8475	8476	8477			
Enviro 200	8107	8108	8109	8488	8491	8492	8493	8494
	8495	8496	8497	8498	8501	8502	8503	8504
	8505	8506	8516	8517	8518	8519	8520	8521
	8522	8523	8524	8525	8526	8527	8528	8775
	8776	8777	8778	8779	8780	8781	8782	8783
	8784	8785	8786	8787				
Volvo B7TL	9021	9022	9023	9024	9025	9026	9027	9028
	9029	9030	9031	9032	9033	9066	9067	9068
	9071	9072	9073					

Byfleet (Wintersells Road) - BF

Solo	8842	8844	8848	8852				
Dart	8001	8002	8003	8004	8042	8046	8047	8048
	8049	8054	8058	8058	8064	8066	8067	8068
	8069	8070	8071	8072	8073	8074	8086	8087
	8088	8089	8090	8091	8092	8093	8094	8095
	8441	8442	8443	8444	8445	8446	8452	9726
	8727	8761	8762	8763	8764	8765	8766	8767
	8768	8769	8770	8771	8772	8773	8774	8842
	8844	8850	8852					

DAF DB250	4001	4002	4003	4004				
Trident	9715	9725	9733	9734	9735	9736	9737	

Hayes (North Hyde Gardens) - WS

Dart	8041	8051	8113	8114	8115	8438	8463	8464
	8465	8467	8468	8469	8470	8471	8472	8490
	8499							
Enviro 200	8583	8584	8585	8586	8587	8588	8589	
	8590	8591						
Trident	9763	9764	9765	9766	9767	9768	9769	9770
	9771	9772						

Twickenham (Stanley Road) - TF

Dart	8033	8101	8101	8102	8103	8104	8105	8106
	8110	8111	8112	8116	8117	8439	8447	8448
	8449	8450	8451	8460	8461	8462	8478	8479
	8480	8481	8482	8483	8484	8485	8486	8487
	8743	8744	8745	8746	8747	8748	8749	8750
	8751	8752	8753					
Enviro 200	8118	8119	8120	8121	8122	8123	8124	8125
	8126	8127	8507	8508	8509	8510	8511	8512
	8513	8514	8515	8529	8530	8531	8532	8533
	8534	8535	8536	8537	8538	8539	8540	8541
	8542	8543	8544	8545	8546	8547	8548	8549
	8550	8551	8567	8568	8569	8570	8571	8572
	8573	8574	8575	8576	8577	8578	8579	8580
	8581	8582	8788	8789	8790	8791	8792	8793
	8806	8807	8808	8809	8810	8811	8812	8813
	8814	8815	8816	8817	8806			
Trident	9715	9723	9725					

Walworth (Camberwell New Road) - WL

Dart	8053		8301	8302	8303	8304	8305	
	8306	8307	8308	8309	8310	8318		
Enviro 200	8321	8322	8323	8324	8325	8326	8327	8328
	8329	8330	8331	8332	8333	8334	8335	8336
	8337	8338	8339	8340	8341	8342		
Volvo B7TL	9001	9002	9003	9004	9005	9006	9007	9008
	9009	9010	9011	9012	9013	9014	9016	9017
	9018	9019	9020	9034	9035	9036	9037	9038
	9039	9040	9041	9042	9043	9044	9045	9046
	9047	9048	9049	9050	9051	9052	9054	9055
	9056	9057	9058	9059	9060	9061	9062	9063
	9064	9065	9069	9070				
Trident	9739	9741	9744	9747	9753	9754	9756	9761
	9828	9829	9830	9832	9833	9834	9835	9836
	9837	9838	9839	9840	9841	9842	9843	
Enviro 400	9812	9428	9429	9430	9431	9432	9433	9434
	9435	9436	9437	9438	9439	9440	9441	9442
	9443	9444	9445	9446	9447	9448	9449	9450
	9451	9452	9453	9454	9455	9456	9457	9458
	9459	9460	9461	9462	9463	9464	9465	9466
Enviro 400 Hybrid	2401	2402	2403	2404	2405	2406	2407	2408
	2409	2410	2411	2412	2413			

Unallocated/stored - u/w

Remainder

ARRIVA LONDON

Arriva London North Ltd, 16 Watsons Road, Wood Green, London, N22 7TZ

Arriva London South Ltd, Croydon Bus Garage, Brighton Road, South Croydon, CR2 6EL

DLA1-125   DAF DB250 10.6m   Alexander ALX400   N45/19D   1998-99

1	Et	R101GNW	25	Et	S225JUA	30	Et	S230JUA
21	Et	S221JUA	26	Et	S226JUA	31	TCt	S231JUA
22	Nt	S322JUA	27	Nt	S227JUA	33	Et	VLT32
23	Et	S223JUA	28	Nt	S228JUA	34	THt	S234JUA
24	Nt	S224JUA	29	THt	S229JUA	35	Et	S235JUA

37	Et	S237JUA
45	THt	S245JUA
56	Et	S256JUA
125	ECt	T325FGN

DLA126-189   DAF DB250 10.2m   Alexander ALX400   N43/18D   1999-2000

126	E	V326DGT	141	w	V341DGT	159	w	V359DGT	178	TCt	W378VGJ
127	E	V327DGT	146	u	V346DGT	160	u	V660LGC	179	N	W379VGJ
128	Et	V628LGC	147	u	V347DGT	161	u	V361DGT	180	w	W433WGJ
129	E	V329DGT	150	TH	V650LGC	162	u	V362DGT	181	BN	W381VGJ
130	E	V330DGT	151	u	V351DGT	163	u	V363DGT	182	BN	W382VGJ
131	w	V331DGT	152	w	V352DGT	164	u	V364DGT	183	BN	W383VGJ
132	E	V332DGT	153	u	V353DGT	165	w	V365DGT	184	BN	W384VGJ
133	Et	V633LGC	154	u	V354DGT	173	N	W373VGJ	185	BN	W385VGJ
135	w	V335DGT	155	u	V355DGT	174	N	W374VGJ	186	BN	W386VGJ
137	u	V337DGT	156	u	V356DGT	175	Et	W432WGJ	187	BN	W387VGJ
138	u	V338DGT	157	u	V357DGT	176	TCt	W376VGJ	188	BN	W388VGJ
139	u	V339DGT	158	TH	V358DGT	177	Nt	W377VGJ	189	w	W389VGJ

DLA199-223   DAF DB250 10.2m   Alexander ALX400   N43/18D   2000

199	u	W399VGJ	209	BN	W409VGJ	214	w	W414VGJ	219	w	X419FGP
205	BN	W436WGJ	210	BN	W438WGJ	215	w	X415FGP	220	w	X501GGO
206	BN	W437WGJ	211	BN	W411VGJ	216	w	X416FGP	221	w	X421FGP
207	BN	W407VGJ	212	BN	W412VGJ	217	w	X417FGP	222	w	X422FGP
208	BN	W408VGJ	213	BN	W413VGJ	218	w	X418FGP	223	w	X423FGP

Arriva's Bus and Coach division is also the importer to the UK of DAF/VDL products, a source frequently used for new buses. Here DB250 DLA132, V332DGT, is seen heading for Norwood Junction. *Terry Longhurst*

Arriva London operates 1500 buses on around seventy services from thirteen garages across London making Arriva one of the largest contractor for TfL. Alexander-bodied DLA339, LJ03MFZ, from Brixton depot is heading for Oxford Circus on route 137. *Terry Longhurst*

DLA224-256

DAF DB250 10.2m   Alexander ALX400   N43/19D   2000-01

224	w	X424FGP	229	AR	X429FGP	242	AR	X442FGP	252	TC	X452FGP
225	u	X425FGP	231	u	X431FGP	243	AR	X443FGP	253	TC	X453FGP
226	u	X426FGP	233	N	X433FGP	245	u	X445FGP	254	N	X454FGP
227	AR	X427FGP	235	N	X435FGP	250	TC	X506GGO	255	TC	X507GGO
228	u	X428FGP	240	w	X503GGO	251	u	X451FGP	256	BN	X508GGO

DLA270-319

DAF DB250 10.2m   Alexander ALX400   N43/19D   2000-01

270	BN	Y452UGC	281	w	Y481UGC	294	AR	Y494UGC	313	BN	Y513UGC
271	BN	Y471UGC	283	w	Y483UGC	295	u	Y495UGC	314	BN	Y514UGC
273	N	Y473UGC	286	u	Y486UGC	297	w	Y497UGC	315	BN	Y529UGC
274	u	Y474UGC	287	AR	Y487UGC	298	AR	Y498UGC	316	BN	Y516UGC
275	N	Y475UGC	289	w	Y489UGC	299	LV	Y499UGC	317	BN	Y517UGC
277	w	Y477UGC	290	u	Y523UGC	311	BN	Y511UGC	318	BN	Y518UGC
278	u	Y478UGC	291	AR	Y491UGC	312	BN	Y512UGC	319	BN	Y519UGC
280	w	Y522UGC	293	AR	Y493UGC						

DLA322-336

DAF DB250 10.2m   TransBus ALX400   N45/19D   2003

322	BN	LG52DAO	326	BN	LG52DBV	330	BN	LG52DCF	334	BN	LG52DCX
323	BN	LG52DAU	327	BN	LG52DBY	331	BN	LG52DCO	335	BN	LG52DCY
324	BN	LG52DBO	328	BN	LG52DBZ	332	BN	LG52DCU	336	BN	LG52DCZ
325	BN	LG52DBU	329	BN	LG52DCE	333	BN	LG52DCV			

DLA337-389

DAF DB250 10.2m   TransBus ALX400   N45/19D   2003

337	BN	LJ03MFX	351	LV	LJ03MKZ	364	LV	LJ03MKL	377	TH	LJ03MTK
338	BN	LJ03MFY	352	LV	LJ03MLE	365	LV	LJ03MWE	378	TH	LJ03MTU
339	BN	LJ03MFZ	353	LV	LJ03MLF	366	LV	LJ03MWF	379	TH	LJ03MTV
340	BN	LJ03MGE	354	LV	LJ03MLK	367	LV	LJ03MWG	380	TH	LJ03MTY
341	BN	LJ03MGU	355	LV	LJ03MJX	368	LV	LJ03MWK	381	TH	LJ03MTZ
342	BN	LJ03MGV	356	LV	LJ03MJY	369	LV	LJ03MWL	382	TH	LJ03MUA
343	BN	LJ03MDV	357	LV	LJ03MKA	370	LV	LJ03MUY	383	TH	LJ03MUB
344	BN	LJ03MDX	358	LV	LJ03MKC	371	BN	LJ03MVC	384	TH	LJ03MYU
345	BN	LJ03MDY	359	LV	LJ03MKD	372	BN	LJ03MVD	385	TH	LJ03MYV
346	BN	LJ03MDZ	360	LV	LJ03MKE	373	TH	LJ03MVE	386	TH	LJ03MYX
347	BN	LJ03MEU	361	LV	LJ03MKF	374	TH	LJ03MSY	387	TH	LJ03MYY
348	LV	LJ03MKU	362	LV	LJ03MKG	375	TH	LJ03MTE	388	TH	LJ03MYZ
349	LV	LJ03MKV	363	LV	LJ03MKK	376	TH	LJ03MTF	389	TH	LJ03MZD
350	LV	LJ03MKX									

In addition to Alexander and Wrightbus bodywork, Plaxton President bodywork also featured in Arriva's orders at the turn of the millennium. Many Presidents have been transferred to other operations, though several remain at Palmers Green depot including DLP100, LF52URE. *Terry Longbottom*

DLP68	AD	LJ51DLF	DAF DB250 10.6m			Plaxton President	N45/21D	2001
DLP72	AD	LJ51DLV	DAF DB250 10.6m			Plaxton President	N45/21D	2001
DLP74	u	LJ51DLY	DAF DB250 10.6m			Plaxton President	N45/21D	2001

DLP76-90 DAF DB250 10.2m TransBus President N43/19D 2002

76	u	LJ51OSX	80	AD	LJ51ORC	84	AD	LJ51ORK	87	E	LF02PKC
77	u	LJ51OSY	81	AD	LJ51ORF	85	AD	LJ51ORL	89	u	LF02PKE
78	u	LJ51OSZ	82	u	LJ51ORG	86	u	LF02PKA	90	AD	LF02PKJ
79	u	LJ51ORA									

DLP91-110 DAF DB250 10.6m TransBus President N45/19D 2002

91	AD	LF52URS	96	u	LF52URX	101	u	LF52URG	106	AD	LF52URM
92	AD	LF52URT	97	AD	LF52URB	102	AD	LF52URH	107	AD	LF52UPP
93	AD	LF52URU	98	AD	LF52URC	103	AD	LF52URJ	108	AD	LF52UPR
94	AD	LF52URV	99	u	LF52URD	104	AD	LF52URK	109	AD	LF52UPS
95	AD	LF52URW	100	AD	LF52URE	105	AD	LF52URL	110	AD	LF52UPT

DW1-50 DAF DB250 10.3m Wrightbus Pulsar Gemini N43/21D 2003

1	TC	801DYE	14	TC	LJ03MWC	27	TC	LJ03MWC	39	TC	LJ53NHF
2	TC	LJ03MWN	15	TC	LJ03MWD	28	TC	LJ53BGO	40	TC	LJ53NHG
3	TC	LJ03MWP	16	TC	LJ03MVF	29	TC	LJ53BGU	41	TC	LJ53NHH
4	TC	LJ03MWU	17	TC	LJ03MWG	30	TC	LJ53NHV	42	BN	LJ53NHK
5	TC	LJ03MWV	18	TC	LJ53NHT	31	TC	LJ53NHX	43	BN	LJ53NHL
6	TC	LJ03MVT	19	TC	WLT719	32	TC	LJ53NHY	44	TC	LJ53NHM
7	TC	WLT807	20	TC	LJ53BFP	33	TC	LJ53NHZ	45	BN	LJ53NHN
8	TC	LJ03MVV	21	TC	LJ53BFU	34	TC	734DYE	46	BN	LJ53NHO
9	TC	LJ03MVW	22	TC	822DYE	35	TC	LJ53NJF	47	BN	LJ53NHP
10	TC	LJ03MVX	23	TC	LJ53BFX	36	TC	LJ53NJK	48	BN	WLT348
11	TC	LJ03MVY	24	TC	LJ53BFY	37	TC	LJ53NJN	49	BN	LJ53NGU
12	TC	LJ03MVZ	25	TC	725DYE	38	TC	LJ53NHE	50	BN	LJ53NGV
13	TC	LJ03MWA	26	TC	LJ53BGF						

DW51-93

VDL Bus DB250 10.3m   Wrightbus Pulsar Gemini   N43/21D   2004

51	BN	LJ04LDX	62	BN	LJ04LDC	73	BN	LJ04LGK	84	BN	LJ04LFX
52	BN	LJ04LDY	63	BN	LJ04LDD	74	BN	LJ04LGL	85	BN	WLT385
53	BN	LJ04LDZ	64	BN	WLT664	75	BN	LJ04LGN	86	BN	LJ04LFZ
54	BN	LJ04LEF	65	BN	LJ04LDF	76	BN	WLT676	87	BN	LJ04LGA
55	BN	LJ04LEU	66	BN	LJ04LDK	77	BN	LJ04LGV	88	BN	LJ04LGC
56	BN	656DYE	67	BN	LJ04LDL	78	BN	LJ04LGW	89	BN	LJ04LGD
57	BN	LJ04LFB	68	BN	LJ04LDN	79	BN	LJ04LGX	90	BN	LJ04LGE
58	BN	LJ04LFD	69	BN	LJ04LDU	80	BN	LJ04LGY	91	BN	LJ04LFG
59	BN	LJ04LFE	70	BN	WLT970	81	BN	LJ04LFU	92	BN	LJ04LFH
60	BN	LJ04LFF	71	BN	LJ04LGF	82	BN	LJ04LFV	93	BN	LJ04LFK
61	BN	LJ04LDA	72	BN	LJ04LGG	83	BN	LJ04LFW			

DW94-102

VDL Bus DB250 10.3m   Wrightbus Pulsar Gemini   N43/21D   2004

94	TC	LJ54BFP	97	TC	WLT997	99	TC	LJ54BFZ	101	TC	LJ54BGF
95	TC	VLT295	98	TC	LJ54BFY	100	TC	LJ54BGE	102	TC	LJ54BGK
96	TC	LJ54BFV									

DW103-133

VDL Bus DB250 10.3m   Wrightbus Pulsar Gemini   N43/21D   2005

103	TC	LJ05BJV	111	TC	LJ05BHP	119	BN	319CLT	127	BN	LJ05BNL
104	TC	LJ05BJX	112	TC	LJ05BHU	120	BN	LJ05BMZ	128	BN	LJ05GKX
105	TC	LJ05BJY	113	TC	LJ05BHV	121	BN	LJ05BNA	129	BN	LJ05GKY
106	TC	LJ05BJZ	114	TC	LJ05BHW	122	BN	LJ05BNB	130	BN	LJ05GKZ
107	TC	LJ05BKA	115	TC	LJ05BHX	123	BN	LJ05BND	131	BN	LJ05GLF
108	TC	LJ05BHL	116	TC	LJ05BHY	124	BN	LJ05BNE	132	BN	LJ05GLK
109	TC	LJ05BHN	117	TC	LJ05BHZ	125	BN	LJ05BNF	133	BN	LJ05GLV
110	TC	LJ05BHO	118	BN	LJ05BMV	126	BN	LJ05BNK			

DW201-262

VDL Bus DB300 10.4m   Wrightbus Pulsar Gemini 2   N41/24D   2009

201	CT	LJ09KRO	217	CT	LJ09STX	233	CT	LJ59AFC	248	CT	LJ59AAO
202	CT	LJ09SUO	218	CT	LJ09STZ	234	CT	LJ59AFD	249	CT	LJ59AAU
203	CT	LJ09SUU	219	CT	LJ09SUA	235	CT	LJ59AFE	250	CT	LJ59AAV
204	CT	LJ09SUV	220	CT	LJ09SUF	236	CT	LJ59AFF	251	CT	LJ59AAX
205	CT	LJ09SUX	221	CT	LJ09SUH	237	CT	LJ59AFG	252	CT	LJ59AAY
206	CT	LJ09SUY	222	CT	LJ59AEO	238	CT	LJ59AFK	253	CT	LJ59AAZ
207	CT	LJ09SVA	223	CT	LJ59AEP	239	CT	LJ59AFL	254	CT	LJ59GVC
208	CT	LJ09SVC	224	CT	LJ59AET	240	CT	LJ59AFM	255	CT	LJ59GVE
209	CT	LJ09SVD	225	CT	LJ59AEU	241	CT	LJ59AFN	256	CT	LJ59GVF
210	CT	LJ09SVE	226	CT	LJ59AEV	242	CT	LJ59ACU	257	CT	LJ59GVG
211	CT	LJ09SVF	227	CT	LJ59AEW	243	CT	LJ59ACV	258	CT	LJ59GVK
212	CT	LJ09SSO	228	CT	LJ59AEX	244	CT	LJ59ACX	259	CT	LJ59GTF
213	CT	LJ09SSU	229	CT	LJ59AEY	245	CT	LJ59AAF	260	CT	LJ59GTU
214	CT	LJ09SSV	230	CT	LJ59AEZ	246	CT	LJ59AAK	261	CT	LJ59GTZ
215	CT	LJ09SSX	231	CT	LJ59AFA	247	CT	LJ59AAN	262	CT	LJ59GUA
216	CT	LJ09SSZ	232	CT	LJ59AFB						

DW263-295

VDL Bus DB300 10.4m   Wrightbus Pulsar Gemini 2   N41/24D   2009-10

263	CT	LJ59LXU	272	BN	LJ59LWV	280	BN	LJ59LWG	288	BN	LJ59LWR
264	CT	LJ59LXV	273	CT	LJ59LWW	281	BN	LJ59LWH	289	BN	LJ59LVH
265	CT	LJ59LXW	274	BN	LJ59LWX	282	BN	LJ59LWK	290	BN	LJ59LVV
266	CT	LJ59LXX	275	BN	LJ59LWY	283	BN	LJ59LWL	291	BN	LJ59LVW
267	CT	LJ59LXY	276	BN	LJ59LWZ	284	BN	LJ59LWM	292	BN	LJ59LVX
268	CT	LJ59LXZ	277	BN	LJ59LXA	285	BN	LJ59LWN	293	BN	LJ59LVY
269	CT	LJ59LWS	278	BN	LJ59LXB	286	BN	LJ59LWO	294	BN	LJ59LVZ
270	CT	LJ59LWT	279	BN	LJ59LWF	287	BN	LJ59LWP	295	BN	LJ59LWA
271	BN	LJ59LWU									

DW296-336

VDL Bus DB300 10.4m   Wrightbus Pulsar Gemini 2   N41/24D   2010

296	BN	LJ10CUH	307	AR	LJ10CVP	317	AR	LJ10CVD	327	AR	LJ60AWK
297	BN	LJ10CUK	308	AR	LJ10CUO	318	AR	LJ60AXX	328	AR	LJ60AWM
298	AR	LJ10CVE	309	AR	LJ10CUU	319	AR	LJ60AXY	329	AR	LJ60AWN
299	AR	LJ10CVF	310	AR	LJ10CUV	320	AR	LJ60AXZ	330	AR	LJ60AWO
300	AR	LJ10CVG	311	AR	LJ10CUW	321	AR	LJ60AYA	331	AR	LJ60AWP
301	AR	LJ10CVH	312	AR	LJ10CUX	322	AR	LJ60AYB	332	AR	LJ60AWR
302	AR	LJ10CVK	313	AR	LJ10CUY	323	AR	LJ60AYC	333	AR	LJ60AWS
303	AR	LJ10CVL	314	AR	LJ10CVA	324	AR	LJ60AYD	334	AR	LJ60AWT
304	AR	LJ10CVM	315	AR	LJ10CVB	325	AR	LJ60AYE	335	AR	LJ60AWU
305	AR	LJ10CVN	316	AR	LJ10CVC	326	AR	LJ60AWH	336	AR	LJ60AWW
306	AR	LJ10CVO									

In 2011 Arriva ordered just over 300 VDL including 104 SB200 single deck chassis. The 207 double deck DB300 chassis carry Wrightbus Gemini 2 DL integral double deck bodies, developed in close co-operation with Arriva and Wrightbus. They are powered by a Cummins 6 cylinder, 6.7 litre Euro 5 engine and a Voith D854.5 automatic transmission and allocated across the UK operation. Seen on route 38 from is DW206, LJ09SUY, one of the earliest deliveries to Arriva. *Richard Godfrey*

DW401-498

VDL Bus DB300 10.4m   Wrightbus Pulsar Gemini 2   N41/24D   2011

401	AR	LJ11AEO	426	AR	LJ61CEO	451	AR	LJ11AAY	475	WN	LJ61CBX
402	AR	LJ11AOP	427	AR	LJ61CEU	452	AR	LJ61CEV	476	WN	LJ61CBY
403	AR	LJ11AOT	428	AR	LJ11ADO	453	AR	LJ61CEX	477	WN	LJ61CCA
404	AR	LJ11AOU	429	AR	LJ11ADU	454	AR	LJ61CEY	478	WN	LJ61CCD
405	AR	LJ11AOV	430	AR	LJ11ADV	455	AR	LJ61CFD	479	WN	LJ61CCE
406	AR	LJ11AOW	431	AR	LJ11ADX	456	AR	LJ61CFE	480	WN	LJ61CCF
407	CT	LJ11AOX	432	AR	LJ11ADZ	457	AR	LJ61CFF	481	WN	LJ61CCK
408	CT	LJ11AOY	433	AR	LJ11AEA	458	AR	LJ61CFG	482	WN	LJ61CCN
409	CT	LJ11AOZ	434	AR	LJ11ABK	459	AR	LJ61CDX	483	WN	LJ61CCO
410	CT	LJ11AFA	435	AR	LJ11ABN	460	AR	LJ61CDY	484	WN	LJ61CCU
411	u	LJ11AFB	436	AR	LJ11ABO	461	AR	LJ61CDZ	485	WN	LJ61CAA
412	AE	LJ11AFC	437	AR	LJ11ABU	462	AR	LJ61CEA	486	WN	LJ61CAE
413	AE	LJ11AFD	438	AR	LJ11ABV	463	AR	LJ61CEF	487	WN	LJ61CAO
414	CT	LJ11AFE	439	AR	LJ11ABX	464	AR	LJ61CEK	488	WN	LJ61CAU
415	CT	LJ11AFF	440	AR	LJ11ABZ	465	AR	LJ61CCV	489	WN	LJ61CAV
416	CT	LJ11AFG	441	AR	LJ11ACF	466	AR	LJ61CCX	490	WN	LJ61CAX
417	CT	LJ11AFK	442	AR	LJ11ACO	467	AR	LJ61CCY	491	WN	LJ61CBF
418	CT	LJ11AFL	443	AR	LJ11ACU	468	AR	LJ61CCZ	492	WN	LJ61CBO
419	AR	LJ11AFM	444	AR	LJ11AAE	469	AR	LJ61CDE	493	WN	LJ61CBU
420	AR	LJ11AFN	445	AR	LJ11AAF	470	WN	LJ61CDF	494	WN	LJ61CBV
421	AR	LJ11ACV	446	AR	LJ61CFA	471	WN	LJ61CDK	495	WN	LJ61CKA
422	AR	LJ11ACX	447	AR	LJ61CFK	472	WN	LJ61CDN	496	WN	LJ61CKC
423	AR	LJ11ACY	448	AR	LJ61CFL	473	WN	LJ61CDO	497	WN	LJ61CKD
424	AR	LJ11ACZ	449	AR	LJ61CDV	474	WN	LJ61CDU	498	WN	LJ61CKE
425	AR	LJ61CEN	450	AR	LJ11AAX						

DW499-539 — VDL Bus DB300 10.4m — Wrightbus Gemini 2 — N41/24D — 2012-13

499	WN	LJ62BKD	510	WN	LJ13CCF	520	AE	LJ13CME	530	AE	LJ13CKV
500	WN	LJ62BKG	511	WN	LJ13CCK	521	AE	LJ13CMF	531	AE	LJ13CKX
501	WN	LJ62BKN	512	WN	LJ13CCL	522	AE	LJ13CMK	532	AE	LJ13CKY
502	WN	LJ62BMO	513	WN	LJ13CCO	523	AE	LJ13CDE	533	AE	LJ13CLF
503	WN	LJ62BNA	514	WN	LJ13CCU	524	AE	LJ13CDF	534	AE	LJ13CLN
504	WN	LJ62BZV	515	WN	LJ13CCV	525	AE	LJ13CDK	535	AR	LJ13CLO
505	WN	LJ62BAA	516	AE	LJ13CCX	526	AE	LJ13CDN	536	AR	LJ13CLV
506	WN	LJ62BBZ	517	AE	LJ13CCY	527	AE	LJ13CDO	537	AR	LJ13CLX
507	WN	LJ62BDF	518	AE	LJ13CCZ	528	AE	LJ13CDU	538	AR	LJ13CLY
508	WN	LJ62BDO	519	AE	LJ13CLZ	529	AE	LJ13CKU	539	AR	LJ13CEV
509	WN	LJ13CCE									

DW540-578 — VDL Bus DB300 10.4m — Wrightbus Gemini 2 — N41/24D — 2013

540	AR	LJ13CEX	550	AR	LJ13CDX	560	E	LJ62FOD	570	E	LJ13CKN
541	AR	LJ13CFA	551	AR	LJ13CDY	561	E	LJ13CEO	571	E	LJ13CKO
542	AR	LJ13CFD	552	AR	LJ13CDZ	562	E	LJ13CEU	572	E	LJ13CKP
543	AR	LJ13CFE	553	AR	LJ13CEA	563	E	LJ13CKC	573	E	LJ13CHZ
544	AR	LJ13CFF	554	AR	LJ13CEF	564	E	LJ13CKD	574	E	LJ13CJE
545	AR	LJ13CFG	555	AR	LJ13CEK	565	E	LJ13CKE	575	E	LJ13CJF
546	AR	LJ13CFK	556	E	LJ13CEN	566	E	LJ13CKF	576	E	LJ13CJO
547	AR	LJ13CFL	557	E	LJ62FNF	567	E	LJ13CKG	577	E	LJ13CJU
548	AR	LJ13CFM	558	E	LJ62FNG	568	E	LJ13CKK	578	E	LJ13CJV
549	AR	LJ13CDV	559	E	LJ62FNR	569	E	LJ13CKL			

DW579-586 — VDL Bus DB300 10.4m — Wrightbus Gemini 2 — N41/24D — 2013

579	AR	LJ13CJX	581	AR	LJ13CJZ	583	AR	LJ13CHF	585	AR	LJ13CHH
580	AR	LJ13CJY	582	AR	LJ13CKA	584	AR	LJ13CHG	586	AR	LJ13CHK

DWL1-16 — DAF SB120 10.2m — Wrightbus Cadet — N27D* — 2001 — *seating varies

1	TH	Y801DGT	4	TH	Y804DGT	7	TH	LJ51DDK	10	TH	LJ51DDO
2	TH	Y802DGT	5	TH	Y805DGT	8	TH	LJ51DDL	11	TH	LJ51DDU
3	TH	Y803DGT	6	TH	Y806DGT	9	TH	LJ51DDN	16	TH	LJ51DEU

DWL30-52 — DAF SB120 10.2m — Wrightbus Cadet — N26D* — 2002 — *seating varies

30	w	LF02PMX	36	u	LF02PNN	42	LV	LF02POA	48	LV	LF52UNZ
31	u	LF02PMY	37	w	LF02PNO	43	LV	LF02POH	49	LV	LF52UOA
32	u	LF02PNE	38	Et	LF02PNU	44	u	LF52UTB	50	u	LF52UOB
33	THt	LF02PNJ	39	u	LF02PNV	45	LV	LF52UNW	51	LV	LF52UOC
34	w	LF02PNK	40	Et	LF02PNX	46	LV	LF52UNX	52	LV	LF52UOD
35	w	LF02PNL	41	w	LF02PNY	47	LV	LF52UNY			

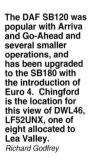

The DAF SB120 was popular with Arriva and Go-Ahead and several smaller operations, and has been upgraded to the SB180 with the introduction of Euro 4. Chingford is the location for this view of DWL46, LF52UNX, one of eight allocated to Lea Valley.
Richard Godfrey

DWS1-18

DAF SB120 9.4m — Wrightbus Cadet2 — N23D — 2003

1	TH	LJ53NGZ	6	TH	LJ53NFT	11	TH	LJ53NFZ	15	TH	LJ53NGN
2	TH	LJ53NHA	7	TH	LJ53NFU	12	TH	LJ53NGE	16	TH	LJ53NFE
3	TH	LJ53NHB	8	TH	LJ53NFV	13	TH	LJ53NGF	17	TH	LJ53NFF
4	TH	LJ53NHC	9	TH	LJ53NFX	14	TH	LJ53NGG	18	TH	LJ53NFG
5	TH	LJ53NHD	10	TH	LJ53NFY						

EN1-13

ADL Dart 4 8.9m — ADL Enviro200 — N26F — 2008

1	LV	LJ57USS	5	LV	LJ57USW	8	LV	LJ57USZ	11	LV	LJ57UTC
2	LV	LJ57UST	6	LV	LJ57USX	9	LV	LJ57UTA	12	LV	LJ57UTE
3	LV	LJ57USU	7	LV	LJ57USY	10	LV	LJ57UTB	13	LV	LJ57UTF
4	LV	LJ57USV									

EN14	LV	LJ12BYW	ADL Dart 4 8.9m	ADL Enviro200	N25F	2012
EN15	LV	LJ12BYX	ADL Dart 4 8.9m	ADL Enviro200	N25F	2012

EN16-22

ADL Dart 4 8.9m — ADL Enviro200 — N26F — 2008 — Arriva Southern Counties

16	LV	GN57BPF	18	LV	GN57BPO	20	LV	GN57BPV	22	LV	GN57BPY
17	LV	GN57BPK	19	LV	GN57BPU	21	LV	GN57BPX			

ENL1-9

ADL Dart 4 10.2m — ADL Enviro 200 — N29D — 2007

1	TC	LJ07ECW	4	TC	LJ07ECZ	6	TC	LJ07EDF	8	TC	LJ07EBP
2	TC	LJ07ECX	5	TC	LJ07EDC	7	TC	LJ07EBO	9	TC	LJ07EBU
3	TC	LJ07ECY									

ENL10-48

ADL Dart 4 10.2m — ADL Enviro 200 — N29D — 2008-09

10	TC	LJ58AVT	25	TC	LJ58AVB	33	WN	LJ09KPV	41	WN	LJ09KPA
18	CT	LJ58AWF	26	TC	LJ58AVC	34	WN	LJ09KPX	42	WN	LJ09KPE
19	LV	LJ58AWG	27	TC	LJ58AVD	35	WN	LJ09KPY	43	WN	LJ09KPF
20	LV	LJ58AVE	28	TC	LJ58AUC	36	WN	LJ09KPZ	44	WN	LJ09KPG
21	TC	LJ58AUV	29	TC	LJ58AUE	37	WN	LJ09KRD	45	WN	LJ09KPK
22	TC	LJ58AUW	30	WN	LJ09KPR	38	WN	LJ09KRE	46	WN	LJ09KPL
23	TC	LJ58AUX	31	WN	LJ09KPT	39	WN	LJ09KRF	47	WN	LJ09KPN
24	TC	LJ58AUY	32	WN	LJ09KPU	40	WN	LJ09KOX	48	WN	LJ09KPO

ENL49-74

ADL Dart 4 10.2m — ADL Enviro 200 — N29D — 2010

49	DX	LJ10CSF	56	DX	LJ10CSX	63	DX	LJ60AYF	69	DX	LJ60AYN
50	DX	LJ10CSO	57	DX	LJ10CSY	64	DX	LJ60AYG	70	DX	LJ60AYO
51	DX	LJ10CSU	58	DX	LJ10CSZ	65	DX	LJ60AYH	71	DX	LJ60AYP
52	DX	LJ59LVL	59	DX	LJ10CTE	66	DX	LJ60AYK	72	DX	LJ60AYS
53	DX	LJ59LVM	60	DX	LJ10CTF	67	DX	LJ60AYL	73	DX	LJ60AXV
54	DX	LJ59LVN	61	DX	LJ10CTK	68	DX	LJ60AYM	74	DX	LJ60AXW
55	DX	LJ10CSV	62	DX	LJ60ATY						

Delivered in 2009, ENL46, LJ09KPL, is seen on route 184 which links Turnpike Lane in Harringay with East Barnet and one of the services which operate 24-hours a day.
Terry Longhurst

The first batch of six Volvo B5LH double-deckers were built in 2008 and after they were fitted with Wright Eclipse Gemini bodywork entered service with Arriva London in 2009. Further deliveries have taken the number of the model with Arriva London to 131. Representing the type is HV75, LJ62BWF, pictured in Park Lane. *Dave Heath*

ENS1-14
ADL Dart 4 9.3m   ADL Enviro 200   N24D   2007

1	CT	LJ07EDK	4	CT	LJ07EDR	9	CT	LJ07EEA	12	CT	LJ07ECN
2	CT	LJ07EDL	5	CT	LJ07EDU	10	CT	LJ07EEB	13	CT	LJ07ECT
3	CT	LJ07EDO	6	CT	LJ07EDV	11	CT	LJ07ECF	14	CT	LJ07ECU
4	CT	LJ07EDP	7	CT	LJ07EDX						

ENS15-28
ADL E20D 9.6m   ADL Enviro 200   N25D   2012

15	LV	LJ12BYY	19	LV	LJ12BZC	23	LV	LJ12BYL	26	LV	LJ12BYO
16	LV	LJ12BYZ	20	LV	LJ12BZD	24	LV	LJ12BYM	27	LV	LJ12BYP
17	LV	LJ12BZA	21	LV	LJ12BZE	25	LV	LJ12BYN	28	LV	LJ12BYR
18	LV	LJ12BZB	22	LV	LJ12BZF						

ENX1-19
ADL E20D 10.6m   ADL Enviro 200   N31D   2011-12

1	E	LJ61CKF	6	E	LJ61CKO	11	TH	LJ12BYU	16	TH	LJ12BYB
2	E	LJ61CKG	7	E	LJ61CHY	12	TH	LJ12BYV	17	TH	LJ12BYC
3	E	LJ61CKK	8	E	LJ61CHZ	13	TH	LJ12BXY	18	TH	LJ12BYD
4	E	LJ61CKL	9	TH	LJ12BYS	14	TH	LJ12BXZ	19	TH	LJ12BYF
5	E	LJ61CKN	10	TH	LJ12BYT	15	TH	LJ12BYA			

HV1-6
Volvo B5LH 10.4m   Wrightbus Gemini 2   N39/21D   2009

1	AR	LJ09KRU	3	AR	LJ09KOH	5	AR	LJ09KOV	6	AR	LJ09KOW
2	AR	LJ09KOE	4	AR	LJ09KOU						

HV7-26
Volvo B5LH 10.4m   Wrightbus Gemini 2   N39/21D   2010-11

7	AR	LJ60AWY	12	AR	LJ60AXD	17	AR	LJ60AWH	22	AR	LJ60AWR
8	AR	LJ60AWZ	13	AR	LJ60AXF	18	AR	LJ60AWM	23	AR	LJ60AWU
9	AR	LJ60AXA	14	AR	LJ60AXG	19	AR	LJ60AWN	24	AR	LJ60AWV
10	AR	LJ60AXB	15	AR	LJ60AWF	20	AR	LJ60AWO	25	AR	LJ60JGY
11	AR	LJ60AXC	16	AR	LJ60AWG	21	AR	LJ60AWP	26	AR	LJ60JGZ

HV27-46
Volvo B5LH 10.4m   Wrightbus Gemini 2   N39/21D   2011

27	SF	LJ11EFT	32	SF	LJ11EFY	37	SF	LJ11EFF	42	SF	LJ11EFN
28	SF	LJ11EFU	33	SF	LJ11EFZ	38	SF	LJ11EFG	43	SF	LJ11EFO
29	SF	LJ11EFV	34	SF	LJ11EGC	39	SF	LJ11EFK	44	SF	LJ11EFP
30	SF	LJ11EFW	35	SF	LJ11EGD	40	SF	LJ11EFL	45	SF	LJ11EFR
31	SF	LJ11EFX	36	SF	LJ11EFE	41	SF	LJ11EFM	46	SF	LJ11EEU

In addition to the Volvo hybrid buses, Arriva also operates five Wrightbus integral examples. These use many of the components of the VDL DB300. Although the type is currently out of service, HW4, LJ09KRK is shown with the 'green leaf' livery additions while operating on route 141. *Terry Longhurst*

HV47-131
Volvo B5LH 10.4m Wrightbus Gemini 2 N39/21D 2013

No	Op	Reg	No	Op	Reg	No	Op	Reg	No	Op	Reg
47	SF	LJ62BEO	69	SF	LJ62BSO	90	WN	LJ13FDO	111	WN	LJ13FCM
48	SF	LJ62BGK	70	SF	LJ62BTO	91	WN	LJ13FDP	112	WN	LJ13FBE
49	SF	LJ62BGX	71	SF	LJ62BTY	92	WN	LJ13FCN	113	WN	LJ13FBF
50	SF	LJ62BHY	72	SF	LJ62BVE	93	WN	LJ13FCO	114	WN	LJ13FBG
51	SF	LJ62BKU	73	SF	LJ62BVP	94	WN	LJ13FCP	115	WN	LJ13FBK
52	SF	LJ62BKX	74	SF	LJ62BVY	95	WN	LJ13FCU	116	WN	LJ13FBL
53	SF	LJ62BMZ	75	SF	LJ62BWF	96	WN	LJ13FCV	117	WN	LJ13FBN
54	SF	LJ62BNE	76	SF	LJ62BWP	97	WN	LJ13FCX	118	WN	LJ13FBO
55	SF	LJ62BNL	77	SF	LJ62BFZ	98	WN	LJ13FCY	119	WN	LJ13FBU
56	SF	LJ62BNW	78	SF	LJ62BGZ	99	WN	LJ13FCZ	120	WN	LJ13FBV
57	SF	LJ62BXD	79	SF	LJ62BHF	100	WN	LJ13FDA	121	WN	LJ13FBX
58	SF	LJ62BXF	80	SF	LJ62BJK	101	WN	LJ13FDC	122	WN	LJ13FAM
59	SF	LJ62BYT	81	SF	LJ62BJX	102	WN	LJ13FBY	123	WN	LJ13FAO
60	SF	LJ62BYU	82	SF	LJ13FDD	103	WN	LJ13FBZ	124	WN	LJ13FAU
61	SF	LJ62BZH	83	SF	LJ13FDE	104	WN	LJ13FCA	125	WN	LJ13FBA
62	SF	LJ62BZR	84	WN	LJ13FDF	105	WN	LJ13FCC	126	WN	LJ13FBB
63	SF	LJ62BZY	85	WN	LJ13FDG	106	-		127		LJ13FBC
64	SF	LJ62BAO	86	WN	LJ13FDK	107	WN	LJ13FCE	128	WN	LJ13FBD
65	SF	LJ62BAU	87	WN	LJ13FDL	108	WN	LJ13FCF	129	WN	LJ13FBO
66	SF	LJ62BCL	88	WN	LJ13FDM	109	WN	LJ13FCG	130	WN	LJ13FEP
67	SF	LJ62BNO	89	WN	LJ13FDN	110	WN	LJ13FCL	131	WN	LJ13FET
68	SF	LJ62BPV									

HV132-151
Volvo B5LH 10.4m Wrightbus Gemini 2 N39/21D 2013

No	Op	Reg	No	Op	Reg	No	Op	Reg	No	Op	Reg
132	-	LJ63	137	-	LJ63	142	-	LJ63	147	-	LJ63
133	-	LJ63	138	-	LJ63	143	-	LJ63	148	-	LJ63
134	-	LJ63	139	-	LJ63	144	-	LJ63	149	-	LJ63
135	-	LJ63	140	-	LJ63	145	-	LJ63	150	-	LJ63
136	-	LJ63	141	-	LJ63	146	-	LJ63	151	-	LJ63

HW1-5
Wrightbus HEV/VDL D300 Wrightbus Gemini 2 N41/24D 2009

No	Op	Reg	No	Op	Reg	No	Op	Reg
1	u	LJ09KRG	3	u	LJ58AVK	4	u	LJ09KRK
2	u	LJ58AVG				5	u	LJ09KRN

LT3-8 — Wrightbus NBfL — N40/22T — 2012 — Owned by TfL

3	AE	LTZ1003	5	AE	LTZ1005	7	AE	LTZ1007	8	AE	LTZ1008
4	AE	LTZ1004	6	AE	LTZ1006						

PDL80-94 — TransBus Dart 8.8m / TransBus Mini Pointer — N23F — 2002

80	WN	LF52UOR	84	WN	LF52USB	89	LV	LF52USJ	92	WN	LF52URO
81	WN	LF52UNV	86	WN	LF52USD	90	LV	LF52USL	93	WN	LF52URP
82	WN	LF52URY	88	LV	LF52USH	91	WN	LF52URN	94	WN	LF52URR
83	WN	LF52URZ									

PDL97-116 — ADL Dart 9.3m / ADL Pointer — N24D — 2005

97	TH	LJ54BAO	102	LV	LJ54BBK	107	LV	LJ54LHG	112	TH	LJ54LHN
98	TH	LJ54BAU	103	LV	LJ54BBN	108	LV	LJ54LHH	113	TH	LJ54LHO
99	TH	LJ54BAV	104	LV	LJ54BBO	109	LV	LJ54LHK	114	TH	LJ54LHP
100	TH	LJ54BBE	105	LV	LJ54BBU	110	LV	LJ54LHL	115	CT	LJ54LHR
101	LV	LJ54BBF	106	LV	LJ54LHF	111	TH	LJ54LHM	116	CT	LJ54LGV

PDL117-123 — ADL Dart 10.1m / ADL Pointer — N29D — 2005

117	TC	LJ05GOP	119	TC	LJ05GOX	121	TC	LJ05GPK	123	TC	LJ05GPU
118	TC	LJ05GOU	120	TC	LJ05GPF	122	TC	LJ05GPO			

PDL124-136 — ADL Dart 9.3m / ADL Pointer — N24D — 2006

124	TH	LJ56APZ	128	TH	LJ56ARX	131	TH	LJ56ASU	134	TH	LJ56AOW
125	TH	LJ56ARF	129	TH	LJ56ARZ	132	TH	LJ56ASV	135	TH	LJ56AOX
126	TH	LJ56ARO	130	TH	LJ56ASO	133	TH	LJ56ASX	136	TH	LJ56AOY
127	TH	LJ56ARU									

PDL137-145 — ADL Dart 8.8m / ADL Mini Pointer — N23F — 2006 — Arriva Southern C, 2011

137	LV	SN06BPE	140	E	SN06BPU	142	E	SN06BPX	144	E	SN06BPZ
138	LV	SN06BPF	141	E	SN06BPV	143	E	SN06BPY	145	E	SN06BRF
139	LV	SN06BPK									

T1-65 — ADL Trident 2 10.1m / ADL Enviro 400 — N41/26D — 2008

1	AD	LJ08CVS	18	DX	LJ08CVO	34	AD	LJ08CTZ	50	TC	LJ08CTO
2	AD	LJ08CVT	19	DX	519CLT	35	AD	LJ08CUA	51	TC	LJ08CYC
3	AD	LJ08CVU	20	DX	LJ08CVR	36	AD	LJ08CUE	52	TC	LJ08CYE
4	AD	LJ08CVV	21	DX	LJ08CUU	37	AD	LJ08CUG	53	TC	LJ08CYF
5	AD	205CLT	22	DX	LJ08CUV	38	AD	LJ08CUH	54	TC	LJ08CYG
6	AD	LJ08CVX	23	DX	LJ08CUW	39	AD	LJ08CUK	55	TC	LJ08CYH
7	AD	LJ08CVY	24	DX	324CLT	40	AD	LJ08CUO	56	TC	LJ08CYK
8	AD	LJ08CVZ	25	DX	LJ08CUY	41	AD	LJ08CSO	57	TC	LJ08CYL
9	AD	LJ08CWA	26	DX	LJ08CVA	42	TC	LJ08CSU	58	TC	LJ08CYO
10	AD	LJ08CWC	27	AD	LJ08CVB	43	TC	LJ08CSV	59	TC	LJ08CYP
11	AD	LJ08CVF	28	AD	LJ08CVC	44	TC	LJ08CSX	60	TC	LJ08CYS
12	DX	LJ08CVG	29	AD	LJ08CVD	45	TC	LJ08CSY	61	TC	LJ08CXR
13	DX	LJ08CVH	30	AD	330CLT	46	TC	LJ08CSZ	62	TC	LJ08CXS
14	DX	LJ08CVK	31	AD	LJ08CTV	47	TC	LJ08CTE	63	TC	LJ08CXT
15	DX	LJ08CVL	32	AD	LJ08CTX	48	TC	LJ08CTF	64	TC	LJ08CXU
16	DX	LJ08CVM	33	AD	LJ08CTY	49	TC	LJ08CTK	65	TC	LJ08CXV
17	DX	217CLT									

T66-83 — ADL Trident 2 10.1m / ADL Enviro 400 — N41/26D — 2009

66	AE	LJ59ACY	71	AE	LJ59ADZ	76	AE	LJ59ABO	80	AE	LJ59ABZ
67	AE	LJ59ACZ	72	AE	LJ59AEA	77	AE	LJ59ABU	81	AE	LJ59ACF
68	AE	LJ59ADO	73	AE	LJ59ABF	78	AE	LJ59ABV	82	AE	LJ59ACO
69	AE	LJ59ADV	74	AE	LJ59ABK	79	AE	LJ59ABX	83	AE	LJ59AAE
70	AE	70CLT	75	AE	LJ59ABN						

Arriva currently operates almost three hundred of the Enviro 400 model with a few of the early examples carrying index numbers initially allocated to Routemasters. One example is T19, 519CLT, seen in Ilford while working route 150. *Dave Heath*

T84-117

						ADL Trident 2 10.1m			ADL Enviro 400			N41/26D	2010		
84	N	LJ59LZD	93	N	593CLT	102	N	LJ59LZB	110	N	LJ59LYK
85	N	185CLT	94	N	LJ59LYT	103	N	LJ59LZC	111	N	LJ59LYO
86	N	LJ59LZF	95	N	LJ59LYU	104	N	LJ59LYA	112	N	LJ59LYP
87	N	LJ59LZG	96	N	LJ59LYV	105	N	LJ59LYC	113	N	LJ59LYS
88	N	LJ59LZH	97	N	LJ59LYW	106	N	LJ59LYD	114	N	LJ59LXP
89	N	LJ59LZK	98	N	398CLT	107	N	LJ59LYF	115	N	LJ59LXR
90	N	LJ59LZL	99	N	LJ59LYY	108	N	LJ59LYG	116	N	LJ59LXS
91	N	LJ59LZM	100	N	LJ59LYZ	109	N	LJ59LYH	117	N	LJ59LXT
92	N	LJ59LZN	101	N	LJ59LZA						

T118-144

						ADL Trident 2 10.1m			ADL Enviro 400			N41/24D	2010		
118	TC	LJ10HVO	125	TH	LJ10HVE	132	TH	LJ10HUA	139	TH	LJ10HUY
119	TC	LJ10HVP	126	TH	LJ10HVF	133	TH	LJ10HUB	140	TH	LJ10HUZ
120	TC	LJ10HVR	127	TH	LJ10HVG	134	TH	LJ10HUK	141	TH	LJ10HTT
121	TC	LJ10HVA	128	TH	LJ10HVH	135	TH	LJ10HUO	142	TH	LJ10HTU
122	TH	LJ10HVB	129	TH	LJ10HVK	136	TH	LJ10HUP	143	TH	LJ10HTV
123	TH	LJ10HVC	130	TH	LJ10HVL	137	TH	LJ10HUU	144	TH	LJ10HTX
124	TH	LJ10HVD	131	TH	LJ10HTZ	138	TH	LJ10HUV			

T145-193

						ADL Trident 2 10.1m			ADL Enviro 400			N41/24D	2010		
145	LV	LJ60AVR	158	LV	LJ60AVF	170	AE	LJ60AUV	182	DX	LJ60AUL
146	LV	LJ60AVT	159	LV	LJ60AVG	171	AE	LJ60AUW	183	DX	LJ60AUM
147	LV	LJ60AVU	160	LV	LJ60AVK	172	AE	LJ60AUX	184	DX	LJ60AUN
148	LV	LJ60AVV	161	LV	LJ60AVL	173	AE	LJ60AUY	185	DX	LJ60ASX
149	LV	LJ60AVW	162	LV	LJ60AVN	174	AE	LJ60AVB	186	DX	LJ60ASZ
150	LV	LJ60AVX	163	LV	LJ60AVO	175	AE	LJ60ATZ	187	DX	LJ60ATF
151	LV	LJ60AVY	164	LV	LJ60AVP	176	AE	LJ60AUA	188	DX	LJ60ATK
152	LV	LJ60AVZ	165	LV	LJ60AUO	177	AE	LJ60AUC	189	DX	LJ60ATN
153	LV	LJ60AWA	166	LV	LJ60AUP	178	AE	LJ60AUE	190	DX	LJ60ATO
154	LV	LJ60AWB	167	LV	LJ60AUR	179	AE	LJ60AUF	191	DX	LJ60ATU
155	LV	LJ60AVC	168	LV	LJ60AUT	180	DX	LJ60AUH	192	DX	LJ60ATV
156	LV	LJ60AVD	169	AE	LJ60AUU	181	DX	LJ60AUK	193	DX	LJ60ATX
157	LV	LJ60AVE									

T201-278 — ADL E40D 10.2m — ADL Enviro 400 — N41/24D — 2012

No		Reg	No		Reg	No		Reg	No		Reg
201	LV	LJ61CHD	221	LV	LJ61CFM	241	E	LJ61LKM	260	LV	LJ61LKL
202	LV	LJ61CHF	222	LV	LJ61CFN	242	E	LJ61LKN	261	AD	LJ61LJC
203	LV	LJ61CHG	223	LV	LJ61CFO	243	E	LJ61LKO	262	AD	LJ61LJE
204	LV	LJ61CHH	224	E	LJ61CFP	244	E	LJ61LKP	263	AD	LJ61LJF
205	LV	LJ61CHK	225	E	LJ61CFU	245	E	LJ61LKU	264	AD	LJ61LJK
206	LV	LJ61CHL	226	E	LJ61CFV	246	E	LJ61LKV	265	WN	LJ61LJL
207	LV	LJ61CHN	227	E	LJ61CFX	247	E	LJ61LKX	266	AD	LJ61LJN
208	LV	LJ61CNO	228	E	LJ61CFY	248	E	LJ61LKY	267	AD	LJ61LJO
209	LV	LJ61CHV	229	E	LJ61CFZ	249	E	LJ61LKZ	268	AD	LJ61LJU
210	LV	LJ61CHX	230	E	LJ61CGE	250	E	LJ61LLA	269	AD	LJ61LJV
211	LV	LJ61CGF	231	E	LJ61LLC	251	E	LJ61LJY	270	AD	LJ61LJX
212	LV	LJ61CGG	232	E	LJ61LLD	252	E	LJ61LJZ	271	WN	LJ61LHP
213	LV	LJ61CGK	233	E	LJ61LLE	253	E	LJ61LKA	272	WN	LJ61LHR
214	LV	LJ61CGO	234	E	LJ61LLF	254	E	LJ61LKC	273	AD	LJ61LHT
215	LV	LJ61CGU	235	E	LJ61LLG	255	E	LJ61LKD	274	AD	LJ61LHU
216	LV	LJ61CGV	236	E	LJ61LLK	256	E	LJ61LKE	275	AD	LJ61LHV
217	LV	LJ61CGX	237	E	LJ61LLM	257	E	LJ61LKF	276	AD	LJ61LHW
218	LV	LJ61CGY	238	E	LJ61LLN	258	E	LJ61LKG	277	AD	LJ61LHX
219	LV	LJ61CGZ	239	E	LJ61LLO	259	E	LJ61LKK	278	AD	LJ61LHY
220	LV	LJ61CHC	240	E	LJ61LLP						

T279-287 — ADL E40D 10.2m — ADL Enviro 400 — N41/24D — 2013

No		Reg	No		Reg	No		Reg	No		Reg
279	TC	LJ13CHL	282	TC	LJ13CHV	284	TC	LJ13CHY	286	TC	LJ13CGK
280	TC	LJ13CHN	283	TC	LJ13CHX	285	TC	LJ13CGG	287	TC	LJ13CGO
281	TC	LJ13CHO									

VLA1-55 — Volvo B7TL 10.6m — TransBus ALX400 4.4m — N49/19D — 2003

No		Reg	No		Reg	No		Reg	No		Reg
1	N	LJ03MYP	15	N	LJ03MXH	29	N	LJ53BDO	43	N	LJ53BCV
2	N	LJ03MYR	16	N	LJ03MXK	30	N	LJ53BDU	44	N	LJ53BCX
3	N	LJ03MYS	17	N	LJ03MXL	31	N	LJ53BDV	45	N	LJ53BCY
4	N	LJ03MYT	18	N	LJ03MXM	32	N	LJ53BDX	46	N	LJ53BAA
5	N	LJ03MXV	19	N	LJ03MXN	33	N	LJ53BDY	47	N	LJ53BAO
6	N	LJ03MXW	20	N	LJ03MXP	34	N	LJ53BDZ	48	N	LJ53BAU
7	N	LJ03MXX	21	N	LJ53BFK	35	N	LJ53BEO	49	N	LJ53BAV
8	N	LJ03MXY	22	N	LJ53BFL	36	N	LJ53BBV	50	N	LJ53BBE
9	N	LJ03MXZ	23	N	LJ53BFM	37	N	LJ53BBX	51	N	LJ53BBF
10	N	LJ03MYA	24	N	LJ53BFN	38	N	LJ53BBZ	52	N	LJ53BBK
11	N	LJ03MYB	25	N	LJ53BFO	39	N	LJ53BCF	53	N	LJ53BBN
12	N	LJ03MYC	26	N	LJ53BCZ	40	N	LJ53BCK	54	N	LJ53BBO
13	N	LJ03MYD	27	N	LJ53BDE	41	N	LJ53BCO	55	N	LJ53BBU
14	N	LJ03MYF	28	N	LJ53BDF	42	N	LJ53BCU			

VLA56-69 — Volvo B7TL 10.6m — TransBus ALX400 4.4m — N49/19D — 2004

No		Reg	No		Reg	No		Reg	No		Reg
56	N	LJ04LFL	60	N	LJ04LFR	64	N	LJ04YWT	67	N	LJ04YWW
57	N	LJ04LFM	61	N	LJ04LFS	65	N	LJ04YWU	68	N	LJ04YWX
58	N	LJ04LFN	62	N	LJ04LFT	66	N	LJ04YWV	69	N	LJ04YWY
59	N	LJ04LFP	63	N	LJ04YWS						

VLA70-73 — Volvo B7TL 10.6m — TransBus ALX400 4.4m — N49/22D — 2004

No		Reg	No		Reg	No		Reg	No		Reg
70	N	LJ04YWZ	71	N	LJ04YXA	72	N	LJ04YXB	73	N	LJ04YWE

VLA74-128 — Volvo B7TL 10.1m — ADL ALX400 — N45/21D — 2004-05

No		Reg	No		Reg	No		Reg	No		Reg
74	N	LJ54BGO	85	AR	LJ54BCY	95	AR	LJ54BBV	105	N	LJ05BKZ
75	N	LJ54BEO	86	AR	LJ54BCZ	96	AR	LJ54BBX	106	BN	LJ05BLF
76	N	LJ54BEU	87	AR	LJ54BDE	97	AR	LJ54BBZ	107	BN	LJ05BLK
77	N	LJ54BFA	88	AR	LJ54BDF	98	AR	LJ54BCE	108	BN	LJ05BLN
78	N	LJ54BFE	89	AR	LJ54BDO	99	AR	LJ54BCF			
79	AR	LJ54BFF	90	AR	LJ54BDU	100	AR	LJ54BCK	124	DX	LJ05BJE
80	AR	LJ54BFKZ	91	AR	LJ54BDV	101	BN	LJ54BCO	125	DX	LJ05BJF
81	AR	LJ54BFL	92	AR	LJ54BDX	102	BN	LJ54BCU	126	DX	LJ05BJK
82	AR	LJ54BFM	93	AR	LJ54BDY	103	DX	LJ54BCV	127	DX	LJ05BJO
83	AR	LJ54BFN	94	AR	LJ54BDZ	104	BN	LJ05BKY	128	DX	LJ05BJU
84	AR	LJ54BFO									

VLA129-143 — Volvo B7TL 10.1m — ADL ALX400 — N45/19D — 2005

129	DX	LJ05GLZ	133	DX	LJ05GPY	137	DX	LJ05GRU	141	DX	LJ05GSU
130	DX	LJ05GME	134	DX	LJ05GPZ	138	DX	LJ05GRX	142	DX	LJ55BTE
131	DX	LJ05GMF	135	DX	LJ05GRF	139	DX	LJ05GRZ	143	DX	LJ55BTF
132	DX	LJ05GPX	136	DX	LJ05GRK	140	DX	LJ05GSO			

VLA144-163 — Volvo B7TL 10.1m — ADL ALX400 — N45/19D — 2005

144	BN	LJ55BTO	149	BN	LJ55BTZ	154	BN	LJ55BRX	159	BN	LJ55BSX
145	BN	LJ55BTU	150	BN	LJ55BUA	155	BN	LJ55BRZ	160	BN	LJ55BSY
146	BN	LJ55BTV	151	BN	LJ55BUE	156	BN	LJ55BSO	161	BN	LJ55BSZ
147	BN	LJ55BTX	152	BN	LJ55BPZ	157	BN	LJ55BSU	162	BN	LJ55BUP
148	BN	LJ55BTY	153	BN	LJ55BRV	158	BN	LJ55BSV	163	BN	LJ55BUR

VLW42-104 — Volvo B7TL 10.1m — Wrightbus Eclipse Gemini — N41/22D — 2002-03

42	u	LF02PKO	58	WN	LF02PTU	74	WN	LF52UTM	90	CT	LF52URA
43	u	LF02PKU	59	WN	LF02PTX	75	WN	LF52USM	91	CT	LF52UPD
44	u	LF02PKV	60	WN	LF02PTY	76	WN	LF52USN	92	CT	WLT892
45	u	LF02PKX	61	WN	LF02PVE	77	WN	LF52USO	93	CT	LF52UPG
46	u	LF02PKY	62	WN	LF02PVJ	78	WN	LF52USS	94	CT	LF52UPH
47	u	LF02PKZ	63	WN	LF02PVK	79	WN	LF52UST	95	CT	WLT895
48	u	LF02PLJ	64	WN	LF02PVL	80	WN	LF52USU	96	CT	LF52UPK
49	E	LF02PLN	65	WN	LF02PVN	81	WN	LF52USV	97	E	LF52UPL
50	E	LF02PLO	66	WN	LF02PVO	82	WN	LF52USW	98	E	LF52UPM
51	u	WLT751	67	WN	LF52UTC	83	WN	LF52USX	99	E	LG52DDA
52	E	LF02PSO	68	WN	LF52UTE	84	WN	LF52USY	100	E	LG52DDE
53	E	LF02PSU	69	WN	LF52USE	85	WN	LF52UPV	101	E	LG52DDF
54	E	WLT554	70	WN	LF52UTG	86	CT	LF52UPW	102	E	LG52DDJ
55	E	LF02PSY	71	WN	LF52UTH	87	CT	LF52UPX	103	E	LG52DDK
56	E	LF02PSZ	72	WN	WLT372	88	CT	WLT888	104	E	LG52DDL
57	E	LF02PTO	73	WN	LF52UTL	89	CT	LF52UPZ			

VLW105-179 — Volvo B7TL 10.1m — Wrightbus Eclipse Gemini — N41/21D — 2002-03

105	E	LJ03MHU	124	E	LF52UOX	143	AE	LJ03MFA	162	AE	LJ03MRX
106	E	LJ03MHV	125	E	LF52UOY	144	AE	LJ03MFE	163	AE	LJ03MRY
107	E	LJ03MHX	126	AE	LF52UPA	145	AE	LJ03MFF	164	AE	LJ03MSU
108	E	LJ03MHY	127	AE	LF52UPB	146	AE	LJ03MFK	165	AE	LJ03MSV
109	E	LJ03MHZ	128	AE	LF52UPC	147	AE	LJ03MBF	166	AE	LJ03MSX
110	E	LJ03MJE	129	AE	LG52DAA	148	AE	LJ03MBU	167	AE	LJ03MMU
111	E	LJ03MJF	130	AE	LJ03MGZ	149	AE	LJ03MBV	168	AE	LJ03MMV
112	E	LJ03MJK	131	AE	LJ03MHA	150	AE	LJ03MBX	169	AE	LJ03MMX
113	E	LJ03MJU	132	AE	LJ03MHE	151	AE	LJ03MBY	170	AE	LJ03MOA
114	E	LJ03MJV	133	AE	LJ03MHF	152	AE	LJ03MDE	171	SF	LJ03MOF
115	E	LJ03MGX	134	AE	LJ03MHK	153	AE	LJ03MDF	172	SF	LJ03MOV
116	E	LJ03MGY	135	AE	LJ03MHL	154	AE	LJ03MDK	173	SF	VLT173
117	E	LF52UPN	136	AE	LJ03MHM	155	AE	LJ03MDN	174	SF	LJ03MPF
118	E	LF52UPO	137	AE	LJ03MHN	156	AE	LJ03MDU	175	SF	LJ03MPU
119	E	LF52UOS	138	AE	LJ03MFN	157	AE	LJ03MPX	176	SF	LJ03MPV
120	E	LF52UOT	139	AE	LJ03MFP	158	AE	LJ03MPY	177	SF	LJ03MLL
121	E	LF52UOU	140	AE	LJ03MFU	159	AE	LJ03MPZ	178	SF	LJ03MLN
122	E	LF52UOV	141	AE	LJ03MFV	160	AE	LJ03MRU	179	SF	LJ03MLV
123	E	LF52UOW	142	AE	LJ03MEV	161	AE	LJ03MRV			

VLW180-199 — Volvo B7TL 10.6m — Wrightbus Eclipse Gemini — N45/24D — 2003

180	SF	LJ03MLX	185	SF	LJ03MMF	190	SF	LJ03MXR	195	SF	LJ53BEU
181	SF	LJ03MLY	186	SF	LJ03MMK	191	SF	LJ03MXS	196	SF	LJ53BEY
182	SF	LJ03MLZ	187	SF	LJ03MKM	192	SF	LJ03MXT	197	SF	LJ53BFA
183	SF	LJ03MMA	188	SF	LJ03MKN	193	SF	LJ03MXU	198	SF	LJ53BFE
184	SF	LJ03MME	189	SF	LJ03MYN	194	SF	LJ03MWX	199	SF	LJ53BFF

Allocated to Norwood are six Routemaster buses that are used on special duties and private hires. Illustrating this iconic vehicle associated with London is an additonal one, RM5, VLT5, a 1959 example which is occasionally used by Arriva and was pictured in Baring Street while operating route 76. *Mark Lyons*

Special event vehicles:

RM5	p	VLT5	AEC Routemaster R2RH	Park Royal	B36/28R	1959	*owned privately*
RM6	N	VLT6	AEC Routemaster R2RH	Park Royal	B36/28R	1959	
RML901	N	WLT901	AEC Routemaster R2RH/1	Park Royal	B40/32R	1963	
RM1124	N	VYJ806	AEC Routemaster R2RH	Park Royal	B36/28R	1965	
RMC1453	N	453CLT	AEC Routemaster R2RH	Park Royal	B32/28R	1962	
RMC1464	N	464CLT	AEC Routemaster R2RH	Park Royal	O32/28R	1962	
RM2217	N	CUV217C	AEC Routemaster R2RH	Park Royal	B36/28R	1965	

Previous registrations:

3CLT	-	LJ53NHM	LJ53NHM, VLT244
70CLT	LJ59AOX	LJ53NHX	LJ53NHX, WLT531
124CLT	124CLT, VYJ806	LJ54BFX	LJ54BFX, WLT997
185CLT	LJ59LZE	LT59GTZ	LJ59GTZ, 361CLT
205CLT	LJ08CVW	LTZ1003	LT61CHT
217CLT	LJ08CVN	LTZ1004	LT12DHT
319CLT	LJ05BMY	LTZ1005	LT12EHT
324CLT	LJ08CUX	LTZ1006	LT12FHT
330CLT	LJ08CVE	LTZ1007	LT12GHT
361CLT	LJ59GTZ	LTZ1008	LT12HHT
398CLT	LJ59LYX	VLT27	-
480CLT	-	VLT32	S233JUA
519CLT	LJ08CVP	VLT173	LJ03MPE
593CLT	LJ59LZO	VLT295	LJ54BFU
656DYE	LJ04LFA	WLT348	LJ53NGO
725DYE	LJ53BGE	WLT372	LF52UTJ
734DYE	LJ53NJE	WLT385	LJ04LFU
801DYE	LJ03MWM	WLT554	LF02PSX
822DYE	LJ53BFV	WLT664	LJ04LDE
LF02PKZ	LF02PKZ, VLT47	WLT676	LJ04LGU
LF52UPJ	LF52UPJ, WLT895	WLT719	LJ53NHU
LF52UPL	LF52UPL, WLT897	WLT751	LF02PRZ
LF52USE	LF52USE, VLT25	WLT807	LJ03MVU
LJ03MMX	LJ03MMX, VLT25	WLT888	LF52UPY
LJ08CVU	LJ08CVU, 3CLT	WLT892	LF52UPE
LJ08CVY	LY08CVY, 7CLT	WLT970	LJ04LDV
LJ51DHE	LJ51DHE, VLT27	WLT997	LJ54BFX
LJ51DHN	LJ51DHW, VLT32		

Depots and allocations:

Barking (Ripple Road, IG11 0ST) - DX

Enviro 200	ENL49	ENL50	ENL51	ENL52	ENL53	ENL54	ENL55	ENL56
	ENL57	ENL58	ENL59	ENL60	ENL61	ENL62	ENL63	ENL64
	ENL65	ENL66	ENL67	ENL68	ENL69	ENL70	ENL71	ENL72
	ENL73	ENL74						
Volvo B7TL	VLA102	VLA103	VLA124	VLA125	VLA126	VLA127	VLA128	VLA129
	VLA130	VLA131	VLA132	VLA133	VLA134	VLA135	VLA136	VLA137
	LA138	VLA139	VLA140	VLA141	VLA142	VLA143	VLA144	
Enviro 400	T12	T13	T14	T15	T16	T17	T18	T19
	T20	T21	T22	T23	T24	T25	T26	T180
	T181	T182	T183	T184	T185	T186	T187	T188
	T189	T190	T191	T192	T193			

Brixton (Streatham Hill, SW2 4TB) - BN

Outstation: Battersea - BA

DB250	DLA181	DLA182	DLA183	DLA184	DLA185	DLA186	DLA187	DLA188
	DLA205	DLA206	DLA207	DLA208	DLA209	DLA212	DLA213	DAL270
	DLA271	DLA311	DLA312	DLA313	DLA314	DLA315	DLA316	DLA317
	DLA318	DLA319	DLA322	DLA323	DLA324	DLA325	DLA326	DLA327
DLA328	DLA329	DLA330	DLA331	DLA332	DLA333	DLA334	DLA335	DLA336
	DLA337	DLA338	DLA339	DLA340	DLA341	DLA342	DLA343	DLA344
	DLA345	DLA346	DLA347	DLA371	DLA372	DW42	DW43	DW45
	DW46	DW47	DW48	DW49	DW50	DW51	DW52	DW53
	DW54	DW55	DW56	DW57	DW58	DW59	DW60	DW61
	DW62	DW63	DW64	DW65	DW66	DW67	DW68	DW69
	DW70	DW71	DW72	DW73	DW74	DW75	DW76	DW77
	DW78	DW79	DW80	DW81	DW82	DW83	DW84	DW85
	DW86	DW87	DW88	DW89	DW90	DW91	DW92	DW93
	DW118	DW119	DW120	DW121	DW122	DW123	DW124	DW125
	DW126	DW127	DW128	DW129	DW130	DW131	DW132	DW133
	DW271	DW272	DW273	DW274	DW275	DW276	DW277	DW278
	DW279	DW280	DW281	DW282	DW283	DW284	DW285	DW286
	DW287	DW288	DW289	DW290	DW291	DW292	DW293	DW294
	DW295	DW296	DW297					
Volvo B7TL	VLA100	VLA102	VLA104	VLA106	VLA107	VLA108	VLA145	VLA146
	VLA147	VLA148	VLA149	VLA150	VLA151	VLA152	VLA153	VLA154
	VLA155	VLA156	VLA157	VLA158	VLA159	VLA160	VLA161	VLA162
	VLA163							

Cambridge Heath (Ash Grove, E8 4RH) - AE

Enviro 400	T66	T67	T68	T69	T70	T71	T72	T73
	T74	T75	T76	T77	T78	T79	T80	T81
	T82	T83	T169	T170	T171	T172	T173	T174
	T175	T176	T177	T178	T179			
Volvo B7TL	VLW126	VLW127	VLW128	VLW129	VLW130	VLW131	VLW132	VLW133
	VLW134	VLW135	VLW136	VLW137	VLW138	VLW139	VLW140	VLW141
	VLW142	VLW143	VLW144	VLW145	VLW146	VLW147	VLW148	VLW149
	VLW150	VLW151	VLW152	VLW153	VLW154	VLW155	VLW156	VLW157
	VLW158	VLW159	VLW160	VLW161	VLW162	VLW163	VLW164	VLW165
	VLW166	VLW167	VLW168	VLW169				
DB300	DW516	DW517	DW518	DW519	DW520	DW521	DW522	DW523
	DW524	DW525	DW526	DW527	DW528	DW529	DW530	DW531
	DW532	DW533	DW534					
NBfL	LT3	LT4	LT5	LT6	LT7	LT8		

Clapton (Bohemia Place, Mare Street, E8 1DU) - CT

Dart	PDL115	PDL116						
Enviro200	ENS1	ENS2	ENS3	ENS4	ENS5	ENS6	ENS7	ENS8
	ENS9	ENS10	ENS11	ENS12	ENS13	ENS14	ENL18	
DB300	DW201	DW202	DW203	DW204	DW205	DW206	DW207	DW208
	DW209	DW210	DW211	DW212	DW213	DW214	DW215	DW216
	DW217	DW218	DW219	DW220	DW221	DW222	DW223	DW224
	DW225	DW226	DW227	DW228	DW229	DW230	DW231	DW232
	DW233	DW234	DW235	DW236	DW237	DW238	DW239	DW240
	DW241	DW242	DW243	DW244	DW245	DW246	DW247	DW248
	DW249	DW250	DW251	DW252	DW253	DW254	DW255	DW256
	DW257	DW258	DW259	DW260	DW261	DW262	DW263	DW264
	DW265	DW266	DW267	DW268	DW269	DW270	DW273	DW407
	DW408	DW409	DW410	DW414	DW415	DW416	DW417	DW418
Volvo B7TL	VLW86	VLW87	VLW88	VLW89	VLW90	VLW91	VLW92	VLW93
	VLW94	VLW95	VLW96					

Croydon (Brighton Road, South Croydon) - TC

Dart	PDL117	PDL118	PDL119	PDL120	PDL121	PDL122	PDL123	
Enviro 200	ENL1	ENL2	ENL3	ENL4	ENL5	ENL6	ENL7	ENL8
	ENL9	ENL10	ENL21	ENL22	ENL23	ENL24	ENL25	ENL26
	ENL27	ENL28	ENL29					
DB250	DLA250	DLA252	DLA253	DLA255	DLA256			
DB300	DW1	DW2	DW3	DW4	DW5	DW6	DW7	DW8
	DW9	DW10	DW11	DW12	DW13	DW14	DW15	DW16
	DW17	DW18	DW19	DW20	DW21	DW22	DW23	DW24
	DW25	DW26	DW27	DW28	DW29	DW30	DW31	DW32
	DW33	DW34	DW35	DW36	DW37	DW38	DW39	DW40
	DW41	DW44	DW94	DW95	DW96	DW97	DW98	DW99
	DW100	DW101	DW102	DW103	DW104	DW105	DW106	DW107
	DW108	DW109	DW110	DW111	DW112	DW113	DW114	DW115
	DW116	DW117						
Enviro 400	T42	T43	T44	T45	T46	T47	T48	T49
	T50	T51	T52	T53	T54	T55	T56	T57
	T58	T59	T60	T61	T62	T63	T64	T65
	T118	T119	T120	T121	T279	T280	T281	T282
	T283	T284	T285	T286	T287			

Enfield (Southbury Road, Ponders End, EN3 4HX) - E

Dart	PDL140	PDL141	PDL142	PDL143	PDL144	PDL145		
Enviro 200	ENX1	ENX2	ENX3	ENX4	ENX5	ENX6	ENX7	ENX8
DAF DB250	DLA126	DLA127	DLA128	DLA130	DLA131	DLA132	DLP87	
Volvo B7TL	VLW49	VLW50	VLW52	VLW53	VLW54	VLW55	VLW56	VLW57
	VLW58	VLW97	VLW98	VLW99	VLW100	VLW101	VLW102	VLW103
	VLW104	VLW105	VLW106	VLW107	VLW108	VLW109	VLW110	VLW111
	VLW112	VLW 113	VLW114	VLW115	VLW116	VLW117	VLW118	VLW119
	VLW120	VLW121	VLW122	VLW123	VLW124	VLW125		
Enviro 400	T224	T225	T226	T227	T228	T229	T230	T231
	T232	T233	T234	T235	T236	T237	T238	T239
	T240	T241	T242	T243	T244	T245	T246	T247
	T248	T249	T250	T251	T252	T253	T254	T255
	T256	T257	T258	T259				
DB300	DW556	DW557	DW558	DW559	DW560	DW561	DW562	DW563
	DW564	DW565	DW566	DW567	DW568	DW569	DW570	DW571
	DW572	DW573	DW574	DW575	DW576	DW577	DW578	

Lea Valley (Leeside Road, Edmonton, N17 0SH) - LV

Dart	PDL88	PDL89	PDL90	PDL101	PDL102	PDL103	PDL104	PDL105
	PDL106	PDL107	PDL108	PDL109	PDL110	PDL137	PDL138	PDL139
DAF SB120	DWL42	DWL43	DWL45	DWL46	DWL47	DWL48	DWL49	DWL51
	DWL52							
Enviro 200	EN1	EN2	EN3	EN4	EN5	EN6	EN7	EN8
	EN9	EN10	EN11	EN12	EN13	EN14	EN15	EN16
	EN17	EN18	EN19	EN20	EN21	EN22	ENS15	ENS16
	ENS17	ENS18	ENS19	ENS20	ENS21	ENS22	ENS23	ENS24
	ENS25	ENS26	ENS28	ENL19	ENL20			
DAF DB250	DLA299	DLA348	DLA349	DLA350	DLA351	DLA352	DLA353	DLA354
	DLA355	DLA356	DLA357	DLA358	DLA359	DLA360	DLA361	DLA362
	DLA363	DLA364	DLA365	DLA366	DLA367	DLA368	DLA369	DLA370
Enviro 400	T42	T145	T146	T147	T148	T149	T150	T151
	T152	T153	T154	T155	T156	T157	T158	T159
	T160	T161	T162	T163	T164	T165	T166	T167
	T168	T201	T202	T203	T204	T205	T206	T207
	T208	T209	T210	T211	T212	T213	T214	T215
	T216	T217	T218	T219	T220	T221	T222	T223
	T260							

Norwood (Ernest Avenue, West Norwood, SE27 0HN) - N

Routemaster	RM6	RML901	RM1124	RMC1453	RMC1464	RM2217		
DAF DB250	DLA173	DLA174	DLA179	DLA180				
Volvo B7TL	VLA1	VLA2	VLA3	VLA4	VLA5	VLA6	VLA7	VLA8
	VLA9	VLA10	VLA11	VLA12	VLA13	VLA14	VLA15	VLA16
	VLA17	VLA18	VLA19	VLA20	VLA21	VLA22	VLA23	VLA24
	VLA25	VLA26	VLA27	VLA28	VLA29	VLA30	VLA31	VLA32
	VLA33	VLA34	VLA35	VLA36	VLA37	VLA38	VLA39	VLA40
	VLA41	VLA42	VLA43	VLA44	VLA45	VLA46	VLA47	VLA48
	VLA49	VLA50	VLA51	VLA52	VLA53	VLA54	VLA55	VLA56
	VLA57	VLA58	VLA59	VLA60	VLA61	VLA62	VLA63	VLA64
	VLA65	VLA66	VLA67	VLA68	VLA69	VLA70	VLA71	VLA72
	VLA73	VLA74	VLA75	VLA76	VLA77	VLA78	VLA101	VLA105
Enviro 400	T84	T85	T86	T87	T88	T89	T90	T91
	T92	T93	T94	T95	T96	T97	T98	T99
	T100	T101	T102	T103	T104	T105	T106	T107
	T108	T109	T110	T111	T112	T113	T114	T115
	T116	T117						

Palmers Green (Regents Avenue, N13 5UR) - AD

DAF DB250	DLP68	DLP72	DLP84	DPL85	DPL90	DPL91	DPL92	DPL93
	DPL94	DPL95	DPL97	DPL98	DPL100	DPL102	DPL103	DPL104
	DPL105	DPL106	DPL107	DLP110				
Trident 2	T1	T2	T3	T4	T5	T6	T7	T8
	T9	T10	T11	T27	T28	T29	T30	T31
	T32	T33	T34	T35	T36	T37	T38	T39
	T40	T41	T261	T262	T263	T264	T266	T267
	T268	T269	T270	T273	T274	T275	T276	T277
	T278							

Stamford Hill (Rookwood Road, N16 6SS) - SF

Volvo B7TL	VLW170	VLW171	VLW172	VLW173	VLW174	VLW175	VLW176	VLW177
	VLW178	VLW179	VLW180	VLW181	VLW182	VLW183	VLW184	VLW185
	VLW186	VLW187	VLW188	VLW189	VLW190	VLW191	VLW192	VLW193
	VLW194	VLW195	VLW196	VLW197	VLW198	VLW199		
VDL DB300	DW534	DW535	DW536	DW537	DW538	DW539		
Volvo B5LH	HV27	HV28	HV29	HV30	HV31	HV32	HV33	HV34
	HV35	HV36	HV37	HV38	HV39	HV40	HV41	HV42
	HV43	HV44	HV45	HV46	HV47	HV48	HV49	HV50
	HV51	HV52	HV53	HV54	HV55	HV56	HV57	HV58
	HV59	HV60	HV61	HV62	HV63	HV64	HV65	HV66
	HV67	HV68	HV69	HV70	HV71	HV72	HV73	HV74
	HV75	HV76	HV77	HV78	HV79	HV80	HV81	HV82
	HV83							

Thornton Heath (London Road, CR7 6AU) - TH

Dart	PDL97	PDL98	PDL99	PDL100	PDL111	PDL112	PDL113	PDL114
	PDL124	PDL125	PDL126	PDL127	PDL128	PDL129	PDL130	PDL131
	PDL132	PDL133	PDL134	PDL135	PDL136			
Enviro 200	ENX9	ENX10	ENX11	ENX12	ENX13	ENX14	ENX15	ENX16
	ENX17	ENX18	ENX19					
DAF SB120	DWL1	DWL2	DWL3	DWL4	DWL5	DWL6	DWL7	DWL8
	DWL9	DWL11	DWS1	DWS2	DWS3	DWS4	DWS5	DWS6
	DWS7	DWS8	DWS9	DWS11	DWS12	DWS13	DWS14	DWS15
	DWS16	DWS17	DWS18					
DAF DB250	DLA158	DLA373	DLA374	DLA375	DLA376	DLA377	DLA378	DLA379
	DLA380	DLA381	DLA382	DLA383	DLA384	DLA385	DLA386	DLA387
	DLA388	DLA389						
Trident 2	T122	T123	T124	T125	T126	T127	T128	T129
	T130	T131	T132	T133	T134	T135	T136	T137
	T138	T139	T140	T141	T142	T143	T144	

Tottenham (Philip Lane, N17 0XR) - AR

DAF DB250	DLA242	DLA243	DLA287	DLA291	DLA293	DLA296	DLA298	
VDL DB300	DW298	DW299	DW300	DW301	DW302	DW303	DW304	DW305
	DW306	DW307	DW308	DW309	DW310	DW311	DW312	DW313
	DW314	DW315	DW316	DW317	DW318	DW319	DW320	DW321
	DW322	DW323	DW324	DW325	DW326	DW327	DW328	DW329
	DW330	DW331	DW332	DW333	DW334	DW335	DW336	DW401
	DW402	DW403	DW404	DW405	DW406	DW412	DW413	
	DW419	DW420	DW421	DW422	DW423	DW424	DW425	DW426
	DW428	DW429	DW430	DW431	DW432	DW433	DW434	DW435
	DW436	DW437	DW438	DW439	DW440	DW441	DW442	DW443
	DW444	DW445	DW446	DW447	DW448	DW449	DW450	DW451
	DW452	DW453	DW454	DW455	DW456	DW457	DW458	DW459
	DW460	DW461	DW462	DW463	DW464	DW465	DW466	DW467
	DW468	DW469	DW535	DW536	DW537	DW538	DW539	DW540
	DW541	DW542	DW543	DW544	DW545	DW546	DW547	DW548
	DW549	DW550	DW551	DW552	DW553	DW554	DW555	DW579
	DW580	DW581	DW582	DW583	DW584	DW585	DW586	
Volvo B5LH	HV1	HV2	HV3	HV4	HV5	HV6	HV7	HV8
	HV9	HV10	HV11	HV12	HV13	HV14	HV15	HV16
	HV17	HV18	HV19	HV20	HV21	HV22	HV23	HV24
	HV25	HV26						
Volvo B7TL	VLA79	VLA80	VLA81	VLA82	VLA83	VLA84	VLA85	VLA86
	VLA87	VLA88	VLA89	VLA90	VLA91	VLA92	VLA93	VLA94
	VLA95	VLA96	VLA97	VLA98	VLA99	VLA100		

Wood Green (High Road) - WN

Dart	PLD80	PLD81	PLD82	PLD83	PLD84	PLD86	PLD91	PLD92
	PLD93	PLD94	PDL144					
Enviro 200	ENL30	ENL31	ENL32	ENL33	ENL34	ENL35	ENL36	ENL37
	ENL38	ENL39	ENL40	ENL41	ENL42	ENL43	ENL44	ENL45
	ENL46	ENL47	ENL48					
Wrightbus Hybrid	HW1	HW2	HW3	HW4	HW5			
Volvo B5LH	HV84	HV85	HV86	HV87	HV88	HV89	HV90	HV91
	HV92	HV93	HV94	HV95	HV96	HV97	HV98	HV99
	HV100	HV101	HV102	HV103	HV104	HV105	HV106	HV107
	HV108	HV109	HV110	HV111	HV112	HV113	HV114	HV115
	HV116	HV117	HV118	HV119	HV120	HV121	HV122	HV123
	HV124	HV125	HV126	HV127	HV128	HV129	HV130	HV131
Volvo B7TL	VLW59	VLW60	VLW61	VLW62	VLW63	VLW64	VLW65	VLW66
	VLW67	VLW68	VLW69	VLW70	VLW71	VLW72	VLW73	VLW74
	VLW75	VLW76	VLW77	VLW78	VLW79	VLW80	VLW81	VLW82
	VLW83	VLW84	VLW85					
VDL DB300	DW465	DW466	DW467	DW468	DW469	DW470	DW471	DW472
	DW473	DW474	DW475	DW476	DW477	DW478	DW479	DW480
	DW481	DW482	DW483	DW484	DW485	DW486	DW487	DW488
	DW489	DW490	DW491	DW492	DW493	DW494	DW495	DW496
	DW497	DW498	DW499	DW500	DW501	DW502	DW503	DW504
	DW505	DW506	DW507	DW508	DW509	DW510	DW511	DW512
	DW513	DW514	DW515					

ARRIVA THE SHIRES

TfL operations:

2468-2472		Optare Solo M780SL		Optare		N24F	2006	
2468	GR	YJ06YRP	**2470**	GR	YJ06YRS	**2471**	GR	YJ06YRT	**2472**	GR	YJ06YRU
2469	GR	YJ06YRR						

3218	GR	S315JUA	Dennis Dart SLF 10.1m	Plaxton Pointer 2	N26D	1998	
3220	GR	S317JUA	Dennis Dart SLF 10.1m	Plaxton Pointer 2	N26D	1998	
3221	GR	S318JUA	Dennis Dart SLF 10.1m	Plaxton Pointer 2	N26D	1998	
3258	GR	V258HBH	Volvo B6BLE	Wright Crusader 2	N30D	1999	
3260	w	V260HBH	Volvo B6BLE	Wright Crusader 2	N30D	1999	
3299	GR	Y299TKJ	Dennis Dart SLF 10.1m	Plaxton Pointer 2	N34D	2001	
3301	GR	Y301TKJ	Dennis Dart SLF 10.1m	Plaxton Pointer 2	N34D	2001	
3515	GR	LJ03MUW	DAF SB120 10.2m	Wrightbus Cadet	N26D	2003	Ariva London, 2012

3704-3710		VDL Bus SB120 10.2m		Wrightbus Cadet 2		N28D	2006	
3704	GR	YJ06LFE	**3706**	GR	YJ06LFG	**3708**	GR	YJ06LFK	**3710**	GR	YJ06LDK
3705	GR	YJ06LFF	**3707**	GR	YJ06LFH	**3709**	GR	YJ06LFL			

3711-3728		VDL Bus SB120 10.8m		Wrightbus Cadet 2		N39F	2006	
3711	GR	YE06HRA	**3716**	GR	YE06HRJ	**3721**	GR	YE06HPK	**3725**	GR	YE06HPP
3712	GR	YE06HRC	**3717**	GR	YE06HPA	**3722**	GR	YE06HPL	**3726**	GR	YE06HPU
3713	GR	YE06HRD	**3718**	GR	YE06HPC	**3723**	GR	YE06HPN	**3727**	GR	YE06HNT
3714	GR	YE06HRF	**3719**	GR	YE06HPF	**3724**	GR	YE06HPO	**3728**	GR	YE06HNU
3715	GR	YE06HRG	**3720**	GR	YE06HPJ						

3804	GR	SN56AXG	ADL Dart 4 10.2m	ADL Enviro 200	N28D	2007	
3805	GR	SN56AXH	ADL Dart 4 10.2m	ADL Enviro 200	N28D	2007	

3811-3819		ADL Dart 4 10.2m		ADL Enviro200		N29D	2008	
3811	GR	LJ58AVU	**3814**	GR	LJ58AVY	**3816**	GR	LJ58AWA	**3818**	GR	LJ58AWF
3812	GR	LJ58AVV	**3815**	GR	LJ58AVZ	**3817**	GR	LJ58AWC	**3819**	GR	LJ58AWG
3813	GR	LJ58AVX									

5448	GR	SN08AAE	ADL Trident 2 10.1m	ADL Enviro 400	N41/26D	2008	

Arriva operations that border the TfL network have gained London contracts. The Shires' commitment to TfL routes is provided by Watford depot. VDL SB120, 3725, YE06HPP, is seen operating route H19 into **Harrow.** *Mark Lyons*

6014-6024   DAF DB250 10.2m   Alexander ALX400   N45/19D   2003

6014	GR	KL52CXF	6017	GR	KL52CXJ	6020	GR	KL52CXN	6023	GR	KL52CXR
6015	GR	KL52CXG	6018	GR	KL52CXK	6021	GR	KL52CXO	6024	GR	KL52CXS
6016	GR	KL52CXH	6019	GR	KL52CXM	6022	GR	KL52CXP			

6025	GR	YJ54CFG	VDL DB250 10.2	Alexander ALX400	N45/19D	2005

6026-6036   VDL DB250 1032m   Wrightbus Pulsar Gemini   N43/21D   2006

6026	GR	YJ55WPO	6029	GR	YJ55WOC	6032	GR	YJ55WOM	6035	GR	YJ55WOV
6027	GR	YJ55WOA	6030	GR	YJ55WOD	6033	GR	YJ55WOR	6036	GR	YJ55WOX
6028	GR	YJ55WOB	6031	GR	YJ55WOH	6034	GR	YJ55WOU			

6041	GR	LJ05GLY	VDL DB250 10.3m	Wrightbus Pulsar Gemini	N45/21D	2005	Arriva London, 2010
6100	GR	KX59AEE	VDL DB300 Hybrid	Wrightbus Gemini 2	N41/24D	2009	
6101	GR	KX59AEF	VDL DB300 Hybrid	Wrightbus Gemini 2	N41/24D	2009	
6109	GR	LJ05BLV	Volvo B7TL 10.1m	ADL ALX400	N45/20D	2004	
6123	GR	LJ05BKX	Volvo B7TL 10.1m	ADL ALX400	N45/20D	2004	Arriva London, 2012

6164-6179   Volvo B7TL 10.1m   ADL ALX400   N45/19D   2005   Arriva London, 2012

6164	GR	LJ55BVS	6168	GR	LJ55BVW	6172	GR	LJ55BVD	6176	GR	LJ55BVH
6165	GR	LJ55BVT	6169	GR	LJ55BVX	6173	GR	LJ55BVE	6177	GR	LJ55BVK
6166	GR	LJ55BVU	6170	GR	LJ55BVY	6174	GR	LJ55BVF	6178	GR	LJ55BVL
6167	GR	LJ55BVV	6171	GR	LJ55BVZ	6175	GR	LJ55BVG	6179	GR	LJ55BVM

Depot and allocation:

Watford (St Albans Road, Garston) - GR

Optare Solo	2468	2469	2470	2471	2472			
Dart	3218	3220	3221	3299	3301	3804	3805	
Volvo B6	3258							
Enviro 200	3811	3812	3813	3814	3815	3816	3817	3818
	3819							
DAF/VDL SB120	3704	3705	3706	3707	3708	3709	3710	3711
	3712	3713	3714	3716	3717	3718	3719	3720
	3721	3722	3723	3724	3725	3726	3727	3728
Trident	5448							
DAF/VDL DB250	6014	6015	6016	6017	6018	6019	6020	6021
	6023	6024	6025	6026	6027	6028	6029	6030
	6031	6032	6033	6034	6035	6036	6041	
Wrightbus/DB300	6100	6101						
Volvo B7TL	6109	6123	6164	6165	6166	6167	6168	6169
	6170	6171	6172	6173	6174	6175	6176	6177
	6178	6179						

The double-deck fleet is represented by VDL DB250 6034, YJ55WOU, one of eleven added to the fleet in 2006. It is seen on route 258 while heading for Watford Junction rail station.
Terry Longhurst

ARRIVA SOUTHERN COUNTIES

TfLoperations:

3293-3302

Dennis Dart SLF 10.7m   Plaxton Pointer 2   N31D   2001

3293	DT	Y293TKJ	3296	DT	Y296TKJ	3298	GY	Y298TKJ	3302	GY	Y302TKJ

3309	GY	LJ54BCX	ADL Dart 9.3m	ADL Pointer	N27D	2005	Arriva London, 2012
3310	GY	LJ54BAA	ADL Dart 9.3m	ADL Pointer	N27D	2005	Arriva London, 2012
3502	GY	KE51PUA	DAF SB120 10.2m	Wrightbus Cadet	N27D	2002	
3514	DA	LJ03MZE	DAF SB120 10.2m	Wrightbus Cadet	N27D	2003	Arriva London, 2012
3524	GY	LJ51DDX	DAF SB120 10.2m	Wrightbus Cadet	N27D	2001	Arriva London, 2012
3525	GY	LJ51DDV	DAF SB120 10.2m	Wrightbus Cadet	N27D	2001	Arriva London, 2012

3945-3957

VDL SB120 9.4m   Wrightbus Cadet 2   N24F   2004

3945	DA	GK53AOH	3948	DA	GK53AON	3953	DA	GK53AOU	3956	DA	GK53AOX
3946	DA	GK53AOJ	3949	DA	GK53AOO	3954	DA	GK53AOV	3957	DA	GK53AOY
3947	DA	GK53AOL	3950	DA	GK53AOP	3955	DA	GK53AOW			

3971	GY	YE06HPX	DAF SB120 10.2m	Wrightbus Cadet 2	N28D	2006
3972	GY	YE06HPY	DAF SB120 10.2m	Wrightbus Cadet 2	N28D	2006
3973	GY	YE06HPZ	DAF SB120 10.2m	Wrightbus Cadet 2	N28D	2006

3982-3996

ADL Dart 4 10.8m   ADL Enviro 200   N32D*   2007   *3997-99 are N29D

3982	DA	GN07DLE	3987	DA	GN07DLU	3992	DA	GN07DME	3996	DA	GN07DMV
3983	DA	GN07DLF	3988	DA	GN07DLV	3993	DA	GN07DMF	3997	DA	GN57BOU
3984	DA	GN07DLJ	3989	DA	GN07DLX	3994	DA	GN07DMO	3998	GY	GN57BOV
3985	DA	GN07DLK	3990	DA	GN07DLY	3995	DA	GN07DMU	3999	GY	GN57BPE
3986	DA	GN07DLO	3991	DA	GN07DLZ						

4000-4010

ADL Dart 4 10.2m   ADL Enviro 200   N29D   2008

4000	GY	GN08CGO	4003	GY	GN08CGX	4006	GY	GO58CHC	4009	GY	GO58CHG
4001	GY	GN08CGU	4004	GY	GN08CGY	4007	GY	GO58CHD	4010	GY	GO58CHH
4002	GY	GN08CGV	4005	GY	GN08CGZ	4008	GY	GO58CHF			

Arriva Southern Counties operates services for TfL in the Dartford area. Welling is the location for this view of SB120 3946, GK53AOJ, seen while operating route B15 in the spring of 2013. *Laurie Rufus*

Transferred from the London fleet to Southern Counties for further use on TfL routes are thirteen Volvo B7TLs with ALX400 bodywork. Now allocated to Grays, 6115, LJ05BKF, is shown working route 370 to the Lakeside shopping centre. *Terry Longhurst*

4023-4027 — ADL Dart 4 10.2m — ADL Enviro 200 — N29D — 2009

4023	DA	GN58BUP	4025	DA	GN58BUV	4026	DA	GN58LVA	4027	DA	GN58LVB
4024	DA	GN58BUU						

4028-4035 — ADL Dart 4 10.8m — ADL Enviro 200 — N32D — 2009

4028	DA	GN09AVV	4030	DA	GN09AVX	4032	DA	GN09AVZ	4034	DA	GN09AWB
4029	DA	GN09AVW	4031	DA	GN09AVY	4033	DA	GN09AWA	4035	DA	GN09AWC

4068-4079 — ADL Dart 4 10.8m — ADL Enviro 200 — N32D — 2010

4068	GY	GN10KWE	4071	GY	GN10KWH	4074	GY	VX10EBN	4077	GY	VX10EBU
4069	GY	GN10KWF	4072	GY	GN10KWJ	4075	GY	VX10EBO	4078	GY	VX10EBV
4070	GY	GN10KWG	4073	GY	GN10KWK	4076	GY	VX10EBP	4079	GY	VX10EBZ

6110-6122 — Volvo B7TL 10.1m — ADL ALX400 — N45/20D — 2005 — Arriva London, 2012

6110	GY	LJ05BLX	6114	GY	LJ05BKD	6117	GY	LJ05BKK	6120	GY	LJ05BKO
6111	GY	LJ05BLZ	6115	GY	LJ05BKF	6118	GY	LJ05BKL	6121	GY	LJ05BKU
6112	GY	LJ05BMO	6116	GY	LJ05BKG	6119	GY	LJ05BKN	6122	GY	LJ05BKV
6113	GY	LJ05BMU						

6213-6219 — DAF DB250 — Wrightbus Pulsar Gemini — N43/21D — 2004

6213	DA	GK53AOA	6215	DA	GK53AOC	6217	DA	GK53AOE	6219	DA	GK53AOG
6214	DA	GK53AOB	6216	DA	GK53AOD	6218	DA	GK53AOF			

6458-6470 — ADL E40D — ADL Enviro 400 — N41/24D — 2011-12

6458	DA	GN61JPY	6462	DA	GN61JRO	6465	DA	GN61JRU	6468	DA	KX61LDO
6459	DA	GN61JGV	6463	DA	GN61JRZ	6466	DA	KX61LDL	6469	DA	KX61LDU
6460	DA	GN61JRV	6464	DA	GN61JSU	6467	DA	KX61LDN	6470	DA	KX61LDV
6461	DA	GN61JRX						

The Beddington Farm depot of Londonlinks transferred from Southern Counties to London South in October 1999 leaving two depots with TfL work, Grays and Dartford. The latest arrivals with Arriva Southern Counties are a batch of Enviro 400s at Dartford. Representing them is 6460, GN61JRV, seen in Eltham while heading for Sidcup station. *Mark Lyons*

Depots and allocations:

Dartford (Central Road) - DA

Dart SLF	3293	3296					
DAF SB120	3514	3945	3946	3947	3948	3949	3950	3951
	3952	3953	3954	3955	3956	3957		
Enviro 200	3982	3983	3984	3985	3986	3987	3988	3989
	3990	3991	3992	3993	3994	3995	3996	4023
	4024	4025	4026	4027	4028	4029	4030	4031
	4032	4033	4034	4035				
VDL DB250	6213	6214	6215	6216	6217	6218	6219	
Enviro 400	6458	6459	6460	6461	6462	6463	6464	6465
	6466	6467	6468	6469	6470			

Grays (Europa Park, London Road) - GY

Dart	3298	3302	3309	3310				
SB120 Cadet	3502	3524	3525	3971	3972	3973		
Enviro 200	3997	3998	3999	4000	4001	4002	4003	4004
	4005	4006	4007	4008	4009	4010	4068	4069
	4070	4071	4072	4073	4074	4075	4076	4077
	4078	4079						
Volvo B7TL	6110	6111	6112	6113	6114	6115	6116	6117
	6118	6119	6120	6121	6122			

ARRIVA - THE ORIGINAL TOUR

The Original Tour Ltd, Jews Road, Wandsworth, SW18 1TB

XMB763	WD	D553YNO	MCW Metrobus DR115/4	MCW		PO65/31D	1988	New World FirstBus, 2001
XMB776	WD	UAR776Y	MCW Metrobus DR115/3	MCW		059/33D	1983	City Sightseeing, 2004
XMB778	WD	OKZ9778	MCW Metrobus DR115/3	MCW		059/33D	1983	City Sightseeing, 2004
XMB779	WD	MXT179	MCW Metrobus DR115/3	MCW		059/33D	1983	City Sightseeing, 2004
XMB780	WD	IIG7780	MCW Metrobus DR115/3	MCW		059/33D	1983	New World FirstBus, 2004
XMB781	WD	IIG7781	MCW Metrobus DR115/3	MCW		059/33D	1983	New World FirstBus, 2004
XMB782	WD	IIG7782	MCW Metrobus DR115/3	MCW		059/33D	1983	New World FirstBus, 2004
XMB783	WD	HIG7783	MCW Metrobus DR115/3	MCW		059/33D	1983	New World FirstBus, 2004
XMB785	WD	NKJ785	MCW Metrobus DR115/3	MCW		059/33D	1983	New World FirstBus, 2004

DLP17-20
DAF DB250 10.6m — Plaxton President — B45/19D — 1999 — Arriva London, 2012

17	WD	T217XBV	18	WD	T218XBV	19	WD	T219XBV	20	WD	T220XBV

DLP201-216
DAF DB250 10.6m — Plaxton President — PO44/21F — 1999 — Arriva London, 2006/12

201	WD	201KYD	205	WD	T205XBV	209	WD	T209XBV	213	WD	T213XBV
202	WD	T202XBV	206	WD	T206XBV	210	WD	T210XBV	214	WD	T214XBV
203	WD	T203XBV	207	WD	T207XBV	211	WD	T211XBV	215	WD	T215XBV
204	WD	T204XBV	208	WD	T208XBV	212	WD	T212XBV	216	WD	T216XBV

DLP240-265
DAF DB250 10.6m — Plaxton President — O47/23F* — 2001 — *several PO47/23F

240	WD	Y532UGC	247	WD	Y547UGC	254	WD	LJ51DJZ	260	WD	LJ51DKL
241	WD	Y541UGC	248	WD	Y548UGC	255	WD	LJ51DKA	261	WD	LJ51DKN
242	WD	Y542UGC	249	WD	Y549UGC	256	WD	LJ51DKD	262	WD	LJ51DKO
243	WD	Y543UGC	250	WD	LJ51DJU	257	WD	LJ51DKE	263	WD	LJ51DKU
244	WD	Y544UGC	251	WD	LJ51DJV	258	WD	LJ51DKF	264	WD	LJ51DKV
245	WD	Y533UGC	252	WD	LJ51DJX	259	WD	LJ51DKK	265	WD	LJ51DKX
246	WD	Y546UGC	253	WD	LJ51DJY						

London Original open-top tour service is provided by Arriva. Early examples for this operation included tri-axle Metrobuses re-imported from Hong Kong, while more recent buses have been transferred from the main London fleet. One of the latter, DLP201, 201KYD, shows the partial open-top conversion. *Mark Lyons*

Looking very smart as it shows off the delights of London to the large numbers of tourists visiting the capital is VLY601, LX05GDV. This is the first of ten Volvo B7Ls with Ayats bodywork. It is seen passing through Trafalgar Square. *Terry Longhurst*

OA315-349

			Leyland Olympian			Alexander RH			PO43/25D* 1992			*321-32/6-8 are CO43/25D
315	WD	J315BSH	323	WD	J323BSH	330	WD	J330BSH	341	WD	J341BSH	
317	WD	J317BSH	324	WD	JNZ8324	331	WD	J331BSH	342	WD	J342BSH	
318	WD	J318BSH	325	WD	J325BSH	332	WD	J332BSH	343	WD	J343BSH	
319	WD	J319BSH	326	WD	J326BSH	333	WD	J333BSH	344	WD	J344BSH	
320	WD	J320BSH	327	WD	J327BSH	335	WD	J335BSH	347	WD	J347BSH	
321	WD	J321BSH	328	WD	J328BSH	336	WD	J336BSH	349	WD	J349BSH	
322	WD	J322BSH	329	WD	J329BSH	338	WD	J338BSH				

VLY601-610

			Volvo B7L 10.6m			Ayats Bravo City			O51/24F 2005			
601	WD	LX05GDV	604	WD	LX05GEJ	607	WD	LX05KNZ	609	WD	EU05DVW	
602	WD	LX05GDY	605	WD	LX05HRO	608	WD	LX05KOA	610	WD	EU05DVX	
603	WD	LX05GDZ	606	WD	LX05HSC							

VLE611-620

			Volvo B9TL 10.9m			East Lancs Visionaire			PO49/31F 2007			
611	WD	LJ07XEN	614	WD	LJ07XER	617	WD	LJ07XEU	619	WD	LJ07XEW	
612	WD	LJ07XEO	615	WD	LJ07XES	618	WD	LJ07XEV	620	WD	LJ07UDD	
613	WD	LJ07XEP	616	WD	LJ07XET							

VXE721-736

			Volvo B9TL 12.3m			Optare Visionaire			PO59/38F 2011			
721	WD	YJ11TVA	725	WD	YJ11TVF	729	WD	YJ11TVN	733	WD	YJ11TVU	
722	WD	YJ11TVC	726	WD	YJ11TVK	730	WD	YJ11TVO	734	WD	YJ11TVV	
723	WD	YJ11TVD	727	WD	YJ11TVL	731	WD	YJ11TVP	735	WD	YJ11TVW	
724	WD	YJ11TVE	728	WD	YJ11TVM	732	WD	YJ11TVT	736	WD	YJ11TVX	

One of the last British manufactuers to offer a new open-top vehicle was East Lancs with its Visionaire model. Based on the Volvo B9TL it sold in limited numbers before the model was withdrawn after East Lancs was sold to Optare, shortly after this batch was built. Illustrating the model is VXE727, YJ11TVL. *Terry Longhurst*

Previous registrations:

201KYD	V601LGC	IIG7782	CZ8974 (HK), A749WEV
D553YNO	DV471 (HK)	JNZ8324	J324BSH
E965JAR	DV4883 (HK)	MXT179	CY9368 (HK), UAR773Y
HIG7783	CZ2554 (HK), UAR247Y	OKZ9778	DA2952(HK), A737WEV
IIG7780	DB1959 (HK), A755WEV	UAR776Y	CZ3659 (HK)
IIG7781	DA3002 (HK), A750WEV	WKJ785	CY7533 (HK), UAR772Y

Depot and allocation:

Jews Road, Wandsworth - WD

An outstaion at Ferry Lane, rainham is also maintained.

Metrobus	XMB763	XMB765	XMB776	XMB778	XMB779	XMB780	XMB781	XMB782
	XMB783	XMB785						
Olympian	OA315	OA317	OA318	OA319	OA321	OA322	OA323	OA324
	OA325	OA326	OA327	OA328	OA329	OA330	OA331	OA332
	OA336	OA341	OA342	OA343				
DAF DB250	DLP17	DLP18	DLP19	DLP20	DLP201	DLP202	DLP203	DLP204
	DLP205	DLP206	DLP207	DLP208	DLP209	DLP210	DLP211	DLP212
	DLP213	DLP214	DLP215	DLP216	DLP240	DLP241	DLP242	DLP243
	DLP244	DLP245	DLP246	DLP247	DLP248	DLP249	DLP250	DLP251
	DLP252	DLP253	DLP254	DLP255	DLP256	DLP257	DLP258	DLP259
	DLP260	DLP261	DLP262	DLP263	DLP264	DLP265		
Volvo V7TL	VLY601	VLY602	VLY603	VLY604	VLY605	VLY606	VLY607	VLY608
	VLY609	VLY610	VLE611	VLE612	VLE613	VLE614	VLE615	VLE616
	VLE617	VLE618	VLE619	VLE620				
Volvo B9TL	VXE721	VXE722	VXE723	VXE724	VXE725	VXE726	VXE727	VXE728
	VXE729	VXE730	VXE731	VXE732	VXE733	VXE734	VXE735	VXE736

BIG BUS TOURS

The Big Bus Company Ltd, 48 Buckingham Palace Road, London, SW1W 0RN

DA1-12 — Dennis Trident 10m — East Lancs Lolyne — O48/23D* — 2001 — *1/3/6/9 are PO48/23D

DA1	LV51YCD	DA4	LV51YCK	DA7	LV51YCO	DA19	LV51YCF
DA2	LV51YCE	DA5	LV51YCJ	DA8	LV51YCC	DA11	LV51YCG
DA3	LV51YCM	DA6	LV51YCH	DA9	LV51YCL	DA12	LV51YCN

DA201-210 — Volvo B9TL 10.9m — East Lancs Visionaire — PO51/31F* — 2008 — *208-10 are O51/31F

DA201	PF08URP	DA204	PF08URU	DA207	PF08URX	DA209	PF08USB
DA202	PF08URR	DA205	PF08URV	DA208	PF08URZ	DA210	PF08USC
DA203	PF08URS	DA206	PF08URW				

DA211-220 — Volvo B9TL 10.9m — Optare Visionaire — O51/31F* — 2009 — *211-3 are PO51/31F

DA211	PN09ENY	DA214	PN09EOC	DA217	PN09EOF	DA219	PN09EOJ
DA212	PN09EOA	DA215	PN09EOD	DA218	PN09EOH	DA220	PN09EOK
DA213	PN09EOB	DA216	PN09EOE				

DA321-326 — Volvo B9TL 12.35m — Optare Visionaire — PO63/38F — 2010

DA321	PN10FOC	DA323	PN10FOF	DA325	PN10FOJ	DA326	PN10FOK
DA322	PN10FOD	DA324	PN10FOH				

AN327-346 — Ankai HFF612121GS 11.9m — Ankai — PO57/25D — 2012 — *331/7-40/2-6 are O57/25D

AN327	LJ12GKL	AN332	LJ12JSY	AN337	LX12AZF	AN342	LJ12JVZ
AN328	LJ12GSZ	AN333	LJ12JWA	AN338	LX12AYN	AN343	LF12ACZ
AN329	LJ12GSZ	AN334	LX12AZL	AN339	LJ12JVK	AN344	LF12ADU
AN330	LJ12GTZ	AN335	LJ12LJL	AN340	LF12AHE	AN345	LJ12MYH
AN331	LJ12JUD	AN336	LJ12JUT	AN341	LJ12JVL	AN346	LJ12MYG

Contrasting the liveries of the rival sightseeing operators is another Visionaire, one of twenty-six operated by Big Bus Tours. DA324, PN10FOH, is seen outside St Paul's Cathedral. *Richard Godfrey*

Big Bus Tours is a family-owned company founded in London in June 1991 with four buses and currently operates over 150 buses worldwide. Brought back from Hong Kong some ten years ago were several Dennis Condor buses, then converted in the UK for use on London tours. D956, G956FVX, is seen in Park Lane. *Richard Godfrey*

DHL14	B14BUS	Dennis Condor DDA1702	Duple Metsec	PO62/40D	1989	New World First Bus, 2003
DM32	G32FWC	Dennis Condor DDA1702	Duple Metsec	O62/40D	1989	New World First Bus, 2003
DHM34	G34FWC	Dennis Condor DDA1702	Duple Metsec	PO62/40D	1989	New World First Bus, 2003
HD42	G42FWC	Dennis Condor DDA1702	Duple Metsec	PO62/40D	1989	New World First Bus, 2003
DM59	F59SYE	Dennis Condor DDA1702	Duple Metsec	O62/40D	1989	New World First Bus, 2003
MBD67	F67SYE	Dennis Condor DDA1702	Duple Metsec	O62/40D	1989	New World First Bus, 2003
DM96	G96SGO	Dennis Condor DDA1702	Duple Metsec	O62/40D	1989	New World First Bus, 2003
D159	G159FWC	Dennis Condor DDA1702	Duple Metsec	O62/40D	1989	New World First Bus, 2003
DL418	F418UJN	Dennis Condor DDA1702	Duple Metsec	O62/40D	1989	New World First Bus, 2003
HD938	G938FVX	Dennis Condor DDA1702	Duple Metsec	PO62/40D	1989	New World First Bus, 2003
HD939	G939FVX	Dennis Condor DDA1702	Duple Metsec	PO62/40D	1989	New World First Bus, 2003
DL943	G943FVX	Dennis Condor DDA1702	Duple Metsec	O62/40D	1989	New World First Bus, 2003
DL952	G952FVX	Dennis Condor DDA1702	Duple Metsec	O62/40D	1989	New World First Bus, 2003
DHM953	G953FVX	Dennis Condor DDA1702	Duple Metsec	PO62/40D	1989	New World First Bus, 2003
DHM954	G954FVX	Dennis Condor DDA1702	Duple Metsec	PO62/40D	1989	New World First Bus, 2003
D956	G956FVX	Dennis Condor DDA1702	Duple Metsec	O62/40D	1989	New World First Bus, 2003
DHM964	G964FVX	Dennis Condor DDA1702	Duple Metsec	PO62/40D	1989	New World First Bus, 2003
DM969	G969FVX	Dennis Condor DDA1702	Duple Metsec	O62/40D	1989	New World First Bus, 2003
D991	G991FVX	Dennis Condor DDA1702	Duple Metsec	O62/40D	1989	New World First Bus, 2003

The latest additions to the Big Bus Tours fleet in London are twenty Ankai HFFs, a purpose-built model which Big Bus also operates in Hong Kong and Shanghai. Anhui Ankai Automobile Co. trading as Ankai is a Chinese automotive manufacturing based in Hefei. AN331, LJ12JUD, is shown. *Richard Godfrey*

Previous registrations:

B14BUS	-	G939FVX	EG857 (HK)
F59SYE	EF4079 (HK)	G943FVX	EH7098 (HK)
F67SYE	EF750 (HK)	G952FVX	EH9876 (HK)
F418UJN	EF3349 (HK)	G953FVX	EG9386 (HK)
G32FWC	EJ2225 (HK)	G954FVX	EH6884 (HK)
G34FWC	EG2166 (HK)	G956FVX	EH4324 (HK)
G42FWC	EH6321 (HK)	G964FVX	EG6964 (HK)
G96SGO	EF5328 (HK)	G969FVX	EJ3811 (HK)
G159FWC	-	G991FVX	EG4627 (HK)
G938FVX	EG9356 (HK)		

Depot and allocation:

EARLSFIELD

Trident	DA1	DA2	DA3	DA4	DA5	DA6	DA7	DA8
	DA9	DA10	DA11	DA12				
Volvo B9TL	DA201	DA202	DA203	DA204	DA205	DA206	DA207	DA208
	DA209	DA210	DA211	DA212	DA213	DA214	DA215	DA216
	DA217	DA218	DA219	DA220	DA321	DA322	DA323	DA324
	DA325	DA326						
Dennis Condor	D32	D59	D96	D159	D418	D943	D952	D956
	D969	D991	DHL14	HD34	HD42	HD938	HD939	HD953
	HD954	HD964	MBD67					
Ankai	AN327	AN328	AN329	AN330	AN331	AN332	AN333	AN334
	AN335	AN336	AN337	AN338	AN339	AN340	AN341	AN342
	AN343	AN344	AN345	AN346				

GO-AHEAD LONDON

London Central Bus Co Ltd; London General Transport Services Ltd

18 Merton High Street, London, SW19 1DN

DMN1	NP	LT02NUK	TransBus Dart 8.9m			Marshall Capital		N25F	2002	First, 2013

DMN2-6			Dennis Dart SLF 10.2m			Marshall Capital		N28D	2001	First, 2013
2	BE	LN51DWL	4	BE	LN51DWO	5	BE	LN51DWP	6	BE	LN51DWU
3	BE	LN51DWN								

DMN7-18			TransBus Dart 8.9m			Marshall Capital		N25F	2002	First, 2013
7	BE	LT02NUM	10	BE	LT02NUU	13	BE	LT52WUP	16	BE	LT02NVJ
8	BE	LT02NUO	11	BE	LT02NUV	14	BE	LT52WUO	17	BE	LT52WUM
9	BE	LT02NUP	12	BE	LT02NVE	15	BE	LT02NVH	18	BE	LT52WUR

DOE1-54			ADL Trident 2 10.3m			Optare Olympus		N43/21D	2008-09
1	A	LX58CWN	15	A	LX58CXE	29	A	LX58CXV	42	A	LX09BXL
2	A	LX58CWO	16	A	LX58CXF	30	A	LX58CXW	43	A	LX09BXM
3	A	LX58CWP	17	A	LX58CXG	31	A	LX58CXY	44	A	LX09BXO
4	A	LX58CWR	18	A	LX58CXH	32	A	LX58CXZ	45	A	LX09AXU
5	A	LX58CWT	19	A	LX58CXJ	33	A	LX58CYA	46	A	LX09AXV
6	A	LX58CWU	20	A	LX58CXK	34	A	LX58CYC	47	A	LX09AXW
7	A	LX58CWV	21	A	LX58CXL	35	A	LX58CYE	48	A	LX09AXY
8	A	LX58CWW	22	A	LX58CXN	36	A	LX58CYF	49	A	LX09AXZ
9	A	LX58CWY	23	A	LX58CXO	37	A	LX58CYG	50	A	LX09AYA
10	A	LX58CWZ	24	A	LX58CXP	38	A	LX09BXG	51	A	LX09AYB
11	A	LX58CXA	25	A	LX58CXR	39	A	LX09BXH	52	A	LX09AYC
12	A	LX58CXB	26	A	LX58CXS	40	A	LX09BXJ	53	A	LX09AYD
13	A	LX58CXC	27	A	LX58CXT	41	A	LX09BXK	54	A	LX09AYE
14	A	LX58CXD	28	A	LX58CXU					

DP192	NX	EJ52WXF	TransBus Dart 10.7m			TransBus Pointer		N36D	2003	Blue Triangle, 2007

Go-Ahead operates its main London operation from thirteen depots across the capital in addition to its Metrobus operation. Fifty Trident 2s bodied by Optare at its former Blackburn facility are operated. Illustrating the style is DOE37, LX58CYG. All are allocated to Sutton depot from where it is seen working route 154. *Richard Godfrey*

DP193-205 — TransBus Dart 10.7m / TransBus Pointer — N33D — 2003-04 — Blue Triangle, 2007

No.		Reg	No.		Reg	No.		Reg	No.		Reg
193	SW	EU53PXY	197	SW	EU53PYD	200	SW	EU53PYH	203	SW	EU53PYO
194	SW	EU53PXZ	198	SW	EU53PYF	201	SW	EU53PYJ	204	SW	EU53PYP
195	SW	EU53PYA	199	SW	EU53PYG	202	SW	EU53PYL	205	SW	BT04BUS
196	SW	EU53PYB									

No.		Reg	Chassis	Body	Layout	Year	Notes
DP208	BE	SN56AYC	ADL Dart 10.7m	ADL Pointer	N33D	2006	Blue Triangle, 2007
DP209	SW	SN56AYD	ADL Dart 10.7m	ADL Pointer	N33D	2006	Blue Triangle, 2007

DW1-12 — DAF SB120 9.4m / Wrightbus Cadet 2 — N23D — 2003 — East Thames, 2009

No.		Reg	No.		Reg	No.		Reg	No.		Reg
1	AL	LF52TKJ	4	AL	LF52TJY	7	AL	LF52TKO	10	AL	LF52TKE
2	AL	LF52TKC	5	AL	LF52TJV	8	AL	LF52TKK	11	AL	LF52TKN
3	AL	LF52TKD	6	AL	LF52TJX	9	AL	LF52TKT	12	AL	LF52TKA

DWL13-37 — VDL Bus SB120 10.8m / Wrightbus Cadet 2 — N30D — 2004 — East Thames, 2009

No.		Reg	No.		Reg	No.		Reg	No.		Reg
13	MW	BX04BX	18	BX	FJ54ZDP	26	NX	FJ54ZFA	33	NX	FJ54
15	BX	BX04BXN	19	BX	FJ54ZDT	27	NX	FJ54ZTV	34	NX	FJ54
16	BX	BX04BXM	21	BX	FJ54ZDV	31	NX	FJ54ZTZ	36	NX	FJ54ZVB
17	BX	FJ54ZDR	22	BX	FJ54ZDW	32	NX	FJ54ZUA	37	MW	FJ54ZDC

E1-39 — ADL Trident 2 10.1m / ADL Enviro 400 — N41/26D* — 2006 — *1-15 are N41/24D

No.		Reg	No.		Reg	No.		Reg	No.		Reg
1	SW	SN06BNA	11	SW	SN06BNV	21	PM	LX06EZR	31	PM	LX06EZF
2	SW	SN06BNB	12	SW	SN06BNX	22	PM	LX06EZS	32	PM	LX06EZG
3	SW	SN06BND	13	SW	SN06BNY	23	PM	LX06EZT	33	PM	LX06EZH
4	SW	SN06BNE	14	SW	SN06BNZ	24	PM	LX06EYY	34	PM	LX06ECT
5	SW	SN06BNF	15	SW	SN06BOF	25	PM	LX06EYZ	35	PM	LX06ECV
6	SW	SN06BNJ	16	SW	LX06EZL	26	PM	LX06EZA	36	PM	LX06FKL
7	SW	SN06BNK	17	PM	LX06EZM	27	PM	LX06EZB	37	PM	LX06FKM
8	SW	SN06BNL	18	PM	LX06EZN	28	PM	LX06EZC	38	SW	LX06FKN
9	SW	SN06BNO	19	PM	LX06EZO	29	PM	LX06EZD	39	BX	LX06FKO
10	SW	SN06BNU	20	PM	LX06EZP	30	PM	LX06EZE			

E40-56 — ADL Trident 2 10.1m / ADL Enviro 400 — N41/26D — 2006-07

No.		Reg	No.		Reg	No.		Reg	No.		Reg
40	BX	LX56ETD	45	BX	LX56ETL	50	BX	LX56ETV	54	BX	LX56EUB
41	BX	LX56ETE	46	BX	LX56ETO	51	BX	LX56ETY	55	BX	LX56EUC
42	BX	LX56ETF	47	BX	LX56ETR	52	BX	LX56ETZ	56	BX	LX56EUD
43	BX	LX56ETJ	48	BX	LX56ETT	53	BX	LX56EUA			
44	BX	LX56ETK	49	BX	LX56ETU						

Further Trident 2s, this time with Alexander Dennis Enviro 400 bodywork, are operated as class E. Stockwell's E75, LX57CKD, is seen heading for Tooting on route 280. *Terry Longhurst*

From the 2011 intake of Enviro 400s, E196, SN61BJZ, is seen at Canada Water while heading for Tottenham Court Road. It is one of almost forty of the type now working from Mandella Way depot, in Southwark.
Dave Heath

E57-99

ADL Trident 2 10.1M   ADL Enviro 400   N39/25D*   2007-08   *57 is N41/26D

57	AL	LX07BYH	68	AL	LX57CJO	79	AL	LX57CKJ	90	AL	LX57CLN
58	A	LX07BYC	69	AL	LX57CJU	80	AL	LX57CKK	91	AL	LX57CLO
59	A	LX07BYD	70	AL	LX57CJV	81	AL	LX57CKL	92	AL	LX57CLV
60	A	LX07BYF	71	AL	LX57CJY	82	AL	LX57CKN	93	AL	LX57CLY
61	PM	LX07BYG	72	AL	LX57CJZ	83	AL	LX57CKO	94	NX	LX08EBP
62	SW	LX57CHV	73	AL	LX57CKA	84	AL	LX57CKP	95	NX	LX08EBU
63	SW	LX57CHY	74	AL	LX57CKC	85	AL	LX57CKU	96	NX	LX08EBV
64	SW	LX57CHZ	75	AL	LX57CKD	86	AL	LX57CKV	97	NX	LX08EBZ
65	SW	LX57CJE	76	AL	LX57CKE	87	AL	LX57CKY	98	NX	LX08ECA
66	SW	LX57CJF	77	AL	LX57CKF	88	AL	LX57CLF	99	NX	LX08ECC
67	BX	LX57CJJ	78	AL	LX57CKG	89	AL	LX57CLJ			

E100-128

ADL Trident 2 10.1M   ADL Enviro 400   N39/26D   2009

100	Q	LX09EZU	108	Q	LX09FAO	115	Q	LX09FBF	122	Q	LX09FBV
101	Q	LX09EZV	109	Q	LX09FAU	116	Q	LX09FBG	123	Q	LX09FBY
102	Q	LX09EZW	110	Q	LX09FBA	117	Q	LX09FBJ	124	Q	LX09FBZ
103	Q	LX09EZZ	111	Q	LX09FBB	118	Q	LX09FBK	125	Q	LX09FCA
104	Q	LX09FAF	112	Q	LX09FBC	119	Q	LX09FBN	126	Q	LX09FCC
105	Q	LX09FAJ	113	Q	LX09FBD	120	Q	LX09FBO	127	Q	LX09FCD
106	Q	LX09FAK	114	Q	LX09FBE	121	Q	LX09FBU	128	Q	LX09FCE
107	Q	LX09FAM									

E129-150

ADL Trident 2 10.1M   ADL Enviro 400   N41/26D   2010

129	SW	SN60BZA	135	SW	SN60BZG	141	AL	SN60BZO	146	AL	SN60BZU
130	SW	SN60BZB	136	SW	SN60BZH	142	AL	SN60BZP	147	AL	SN60BZV
131	SW	SN60BZC	137	SW	SN60BZJ	143	AL	SN60BZR	148	AL	SN60BZW
132	SW	SN60BZD	138	AL	SN60BZK	144	AL	SN60BZS	149	AL	SN60BZX
133	SW	SN60BZE	139	AL	SN60BZL	145	AL	SN60BZT	150	AL	SN60BZY
134	SW	SN60BZF	140	AL	SN60BZM						

Further Enviro 400s continue to join Go-Ahead London. Here, E212, SN61DDJ, from the London Central operation is seen at Victoria while working route 36. Several of the 2012 intake were assembled by Plaxton at Scarborough where a production line for the Enviro 400 has been established alongside the Enviro 200 line. *Laurie Rufus*

E151-204

		ADL Trident 2	10.1M			ADL Enviro 400		N41/24D*	2011		*saeting varies
151	SW	SN11BTY	165	MW	SN61BGO	179	MW	SN61BHO	192	MW	SN61BJU
152	SW	SN11BTZ	166	MW	SN61BGU	180	MW	SN61BHP	193	MW	SN61BJV
153	SW	SN11BUA	167	MW	SN61BGV	181	MW	SN61BHU	194	MW	SN61BJX
154	SW	SN11BUE	168	MW	SN61BGX	182	MW	SN61BHV	195	MW	SN61BJY
155	SW	SN11BUF	169	MW	SN61BGY	183	MW	SN61BHW	196	MW	SN61BJZ
156	SW	SN11BUH	170	MW	SN61BGZ	184	MW	SN61BHX	197	MW	SN61BKA
157	SW	SN11BUJ	171	MW	SN61BHA	185	MW	SN61BHY	198	MW	SN61BKD
158	SW	SN11BUO	172	MW	SN61BHD	186	MW	SN61BHZ	199	MW	SN61BKE
159	SW	SN11BUP	173	MW	SN61BGE	187	MW	SN61BJE	200	MW	SN61BKF
160	SW	SN11BUU	174	MW	SN61BHE	188	MW	SN61BJF	201	MW	SN61BKG
161	SW	SN11BUV	175	MW	SN61BHF	189	MW	SN61BJJ	202	BX	SN61BKJ
162	SW	SN11BUW	176	MW	SN61BHJ	190	MW	SN61BJK	203	BX	SN61BKK
163	MW	SN61BGF	177	MW	SN61BHK	191	MW	SN61BJO	204	BX	SN61BKL
164	MW	SN61BGK	178	MW	SN61BHL						

E205-245

		ADL E40D	10.2m			ADL Enviro 400		N41/24D	2011-12		
205	BX	SN61DCV	216	NX	SN61DDU	226	NX	SN61DFF	236	BX	YX61DTK
206	BX	SN61DCX	217	NX	SN61DDV	227	NX	SN61DFG	237	BX	YX61DTN
207	BX	SN61DCY	218	NX	SN61DDX	228	NX	SN61DFJ	238	BX	YX61DPF
208	NX	SN61DCZ	219	NX	SN61DDY	229	BX	YX61DSE	239	BX	YX61DPK
209	NX	SN61DDA	220	NX	SN61DDZ	230	BX	YX61DSV	240	BX	YX61DPN
210	NX	SN61DDE	221	NX	SN61DEU	231	BX	YX61DSO	241	BX	YX61DPO
211	NX	SN61DDF	222	NX	SN61DFA	232	BX	YX61DSU	242	BX	YX61DPU
212	NX	SN61DDJ	223	NX	SN61DFC	233	BX	YX61DSY	243	BX	YX61DPV
213	NX	SN61DDK	224	NX	SN61DFD	234	BX	YX61DSZ	244	BX	YX61DPY
214	NX	SN61DDL	225	NX	SN61DFE	235	BX	YX61DTF	245	BX	YX61DPZ
215	NX	SN61DDO									

E246-260

		ADL E40D	10.2m			ADL Enviro 400		N41/24D	2012		
246	NX	YX12FPA	250	NX	YX12FPF	254	NX	YX12FPL	258	NX	YX12FPT
247	NX	YX12FPC	251	NX	YX12FPG	255	NX	YX12FPN	259	NX	YX12FPU
248	NX	YX12FPD	252	NX	YX12FPJ	256	NX	YX12FPO	260	NX	YX12FPV
249	NX	YX12FPE	253	NX	YX12FPK	257	NX	YX12FPP			

MCV Evolution bodywork is fitted to three batches of Darts. Egyptian Bus and Coach Manufacturer MCV has developed the former Stirling model now imported to the UK on a variety of chassis. Illustrating the styling is ED1, AE06HCA, seen at Stratford while working route 108. *Dave Heath*

E261-280

ADL E40D 10.2m | ADL Enviro 400 | N41/24D 2013

261	NX	SN62DDE	266	NX	SN62DGF	271	NX	SN62DJO	276	NP	SN13CJE
262	NX	SN62DDO	267	NX	SN62DGU	272	NX	SN62DHJ	277	AL	SN13CJF
263	NX	SN62CCX	268	NX	SN62DHA	273	NX	SN62DLY	278	AL	SN13CJJ
264	NX	SN62DFL	269	NX	SN62DHX	274	NX	SN62DLZ	279	AL	SN13CJO
265	NX	SN62DFX	270	NX	SN62DHZ	275	NX	SN62SMV	280	AL	SN13CJU

ED1-8

ADL Dart 4 10.8m | MCV Evolution | N29D 2006

1	NX	AE06HCA	3	NX	AE06HCD	5	NX	AE06HCG	7	NX	AE06HCJ
2	NX	AE06HCC	4	NX	AE06HCF	6	NX	AE06HCH	8	NX	AE06HCK

ED9-17

ADL Dart 4 9.2m | MCV Evolution | N23D 2006

9	BE	AE56OUH	12	BE	AE56OUL	14	BE	AE56OUN	16	BE	AE56OUP
10	BE	AE56OUJ	13	BE	AE56OUM	15	BE	AE56OUO	17	BE	AE56OUS
11	BE	AE56OUK									

ED18-28

ADL Dart 4 10.4m | MCV Evolution | N29D 2007

18	BE	LX07BYJ	21	BE	LX07BYM	24	BE	LX07BYP	27	BE	LX07BYT
19	BE	LX07BYK	22	BE	LX07BYN	25	BE	LX07BYR	28	SI	LX07BYU
20	BE	LX07BYL	23	BE	LX07BYO	26	BE	LX07BYS			

EH1-5

ADL Trident E400H 10.1m | ADL Enviro 400 | N37/25D 2008-09

1	SW	LX58DDJ	3	SW	LX58DDL	4	SW	LX58DDN	5	SW	LX58DDO
2	SW	LX58DDK									

EH6-20

ADL E40H 10.2m | ADL Enviro 400 | N37/24D 2011

6	NX	SN61BLJ	10	NX	SN61DAO	14	NX	SN61DBV	18	NX	SN61DCE
7	NX	SN61BLK	11	NX	SN61DAU	15	NX	SN61DBX	19	NX	SN61DCO
8	NX	SN61BLV	12	NX	SN61DBO	16	NX	SN61DBY	20	NX	SN61DCU
9	NX	SN61DAA	13	NX	SN61DBU	17	NX	SN61DBZ			

EH21-38

ADL E40H 10.2m | ADL Enviro 400 | N37/24D 2013

21	SW	YX13BJE	26	SW	YX13BJU	31	SW	YX13BKD	35	SW	YX13BKJ
22	SW	YX13BJF	27	SW	YX13BJV	32	SW	YX13BKE	36	SW	YX13BKK
23	SW	YX13BJJ	28	SW	YX13BJY	33	SW	YX13BKF	37	SW	YX13BKL
24	SW	YX13BJK	29	SW	YX13BJZ	34	SW	YX13BKG	38	SW	YX13BKN
25	SW	YX13BJO	30	SW	YX13BKA						

Acquired with the East London operation in 2009 were fourteen Scania N94s with East Lancashire Myllennium bodywork. Now allocated to Southwark, ELS11, YR52VFK, represents the batch as it heads for Denmark Hill while working route 42. *Dave Heath*

ELS1-14

Scania N94 UB 10.6m   East Lancashire Myllennium   N29D   2002   East Thames, 2009

1	MW	YU02GHG	5	MW	YU02GHD	9	MW	YR52VFJ	12	MW	YR52VFL
2	MW	YU02GHH	6	MW	YU02GHA	10	MW	YR52VFH	13	MW	YR52VFM
3	MW	YU02GHJ	7	MW	YU02GHN	11	MW	YR52VFK	14	MW	YR52VFN
4	MW	YU02GHK	8	MW	YU02GHO						

EN1-24

ADL Trident 2 10.1m   ADL Enviro 400   N41/26D   2008   First, 2012

1	NP	SN58CDY	7	NP	SN58CEO	13	NP	SN58CFD	19	NP	LK08FLJ
2	NP	SN58CDZ	8	NP	SN58CEU	14	NP	SN58CFE	20	NP	LK08FLL
3	NP	SN58CEA	9	NP	SN58CEV	15	NP	SN58CFF	21	NP	LK08FLM
4	NP	SN58CEF	10	NP	SN58CEX	16	NP	SN58CFG	22	NP	LK08FLN
5	NP	SN58CEJ	11	NP	SN58CEY	17	NP	SN58CFJ	23	NP	LK08FLP
6	NP	SN58CEK	12	NP	SN58CFA	18	NP	LK08FLH	24	NP	LK08FLR

EN25	BE	LK57EJN	ADL Trident 2 10.1m	ADL Enviro 400	N41/26D	2008	First, 2013
EN26	BE	LK57EJO	ADL Trident 2 10.1m	ADL Enviro 400	N41/26D	2008	First, 2013
EN27	BE	LK08FLX	ADL Trident 2 10.1m	ADL Enviro 400	N41/26D	2008	First, 2013
LDP151	PL	Y851TGH	Dennis Dart SLF 8.8m	Plaxton Pointer MPD	N29F	2001	
LDP183	AF	Y983TGH	Dennis Dart SLF 9.3m	Plaxton Pointer 2	N28F	2001	
LDP186	SW	Y986TGH	Dennis Dart SLF 9.3m	Plaxton Pointer 2	N28F	2001	
LDP187	SW	Y987TGH	Dennis Dart SLF 9.3m	Plaxton Pointer 2	N28F	2001	

LDP191-227

Dennis Dart SLF 10.1m   Plaxton Pointer 2   N30D*   2002   *203-27 are N27D

191	BE	SN51UAD	201	AL	SN51UAP	210	NX	SN51UAZ	219	PL	SK52MPF
192	BE	SN51UAE	202	BX	SN51UAR	211	PL	SK52MMU	220	PL	SK52MPO
193	BE	SN51UAF	203	AF	SN51UAS	212	PL	SK52MMV	221	PL	SK52MLU
194	BE	SN51UAG	204	SW	SN51UAT	213	PL	SK52MMX	222	PL	SK52MLV
195	BE	SN51UAH	205	BX	SN51UAU	214	PL	SK52MOA	223	PL	SK52MLX
196	BE	SN51UAJ	206	MW	SN51UAV	215	PL	SK52MOF	224	PL	SK52MLY
197	u	SN51UAK	207	BX	SN51UAW	216	PL	SK52MOU	225	PL	SK52MLZ
198	u	SN51UAL	208	PL	SN51UAX	217	PL	SK52MOV	226	PL	SK52MMA
199	BE	SN51UAM	209	NX	SN51UAY	218	PL	SK52MPE	227	PL	SK52MME
200	u	SN51UAO									

LDP249-262

TransBus Dart 10.1m   TransBus Pointer   N27D   2003

249	Q	SN53KKF	253	Q	SN53KKL	257	Q	SN53KKR	260	Q	SN53KKV
250	Q	SN53KKG	254	Q	SN53KKM	258	Q	SN53KKT	261	Q	SN53KKW
251	Q	SN53KKH	255	Q	SN53KKO	259	Q	SN53KKU	262	Q	SN53KKX
252	Q	SN53KKJ	256	Q	SN53KKP						

Delivered in 2009 to replace articulated buses on Red Arrow service were fifty Mercedes-Benz Citaro buses now operating successfully elsewhere. Putney Bridge is the location for this view of MEC18, BD09ZPY, which, as shown, was working a rail replacement service. *Dave Heath*

LDP263-272

ADL Dart 8.8m — ADL Pointer — N23F — 2005

263	PL	LX05EYP	266	PL	LX05EYT	269	PL	LX05EYW	271	PL	LX05EXZ
264	PL	LX05EYR	267	PL	LX05EYU	270	PL	LX05EYY	272	PL	LX05EYA
265	PL	LX05EYS	268	PL	LX05EYV						

LDP273-280

ADL Dart 10.1m — ADL Pointer — N28D — 2006

273	NX	LX06EYT	275	NX	LX06EYV	277	NX	LX06FBD	279	NX	LX06FAA
274	NX	LX06EYU	276	NX	LX06EYW	278	NX	LX06FBE	280	NX	LX06FAF

LDP281-291

ADL Dart 8.8m — ADL Pointer — N23F — 2006

281	AF	LX06FAJ	284	AF	LX06FAO	287	SW	LX06FBB	290	SW	LX06EZV
282	AF	LX06FAK	285	AF	LX06FAU	288	SW	LX06FBC	291	SW	LX06EZW
283	AF	LX06FAM	286	AF	LX06FBA	289	SW	LX06EZU			

LDP292	PL	LX06EZZ	ADL Dart 10.1m	ADL Pointer	N28D	2006
LDP293	PL	LX06EZJ	ADL Dart 10.1m	ADL Pointer	N28D	2006
LDP294	PL	LX06EZK	ADL Dart 10.1m	ADL Pointer	N28D	2006

LT41-68

Wrightbus NBfL — Wrightbus — N40/22T — On order

41	SW	LTZ1041	48	SW	LTZ1048	55	SW	LTZ1055	62	SW	LTZ1062
42	SW	LTZ1042	49	SW	LTZ1049	56	SW	LTZ1056	63	SW	LTZ1063
43	SW	LTZ1043	50	SW	LTZ1050	57	SW	LTZ1057	64	SW	LTZ1064
44	SW	LTZ1044	51	SW	LTZ1051	58	SW	LTZ1058	65	SW	LTZ1065
45	SW	LTZ1045	52	SW	LTZ1052	59	SW	LTZ1059	66	SW	LTZ1066
46	SW	LTZ1046	53	SW	LTZ1053	60	SW	LTZ1060	67	SW	LTZ1067
47	SW	LTZ1047	54	SW	LTZ1054	61	SW	LTZ1061	68	SW	LTZ1068

MEC1-50

Mercedes-Benz Citaro O530 — Mercedes-Benz — N21D — 2009

1	RA	BG09JJK	14	RA	BD09ZPU	27	RA	BD09ZVS	39	RA	BD09ZWF
2	RA	BG09JJL	15	RA	BD09ZPV	28	RA	BD09ZVT	40	MW	BD09ZWG
3	RA	BG09JJU	16	RA	BD09ZPW	29	RA	BD09ZVU	41	RA	BD09ZWH
4	RA	BG09JJV	17	RA	BD09ZPX	30	RA	BD09ZVV	42	RA	BT09GOH
5	RA	BG09JJX	18	RA	BD09ZPY	31	RA	BD09ZVW	43	RA	BT09GOJ
6	RA	BG09JJY	19	RA	BD09ZPZ	32	MW	BD09ZVX	44	RA	BT09GOK
7	RA	BG09JJZ	20	RA	BD09ZRA	33	RA	BD09ZVY	45	MW	BT09GOP
8	RA	BG09JKE	21	RA	BD09ZRC	34	RA	BD09ZVZ	46	RA	BT09GOU
9	RA	BG09JKF	22	RA	BD09ZRE	35	RA	BD09ZWA	47	RA	BT09GOX
10	RA	BG09JKJ	23	RA	BD09ZRF	36	RA	BD09ZWB	48	MW	BT09GPE
11	RA	BD09ZPR	24	RA	BD09ZRG	37	MW	BD09ZWC	49	MW	BT09GPF
12	RA	BD09ZPS	25	RA	BD09ZRJ	38	MW	BD09ZWE	50	RA	BT09GPJ
13	RA	BD09ZPT	26	RA	BD09ZRK						

The President body was the successor to the Northern Counties Palatine and was introduced as the Plaxton name started to be used for production at Wigan, a facility closed down following the rescue of TransBus by a group of Scottish businessmen. The model is still popular with PVL347, PF52WPX, seen at New Cross. *Richard Godfrey*

NV170	AL	R370LGH	Volvo Olympian			Northern Counties Palatine II	CO47/24D	1997		
NV171	AL	R371LGH	Volvo Olympian			Northern Counties Palatine II	CO47/24D	1998		

PVL59-143
Volvo B7TL 10m   Plaxton President   N41/19D   2000

59	Qt	W459WGH	76	Qt	W476WGH	97	BE	W497WGH	133	Qt	W533WGH
60	Qt	W996WGH	79	u	W479WGH	110	BE	W401WGH	134	Qt	W534WGH
61	PM	W461WGH	80	Qt	W408WGH	112	AL	W512WGH	135	Qt	W435WGH
62	Qt	W462WGH	82	Qt	W482WGH	113	NP	W513WGH	136	Qt	W536WGH
64	Q	W464WGH	83	w	W483WGH	115	BE	W415WGH	137	Qt	W537WGH
66	SI	W466WGH	85	BXW	W485WGH	120	Qt	W402WGH	138	Qt	W538WGH
67	SI	W467WGH	86	Qt	W486WGH	123	Qt	W523WGH	139	Qt	W539WGH
68	BE	W468WGH	92	Qt	W492WGH	129	Qt	W529WGH	140	Qt	W404WGH
69	BE	W469WGH	94	BX	W494WGH	130	Qt	W403WGH	141	Qt	W541WGH
70	BE	W578DGU	95	BE	W495WGH	131	Qt	W531WGH	142	Qt	W542WGH
75	Qt	W475WGH	96	BE	W496WGH	132	Qt	W532WGH	143	Qt	W543WGH

PVL145-208
Volvo B7TL 10m   Plaxton President   N41/20D   2000

145	BX	X745EGK	153	BX	X553EGK	163	BX	X563EGK	189	w	X589EGK
146	w	X546EGK	154	BX	X554EGK	164	BX	X564EGK	203	SW	X503EGK
147	u	X547EGK	155	BX	X615EGK	165	BX	X656EGK	204	u	X504EGK
148	u	X548EGK	159	NX	X559EGK	166	BX	X566EGK	205	u	X705EGK
149	u	X549EGK	160	BX	X616EGK	167	BX	X567EGK	206	u	X506EGK
150	u	X599EGK	161	BX	X561EGK	169	u	X569EGK	207	u	X507EGK
151	NX	X551EGK	162	BX	X562EGK	170	NX	X707EGK	208	BE	X508EGK
152	BX	X552EGK									

PVL209-272
Volvo B7TL 10m   Plaxton President   N41/20D*   2001-02   *263-5 are NC41/20D
*219/21-3 are N41/25F, 224 is PO41/20D

209	BE	Y809TGH	221	AF	Y821TGH	231	BE	Y731TGH	244	SW	Y744TGH
214	u	Y814TGH	222	AF	Y822TGH	232	MW	Y732TGH	245	AF	Y745TGH
215	AL	Y815TGH	223	BE	Y823TGH	233	MW	Y733TGH	248	NX	Y748TGH
216	BX	Y816TGH	224	BE	Y824TGH	234	u	Y734TGH	263	AF	PN02XBL
217	BX	Y817TGH	225	NX	Y825TGH	235	u	Y735TGH	264	NX	PN02XBM
218	AF	Y818TGH	226	AF	Y826TGH	236	u	Y736TGH	265	AF	PN02XBO
219	NX	Y819TGH	229	BX	Y729TGH	237	u	Y737TGH	272	Q	PN02XBW
220	SW	Y802TGH	230	u	Y703TGH	238	u	Y738TGH			

PVL276-354 — Volvo B7TL 10m — TransBus President — N41/20D — 2002-03

No.		Reg	No.		Reg	No.		Reg	No.		Reg
276	w	PJ02RBO	299	Q	PJ02RFL	318	Q	PJ52LVV	337	PM	PJ52LWS
281	A	PJ02RBZ	300	Q	PJ02RFN	319	NX	PJ52LVW	338	PM	PJ52LWT
282	A	PJ02RCF	301	Q	PJ02RFO	320	NX	PJ52LVX	339	PM	PJ52LWU
283	A	PJ02RCO	302	Q	PJ02RFX	321	NX	PJ52LVY	340	PM	PJ52LWV
284	A	PJ02RCU	303	Q	PJ02RFY	322	NX	PJ52LVZ	341	PM	PJ52LWW
285	A	PJ02RCV	304	Q	PJ02RFZ	323	NX	PJ52LWA	342	PM	PJ52LWX
286	A	PJ02RCX	305	Q	PJ02RGO	324	NX	PJ52LWC	343	NX	PF52WPT
287	A	PJ02RCY	306	Q	PJ02RGU	325	NX	PJ52LWD	344	NX	PF52WPU
288	A	PJ02RCZ	307	Q	PJ02RGV	326	Q	PJ52LWE	345	NX	PF52WPV
289	A	PJ02RDO	308	Q	PJ02TVN	327	Q	PJ52LWF	346	NX	PF52WPW
290	A	PJ02RDU	309	Q	PJ02TVO	328	Q	PJ52LWG	347	NX	PF52WPX
291	A	PJ02RDV	310	Q	PJ02TVP	329	PM	PJ52LWH	348	NX	PF52WPY
292	A	PJ02RDX	311	Q	PJ02TVT	330	PM	PJ52LWK	349	NX	PF52WPZ
293	A	PJ02RDY	312	Q	PJ02TVU	331	PM	PJ52LWL	350	NX	PF52WRA
294	A	PJ02RDZ	313	Q	PJ52LVP	332	PM	PJ52LWM	351	NX	PF52WRC
295	A	PJ02REU	314	Q	PJ52LVR	333	PM	PJ52LWN	352	NX	PF52WRD
296	A	PJ02RFE	315	Q	PJ52LVS	334	PM	PJ52LWO	353	NX	PF52WRE
297	A	PJ02RFF	316	Q	PJ52LVT	335	PM	PJ52LWP	354	NX	PF52WRG
298	Q	PJ02RFK	317	Q	PJ52LVU	336	PM	PJ52LWR			

PVL355-389 — Volvo B7TL 10m — TransBus President — N41/20D — 2003

No.		Reg	No.		Reg	No.		Reg	No.		Reg
355	NX	PL03AGZ	369	BX	PJ53SRO	376	AL	PJ53NKN	383	AL	PJ53NKX
362	BX	PJ53SOF	370	BX	PJ53SRU	377	AL	PJ53NKO	384	AL	PJ53NKZ
363	BX	PJ53SOH	371	AL	PJ53NKG	378	AL	PJ53NKP	385	AL	PJ53NLA
364	BX	PJ53SOU	372	AL	PJ53NKH	379	AL	PJ53NKR	386	AL	PJ53NLC
365	BX	PJ53SPU	373	AL	PJ53NKK	380	AL	PJ53NKS	387	AL	PJ53NLD
366	BX	PJ53SPV	374	AL	PJ53NKL	381	AL	PJ53NKT	388	AL	PJ53NLE
367	BX	PJ53SPX	375	AL	PJ53NKM	382	AL	PJ53NKW	389	AL	PJ53NLF
368	BX	PJ53SPZ									

PVL390-419 — Volvo B7TL 10m — ADL President — N41/20D — 2005

No.		Reg	No.		Reg	No.		Reg	No.		Reg
390	AL	LX54HAA	398	AL	LX54GZK	406	AL	LX54GYV	413	AL	LX54GZE
391	AL	LX54HAE	399	AL	LX54GZL	407	AL	LX54GYW	414	AL	LX54GZF
392	AL	LX54HAO	400	AL	LX54GZM	408	AL	LX54GYY	415	AL	LX54GZU
393	AL	LX54HAU	401	AL	LX54GZN	409	AL	LX54GYZ	416	AL	LX54GZV
394	AL	LX54HBA	402	AL	LX54GZO	410	AL	LX54GZB	417	AL	LX54GZW
395	AL	LX54HBB	403	AL	LX54GZP	411	AL	LX54GZC	418	AL	LX54GZY
396	AL	LX54GZG	404	AL	LX54GZR	412	AL	LX54GZD	419	AL	LX54GZZ
397	AL	LX54GZH	405	AL	LX54GZT						

PVN1-17 — Volvo B7TL 10.6m — TransBus President 4.4m — N44/21D — 2003 — First, 2012

No.		Reg	No.		Reg	No.		Reg	No.		Reg
1	NP	LK03NHF	6	NP	LK03NHX	10	BE	LK03NJF	14	BE	LK03NJX
2	NP	LK03NHG	7	BE	LK03NHY	11	BE	LK03NJJ	15	BE	LK03NJY
3	NP	LK03NHP	8	BE	LK03NHZ	12	BE	LK03NJN	16	BE	LK03NJZ
4	NP	LK03NHT	9	BE	LK03NJE	13	BE	LK03NJV	17	BE	LK03NKA
5	NP	LK03NHV									

RM9	NX	VLT9	AEC Routemaster R2RH	Park Royal	B36/28R	1959

RML2305-2604 — AEC Routemaster R2RH1 — Park Royal — B40/32R* — 1961-67 — *2318 is O40/32R

*2516 is B40/32R, classified DRM

No.		Reg	No.		Reg	No.		Reg	No.		Reg
2305	AL	CUV305C	2472	NX	JJD472D	2520	Q	JJD520D	2604	AL	NML604E
2318	NX	CUV318C	2516	PL	WLT516						

SE1-17 — ADL Dart 4 10.2m — ADL Enviro 200 — N29D — 2007

No.		Reg	No.		Reg	No.		Reg	No.		Reg
1	AL	LX07BXH	6	AL	LX07BXN	10	AL	LX07BXS	14	AL	LX07BXY
2	AL	LX07BXJ	7	AL	LX07BXO	11	AL	LX07BXU	15	AL	LX07BZH
3	AL	LX07BXK	8	AL	LX07BXP	12	AL	LX07BXV	16	AL	LX07BYA
4	AL	LX07BXL	9	AL	LX07BXR	13	AL	LX07BXW	17	AL	LX07BYB
5	AL	LX07BXM									

SE18-36 — ADL Dart 4 10.8m — ADL Enviro 200 — N32D — 2007-08

No.		Reg	No.		Reg	No.		Reg	No.		Reg
18	BE	SK07DZM	23	BE	SK07DWK	28	BE	SK07DWU	33	BE	SK07DWZ
19	BE	SK07DZN	24	BE	SK07DWL	29	BE	SK07DWV	34	BE	SK07DXA
20	BE	SK07DZO	25	BE	SK07DWM	30	BE	SK07DWW	35	BE	SK07DXB
21	BE	SK07DWG	26	BE	SK07DWO	31	BE	SK07DWX	36	BE	YN08DMY
22	BE	SK07DWJ	27	BE	SK07DWP	32	BE	SK07DWY			

Go-Ahead London operates various lengths of the Enviro 200. Illustrating the most popular, the 10.8 metre model, is SE141, YX61BVZ, seen in Hackney while heading towards the Isle of Dogs. *Richard Godfrey*

SE37-46

			ADL Dart 4 10.2m			ADL Enviro 200		N29D	2010		
37	W	LX10AUP	40	BE	LX10AUU	43	BE	LX10AUY	45	BE	LX10AVC
38	BE	LX10AUR	41	BE	LX10AUV	44	BE	LX10AVB	46	BE	LX10AVD
39	BE	LX10AUT	42	BE	LX10AUW						

SE47-54

			ADL Dart 4 10.8m			ADL Enviro 200		N32D	2010		
47	SW	YX60EOE	49	SW	YX60EOG	51	SW	YX60EOJ	53	SW	YX60EOL
48	SW	YX60EOF	50	SW	YX60EOH	52	SW	YX60EOK	54	SW	YX60EOO

SE55-84

			ADL Dart 4 10.2m			ADL Enviro 200		N29D	2010		
55	BV	YX60DXT	63	BV	YX60FSU	71	BX	YX60FBZ	78	BX	YX60FCL
56	BV	YX60FSN	64	BV	YX60EPP	72	BX	YX60FCA	79	BX	YX60FCM
57	BV	YX60DXU	65	BV	YX60EPU	73	BX	YX60FCC	80	BX	YX60FCO
58	BV	YX60FSO	66	BV	YX60EOP	74	BX	YX60FCD	81	BX	YX60FCP
59	BX	YX60FSP	67	BV	YX60FCZ	75	BX	YX60FCE	82	BX	YX60FCU
60	BV	YX60FSS	68	BV	YX60FDA	76	BX	YX60FCF	83	BX	YX60FCV
61	BV	YX60DXW	69	BX	YX60FBU	77	BX	YX60FCG	84	BX	YX60FCY
62	BV	YX60EPO	70	BX	YX60FBY						

SE85-93

			ADL Dart 4 9.3m			ADL Enviro 200		N24D	2011		
85	Q	YX11CPE	88	Q	YX11CPN	90	Q	YX11CPU	92	Q	YX11CPY
86	Q	YX11CPF	89	Q	YX11CPO	91	Q	YX11CPV	93	Q	YX11CPZ
87	Q	YX11CPK									

SE94-103

			ADL Dart 4 10.8m			ADL Enviro 200		N32D	2011		
94	BE	SN11FFZ	97	BE	SN11FGD	100	BE	SN61BKV	102	BE	SN61BKY
95	BE	SN11FGA	98	BE	SN61BKO	101	BE	SN61BKX	103	BE	SN61BKZ
96	BE	SN11FGC	99	BE	SN61BKU						

SE104-119

			ADL Dart 4 10.8m			ADL Enviro 200		N32D	2011		
104	SI	YX61BWA	108	SI	YX61BWE	112	SI	YX61BXR	116	SI	YX61BXW
105	SI	YX61BWB	109	SI	YX61BYD	113	SI	YX61BXS	117	SI	YX61BXY
106	SI	YX61BWC	110	SI	YX61BYF	114	SI	YX61BXU	118	SI	YX61BXZ
107	SI	YX61BWD	111	SI	YX61BYG	115	SI	YX61BXV	119	SI	YX61BYA

SE120-166   ADL Dart 4 10.8m   ADL Enviro 200   N29D*   2011   *120-41 are N32D

120	SI	YX61BWU	132	SI	YX61BWH	144	SI	YX61BXM	156	PM	YX61DVF
121	SI	YX61BWV	133	SI	YX61BWJ	145	SI	YX61BXN	157	PM	YX61DVG
122	SI	YX61BWW	134	SI	YX61BWK	146	SI	YX61BXO	158	PM	YX61DVH
123	SI	YX61BWY	135	SI	YX61BWL	147	SI	YX61BXP	159	PM	YX61DVJ
124	SI	YX61BWZ	136	SI	YX61BWM	148	SI	YX61DTO	160	PM	YX61DVK
125	SI	YX61BXA	137	SI	YX61BWN	149	SI	YX61DTU	161	PM	YX61DVL
126	SI	YX61BXB	138	SI	YX61BWO	150	SI	YX61DTV	162	PM	YX61DVM
127	SI	YX61BXC	139	SI	YX61BWP	151	SI	YX61DTY	163	PM	YX61DVN
128	SI	YX61BXD	140	SI	YX61BVY	152	SI	YX61DTZ	164	PM	YX61DVO
129	SI	YX61BXE	141	SI	YX61BVZ	153	PM	YX61DVA	165	PM	YX61DVP
130	SI	YX61BWF	142	SI	YX61BXK	154	PM	YX61DVB	166	PM	YX61DVR
131	SI	YX61BWG	143	SI	YX61BXL	155	PM	YX61DVC			

SE167-174   ADL E20D 10.2m   ADL Enviro 200   N29D   2011

167	A	YX61EKF	169	A	YX61EKH	171	A	YX61EKK	173	A	YX61EKM
168	A	YX61EKG	170	A	YX61EKJ	172	A	YX61EKL	174	A	YX61EKN

SE175-193   ADL E20D 10.2m   ADL Enviro 200   N29D   2012

175	PL	SN12AUM	180	PL	SN12AUU	185	PL	SN12AVB	190	PL	SN12AVG
176	PL	SN12AUO	181	PL	SN12AUV	186	PL	SN12AVC	191	PL	SN12AVJ
177	PL	SN12AUP	182	PL	SN12AUW	187	PL	SN12AVD	192	PL	SN12AVK
178	PL	SN12AUR	183	PL	SN12AUX	188	PL	SN12AVE	193	PL	SN12AVL
179	PL	SN12AUT	184	PL	SN12AUY	189	PL	SN12AVF			

SEN1-12   ADL Dart 4 8.9m   ADL Enviro 200   N26F   2011   First, 2012

1	NP	YX60FUA	4	NP	YX60FUE	7	NP	YX60FUH	10	NP	YX60FUO
2	NP	YX60FUB	5	NP	YX60FUF	8	NP	YX60FUJ	11	NP	YX60FUP
3	NP	YX60FUD	6	NP	YX60FUG	9	NP	YX60FUM	12	NP	YX60FUT

SEN13-20   ADL Dart 4 9.3m   ADL Enviro 200   N24D   2011   First, 2012

13	NP	YX11FYS	15	NP	YX11FYU	17	NP	YX11FYW	19	NP	YX11FYZ
14	NP	YX11FYT	16	NP	YX11FYV	18	NP	YX11FYY	20	NP	YX11AGU

SEN21-29   ADL E20D 9.6m   ADL Enviro 200   N25D   2012   First, 2012

21	NP	YX61FYT	24	NP	YX61FYW	26	NP	YX61FYZ	28	NP	YX61FZB
22	NP	YX61FYU	25	NP	YX61FYY	27	NP	YX61FZA	29	NP	YX61FZZ
23	NP	YX61FYV									

SEN30-37   ADL E20D 9.6m   ADL Enviro 200   N25D   2012   First, 2012

30	BE	YX61FXO	32	BE	YX61FXR	34	BE	YX61FXT	36	BE	YX61FXV
31	BE	YX61FXP	33	BE	YX61FXS	35	BE	YX61FXU	37	BE	YX61FXW

SO1-5   Scania N94 UD 10.6m   East Lancs OmniDekka 4.4m   N45/27D   2005   Blue Triangle, 2007

1	SI	BV55UCT	3	SI	BV55UCW	4	SI	BV55UCX	5	SI	BV55UCY
2	SI	BV55UCU									

SOC1	SI	LX08ECD	Scania OmniCity N230 UD 10.8m Scania	N41/22D	2008
SOC2	SI	LX08ECE	Scania OmniCity N230 UD 10.8m Scania	N41/22D	2008
SOC3	u	LX08ECF	Scania OmniCity N230 UD 10.8m Scania	N41/22D	2008

SOE1-40   ADL Dart 4 8.9m   Optare Esteem   N29D   2009

1	AL	LX09AYF	11	AL	LX09AYS	21	AL	LX09AZD	31	A	LX09BXP
2	AL	LX09AYG	12	AL	LX09AYT	22	AL	LX09AZF	32	A	LX09BXR
3	AL	LX09AYH	13	AL	LX09AYU	23	AL	LX09AZG	33	A	LX09BXS
4	AL	LX09AYJ	14	AL	LX09AYV	24	AL	LX09AZJ	34	A	LX09EVB
5	AL	LX09AYK	15	AL	LX09AYW	25	AL	LX09AZL	35	A	LX09EVC
6	AL	LX09AYL	16	AL	LX09AYY	26	AL	LX09AZN	36	A	LX09EVD
7	AL	LX09AYM	17	AL	LX09AYZ	27	AL	LX09AZO	37	A	LX09EVF
8	AL	LX09AYN	18	AL	LX09AZA	28	AL	LX09AZP	38	A	LX09EVG
9	AL	LX09AYO	19	AL	LX09AZB	29	A	LX09AZR	39	A	LX09EVH
10	AL	LX09AYP	20	AL	LX09AXC	30	A	LX09AZT	40	A	LX09EVJ

VE1	AF	LX58CWK	Volvo B9TL 10.4m	ADL Enviro 400	N41/24D	2008
VE2	AF	LX58CWL	Volvo B9TL 10.4m	ADL Enviro 400	N41/24D	2008
VE3	AF	LX58CWM	Volvo B9TL 10.4m	ADL Enviro 400	N41/24D	2008
VM1	SI	BJ11XGZ	Volvo B9TL 10.3m	MCV	N41/22D	2011	development vehicle

Go-Ahead London's Hybrid Volvo B5LHs carry class letters WHV. Pictured on route 19 at Hyde Park Corner is WHV20, LJ61NVF, from the 2012 intake all of which are allocated to Stockwell depot. *Dave Heath*

VP1-19
Volvo B7TL 10m · Plaxton President · N41/23D · 2011 · East Thames, 2009

1	Q	X149FBB	6	Q	X157FBB	11	Q	X163FBB	16	BX	X168FBB
2	Q	X151FBB	7	Q	X158FBB	12	Q	X164FBB	17	BX	X169FBB
3	Q	X152FBB	8	Q	X159FBB	13	Q	X165FBB	18	Qt	X171FBB
4	Q	X153FBB	9	Q	X161FBB	14	Q	X166FBB	19	Qt	X172FBB
5	Q	X154FBB	10	Q	X162FBB	15	BX	X167FBB			

VWL1-31
Volvo B7TL 10.6m · Wrightbus Eclipse Gemini · N43/22D · 2002 · East Thames, 2009

1	Q	LB02YWX	9	Q	LB02YXG	17	BV	LF52TGO	25	BV	LF52THN
2	Q	LB02YWY	10	Q	LB02YXH	18	BV	LF52TGU	26	BV	LF52THU
3	Q	LB02YWZ	11	BV	LB02YXJ	19	BV	LF52TGV	27	MW	LF52THV
4	Q	LB02YXA	12	BV	LB02YXK	20	BV	LF52TGX	28	MW	LF52THX
5	Q	LB02YXC	13	BV	LB02YXL	21	BV	LF52TGY	29	MW	LF52THZ
6	Q	LB02YXD	14	BV	LB02YXM	22	BV	LF52TGZ	30	MW	LF52TJO
7	Q	LB02YXE	15	BV	LB02YXN	23	BV	LF52THG	31	MW	LF52TJU
8	Q	LB02YXF	16	BV	LF52TGN	24	BV	LF52THK			

VWL32-44
Volvo B7TL 10.6m · Wrightbus Eclipse Gemini · N43/23D · 2004

32	MW	BX04AZW	36	MW	BX04BAA	39	MW	BX04BBE	42	MW	BX04BKL
33	MW	BX04AZV	37	MW	BX04BAU	40	MW	BX04BBF	43	MW	BX04BKK
34	MW	BX04AZU	38	MW	BX04BAV	41	MW	BX04BBJ	44	MW	BX04BKJ
35	MW	BX04AZZ									

WDL1
AL · LX58CWG · VDL/Wrightbus DL 10.4m · Wrightbus Gemini 2 · N41/24D · 2009

WHV1-16
Volvo B5LH · Wrightbus Gemini 2 · N39/21D · 2011

1	Q	LJ61GVW	5	Q	LJ61GWA	9	Q	LJ61GXG	13	Q	LJ61GXM
2	Q	LJ61GVX	6	Q	LJ61GWC	10	Q	LJ61GXH	14	Q	LJ61GXN
3	Q	LJ61GVY	7	Q	LJ61GXE	11	Q	LJ61GXK	15	Q	LJ61GXO
4	Q	LJ61GVZ	8	Q	LJ61GXF	12	Q	LJ61GXL	16	Q	LJ61GXP

WHV17-31
Volvo B5LH · Wrightbus Gemini 2 · N39/21D · 2012

17	SW	LJ61NVC	21	SW	LJ61NVG	25	SW	LJ61NVM	29	SW	LJ61NVR
18	SW	LJ61NVD	22	SW	LJ61NVH	26	SW	LJ61NVN	30	SW	LJ61NVS
19	SW	LJ61NVE	23	SW	LJ61NVK	27	SW	LJ12CHH	31	SW	LJ12CHK
20	SW	LJ61NVF	24	SW	LJ61NVL	28	SW	LJ61NVP			

The Wrightbus StreetLight is available in two configurations, one with the door located behind the front axle (Wheel Forward) and one with the door located ahead of the front wheel (Door Forward). There is a standard 2445mm width across the range with a variety of body lengths and seating layouts available. The shortest is the 8.8 metre Wheel Forward model which is class WS at Go-Ahead London. WS2, LJ12CGG, is shown passing along Grange Hill while working route 467. *Richard Godfrey*

WHV32-41   Volvo B5LH   Wrightbus Gemini 2   N39/21D   2012

32	AF	LJ62KED	35	AF	LJ62KGF	38	AF	LJ62KGY	40	AF	LJ62KHV
33	AF	LJ62KEF	36	AF	LJ62KGG	39	AF	LJ62KHF	41	AF	LJ62KKP
34	AF	LJ62KFU	37	AF	LJ62KGN						

WHY1-7   VDL Bus Hybrid 10.4m   Wrightbus Electrocity   N26D*   2006-08   *7 is B28D

| 1 | Q | LX06ECN | 3 | Q | LX55EAE | 6 | Q | LX55EAJ | 7 | Q | LX57CLZ |
| 2 | Q | LX55EAC | 4 | Q | LX55EAF | 5 | Q | LX55EAG | | | |

WHY8-13   VDL Bus Hybrid 10.4m   Wrightbus Electrocity   N25D   2011

| 8 | Q | LX11DVA | 10 | Q | LX11DVC | 12 | Q | LX11DVG | 13 | Q | LX11DVH |
| 9 | Q | LX11DVB | 11 | Q | LX11DVF | | | | | | |

WS1-9   Wrightbus StreetLite WF 8.8m   Wrightbus   N28F   2012

1	BE	LJ12CGF	4	BE	LJ12CGO	6	BE	LJ12CGV	8	BE	LJ12CGY
2	BE	LJ12CGG	5	BE	LJ12CGU	7	BE	LJ12CGX	9	BE	LJ12CGZ
3	BE	LJ12CGK									

WS10-20   Wrightbus StreetLite DF 10.9m   Wrightbus   N31D   2013

10	AL	LJ13GJU	13	AL	LJ13GJY	16	AL	LJ13GKC	19	AL	LJ13GKF
11	AL	LJ13GJV	14	AL	LJ13GJZ	17	AL	LJ13GKD	20	AL	LJ13GKG
12	AL	LJ13GJX	15	AL	LJ13GKA	18	AL	LJ13GKE			

WS21-32   Wrightbus StreetLite DF 10.4m   Wrightbus   N31D   2013

21	NP	LJ13GKK	24	NP	LJ13GKO	27	NP	LJ13GKV	30	NP	LJ13GKZ
22	NP	LJ13GKL	25	NP	LJ13GKP	28	NP	LJ13GKX	31	NP	LJ13GLF
23	NP	LJ13GKN	26	NP	LJ13GKU	29	NP	LJ13GKY	32	NP	LJ13GLK

Mornington Cresent is the location for this view of WVL110, LX03EDU, one of five hundred in the Volvo-Wrightbus Eclipse Gemini combination currently operated. This example is a Volvo B7TL chassis which was launched in 1999 as a successor to the Olympian. Subsequent deliveries use the Volvo B9TL chassis that was introduced in 2006, initially as tri-axle model for the Hong Kong market. *Dave Heath*

WVL1-121

Volvo B7TL 10.1m   Wrightbus Eclipse Gemini 4.2m N41/22D* 2002-03   *93 is CO41/22D

1	SW	LG02KGP	32	AF	LF52ZRO	62	AF	LF52ZTG	92	BX	LF52ZND
2	SW	LG02KGU	33	AF	LF52ZRP	63	AF	LF52ZTH	93	u	LF52ZNE
3	SW	LG02KGV	34	AF	LF52ZRR	64	AF	LF52ZTJ	94	AL	LF52ZNG
4	SW	LG02KGX	35	AF	LF52ZRT	65	AF	LF52ZTK	95	BX	LF52ZNH
5	SW	LG02KGY	36	AF	LF52ZRU	66	AF	LF52ZTL	96	SW	LF52ZNJ
6	SW	LG02KGZ	37	AF	LF52ZRV	67	AF	LF52ZTM	97	BE	LF52ZNK
7	SW	LG02KHA	38	AF	LF52ZRX	68	AF	LF52ZTN	98	BE	LF52ZNL
8	SW	LG02KHE	39	AF	LF52ZRY	69	AF	LF52ZTO	99	AL	LF52ZNM
9	SW	LG02KHF	40	AF	LF52ZRZ	70	AF	LF52ZTP	100	AL	LF52ZNN
10	SW	LG02KHH	41	AF	LF52ZSD	71	AF	LF52ZTR	101	SW	LF52ZNO
11	SW	LG02KHJ	42	AF	LF52ZPZ	72	AL	LF52ZPB	102	SW	LF52ZLZ
12	SW	LG02KHK	43	AF	LF52ZRA	73	AL	LF52ZPC	103	BE	LF52ZMO
13	SW	LG02KHL	44	AF	LF52ZRC	74	SW	LF52ZPD	104	BE	LF52ZMU
14	AF	LG02KHM	45	AF	LF52ZRD	75	BE	LF52ZPE	105	SW	LX03EXV
15	AF	LG02KHO	46	AF	LF52ZRE	76	SW	LF52ZPG	106	SW	LX03EXW
16	AF	LG02KHP	47	AF	LF52ZRG	77	BE	LF52ZPH	107	SW	LX03EXZ
17	AF	LG02KHR	48	AF	LF52ZRJ	78	AL	LF52ZPJ	108	SW	LX03EXU
18	AF	LG02KHT	49	AF	LF52ZRK	79	AL	LF52ZPK	109	SW	LX03EDR
19	AF	LG02KHU	50	AF	LF52ZRL	80	AL	LF52ZPL	110	SW	LX03EDU
20	AF	LG02KHV	51	AF	LF52ZRN	81	PM	LF52ZPM	111	SW	LX03EDV
21	AF	LG02KHW	52	AF	LF52ZPN	82	PM	LF52ZNP	112	SW	LX03EEA
22	AF	LG02KHX	53	AF	LF52ZPO	83	BX	LF52ZNR	113	SW	LX03EEB
23	AF	LG02KHY	54	AF	LF52ZPP	84	AL	LF52ZNS	114	SW	LX03EEF
24	AF	LG02KHZ	55	AF	LF52ZPR	85	AL	LF52ZNT	115	SW	LX03EEG
25	AF	LG02KJA	56	AF	LF52ZPS	86	PM	LF52ZNU	116	SW	LX03EEH
26	AF	LG02KJE	57	AF	LF52ZPU	87	Q	LF52ZNV	117	SW	LX03EEJ
27	AF	LG02KJF	58	AF	LF52ZPV	88	SW	LF52ZNW	118	SW	LX03EEM
28	AF	LF52ZSO	59	AF	LF52ZPW	89	AL	LF52ZNX	119	SW	LX03ECV
29	AF	LF52ZSP	60	AF	VLT60	90	BE	LF52ZNY	120	SW	LX03ECW
30	AF	LF52ZSR	61	AF	LF52ZPY	91	BE	LF52ZNZ	121	SW	LX03ECY
31	AF	LF52ZST									

WVL122-159   Volvo B7TL 10.1m   Wrightbus Eclipse Gemini 4.2m N41/22D* 2003-04   *150 is N41/21D

122	SW	LX53AZP	133	SW	LX53AZF	142	SW	LX53AYP	151	SW	LX53BJU
123	SW	LX53AZR	134	SW	LX53AZG	143	SW	LX53AYT	152	AL	LX53BEY
124	w	LX53AZT	135	SW	LX53AZJ	144	SW	LX53AYU	153	AF	LX53BGE
125	w	LX53AZU	136	SW	LX53AZL	145	SW	LX53AYV	154	AF	LX53BFK
126	w	LX53AZV	137	SW	LX53AZN	146	SW	LX53AYW	155	AF	LX53BDY
129	SW	LX53AZA	138	SW	LX53AZO	147	SW	LX53AYY	156	AF	LX53BBZ
130	SW	LX53AZB	139	SW	LX53AYM	148	SW	LX53AYZ	157	AF	LX53BAA
131	SW	LX53AZC	140	SW	LX53AYN	149	SW	LX53BJK	158	AF	LX53BDO
132	SW	LX53AZD	141	SW	LX53AYO	150	SW	LX53BJO	159	AF	LX53BAO

WVL160-211   Volvo B7TL 10.1m   Wrightbus Eclipse Gemini 4.2m N41/22D 2005

160	AF	LX05FBY	173	AF	LX05FBN	186	AF	LX05FAU	199	NP	LX05EZR
161	AF	LX05FBZ	174	AF	LX05FBO	187	AF	LX05FBA	200	NP	LX05EZS
162	AF	LX05FCA	175	AF	LX05FBU	188	AF	LX05FBB	201	NP	LX05EZT
163	AF	LX05FCC	176	AF	LX05EZJ	189	NP	LX05FBC	202	NP	LX05EZU
164	AF	LX05FCD	177	AF	LX05EYM	190	NP	LX05EZV	203	NP	LX05EYZ
165	AF	LX05FCE	178	AF	LX05EYO	191	NP	LX05EZW	204	NP	LX05EZA
166	AF	LX05FCF	179	AF	LX05FBV	192	NP	LX05EZZ	205	NP	LX05EZB
167	AF	LX05FBD	180	AF	LX05FAA	193	NP	LX05EZK	206	AL	LX05EZC
168	AF	LX05FBE	181	AF	LX05FAF	194	NP	LX05EZL	207	AL	LX05EZD
169	AF	LX05FBF	182	AF	LX05FAJ	195	NP	LX05EZM	208	AL	LX05EZE
170	AF	LX05FBJ	183	AF	LX05FAK	196	NP	LX05EZN	209	AL	LX05EZF
171	AF	LX05FBK	184	AF	LX05FAM	197	NP	LX05EZO	210	NP	LX05EZG
172	AF	LX05FBL	185	AF	LX05FAO	198	NP	LX05EZP	211	AL	LX05EZH

WVL212-273   Volvo B7TL 10.1m   Wrightbus Eclipse Gemini 4.2m N41/21D 2006

212	Q	LX06DYS	229	Q	LX06DZM	244	Q	LX06EAG	259	Q	LX06EBK
213	Q	LX06DYT	230	Q	LX06DZN	245	Q	LX06EAJ	260	Q	LX06EBL
214	Q	LX06DYU	231	Q	LX06DZO	246	Q	LX06EAK	261	Q	LX06EBM
215	Q	LX06DYV	232	Q	LX06DZP	247	Q	LX06EAL	262	Q	LX06EBN
216	Q	LX06DYW	233	Q	LX06DZR	248	Q	LX06EAM	263	Q	LX06EBO
217	Q	LX06DYY	234	Q	LX06DZS	249	Q	LX06EAO	264	Q	LX06EBP
218	Q	LX06DZA	235	Q	LX06DZT	250	Q	LX06EAP	265	Q	LX06EBU
219	Q	LX06DZB	236	Q	LX06DZU	251	Q	LX06EAW	266	Q	LX06EBV
220	Q	LX06DZC	237	Q	LX06DZV	252	Q	LX06EAY	267	Q	LX06EBZ
222	Q	LX06DZE	238	Q	LX06DZW	253	Q	LX06EBA	268	Q	LX06ECA
223	Q	LX06DZF	239	Q	LX06DZY	254	Q	LX06EBC	269	Q	LX06ECC
224	Q	LX06DZG	240	Q	LX06DZZ	255	Q	LX06EBD	270	Q	LX06ECD
225	Q	LX06DZH	241	Q	LX06EAA	256	Q	LX06EBE	271	MW	LX06ECE
226	Q	LX06DZJ	242	Q	LX06EAC	257	Q	LX06EBG	272	BX	LX06ECF
227	Q	LX06DZK	243	Q	LX06EAF	258	Q	LX06EBJ	273	BX	LX06ECJ
228	Q	LX06DZL									

WVL274-349   Volvo B9TL 10.4m   Wrightbus Eclipse Gemini 2   N39/23D   2009-10

274	NX	LX59CYL	293	NX	LX59CZL	312	PM	LX59CZY	331	PM	LX59DDF
275	NX	LX59CYO	294	NX	LX59CZM	313	PM	LX59CZZ	332	PM	LX59DDJ
276	NX	LX59CYP	295	NX	LX59CZN	314	PM	LX59DAA	333	PM	LX59DDK
277	NX	LX59CYS	296	NX	LX59CZO	315	PM	LX59DAO	334	BE	LX59DDL
278	NX	LX59CYT	297	NX	LX59CZP	316	PM	LX59DAU	335	BE	LX59DDN
279	NX	LX59CYU	298	NX	LX59CZR	317	PM	LX59DBO	336	BE	LX59DDO
280	NX	LX59CYV	299	NX	LX59CZS	318	PM	LX59DBU	337	BE	LX59DDU
281	NX	LX59CYW	300	NX	LX59CZT	319	PM	LX59DBV	338	BE	LX59DDV
282	NX	LX59CYY	301	NX	LX59CZU	320	PM	LX59DBY	339	BE	LX59DDY
283	NX	LX59CYZ	302	NX	LX59CZV	321	PM	LX59DBZ	340	BE	LX59DDZ
284	NX	LX59CZA	303	PM	LX59CYA	322	PM	LX59DCE	341	BE	LX59DEU
285	NX	LX59CZB	304	PM	LX59CYC	323	PM	LX59DCF	342	BE	LX59DFA
286	NX	LX59CZC	305	PM	LX59CYE	324	PM	LX59DCO	343	BE	LX59DFC
287	NX	LX59CZD	306	PM	LX59CYF	325	PM	LX59DCU	344	BE	LX59DFD
288	NX	LX59CZF	307	PM	LX59CYG	326	PM	LX59DCV	345	BE	LX59DFE
289	NX	LX59CZG	308	PM	LX59CYH	327	PM	LX59DCY	346	BE	LX59DFF
290	NX	LX59CZH	309	PM	LX59CYJ	328	PM	LX59DCZ	347	BE	LX59DFG
291	NX	LX59CZJ	310	PM	LX59CYK	329	PM	LX59DDA	348	BE	LX59DFJ
292	NX	LX59CZK	311	PM	LX59CZW	330	PM	LX59DDE	349	BE	LX59DFK

Almost a hundred WVL class buses are allocated to Camberwell represented here by WVL452, LJ61GWN. It was pictured at the Elephant & Castle, one fine autumn day. *Richard Godfrey*

WVL350-385

Volvo B9TL 10.4m   Wrightbus Eclipse Gemini 2   N39/23D   2010-11

350	BX	LX60DVY	**359**	BX	LX60DWK	**368**	BX	LX60DWY	**377**	BX	LX60DXH
351	BX	LX60DVZ	**360**	BX	LX60DWL	**369**	BX	LX60DWZ	**378**	BX	LX60DXJ
352	BX	LX60DWA	**361**	BX	LX60DWM	**370**	BX	LX60DXA	**379**	BE	LX60DXK
353	BX	LX60DWC	**362**	BX	LX60DWN	**371**	BX	LX60DXB	**380**	Q	LX60DXM
354	BX	LX60DWD	**363**	BX	LX60DWO	**372**	BX	LX60DXC	**381**	Q	LX60DXO
355	BX	LX60DWE	**364**	BX	LX60DWP	**373**	BX	LX60DXD	**382**	Q	LX60DXP
356	BX	LX60DWF	**365**	BX	LX60DWU	**374**	BX	LX60DXE	**383**	Q	LX60DXR
357	BX	LX60DWG	**366**	BX	LX60DWV	**375**	BX	LX60DXF	**384**	Q	LX60DXS
358	BX	LX60DWJ	**367**	BX	LX60DWW	**376**	BX	LX60DXG	**385**	Q	LX60DXT

WVL386-421

Volvo B9TL 10.4m   Wrightbus Eclipse Gemini 2   N39/23D   2011

386	NX	LX11CVL	**395**	NX	LX11CVV	**404**	NX	LX11CWJ	**413**	SI	LX11CWU
387	NX	LX11CVM	**396**	NX	LX11CVW	**405**	NX	LX11CWK	**414**	SI	LX11CWV
388	NX	LX11CVN	**397**	NX	LX11CVY	**406**	NX	LX11CWL	**415**	SI	LX11CWW
389	NX	LX11CVO	**398**	NX	LX11CVZ	**407**	NX	LX11CWM	**416**	SI	LX11CWY
390	NX	LX11CVP	**399**	NX	LX11CWA	**408**	NX	LX11CWN	**417**	SI	LX11CWZ
391	NX	LX11CVR	**400**	NX	LX11CWC	**409**	NX	LX11CWO	**418**	SI	LX11CXA
392	NX	LX11CVS	**401**	NX	LX11CWD	**410**	NX	LX11CWP	**419**	SI	LX11CXB
393	NX	LX11CVT	**402**	NX	LX11CWE	**411**	NX	LX11CWR	**420**	SI	LX11CXC
394	NX	LX11CVU	**403**	NX	LX11CWG	**412**	NX	LX11CWT	**421**	SI	LX11CXD

WVL422-456

Volvo B9TL 10.4m   Wrightbus Eclipse Gemini 2   N39/23D   2011

422	SI	LX11FHV	**431**	SI	LX11FJJ	**440**	Q	LJ61GWZ	**449**	Q	LJ61GWK
423	SI	LX11FHW	**432**	SI	LX11FJK	**441**	Q	LJ61GXA	**450**	Q	LJ61GWL
424	SI	LX11FHY	**433**	SI	LX11FJN	**442**	Q	LJ61GXB	**451**	Q	LJ61GWM
425	SI	LX11FHZ	**434**	SI	LX11FJO	**443**	Q	LJ61GXC	**452**	Q	LJ61GWN
426	SI	LX11FJA	**435**	Q	LJ61GWU	**444**	Q	LJ61GXD	**453**	Q	LJ61GWO
427	SI	LX11FJC	**436**	Q	LJ61GWV	**445**	Q	LJ61GWD	**454**	Q	LJ61GWP
428	SI	LX11FJD	**437**	Q	LJ61GWW	**446**	Q	LJ61GWE	**455**	BX	LJ61GVP
429	SI	LX11FJE	**438**	Q	LJ61GWX	**447**	Q	LJ61GWF	**456**	BX	LJ61GVT
430	SI	LX11FJF	**439**	Q	LJ61GWY	**448**	Q	LJ61GWG			

WVL457-495

Volvo B9TL 10.5m — Wrightbus Eclipse Gemini 2 — N39/23D — 2012

No		Reg	No		Reg	No		Reg	No		Reg
457	NP	LJ61NUM	467	NP	LJ61NWW	477	AL	LJ61NWL	487	SW	LJ61NVZ
458	NP	LJ61NUO	468	AL	LJ61NWX	478	AL	LJ61NWM	488	SW	LJ61NWA
459	NP	LJ61NUP	469	AL	LJ12CHC	479	AL	LJ61NWN	489	SW	LJ61NWB
460	NP	LJ61NUU	470	AL	LJ61NWZ	480	AL	LJ61NWO	490	SW	LJ61NWC
461	NP	LJ61NUV	471	AL	LJ61NXA	481	SW	LJ12CHD	491	SW	LJ61NWD
462	NP	LJ61NUW	472	AL	LJ61NXB	482	SW	LJ61NWR	492	SW	LJ61NWE
463	NP	LJ61NUX	473	AL	LJ61NXC	483	SW	LJ12CHF	493	SW	LJ61NWF
464	NP	LJ61NUY	474	AL	LJ61NXD	484	SW	LJ12CHG	494	SW	LJ61NWG
465	NP	LJ61NVA	475	AL	LJ61NXE	485	SW	LJ61NWU	495	SW	LJ61NWH
466	NP	LJ61NVB	476	AL	LJ61NXF	486	SW	LJ61NWV			

WVL496-508

Volvo B9TL 10.5m — Wrightbus Eclipse Gemini 2 — N39/23D — 2012

No		Reg	No		Reg	No		Reg	No		Reg
496	AF	LJ62KXX	500	AF	LJ62KOX	503	AF	LJ62KBY	506	AF	LJ62KDZ
497	AF	LJ62KXZ	501	AF	LJ62KZD	504	AF	LJ62KCU	507	AF	LJ62KLC
498	AF	LJ62KYA	502	AF	LJ62KZP	505	AF	LJ62KDV	508	AF	LJ62KLS
499	AF	LJ62KYG									

WVN1-23

Volvo B9TL 10.4m — Wrightbus Eclipse Gemini 2 — N39/23D — 2009-10 — First, 2012

No		Reg	No		Reg	No		Reg	No		Reg
1	NP	LK59FEP	7	NP	LK59FDZ	13	NP	LK59FEO	19	NP	LK59FDM
2	NP	LK59FET	8	NP	LK59FEF	14	NP	LK59FDE	20	NP	LK59FDN
3	NP	LK59FEU	9	NP	LK59FEG	15	NP	LK59FDF	21	NP	LK59FDO
4	NP	LK59FDV	10	NP	LK59FEH	16	NP	LK59FDG	22	NP	LK59FDP
5	NP	LK59FDX	11	NP	LK59FEJ	17	NP	LK59FDJ	23	NP	LK59FDU
6	NP	LK59FDY	12	NP	LK59FEM	18	NP	LK59FDL			

WVN24-45

Volvo B9TL 10.4m — Wrightbus Eclipse Gemini 2 — N39/23D — 2009-10 — First, 2012

No		Reg	No		Reg	No		Reg	No		Reg
24	NP	BG59FXA	30	NP	BG59FXH	36	NP	BV10WVJ	41	NP	BV10WWD
25	NP	BG59FXB	31	NP	BV10WVD	37	NP	BV10WVK	42	NP	BV10WWF
26	NP	BG59FXC	32	NP	BV10WVE	38	NP	BV10WVL	43	NP	BV10WWO
27	NP	BG59FXD	33	NP	BV10WVF	39	NP	BV10WWA	44	NP	BV10WWP
28	NP	BG59FXE	34	NP	BV10WVG	40	NP	BV10WWC	45	NP	BV10WWR
29	NP	BG59FXF	35	NP	BV10WVH						

WVN46-53

Volvo B9TL 10.5m — Wrightbus Eclipse Gemini 2 — N39/23D — 2012 — First, 2012

No		Reg	No		Reg	No		Reg	No		Reg
46	NP	BL61ACY	48	NP	BL61ADU	50	NP	BL61ADV	52	NP	BL61ADX
47	NP	BL61ACX	49	NP	BL61ACZ	51	NP	BL61ADO	53	NP	BL61ADZ

Previous registrations:

R370LGH	R370LGH, WLT470	WLT516	CUV283C
VLT9	VLT9, OYM374A		

On order: 2 BYD Electric buses.

On 31st March 2012, Northumberland Park depot, along with its vehicles and routes, was sold by First to Go-Ahead, which integrated it into its London General operation. One of the buses included in the sale was WVN32, BV10WVE.
Terry Longhurst

Depots and allocations:

Belvedere (Burt's Wharf, Crabtree Manor Way, DA17 6LJ) - BV

Enviro 200	SE55	SE56	SE57	SE58	SE60	SE61	SE62	SE63
	SE64	SE65	SE66	SE67	SE68			
Volvo B7TL	VWL11	VWL12	VWL13	VWL14	VWL15	VWL16	VWL17	VWL18
	VWL19	VWL20	VWL21	VWL22	VWL23	VWL24	VWL25	VWL26

Bexleyheath (Erith Road, DA7 6BX) - BX

Dart	LDP202	LDP205	LDP207					
Enviro 200	SE69	SE70	SE71	SE72	SE73	SE74	SE75	SE76
	SE77	SE79	SE80	SE81	SE82	SE83	SE84	
SB120	DWL15							
Volvo B7TL	VP15	VP16	VP17	PVL94	PVL152	PVL153	PVL154	PVL155
	PVL160	PVL161	PVL162	PVL163	PVL164	PVL165	PVL166	PVL167
	PVL362	PVL363	PVL364	PVL365	PVL366	PVL367	PVL368	PVL369
	PVL370	WVL81	WVL82	WVL83	WVL95	WVL272	WVL273	
Volvo B9TL	WVL350	WVL351	WVL352	WVL353	WVL354	WVL355	WVL356	WVL357
	WVL358	WVL359	WVL360	WVL361	WVL362	WVL363	WVL364	WVL365
	WVL366	WVL367	WVL368	WVL369	WVL370	WVL371	WVL372	WVL373
	WVL374	WVL375	WVL376	WVL377	WVL378	WVL379	WVL455	WVL456
Enviro 400	E39	E40	E41	E42	E43	E44	E45	E46
	E47	E48	E49	E50	E51	E52	E53	E54
	E55	E56	E67	E202	E203	E204	E205	E206
	E207	E229	E230	E231	E232	E233	E234	E235
	E236	E237	E238	E239	E240	E241	E242	E243
	E244	E245						

Camberwell (Warner Road, SE5 9LU) - Q

Dart	LDP249	LDP250	LDP251	LDP252	LDP253	LDP254	LDP255	LDP256
	LDP257	LDP258	LDP259	LDP260	LDP261	LDP262		
Enviro 200	SE85	SE86	SE87	SE88	SE89	SE90	SE91	SE92
	SE93							
Scania N94	ELS1	ELS2	ELS3	ELS4	ELS5	ELS6	ELS7	ELS8
	ELS9	ELS10	ELS11	ELS12	ELS13	ELS14		
Optare Versa	HOV1							
VDL/Wrightbus Hybrid	WDL1	WHY1	WHY2	WHY3	WHY4	WHY5	WHY6	WHY7
	WHY8	WHY9	WHY10	WHY11	WHY12	WHY13	WHY14	WHY15
	WHY16							
Routemaster	RML2472	RML2520						
Volvo B7TL	EVL5	EVL15	EVL17	PVL272	PVL298	PVL299	PVL300	PVL301
	PVL302	PVL303	PVL304	PVL305	PVL306	PVL307	PVL308	PVL309
	PVL310	PVL311	PVL312	PVL313	PVL314	PVL315	PVL316	PVL317
	PVL318	PVL326	PVL327	PVL328				
	VP1	VP2	VP3	VP4	VP5	VP6	VP7	VP8
	VP9	VP10	VP11	VP12	VP13	VP14	VWL1	VWL2
	VWL3	VWL4	VWL6	VWL7	VWL8	VWL9	VWL10	VWL212
	WVL213	WVL214	WVL215	WVL216	WVL217	WVL218	WVL219	WVL220
	WVL222	WVL223	WVL224	WVL225	WVL226	WVL227	WVL228	WVL229
	WVL230	WVL231	WVL232	WVL233	WVL234	WVL235	WVL236	WVL237
	WVL238	WVL239	WVL240	WVL241	WVL242	WVL243	WVL244	WVL245
	WVL246	WVL247	WVL248	WVL249	WVL250	WVL251	WVL252	WVL253
	WVL254	WVL255	WVL256	WVL257	WVL259	WVL260	WVL261	WVL262
	WVL263	WVL264	WVL265	WVL266	WVL267	WVL268	WVL269	WVL270
	WVL271	WVL272	WVL273					
Volvo B9TL	WVL380	WVL381	WVL382	WVL383	WVL384	WVL385	WVL435	WVL436
	WVL437	WVL438	WVL439	WVL440	WVL441	WVL442	WVL443	WVL444
	WVL445	WVL447	WVL448	WVL449	WVL450	WVL451	WVL452	WVL453
	WVL454							
Volvo B5LH	WHV1	WHV2	WHV3	WHV4	WHV5	WHV6	WHV7	WHV8
	WHV9	WHV10	WHV11	WHV12	WHV13	WHV14	WHV15	WHV16
Enviro 400	E100	E101	E102	E103	E104	E105	E106	E107
	E108	E109	E110	E111	E112	E113	E114	E115
	E116	E117	E118	E119	E120	E121	E122	E123
	E124	E125	E126	E127	E128			

Merton (High Street, SW19 1DN) - AL

Dart	LDP197	LDP198	LDP199	LDP200	LDP201		
SB120	DW1	DW2	DW3	DW4	DW5	DW6	DW7	DW8
	DW9	DW11	DW12					
Enviro 200	SE1	SE2	SE3	SE4	SE5	SE6	SE7	SE8
	SE9	SE10	SE11	SE12	SE13	SE14	SE15	SE16
	SE17	SOE1	SOE2	SOE3	SOE4	SOE5	SOE6	SOE7
	SOE8	SOE9	SOE10	SOE11	SOE12	SOE13	SOE14	SOE15
	SOE16	SOE17	SOE18	SOE19	SOE20	SOE21	SOE22	SOE23
	SOE24	SOE25	SOE26	SOE27	SOE28			
Streetlite	WS10	WS11	WS12	WS13	WS14	WS15	WS16	WS17
	WS18	WS19	WS20					
Routemaster	RML2305	RML2604						
Olympian	NV170	NV171						
Enviro 400	E57	E68	E69	E70	E71	E72	E73	E74
	E75	E76	E77	E78	E79	E80	E81	E82
	E83	E84	E85	E86	E87	E88	E89	E90
	E91	E92	E93	E138	E139	E140	E141	E142
	E143	E144	E145	E146	E147	E148	E149	E150
	E276	E277	E278	E279	E280			
Volvo B7TL	PVL112	PVL371	PVL372	PVL373	PVL374	PVL375	PVL376	
	PVL377	PVL378	PVL379	PVL380	PVL381	PVL382	PVL383	PVL384
	PVL385	PVL386	PVL387	PVL388	PVL389	PVL390	PVL391	PVL392
	PVL393	PVL394	PVL395	PVL396	PVL397	PVL398	PVL399	PVL400
	PVL401	PVL402	PVL403	PVL404	PVL405	PVL406	PVL407	PVL408
	PVL409	PVL410	PVL411	PVL412	PVL413	PVL414	PVL415	PVL416
	PVL417	PVL418	PVL419					
Volvo B7TL	WVL72	WVL73	WVL78	WVL79	WVL80	WVL84	WVL85	WVL89
	WVL94	WVL99	WVL152	WVL206	WVL207	WVL208	WVL209	
Volvo B9TL	WVL468	WVL469	WVL470	WVL471	WVL472	WVL473	WVL474	WVL475
	WVL476	WVL477	WVL478	WVL479	WVL480			

New Cross (New Cross Road, SE14 5UH) - NX

Dart	DP192	LDP209	LDP210	LDP273	LDP274	LDP275	LDP276	LDP277
	LDP278	LDP279	LDP280					
Enviro 200	ED1	ED2	ED3	ED4	ED5	ED6	ED7	ED8
SB120	DWL16	DWL18	DWL19	DWL21	DWL22	DWL26		
	DWL27	DWL31	DWL32	DWL36	DWL37			
Enviro 400	E94	E95	E96	E97	E98	E99	E208	E209
	E210	E211	E212	E213	E214	E215	E216	E217
	E218	E219	E220	E221	E222	E223	E224	E225
	E226	E227	E228	E246	E247	E248	E249	E250
	E251	E252	E253	E254	E255	E256	E257	E258
	E259	E260	E261	E262	E263	E264	E265	E266
	E267	E268	E269	E270	E271	E272	E273	E274
	E275							
E400 Hybrid	EH6	EH7	EH8	EH9	EH10	EH11	EH12	EH13
	EH14	EH15	EH16	EH17	EH18	EH19	EH20	
Volvo B7TL	PVL151	PVL159	PVL170	PVL216	PVL225	PVL229	PVL264	PVL319
	PVL320	PVL321	PVL322	PVL323	PVL324	PVL325	PVL343	PVL344
	PVL345	PVL346	PVL347	PVL348	PVL349	PVL350	PVL351	PVL352
	PVL353	PVL354	PVL355					
Routemaster	RM9	RML2318						
Volvo B9TL	WVL274	WVL275	WVL276	WVL277	WVL278	WVL279	WVL280	WVL281
	WVL282	WVL283	WVL284	WVL285	WVL286	WVL287	WVL288	WVL289
	WVL290	WVL291	WVL292	WVL293	WVL294	WVL295	WVL296	WVL297
	WVL298	WVL299	WVL300	WVL301	WVL302	WVL386	WVL387	WVL388
	WVL389	WVL390	WVL391	WVL392	WVL393	WVL394	WVL395	WVL396
	WVL397	WVL398	WVL399	WVL400	WVL401	WVL402	WVL403	WVL404
	WVL405	WVL406	WVL407	WVL408	WVL409	WVL410	WVL411	WVL412

Northumberland Park (Marsh Lane, Tottenham, N17 0HY) - NP

Dart	DMN1							
Enviro 200	SE1	SE2	SE3	SE4	SE5	SE6	SE7	SE8
	SE9	SE10	SE11	SE12	SE13	SE14	SE15	SE16
	SE17	SE18	SE19	SE20	SE21	SE22	SE23	SE24
	SE25	SE26	SE27	SE28	SE29			
Streetlite	WS21	WS22	WS23	WS24	WS25	WS26	WS27	WS28
	WS29	WS30	WS31	WS32				
Volvo B7TL	PVN1	PVN2	PVN3	PVN4	PVN5	PVN6	WVL189	WVL190
	WVL191	WVL192	WVL193	WVL194	WVL195	WVL196	WVL197	WVL198
	WVL199	WVL200	WVL201	WVL202	WVL203	WVL204	WVL205	WVL210
Volvo B9TL	WVN1	WVN2	WVN3	WVN4	WVN5	WVN6	WVN7	WVN8
	WVN9	WVN10	WVN11	WVN12	WVN13	WVN14	WVN15	WVN16
	WVN17	WVN18	WVN19	WVN20	WVN21	WVN22	WVN23	WVN24
	WVN25	WVN26	WVN27	WVN28	WVN29	WVN30	WVN31	WVN32
	WVN33	WVN34	WVN35	WVN36	WVN37	WVN38	WVN39	WVN40
	WVN41	WVN42	WVN43	WVN44	WVN45	WVN46	WVN47	WVN48
	WVN49	WVN50	WVN51	WVN52	WVN53			
	WVL457	WVL458	WVL459	WVL460	WVL461	WVL462	WVL463	WVL464
	WVL465	WVL466	WVL467					
Enviro 400	EN1	EN2	EN3	EN4	EN5	EN6	EN7	EN8
	EN9	EN10	EN11	EN12	EN13	EN14	EN15	EN16
	EN17	EN18	EN19	EN20	EN21	EN22	EN23	EN24

Peckham (Blackpool Road, SE15 3SU) - PM

Dart	LDP206							
Enviro 200	SE153	SE154	SE155	SE156	SE157	SE158	SE159	SE160
	SE161	SE162	SE163	SE164	SE165	SE166		
Volvo B7TL	PVL61	PVL329	PVL330	PVL331	PVL332	PVL333	PVL334	PVL335
	PVL336	PVL337	PVL338	PVL339	PVL340	PVL341	PVL342	
Volvo B9TL	WVL303	WVL304	WVL305	WVL306	WVL307	WVL308	WVL309	WVL310
	WVL311	WVL312	WVL313	WVL314	WVL315	WVL316	WVL317	WVL318
	WVL319	WVL320	WVL321	WVL322	WVL323	WVL324	WVL325	WVL326
	WVL327	WVL328	WVL329	WVL330	WVL331	WVL332	WVL333	
Enviro 400	E17	E18	E19	E20	E21	E22	E23	E24
	E25	E26	E27	E28	E29	E30	E31	E32
	E33	E34	E35	E36	E37	E61		

Putney (Chelverton Road, SW15 1RN) - AF

Dart	LDP183	LDP203	LDP281	LDP282	LDP283	LDP284	LDP285	LDP286
Routemaster	RML887	RML2318	RML2472					
Olympian	NV170	NV171						
Volvo B7TL	PVL218	PVL221	PVL222	PVL226	PVL245	PVL263	PVL265	
	WVL14	WVL15	WVL16	WVL17	WVL18	WVL19	WVL20	WVL21
	WVL22	WVL23	WVL24	WVL25	WVL26	WVL27	WVL28	WVL29
	WVL30	WVL31	WVL32	WVL33	WVL34	WVL35	WVL36	WVL37
	WVL38	WVL39	WVL40	WVL41	WVL42	WVL43	WVL44	WVL45
	WVL46	WVL47	WVL48	WVL49	WVL50	WVL51	WVL52	WVL53
	WVL54	WVL55	WVL56	WVL57	WVL58	WVL59	WVL60	WVL61
	WVL62	WVL63	WVL64	WVL65	WVL66	WVL67	WVL68	WVL69
	WVL70	WVL71	WVL153	WVL154	WVL155	WVL156	WVL157	WVL158
	WVL159	WVL160	WVL161	WVL162				
	WVL163	WVL164	WVL165	WVL166	WVL167	WVL168	WVL169	WVL170
	WVL171	WVL172	WVL173	WVL174	WVL175	WVL176	WVL177	WVL178
	WVL179	WVL180	WVL181	WVL182	WVL183	WVL184	WVL185	WVL186
	WVL187	WVL188	WVL211					
Volvo B9TL	VE1	VE2	VE3	WVL496	WVL497	WVL498	WVL499	WVL500
	WVL501	WVL502	WVL503	WVL504	WVL505	WVL506	WVL507	WVL508
Volvo B5TL	WHV32	WHV33	WHV34	WHV35	WHV36	WHV37	WHV38	WHV39
	WHV40	WHV41						

Rainham (Denver Industrial Estate, Ferry Lane, RM13 9DD) - BE

Type								
Streetlite	WS1	WS2	WS3	WS4	WS5	WS6	WS7	WS8
	WS9							
Dart	LDP191	LDP192	LDP193	LDP194	LDP195	LDP196	LDP199	DMN2
	DMN3	DMN4	DMN5	DMN6	DMN7	DMN8	DP208	
Enviro 200	ED9	ED10	ED11	ED12	ED13	ED14	ED15	ED16
	ED17	ED18	ED19	ED20	ED21	ED22	ED23	ED24
	ED25	ED26	ED27	SE18	SE19	SE20	SE21	SE22
	SE23	SE24	SE25	SE26	SE27	SE28	SE29	SE30
	SE31	SE32	SE33	SE34	SE35	SE36	SE37	SE38
	SE39	SE40	SE41	SE42	SE43	SE44	SE45	SE46
	SE94	SE95	SE96	SE97	SE98	SE99	SE100	SE101
	SE102	SE103	SEN30	SEN31	SEN32	SEN33	SEN34	SEN35
	SEN36	SEN37						
Trident	EN25	EN26	EN27					
Scania	SOC1							
Volvo B7TL	PVL66	PVL67	PVL68	PVL69	PVL95	PVL96	PVL97	PVL115
	PVL116	PVL217	PVL219	PVL223	PVL224	PVN7	PVN8	PVN9
	PVN10	PVN11	PVN12	PVN13	PVN14	PVN15	PVN16	PVN17
	WVL75	WVL77	WVL90	WVL91	WVL97	WVL98	WVL103	WVL104
Volvo B9TL	WVL334	WVL335	WVL336	WVL337	WVL338	WVL339	WVL340	WVL341
	WVL342	WVL343	WVL344	WVL345	WVL346	WVL347	WVL348	WVL349
	WVL457	WVL458	WVL459	WVL460	WVL461	WVL462	WVL463	WVL464
	WVL465	WVL466	WVL467					

Silvertown (Factory Road, E16 2EL) - SI

Dart	ED28							
Enviro 200	SE104	SE105	SE106	SE107	SE108	SE109	SE110	SE111
	SE112	SE113	SE114	SE115	SE116	SE117	SE118	SE119
	SE120	SE121	SE122	SE123	SE124	SE125	SE126	SE127
	SE128	SE129	SE130	SE131	SE132	SE133	SE134	SE135
	SE136	SE137	SE138	SE139	SE140	SE141	SE142	SE143
	SE144	SE145	SE146	SE147	SE148	SE149	SE150	SE151
	SE152							
Volvo B7TL	PVL70	PVL110	PVL209					
Volvo B9TL	VM1	WVL413	WVL414	WVL415	WVL416	WVL417	WVL418	WVL419
	WVL420	WVL421	WVL422	WVL423	WVL424	WVL425	WVL426	WVL427
	WVL428	WVL429	WVL430	WVL431	WVL432	WVL433	WVL434	

Southwark (Unit 2, 5 Mandela Way, SE1 5SS) - MW

Dart	LDP206							
Citaro	MEC32	MEC37	MEC38	MEC40	MEC45	MEC48	MEC49	
Volvo B7TL	PVL232	PVL233	VWL27	VWL28	VWL29	VWL30	VWL31	VWL32
	VWL33	VWL34	VWL35	VWL36	VWL37	VWL38	VWL39	VWL40
	VWL41	VWL42	VWL43	VWL44	WVL271			
Scania N94	ELS1	ELS2	ELS3	ELS4	ELS5	ELS6	ELS7	ELS8
	ELS9	ELS10	ELS11	ELS12	ELS13	ELS14		
Enviro 400	E163	E164	E165	E166	E167	E168	E169	E170
	E171	E172	E173	E174	E175	E176	E177	E178
	E179	E180	E181	E182	E183	E184	E185	E186
	E187	E188	E189	E190	E191	E192	E193	E194
	E195	E196	E197	E198	E199	E200	E201	

Stockwell (Binfield Road, SW4 6ST) - SW

Type								
Dart	DP193	DP194	DP195	DP196	DP197	DP198	DP199	DP200
	DP201	DP202	DP203	DP204	DP205	DP209	LDP186	LPD187
	LDP204	LDP287	LDP288	LDP289	LDP290	LDP291		
Enviro 200	SE47	SE48	SE49	SE50	SE51	SE52	SE53	SE54
Enviro 400	E1	E2	E3	E4	E5	E6	E7	E8
	E9	E10	E11	E12	E13	E14	E15	E38
	E62	E63	E64	E65	E66	E129	E130	E131
	E132	E133	E134	E135	E136	E137	E151	E152
	E153	E154	E155	E156	E157	E158	E159	E160
	E161	E162						

Trident E400H	EH1	EH2	EH3	EH4	EH5	EH21	EH22	EH23
	EH24	EH25	EH26	EH27	EH28	EH29	EH30	EH31
	EH32	EH33	EH34	EH35	EH36	EH37	EH38	
VDL/Wrightbus	WHD1							
Volvo B5LH	WHY17	WHY18	WHY19	WHY20	WHY21	WHY22	WHY23	WHY24
	WHY25	WHY26	WHY27	WHY28	WHY29	WHY30	WHY31	
Volvo B7TL	PVL85	PVL203	PVL220	PVL244	WVL1	WVL2	WVL3	WVL4
	WVL5	WVL6	WVL7	WVL8	WVL9	WVL10	WVL11	WVL12
	WVL13	WVL74	WVL76	WVL88	WVL96	WVL101	WVL102	WVL105
	WVL106	WVL107	WVL108	WVL109	WVL110	WVL111	WVL112	WVL113
	WVL114	WVL115	WVL116	WVL117	WVL118	WVL119	WVL120	WVL121
	WVL122	WVL123	WVL125	WVL126	WVL129	WVL130	WVL131	WVL132
	WVL133	WVL134	WVL135	WVL136	WVL137	WVL138	WVL139	WVL140
	WVL141	WVL142	WVL143	WVL144	WVL145	WVL146	WVL147	WVL148
	WVL149	WVL150	WVL151	WVL481	WVL482	WVL483	WVL484	WVL485
	WVL486	WVL487	WVL488	WVL489	WVL490	WVL491	WVL492	WVL493
	WVL494	WVL495						

Sutton (Bushey Road, SM1 1QJ) - A

Dart	LDP183							
Enviro 200	SE167	SE168	SE169	SE170	SE171	SE172	SE173	SE174
	SOE29	SOE30	SOE31	SOE32	SOE33	SOE34	SOE35	SOE36
	SOE37	SOE38	SOE39	SOE40				
Trident 2	DOE1	DOE2	DOE3	DOE4	DOE5	DOE6	DOE7	DOE8
	DOE8	DOE10	DOE11	DOE12	DOE13	DOE14	DOE15	DOE16
	DOE17	DOE18	DOE19	DOE20	DOE21	DOE22	DOE23	DOE24
	DOE25	DOE26	DOE27	DOE28	DOE29	DOE30	DOE31	DOE32
	DOE33	DOE34	DOE35	DOE36	DOE37	DOE38	DOE39	DOE40
	DOE41	DOE42	DOE43	DOE44	DOE45	DOE46	DOE47	DOE48
	DOE49	DOE50	DOE51	DOE52	DOE53	DOE54		
Enviro 400	E58	E59	E60					
Volvo B7TL	PVL281	PVL282	PVL283	PVL284	PVL285	PVL286	PVL287	PVL288
	PVL289	PVL290	PVL291	PVL292	PVL293	PVL294	PVL295	PVL296
	PVL297							

Waterloo (Cornwall Road, SE1 8TE) - RA

MB Citaro O530	MEC1	MEC2	MEC3	MEC4	MEC5	MEC6	MEC7	MEC8
	MEC9	MEC10	MEC11	MEC12	MEC13	MEC14	MEC15	MEC16
	MEC17	MEC18	MEC19	MEC20	MEC21	MEC22	MEC23	MEC24
	MEC25	MEC26	MEC27	MEC28	MEC29	MEC30	MEC31	MEC33
	MEC34	MEC35	MEC36	MEC39	MEC41	MEC42	MEC43	MEC44
	MEC46	MEC47	MEC49	MEC50				

Wimbledon (Waterside Way, SW17 0HB) - PL

Dart	LDP151	LDP208	LDP211	LDP212	LDP213	LDP214	LDP215	LDP216
	LDP217	LDP218	LDP219	LDP220	LDP221	LDP222	LDP223	LDP224
	LDP225	LDP226	LDP227	LDP263	LDP264	LDP265	LDP266	LDP267
	LDP268	LDP269	LDP270	LDP271	LDP272	LDP292	LDP293	LDP294
Enviro 200	SE175	SE176	SE177	SE178	SE179	SE180	SE181	SE182
	SE183	SE184	SE185	SE186	SE187	SE188	SE189	SE190
	SE191	SE192	SE193					

unallocated/stored/refurbishing - u/w

remainder

CT Plus Ltd, Ash Grove Depot, Mare Street, Hackney, E8 4RH

BT1	HK	YX10AYD	Volkswagen T5	Bluebird Tucana	N12F	2010	
BT2	HK	YX10AYF	Volkswagen T5	Bluebird Tucana	N12F	2010	
BT3	HK	YX10FFW	Volkswagen T5	Bluebird Tucana	N12F	2010	
DA1	HK	MX10DXR	ADL Dart 4 10.8m	ADL Enviro 200	N37F	2010	

DA2-12 ADL Dart 4 10.8m ADL Enviro 200 N31D 2012

2	HK	YX62DHC	5	HK	YX62DKD	8	HK	YX62DMU	11	HK	YX62DTV
3	HK	YX62DHD	6	HK	YX62DKE	9	HK	YX62DPF	12	HK	YX62DTY
4	HK	YX62DHY	7	HK	YX62DKL	10	HK	YX62DSZ		

DAS1	HK	SN57DWE	ADL Dart 4 8.9m	ADL Enviro 200	N26F	2007
DAS2	HK	SN57DWF	ADL Dart 4 8.9m	ADL Enviro 200	N26F	2007

DCS1-9 TransBus Dart 8.9m Caetano Slimbus N30F 2003

1	HK	E8NJB	4	HK	KV03ZFH	6	HK	HX03MGU	8	HK	HX03MGY
2	HK	KV03ZFF	5	HK	HX03MGV	7	HK	HX03MGJ	9	HK	HX03MGZ
3	HK	KV03ZFG								

DE1-6 ADL Dart 4 10.4m East Lancs Esteem N28D 2007

1	HK	PN07KPY	3	HK	PN07KRD	5	HK	PN07KRF	6	HK	PN07KRG
2	HK	PN07KPZ	4	HK	PN07KRE					

DP1	HK	SN53EUD	TransBus Dart 10.1m	TransBus Pointer	N30D	2003	Go-Ahead London, 2012
DPS1	HK	P508RYM	Dennis Dart 9.2m	Plaxton Pointer	N31F	1996	
DPS2	AW	BU05HFG	ADL Dart 8.8m	ADL Mini Pointer	N29F	2005	
DPS3	AW	MM51XVB	Dennis Dart 8.8m	Plaxton Pointer MPD	N29F	2001	
DPS4	AW	BX54DLK	ADL Dart 9.3m	ADL Pointer 2	N27D	2004	Abellio, 2012
EO1	HK	PN08SWJ	ADL Trident 2 10.3m	East Lancs Olympus	N43/21D	2008	
HEA1	HK	SN62DND	ADL E40H 10.4m	ADL Enviro 400	N37/24D	2012	

HDC1-11 Dennis Dart SLF 10.5m Caetano Nimbus N24D 2001

1	HK	X584ORV	4	HK	X587ORV	7	HK	X591ORV	10	HK	X594ORV
2	HK	X585ORV	5	HK	X588ORV	8	HK	X592ORV	11	HK	X595ORV
3	HK	X586ORV	6	HK	X589ORV	9	HK	X593ORV		

HTL1-13 TransBus Trident 10m East Lancs Myllenium Lolyne N45/17D 2003

1	HK	LR52LTO	5	HK	LR52LWE	8	HK	LR52LWH	11	HK	PF52TGZ
2	HK	LR52LTN	6	HK	LR52LTK	9	HK	LR52LWJ	12	HK	LR52LYC
3	HK	LR52LTJ	7	HK	LR52LWF	10	HK	PF52TFX	13	HK	LR52LYJ
4	HK	LR52LTF								

HTP3	HK	PN03UMB	TransBus Trident 9.9m	TransBus President	N41/23D	2003	Go-Ahead London, 2009
HTP4	HK	PN03UMK	TransBus Trident 9.9m	TransBus President	N41/23D	2003	Go-Ahead London, 2009
HTP6	AW	PN03ULY	TransBus Trident 9.9m	TransBus President	N41/23D	2003	Go-Ahead London, 2009

LFO3-6 Optare Alero Optare BC13F* 2003-04 *seating varies

3	HK	YN53ENH	4	HK	YN53ENM	5	HK	YN54LLA	6	HK	YN54LKU

OS2-8 Optare Solo M780 SE Optare N21F 2010-11

2	AW	YJ59NRN	4	AW	YJ10EYF	6	AW	YJ10EYH	8	AW	YJ10EYL
3	AW	YJ59NRO	5	AW	YJ10EYG	7	AW	YJ10EYK		

OS9-18 Optare Solo M880 Optare N23F 2011

9	HK	YJ11PFA	12	HK	YJ11PFF	15	HK	YJ11PFN	17	HK	YJ60LRX
10	HK	YJ11PFD	13	HK	YJ11PFG	16	HK	YJ11PFO	18	HK	YJ60LRY
11	HK	YJ11PFE	14	HK	YJ11PFK					

OS19-27 Optare Solo M950 Optare N26D 2012

19	HK	YJ61MKA	22	HK	YJ12GVU	24	HK	YJ12GVW	26	HK	YJ12GVY
20	HK	YJ12GVR	23	HK	YJ12GVV	25	HK	YJ12GVX	27	HK	YJ12GVZ
21	HK	YJ12GVT								

CT Plus is a part of the HCT Group and in London provides bus services for TfL on ten routes. Pictured operating route 212 from Walthamstow to Chingford is Scania N230 number SD4, YR59NPF.
Terry Longhurst

SD1-10

		Scania N230 UD 10.8m			East Lancs OmniDekka			N41/22D	2010		
1	AW	YR59NPA	4	AW	YR59NPF	7	AW	YR59NPN	9	AW	YR59NPK
2	AW	YR59NPC	5	AW	YR59NPG	8	AW	YR59NPE	10	AW	YR59NPO
3	AW	YR59NPD	6	AW	YR59NPJ						

Ancillary vehicles:

-	HKt	YK10AVV	BMC Condor 225	BMC		B45F	2012
-	HK	HV02PDO	Dennis Dart SLF	Caetano Nimbus		N31D	2002

Note: The operator also provides over forty non-PCV vehicles for welfare related work in London using the CT Plus name. Its associate, Hackney Community Transport, operates more than thirty similar vehicles. There is also an extensive operation in Bristol, Jersey and Yorkshire.

Previous registration:
E8NJB   KV03ZFE

Depots and allocations:

Hackney (Mare Street,) - HK

Volkswagen	BT1	BT2	BT3					
Optare Alero	LFO3	LFO4	LFO5	LFO6				
Optare Solo	OS9	OS10	OS11	OS12	OS13	OS14	OS15	OS16
	OS17	OS18	OS19	OS20	OS21	OS22	OS23	OS24
	OS25	OS26	OS27					
Dart	DCS1	DCS2	DCS3	DCS4	DCS5	DCS6	DCS7	DCS8
	DCS9	DE1	DE2	DE3	DE4	DE5	DE6	DP1
	DPS1	DPS2	DPS3	DPS4				
Enviro 200	DA1	DA2	DA3	DA4	DA5	DA6	DA7	DA8
	DA9	DA10	DA11	DA12	DAS1	DAS2		
Trident	EO1	HTL1	HTL2	HTL3	HTL4	HTL5	HTL6	HTL7
	HTL8	HTL9	HTL10	HTL11	HTL12	HTL13	HTP3	HTP4
Enviro 400	HEA1							

Ash Grove ( ) - AW

Optare Solo	OS2	OS3	OS4	OS5	OS6	OS7	OS8	
Dart	DPS2							
Trident	HTP6							
Scania OmniDekka	SD1	SD2	SD3	SD4	SD5	SD6	SD7	SD8
	SD9	SD10						

LONDON DIAL-A-RIDE

Transport for London, Dial-a-Ride, 5 Mandela Way, London, SE1 5SS

D7001-7068 — Volkswagen T5 / Bluebird Tucana / N8F / 2008

7001	DR	YX57HBZ	7018	DR	YX08GVT	7035	DR	YX58EGD	7052	DR	YX58EEZ
7002	DR	YX08FKE	7019	DR	YX08GVU	7036	DR	YX08KXT	7053	DR	YX58EFC
7003	DR	YX08FKF	7020	DR	YX08GWF	7037	DR	YX08KXW	7054	DR	YX58EHB
7004	DR	YX08FKO	7021	DR	YX08GVW	7038	DR	YX58EGE	7055	DR	YX58EFA
7005	DR	YX08FKP	7022	DR	YX08GVY	7039	DR	YX58EGF	7056	DR	YX58EHG
7006	DR	YX08FKR	7023	DR	YX08GVZ	7040	DR	YX58EGJ	7057	DR	YX58EHH
7007	DR	YX08FKS	7024	DR	YX08GWA	7041	DR	YX58EGZ	7058	DR	YX58EHJ
7008	DR	YX08FKU	7025	DR	YX08GWC	7042	DR	YX58EFD	7059	DR	YX58EHK
7009	DR	YX08FKT	7026	DR	YX08GVV	7043	DR	YX58EFE	7060	DR	YX58EHL
7010	DR	YX08FKZ	7027	DR	YX08GWG	7044	DR	YX58EFF	7061	DR	YX58EHR
7011	DR	YX08FKV	7028	DR	YX08KXJ	7045	DR	YX58EFO	7062	DR	YX58GSO
7012	DR	YX08FKW	7029	DR	YX08KXK	7046	DR	YX58EFN	7063	DR	YX58GSY
7013	DR	YX08FKG	7030	DR	YX08KXL	7047	DR	YX58EEU	7064	DR	YX58GSZ
7014	DR	YX08FKK	7031	DR	YX08KXP	7048	DR	YX58EET	7065	DR	YX58GTF
7015	DR	YX08FKJ	7032	DR	YX08KXR	7049	DR	YX58EEW	7066	DR	YX58GTU
7016	DR	YX08FKL	7033	DR	YX08KXM	7050	DR	YX58EEV	7067	DR	YX58GTY
7017	DR	YX08FKM	7034	DR	YX08KXN	7051	DR	YX58EEY	7068	DR	YX58GTZ

D7069-7104 — Volkswagen T5 / Bluebird Tucana / N8F / 2009

7069	DR	YX09ETA	7078	DR	YX09ETR	7087	DR	YX09EUH	7096	DR	YX09EUZ
7070	DR	YX09ETD	7079	DR	YX09ETU	7088	DR	YX09EUJ	7097	DR	YX09EVB
7071	DR	YX09ETE	7080	DR	YX09ETV	7089	DR	YX09EUK	7098	DR	YX09EVC
7072	DR	YX09ETF	7081	DR	YX09ETY	7090	DR	YX09EUL	7099	DR	YX09EVF
7073	DR	YX09ESY	7082	DR	YX09ETZ	7091	DR	YX09EUP	7100	DR	YX09EVK
7074	DR	YX09ETJ	7083	DR	YX09EUA	7092	DR	YX09EUR	7101	DR	YX09HRL
7075	DR	YX09ETK	7084	DR	YX09EUB	7093	DR	YX09EUT	7102	DR	YX09HRM
7076	DR	YX09ETL	7085	DR	YX09EUC	7094	DR	YX09EUW	7103	DR	YX09HRN
7077	DR	YX09ETO	7086	DR	YX09EUF	7095	DR	YX09EUY	7104	DR	YX09HRO

London Buses Limited is responsible for operating the Dial-a-Ride service, which provides door-to-door transport for people with disabilities. In November 2011 Transport for London instigated a year-long trial of environmentally friendly biofuel in twelve of its Dial-a-Ride vehicles. Seen at Norwood Green is 7053, YX58EFC. *Mark Lyons*

Bluebird Tucana-bodied Volkswagen 7008, YX08FKU, is seen in Chepstow Road. *Mark Lyons*

D7105-7141

		Volkswagen T5			Bluebird Tucana			N8F	2009-10		
7105	DR	YX59AAO	7115	DR	YX59ACY	7124	DR	YX10FGA	7133	DR	YX60CJV
7106	DR	YX59ABN	7116	DR	YX59ADO	7125	DR	YX10FGD	7134	DR	YX60CJY
7107	DR	YX59ABV	7117	DR	YX59ADU	7126	DR	YX10FGC	7135	DR	YX60CJE
7108	DR	YX59ABU	7118	DR	YX59ADV	7127	DR	YX10FGE	7136	DR	YX60CKG
7109	DR	YX59ABZ	7119	DR	YX59ADZ	7128	DR	YX10FGF	7137	DR	YX60CKJ
7110	DR	YX59ACF	7120	DR	YX59AEA	7129	DR	YX10FGG	7138	DR	YX60CJF
7111	DR	YX59ACJ	7121	DR	YX59AEB	7130	DR	YX60CJJ	7139	DR	YX60CKK
7112	DR	YX59ACO	7122	DR	YX10FFY	7131	DR	YX60CJO	7140	DR	YX60CKU
7113	DR	YX59ACU	7123	DR	YX10FFZ	7132	DR	YX60CJU	7141	DR	YX60CKV
7114	DR	YX59ACV									

D7142-7161

		Volkswagen T5			Bluebird Tucana			N8F	2011		
7142	DR	YX60DYN	7147	DR	YX60DYU	7152	DR	YX60DZF	7157	DR	YX11EVG
7143	DR	YX60DYO	7148	DR	YX60DYY	7153	DR	YX60DZG	7158	DR	YX11CVV
7144	DR	YX60DYP	7149	DR	YX60DZA	7154	DR	YX60DZJ	7159	DR	YX11CVW
7145	DR	YX60DYS	7150	DR	YX60CLY	7155	DR	YX60DZL	7160	DR	YX11CVY
7146	DR	YX60DYT	7151	DR	YX60CLV	7156	DR	YX60EVR	7161	DR	YX11CVZ

D7162-7203

		Volkswagen T5			Bluebird Tucana			N8F	2011		
7162	DR	YX11FSF	7173	DR	YX11FSY	7184	DR	YX61DWC	7194	DR	YX61DWO
7163	DR	YX11FSG	7174	DR	YX11FSZ	7185	DR	YX61DWD	7195	DR	YX61DWP
7164	DR	YX11FSJ	7175	DR	YX11FTA	7186	DR	YX61DWE	7196	DR	YX61DWU
7165	DR	YX11FSK	7176	DR	YX11CVC	7187	DR	YX61DWF	7197	DR	YX61DWV
7166	DR	YX11FSL	7177	DR	YX11CVD	7188	DR	YX61DWG	7198	DR	YX61DWW
7167	DR	YX11FSN	7178	DR	YX11CVE	7189	DR	YX61DWJ	7199	DR	YX61DWY
7168	DR	YX11FSO	7179	DR	YX11CVF	7190	DR	YX61DWK	7200	DR	YX61DWZ
7169	DR	YX11FSP	7180	DR	YX11CVG	7191	DR	YX61DWL	7201	DR	YX61DXA
7170	DR	YX11FSS	7181	DR	YX61DVY	7192	DR	YX61DWM	7202	DR	YX61DXB
7171	DR	YX11FSU	7182	DR	YX61DVZ	7193	DR	YX61DWN	7203	DR	YX61DXC
7172	DR	YX11FSV	7183	DR	YX61DWA						

D7204-7229

		Volkswagen T5			Bluebird Tucana			N8F	2012		
7204	DR	YX12CGE	7211	DR	YX62AEC	7218	DR	YX62AKK	7224	DR	YX62AWH
7205	DR	YX12CGF	7212	DR	YX62AED	7219	DR	YX62AKZ	7225	DR	YX62AWJ
7206	DR	YX12CGG	7213	DR	YX62AEJ	7220	DR	YX62AVJ	7226	DR	YX62AYB
7207	DR	YX12CGK	7214	DR	YX62AEK	7221	DR	YX62AVN	7227	DR	YX62AYC
7208	DR	YX12CGO	7215	DR	YX62AHU	7222	DR	YX62AVY	7228	DR	YX62AYD
7209	DR	YX12CGU	7216	DR	YX62AKG	7223	DR	YX62AWA	7229	DR	YX62AYF
7210	DR	YX62ACV	7217	DR	YX62AKJ						

Note: Also operated is a fleet of Mercedes-Benz minibuses which are in the process of being replaced and are not listed here.

Metrobus Ltd, Wheatstone Close, Crawley, RH10 9UA

101	MB	YJ56WVF	Optare Solo M710 SE	Optare	N17F	2006	
102	MB	YJ56WVG	Optare Solo M710 SE	Optare	N17F	2006	
142	C	LT02ZDR	TransBus Dart 8.9m	Marshall Capital	N25F	2002	FirstBus, 2007
143	MB	LT02ZDS	TransBus Dart 8.9m	Marshall Capital	N25F	2002	FirstBus, 2007

148-162   ADL Dart 4 8.9m   ADL Enviro 200   N26F   2011

148	MB	YX60FTO	152	MB	YX60FTV	156	MB	YX60FUW	160	MB	YX60FVC
149	MB	YX60FTP	153	MB	YX60FTY	157	MB	YX60FUY	161	MB	YX60FVD
150	MB	YX60FTT	154	MB	YX60FTZ	158	MB	YX60FVA	162	MB	YX60FVE
151	MB	YX60FTU	155	MB	YX60FUV	159	MB	YX60FVB			

163-178   ADL Dart 4 8.9m   ADL Enviro 200   N25F   2011

163	MB	YX61ENC	167	MB	YX61ENJ	171	MB	YX61ENN	175	MB	YX61ENT
164	MB	YX61ENE	168	MB	YX61ENK	172	MB	YX61ENO	176	MB	YX61ENU
165	MB	YX61ENF	169	MB	YX61ENL	173	MB	YX61ENP	177	MB	YX61ENV
166	MB	YX61ENH	170	MB	YX61ENM	174	MB	YX61ENR	178	MB	YX61ENW

179-192   ADL Dart 4 8.9m   ADL Enviro 200   N20D   2013

179	MB	YX62DYH	183	MB	YX62DZN	187	MB	YX13AJV	190	MB	YY13VKP
180	MB	YX62DYN	184	MB	YX62DZU	188	MB	YX13AJY	191	MB	YY13VKR
181	MB	YX62DYS	185	MB	YX13AJO	189	MB	YY13VKO	192	MB	YY13VKS
182	MB	YX62DZE	186	MB	YX13AJU						

201-219   TransBus Dart 10.7m   TransBus Pointer   N36D   2003

201	CY	SN03WKU	206	CY	SN03WLH	212	C	SN03WMC	216	C	SN03WMP
202	CY	SN03WKY	207	CY	SN03WLL	213	C	SN03WMF	217	CY	SN03WMT
203	CY	SN03WLA	210	C	SN03WLX	214	C	SN03WMG	218	CY	SN03WMV
204	CY	SN03WLE	211	C	SN03WLZ	215	C	SN03WMK	219	C	SN03WMY
205	CY	SN03WLF									

228-236   ADL Dart 4 9m   East Lancs Esteem   N24F   2006

228	MB	PO56JEU	231	MB	PO56JFF	233	MB	PO56JFJ	235	MB	PO56JFN
229	MB	PO56JFA	232	MB	PO56JFG	234	MB	PO56JFK	236	MB	PO56JFU
230	MB	PO56JFE									

241	CY	R741BMY	Dennis Dart SLF 10.1m	Plaxton Pointer	N32F	1998
244	CY	R744BMY	Dennis Dart SLF 10.1m	Plaxton Pointer	N35F	1998
247	CY	R747BMY	Dennis Dart SLF 10.1m	Plaxton Pointer	N35F	1998

251-256   ADL Dart 8.8m   ADL Mini Pointer   N23F   2004

251	MB	SN54GPV	253	MB	SN54GPY	255	MB	SN54GRF	256	MB	SN54GRK
252	MB	SN54GPX	254	MB	SN54GPZ						

257-268   ADL Dart 9m   East Lancs Esteem   N27F   2006

257	MB	PN06UYL	260	MB	PN06UYP	263	MB	PN06UYT	266	MB	PN06UYW
258	MB	PN06UYM	261	MB	PN06UYR	264	MB	PN06UYU	267	MB	PN06UYX
259	MB	PN06UYO	262	MB	PN06UYS	265	MB	PN06UYV	268	MB	PN06UYY

271-289   TransBus Dart 8.8m   TransBus Mini Pointer   N27F*   2003   *287-9 are N29F

271	MB	SN03YBA	276	MB	SN03YBK	281	MB	SN03YBY	286	MB	SN03YCK
272	MB	SN03YBB	277	MB	SN03YBR	282	MB	SN03YBZ	287	CY	SN03YCL
273	MB	SN03YBC	278	MB	SN03YBS	283	MB	SN03YCD	288	CY	SN03YCM
274	MB	SN03YBG	279	MB	SN03YBT	284	MB	SN03YCE	289	CY	SN03YCT
275	MB	SN03YBH	280	MB	SN03YBX	285	MB	SN03YCF			

310	u	T310SMV	Dennis Dart SLF 10.2m	Alexander ALX200	N32F	1999
311	u	T311SMV	Dennis Dart SLF 10.2m	Alexander ALX200	N32F	1999
320	CY	LX03OJP	TransBus Dart SLF 10.7m	TransBus Pointer	N37F	2003
321	CY	LX03OJN	TransBus Dart SLF 10.7m	TransBus Pointer	N37F	2003
334	C	W334VGX	Dennis Dart SLF 10.7m	Plaxton Pointer 2	N31D	2000
344	CY	X344YGU	Dennis Dart SLF 8.8m	Plaxton Pointer MPD	N29F	2000

Metrobus was formed in 1983 to operate the bus and coach services previously provided by Tillingbourne (Metropolitan) Ltd; the business consisted of six vehicles based at Green Street Green near Orpington. The opportunity to expand was soon realised and the company was to benefit from the London tendering system set up in 1985. Expansion on London Transport contracts and commercial initiatives increased the fleet to over a hundred buses by 1997. A recent addition to the fleet is Enviro 200 180, YX62DYN, seen in Bromley while operating route 138 to Colney Hall. *Richard Godfrey*

359-379   Dennis Dart SLF 11m   Caetano Nimbus   N38F*   2001   *seating varies

359	CY	Y359HMY	365	CY	Y365HMY	371	CY	Y371HMY	376	CY	Y376HMY
361	CY	Y361HMY	366	CY	Y366HMY	372	CY	Y372HMY	377	CY	Y377HMY
362	CY	Y362HMY	367	CY	Y367HMY	373	CY	Y373HMY	378	CY	Y378HMY
363	CY	Y363HMY	368	CY	Y368HMY	374	CY	Y374HMY	379	CY	Y379HMY
364	CY	Y364HMY									

390	CY	P380FPK	Dennis Dart SLF 10.7m	Plaxton Pointer	B39F	1997	Arriva S Counties, 2009
393	CY	P283FPK	Dennis Dart SLF 10.7m	Plaxton Pointer	B39F	1997	Arriva S Counties, 2009
394	CY	P274FPK	Dennis Dart SLF 10.7m	Plaxton Pointer	B39F	1997	Arriva S Counties, 2009
395	CY	P285FPK	Dennis Dart SLF 10.7m	Plaxton Pointer	B39F	1997	Arriva S Counties, 2009
396	CY	N232TPK	Dennis Dart SLF 10.1m	Plaxton Pointer	B35F	1996	Arriva S Counties, 2009
398	CY	P278FPK	Dennis Dart SLF 10.7m	Plaxton Pointer	B39F	1997	Arriva S Counties, 2009

431-447   Scania N94UD 10.6m   East Lancs OmniDekka 4.4m   N45/29D*   2003   *seating varies

431	C	YV03PZW	436	C	YV03PZF	440	C	YV03PZK	444	C	YV03RCZ
432	C	YV03PZX	437	C	YV03PZG	441	C	YV03PZL	445	C	YV03RAU
433	C	YV03PZY	438	C	YV03PZH	442	C	YV03PZM	446	C	YV03RAX
434	C	YV03PZZ	439	C	YV03PZJ	443	C	YV03RCY	447	C	YV03RBF
435	C	YV03PZE									

451-471   Scania N94UD 10.6m   East Lancs OmniDekka 4.4m   N45/29D*   2003   *seating varies

451	C	YU52XVK	458	MB	YN03DFD	462	MB	YN03DFK	468	MB	YN03DFY
455	C	YN03DFA	459	MB	YN03DFE	465	MB	YN03DFU	469	CY	YV03RBU
456	C	YN03DFC	460	MB	YN03DFG	466	MB	YN03DFV	470	CY	YV03RBX
457	MB	YU52XVR	461	MB	YN03DFJ	467	MB	YN03DFX	471	CY	YN53USG

472-497   Scania N94UD 10.6m   East Lancs OmniDekka 4.4m   N45/29D*   2003-05   *seating varies

472	CY	YN53RYA	479	MB	YN53RYM	486	CY	YN53RYY	492	CY	YN53RZE
473	CY	YN53RYB	480	C	YN53RYP	487	CY	YN53RYZ	493	CY	YN53RZF
474	CY	YN53RYC	481	C	YN53RYR	488	CY	YN53RZA	494	CY	YN54AJU
475	CY	YN53RYD	482	CY	YN53RYT	489	CY	YN53RZB	495	CY	YN54AJV
476	CY	YN53RYF	483	CY	YN53RYV	490	CY	YN53RZC	496	CY	YN54AJX
477	CY	YN53RYH	484	CY	YN53RYW	491	CY	YN53RZD	497	CY	YN54AJY
478	CY	YN53RYK	485	CY	YN53RYX						

Metrobus made a further expansion within London in late 2007 when the Orpington operation belonging to First London was taken over. Included in the transfer were seven TfL services and thirty-five Dennis Darts. Integral Scania OmniCity single-deck buses have been selected for several purchases with 523, YN53RXR, from the 2003 intake shown. *Terry Longhurst*

| 513 | CY | YP52CTO | Scania OmniCity CN94 UB 12m | Scania | | | | N42F | 2002 | | |

514-530 — Scania OmniCity CN94 UB 12m — Scania — N32D — 2003

514	MB	YN53RXF	519	MB	YN53RXL	523	MB	YN53RXR	527	MB	YN53RXW
515	MB	YN53RXG	520	MB	YN53RXM	524	MB	YN53RXT	528	MB	YN53RXX
516	MB	YN53RXH	521	MB	YN53RXO	525	MB	YN53RXU	529	MB	YN53RXY
517	MB	YN53RXJ	522	MB	YN53RXP	526	MB	YN53RXV	530	MB	YN53RXZ
518	MB	YN53RXK									

531-535 — Scania OmniCity CN94 UB 12m — Scania — N37D — 2003

| 531 | CY | YN03UWU | 533 | CY | YN03UPM | 534 | CY | YN03WPP | 535 | CY | YN03WPR |
| 532 | CY | YN03UWY | | | | | | | | | |

546-558 — Scania OmniCity CN94 UB 12m — Scania — N37D* — 2005 — *552-8 N34D

546	CY	YN05HCA	550	CY	YN05HCF	553	CY	YN55PWK	556	CY	YN55PWU
547	CY	YN05HCC	551	CY	YN05HCG	554	CY	YN55PWL	557	CY	YN55PWV
548	CY	YN05HCD	552	CY	YN55PWJ	555	CY	YN55PWO	558	CY	YN55PWX
549	CY	YN05HCE									

559-567 — Scania OmniCity CN230 UB 12m — Scania — N33D* — 2007-08 — *559/60 are N36D

559	CY	YN07LKF	562	C	YN58BNA	564	C	YN08OAW	566	C	YN08OAY
560	CY	YN07LKG	563	C	YN08OAV	565	C	YN08OAX	567	C	YN08OAZ
561	C	YN08OAS									

568-581 — Scania OmniCity CN230 UB 12m — Scania — N36D — 2009

568	CY	YT09BKD	572	CY	YT09BKJ	576	CY	YT09BKO	579	CY	YT09BKX
569	CY	YT09BKE	573	CY	YT09BKK	577	CY	YT09BKU	580	CY	YT09BKY
570	CY	YT09BKF	574	CY	YT09BKL	578	CY	YT09BKV	581	CY	YT09BKZ
571	CY	YT09BKG	575	CY	YT09BKN						

| 582 | CY | YN62CLF | Scania OmniCity CN230 UB 12m | Scania | | | | N35D | 2012 | | |

Metrobus operates several MAN single-decks with East Lancs Esteem, Alexander Dennis Enviro and MCV Evolution bodywork. Illustrating the latter is 718, AE09DHU, as it passes through Catford Hill en route for Blackheath. *Mark Lyons*

601-623
Scania OmniTown N94 UB 10.6m East Lancs Esteem   N29D*   2006   *616-23 N36F

601	MB	YM55SWU	607	MB	YM55SXA	613	MB	YN06JXT	619	CY	YM55SXO
602	MB	YM55SWV	608	MB	YM55SXB	614	MB	YM55SXH	620	CY	YM55SXP
603	MB	YN06JXR	609	MB	YM55SXC	615	c	YN06JXU	621	CY	YM55SXR
604	MB	YM55SWX	610	MB	YM55SXD	616	CY	YN06JXV	622	CY	YN06JXY
605	MB	YM55SWY	611	MB	YM55SXE	617	CY	YN06JXW	623	CY	YN06JXZ
606	MB	YN06JXS	612	MB	YM55SXF	618	CY	YN06JXX			

624-633
Scania OmniCity N230 UB 10.9m Scania   N33F   2008

624	CY	YN08DFJ	627	CY	YN08DFO	630	CY	YN08DFV	632	CY	YN08DFY
625	CY	YN08DFK	628	CY	YN08DFP	631	CY	YN08DFX	633	CY	YN08DFZ
626	CY	YN08DFL	629	CY	YN08DFU						

701-705
MAN 12.240 10.3m   East Lancs Esteem   N27D   2007

701	MB	PN07KRK	703	MB	PN07KRU	704	MB	PN07KRV	705	MB	PN07KRX
702	MB	PN07KRO									

706	C	YX58DXB	MAN 14.240	10.8m	ADL Enviro 200	N34D	2009
707	C	YX58DXC	MAN 14.240	10.8m	ADL Enviro 200	N34D	2009
708	C	YX58DXD	MAN 14.240	10.8m	ADL Enviro 200	N34D	2009

709-723
MAN 14.240 10.8m   MCV Evolution   N28D   2009

709	C	AE09DHG	713	C	AE09DHP	717	C	AJ58WBG	721	C	AJ58WBK
710	C	AE09DHK	714	C	AJ58WBE	718	C	AE09DHU	722	C	AJ58WBF
711	C	AJ58WBD	715	C	AE09DHJ	719	C	AE09DHN	723	C	AE09DHV
712	C	AE09DHM	716	C	AE09DHO	720	C	AE09DHL			

725-730
ADL Dart 4 10.2m   ADL Enviro 200   N36F   2007   Arriva S Counties, 2009

725	CY	GN07AVR	727	CY	GN07AVU	729	CY	GN07AVW	730	CY	GN07AUY
726	CY	GN07AVT	728	CY	GN07AVV						

731	MB	YX11CTE	ADL Dart 4 10.2m	ADL Enviro 200	N29D	2011
732	MB	YX11CTF	ADL Dart 4 10.2m	ADL Enviro 200	N29D	2011
733	MB	YX11CTK	ADL Dart 4 10.2m	ADL Enviro 200	N29D	2011

734-739
ADL E20D 10.8m ADL Enviro 200 N38F 2012

734	CY	SN12AAE	736	CY	SN12AAJ	738	CY	SN12AAO	739	CY	SN12AAU
735	CY	SN12AAF	737	CY	SN12AAK						

740-762
ADL E20D 10.8m ADL Enviro 200 N31D 2013

740	MB	YX13AFF	746	MB	YX13AFV	752	MB	YX13AGY	758	MB	YX13AHF
741	MB	YX13AFJ	747	MB	YX13AFY	753	MB	YX13AGZ	759	MB	YX13AHG
742	MB	YX13AFK	748	MB	YX13AFZ	754	MB	YX13AHA	760	MB	YX13AHJ
743	MB	YX13AFN	749	MB	YX13AGO	755	MB	YX13AHC	761	MB	YX13AHK
744	MB	YX13AFO	750	MB	YX13AGU	756	MB	YX13AHD	762	MB	YX13AHL
745	MB	YX13AFU	751	MB	YX13AGV	757	MB	YX13AHF			

870-899
Scania OmniCity N230 UD 10.8m Optare Olympus N45/23D 2009

870	C	PN09EKR	878	C	PN09ELU	886	C	PN09ENC	893	C	PN09ENO
871	C	PN09EKT	879	C	PN09ELV	887	C	PN09ENE	894	C	PN59KFW
872	C	PN09EKU	880	C	PN09ELW	888	C	PN09ENF	895	C	PN59KFX
873	C	PN09EKV	881	C	PN09ELX	889	C	PN09ENH	896	C	PN59KFY
874	C	PN09EKW	882	C	PN09EMF	890	C	PN09ENK	897	C	PN59KFZ
875	C	PN09EKX	883	C	PN09EMK	891	C	PN09ENL	898	C	PN59KGA
876	C	PN09EKY	884	C	PN09EMV	892	C	PN09ENM	899	C	PN59KGE
877	C	PN09ELO	885	C	PN09EMX						

901-927
Scania N94 UD 10.6m East Lancs OmniDekka N45/26D 2006

901	MB	YN55PZC	908	MB	YN55PZL	915	MB	YN55PZW	922	C	YN06JYG
902	MB	YN55PZD	909	MB	YN55PZM	916	MB	YN55PZX	923	C	YN06JYH
903	MB	YN55PZE	910	MB	YN55PZO	917	C	YN06JYB	924	C	YN06JYJ
904	MB	YN55PZF	911	MB	YN55PZP	918	C	YN06JYC	925	C	YN06JYK
905	MB	YN55PZG	912	MB	YN55PZR	919	C	YN06JYD	926	C	YN06JYL
906	MB	YN55PZH	913	MB	YN55PZU	920	C	YN06JYE	927	C	YN06JYO
907	MB	YN55PZJ	914	MB	YN55PZV	921	C	YN06JYF			

928-946
Scania N94 UD 10.6m East Lancs OmniDekka N45/26D 2006

928	C	YN56FDA	933	MB	YN56FDG	938	MB	YN56FDO	943	MB	YN56FDY
929	C	YN56FDC	934	MB	YN56FDJ	939	MB	YN56FDP	944	MB	YN56FDZ
930	MB	YN56FDD	935	MB	YN56FDK	940	MB	YN56FDU	945	MB	YN56FEF
931	MB	YN56FDE	936	MB	YN56FDL	941	MB	YN56FDV	946	MB	YN56FEG
932	MB	YN56FDF	937	MB	YN56FDM	942	MB	YN56FDX			

947-952
Scania N230 UD 10.8m East Lancs OmniDekka N45/23D 2007

947	C	YN07EXF	949	C	YN07EXH	951	C	YN07EXM	952	C	YN07EXO
948	C	YN07EXG	950	C	YN07EXK						

953-978
Scania OmniCity N230 UD 10.8m Scania N41/22D 2008-10 *953-4 are N41/31F

953	CY	YN08OBP	960	C	YT59DYC	967	C	YT59DYM	973	C	YT59DYW
954	CY	YN08OBR	961	C	YT59DYD	968	C	YT59DYO	974	MB	YR10BCE
955	C	YR58SNY	962	C	YT59DYF	969	C	YT59DYP	975	MB	YR10BCF
956	C	YR58SNZ	963	C	YT59DYG	970	C	YT59DYS	976	MB	YR10BCK
957	C	YP58UFV	964	C	YT59DYH	971	C	YT59DYU	977	MB	YR10BCO
958	C	YT59DYA	965	C	YT59DYN	972	C	YT59DYV	978	MB	YR10BCU
959	C	YT59DYB	966	C	YT59DYJ						

Ancillary vehicles:

7208	CYt	SN03WLP	TransBus Dart 10.7m	TransBus Pointer	TV	2003	
7209	CYt	SN03WLU	TransBus Dart 10.7m	TransBus Pointer	TV	2003	
7380	CYt	LK51LYJ	Dennis Dart SLF 10.2m	Marshall Capital	TV	2001	FirstBus, 2007
7381	CYt	LK51JYL	Dennis Dart SLF 10.2m	Marshall Capital	TV	2001	FirstBus, 2007
7382	CYt	LK51JYN	Dennis Dart SLF 10.2m	Marshall Capital	TV	2001	FirstBus, 2007
7764	CYt	M516VJO	Dennis Dart 9.8m	Marshall C37	TV	1995	Oxford Citybus, 2004
7767	CYt	M507VJO	Dennis Dart 9.8m	Marshall C37	TV	1995	Oxford Citybus, 2004

Shirley Road in Shirley forms the backdrop to this view of Scania OmniDekka 956, YR58SNZ, one of the dual-doored examples in the fleet. After success with the single-deck, Scania announced the introduction in 2005 of the OmniCity double decker in order to complement its OmniDekka citybus sold mostly in the UK. The initial double-deck OmniCity used the N94UD chassis, but now uses the N230UD, seen here. *Richard Godfrey*

Depots and allocations:

Crawley (Wheatstone Close, RH10 9UA) - CY

Dart	201	202	203	204	205	206	207	217
	218	241	244	247	287	288	289	320
	321	344	359	361	362	363	364	365
	366	367	368	371	372	373	374	376
	377	378	379˙	390	393	394	395	396
	398							
Enviro 200	725	726	727	728	729	730	734	735
	736	737	738	739				
Scania sd	513	531	532	533	534	535	546	547
	548	549	550	551	552	553	554	555
	556	557	558	559	560	568	569	570
	571	572	573	574	575	576	577	578
	579	580	581	582	616	617	618	619
	620	621	622	623	624	625	626	627
	628	629	630	631	632	633		
Scania dd	469	470	471	472	473	474	475	476
	477	478	482	483	484	485	486	487
	488	489	490	491	492	493	494	495
	496	497	953	954				
Ancillary	7208	7209	7380	7381	7382	7764	7767	

Croydon (Beddington Lane) - C

Dart	142	210	211	212	213	214	215	216
	219	334						
Enviro 200	189	190	191	192				
MAN 12.240	706	707	708	709	710	711	712	713
	714	715	716	717	718	719	720	721
	722	723						
Scania sd	561	562	563	564	565	566	567	
Scania dd	431	432	433	434	435	436	437	438
	439	440	441	442	443	444	445	446
	447	451	455	456	480	481	870	871
	872	873	874	875	876	877	878	879
	880	881	882	883	884	885	886	887
	888	889	890	891	892	893	894	895
	896	897	898	899	917	918	919	920
	921	922	923	924	925	926	927	928
	929	947	948	949	950	951	952	955
	956	957	958	959	960	961	962	963
	964	965	966	967	968	969	970	971
	972	973						

Orpington (Farnborough Hill, Green Street Green) - MB

Solo	101	102						
Dart	142	228	229	230	231	232	233	234
	235	236	251					
	252	253	254	255	256	257	258	259
	260	261	262	263	264	265	266	267
	268	271	272	273	274	275	276	277
	278	279	280	281	282	283	284	285
	286							
Enviro 200	148	149	150	151	152	153	154	155
	156	157	158	159	160	161	162	163
	164	165	166	167	168	169	170	171
	172	173	174	175	176	177	178	179
	180	181	182	183	184	185	186	187
	188	731	732	733	740	741	742	743
	744	745	746	747	748	749	750	751
	752	753	754	755	756	757	758	759
	760	761	762					
MAN 12.240	701	702	703	704	705			
Scania OmniCity	514	515	516	517	518	519	520	521
	522	523	524	525	526	527	528	529
	530							
Scania OmniTown	601	602	603	604	605	606	607	608
	609	610	611	612	613	614	615	616
	617	618	619	620	621	622	623	
Scania OmniDekka	456	457	458	459	460	461	462	465
	466	467	468	479	901	902	903	904
	905	906	907	908	909	910	911	912
	913	914	915	916	930	931	932	933
	934	935	936	937	938	939	940	941
	942	943	944	945	946	974	975	976
	977	978						

unallocated/stored/refurbishing - u/w

remainder

METROLINE

Metroline Travel Ltd, Comfort Delgro House, 329 Edgware Road, London NW2 6JP

| **DLD178** | KC | Y238NLK | Dennis Dart SLF 10.1m | | | Plaxton Pointer 2 | | N27D* | 2001 | | |

DLD198-207			Dennis Dart SLF 10.1m			Plaxton Pointer 2		N30D*	2002	*seating varies	
198	w	LN51KXD	201	w	LN51KXG	204	w	LN51KXK	206	AHt	LN51KXM
199	AHt	LN51KXE	202	AHt	LN51KXH	205	w	LN51KXL	207	w	LN51KXO
200	AHt	LN51KXF									

DSD209-215			TransBus Dart 9.3m			TransBus Pointer		N24D	2002		
209	PB	LR02BDX	212	PB	LR02BEJ	214	PB	LR02BEU	215	PB	LR02BEY

DP1009-1016			Dennis Dart SLF 10.1m			Plaxton Pointer 2		N27D	2001-02		
1009	u	RL51DOA	1011	PA	RL51DOJ	1013	PA	RL51DNY	1016	PA	RL51DNU
1010	PA	RL51DNX	1012	PA	RL51DOH	1015	PA	RL51DOU			

VPL143-157			Volvo B7TL 10.6m			Plaxton President 4.4m		N43/23D	2000-01		
143	w	X643LLX	144	w	X644LLX	149	w	X649LLX	157	EW	X657LLX

VPL163-236			Volvo B7TL 10.6m			Plaxton President 4.4m		N43/24D	2001		
163	u	Y163NLK	187	u	Y187NLK	210	EW	Y143NLK	222	HD	LK51XGS
165	u	Y165NLK	188	u	Y188NLK	211	u	LK51XGE	224	HT	LK51XGU
168	u	Y168NLK	191	AC	Y191NLK	213	EW	LK51XGG	226	HT	LK51XGW
169	u	Y169NLK	196	u	Y146NLK	214	u	LK51XGH	229	HT	LK51XGZ
175	u	Y195NLK	199	u	Y199NLK	215	u	LK51XGJ	231	HT	LK51XHB
177	u	Y177NLK	200	EW	Y149NLK	216	u	LK51XGL	232	HT	Y232NLK
181	u	Y181NLK	201	EW	Y201NLK	217	w	LK51XGM	233	HT	Y233NLK
184	w	Y184NLK	203	EW	Y203NLK	218	EW	LK51XGN	234	HT	Y234NLK
185	u	Y185NLK	205	EW	LK51XGD	219	u	LK51XGO	235	HT	Y235NLK
186	AC	Y186NLK	207	HD	Y207NLK	221	EW	LK51XGR	236	u	Y236NLK

Metroline operates almost 1700 buses from fourteen garages across London. Since March 2000, Metroline has been a wholly owned subsidiary of Singapore based ComfortDelGro, one of the world's largest passenger land transport companies. Seen operating route 390 at Euston is VPL585, LK04NMJ. This route is due to receive twenty examples of the New Bus for London by the end of 2013. *Dave Heath*

Metroline operates a large number of the Plaxton President double-deck on both Trident and Volvo chassis and in two lengths of each. Craven Park is the location for this view of VP537, LK04CUW, one of the standard length Volvo B7TLs, seen here on route 260 to Golders Green. *Richard Godfrey*

TPL241-292

Dennis Trident 10.6m   Plaxton President 4.4m   N43/23D   2002

241	u	LN51KXU	264	AHt	LN51KYY	273	PB	LR02BAV	282	u	LR02BBX
244	u	LN51KXY	265	HT	LN51KYZ	274	PB	LR02BAU	284	AHt	LR02BCE
247	u	LN51KYB	266	AHt	LN51KZA	277	w	LR02BBK	287	AHt	LR02BCO
249	u	LN51KYE	267	HT	LN51KZB	278	u	LR02BBN	289	w	LR02BCV
253	u	LN51KYJ	268	HT	LN51KZC	279	w	LR02BBO	291	u	LR02BCY
261	u	LN51KYV	269	u	LN51KZD	280	u	LR02BBU	292	w	LR02BC
263	HT	LN51KYX	270	HT	LR02BAA						

VP317-347

Volvo B7TL 10m   Plaxton President 4.4m   N39/20D   2002

317	HD	LR52BLK	325	HD	LR52BMY	333	HD	LR52BNK	341	HD	LR52BNZ
318	HD	LR52BLN	326	HD	LR52BMZ	334	HD	LR52BNL	342	HD	LR52BOF
319	HD	LR52BLV	327	HD	LR52BNA	335	HD	LR52BNN	343	HD	LR52BOH
320	HD	LR52BLX	328	HD	LR52BNB	336	HD	LR52BNO	344	HD	LR52BOJ
321	HD	LR52BLZ	329	HD	LR52BND	337	HD	LR52BNU	345	HD	LR52BOU
322	HD	LR52BMO	330	HD	LR52BNE	338	HD	LR52BNV	346	HD	LR52BOV
323	HD	LR52BMU	331	HD	LR52BNF	339	HD	LR52BNX	347	HD	LR52BPE
324	HD	LR52BMV	332	HD	LR52BNJ	340	HD	LR52BNY			

TP403-428

TransBus Trident 9.9m   TransBus President 4.4m   N39/20D*   2003   *seating varies

403	PB	LK03CEJ	410	HT	LK03CDD	417	HT	LK03CDN	423	HT	LK03CDZ
404	HT	LK03CEN	411	AH	LK03CDE	418	HT	LK03CDP	424	AH	LK03CGE
405	PB	LK03CEU	412	AH	LK03CDF	419	HT	LK03CDU	425	AH	LK03CGF
406	AH	LK03CEV	413	AH	LK03CDG	420	HT	LK03CDV	426	HT	LK03CGG
407	PB	LK03CEX	414	HT	LK03CDJ	421	HT	LK03CDX	427	HT	LK03CGU
408	HT	LK03CEY	415	AH	LK03CDL	422	HT	LK03CDY	428	HT	LK03CGV
409	HT	LK03CDA	416	AH	LK03CDM						

TP429-465   TransBus Trident 9.9m   TransBus President 4.4m   N39/20D   2003

429	AH	LK03GFU	439	PB	LK03GGV	448	PB	LK03GHH	457	PB	LK03GJG
430	W	LK03GFV	440	PB	LK03GGX	449	PB	LK03GHJ	458	PB	LK03GJU
431	PB	LK03GFX	441	PB	LK03GGY	450	PB	LK03GHN	459	PB	LK03GJV
432	HT	LK03GFY	442	PB	LK03GGZ	451	HT	LK03GHU	460	PB	LK03GJX
433	UX	LK03GFZ	443	PB	LK03GHA	452	PB	LK03GHV	461	PB	LK03GJY
434	PB	LK03GGA	444	PB	LK03GHB	453	PB	LK03GHX	462	PB	LK03GJZ
435	PB	LK03GGF	445	PB	LK03GHD	454	PB	LK03GHY	463	PB	LK03GKA
436	PB	LK03GGJ	446	PB	LK03GHF	455	PB	LK03GHZ	464	PB	LK03GKC
437	PB	LK03GGP	447	PB	LK03GHG	456	PB	LK03GJF	465	PB	LK03GKD
438	PB	LK03GGU									

VP466-511   Volvo B7TL 10m   TransBus President 4.4m   N39/20D   2003

466	HD	LK03GKE	478	AC	LK03GLF	490	AC	LK03GMZ	501	AC	LK53LXU
467	HD	LK03GKF	479	AC	LK03GLJ	491	AC	LK03GNF	502	AC	LK53LXV
468	HD	LK03GKG	480	AC	LK03GLV	492	AC	LK03GNJ	503	AC	LK53LXW
469	HD	LK03GKJ	481	AC	LK03GLY	493	AC	LK03GNN	504	AC	LK53LXX
470	HD	LK03GKL	482	AC	LK03GLZ	494	AC	LK03GNP	505	AC	LK53LXY
471	HD	LK03GKN	483	HD	LK03GME	495	AC	LK53LXM	506	AC	LK53LXZ
472	HD	LK03GKP	484	HD	LK03GMF	496	AC	LK53LXN	507	AC	LK53LYA
473	AC	LK03GKU	485	HD	LK03GMG	497	AC	LK53LXO	508	AC	LK53LYC
474	AC	LK03GKV	486	HD	LK03GMU	498	AC	LK53LXP	509	AC	LK53LYD
475	AC	LK03GKX	487	HD	LK03GMV	499	AC	LK53LXR	510	AC	LK53LYF
476	AC	LK03GKY	488	HD	LK03GMX	500	AC	LK53LXT	511	AC	LK53LYG
477	AC	LK03GKZ	489	AC	LK03GMY						

VP512-580   Volvo B7TL 10m   TransBus President 4.4m   N39/20D   2004

512	AC	LK04CPY	530	AC	LK04CTZ	547	AC	LK04CVH	564	AC	LK04EKY
513	AC	LK04CPZ	531	AC	LK04CUA	548	AC	LK04CVJ	565	AC	LK04EKZ
514	AC	LK04CRF	532	AC	LK04CUC	549	AC	LK04CVL	566	AC	LK04ELC
515	AC	LK04CRJ	533	AC	LK04CUG	550	AC	LK04CVM	567	AC	LK04ELH
516	AC	LK04CRU	534	AC	LK04CUH	551	AC	LK04CVN	568	AC	LK04ELJ
517	AC	LK04CRV	535	AC	LK04CUJ	552	AC	LK04CVP	569	AC	LK04ELU
518	AC	LK04CRZ	536	AC	LK04CUU	553	AC	LK04CVR	570	AC	LK04ELV
519	AC	LK04CSF	537	AC	LK04CUW	554	AC	LK04CVS	571	AC	LK04ELW
520	AC	LK04CSU	538	AC	LK04CUX	555	AC	LK04CVT	572	AC	LK04ELX
521	AC	LK04CSV	539	AC	LK04CUY	556	AC	LK04CVU	573	AC	LK04EMF
522	AC	LK04CSX	540	AC	LK04CVA	557	AC	LK04CVV	574	AC	LK04EMJ
523	AC	LK04CSY	541	AC	LK04CVB	558	AC	LK04CVW	575	AC	LK04EMV
524	AC	LK04CSZ	542	AC	LK04CVC	559	AC	LK04CVX	576	AC	LK04EMX
525	AC	LK04CTE	543	AC	LK04CVD	560	AC	LK04EKU	577	AC	LK04ENE
526	AC	LK04CTF	544	AC	LK04CVE	561	AC	LK04EKV	578	AC	LK04ENF
527	AC	LK04CTU	545	AC	LK04CVF	562	AC	LK04EKW	579	AC	LK04ENH
528	AC	LK04CTV	546	AC	LK04CVG	563	AC	LK04EKX	580	AC	LK04ENJ
529	AC	LK04CTX									

VPL581-603   Volvo B7TL 10.6m   TransBus President 4.4m   N43/23D   2004

581	HT	LK04NLZ	587	HT	LK04NMU	593	HT	LK04NNB	599	HT	LK04NNH
582	HT	LK04NMA	588	HT	LK04NMV	594	HT	LK04NNC	600	HT	LK04NNJ
583	HT	LK04NME	589	HT	LK04NMX	595	HT	LK04NND	601	HT	LK04NNL
584	HT	LK04NMF	590	HT	LK04NMY	596	HT	LK04NNE	602	HT	LK04NNM
585	HT	LK04NMJ	591	HT	LK04NMZ	597	HT	LK04NNF	603	HT	LK04NNP
586	HT	LK04NMM	592	HT	LK04NNA	598	HT	LK04NNG			

VP604-628   Volvo B7TL 10m   TransBus President 4.4m   N39/20D   2004

604	HD	LK04UWJ	611	HD	LK04UWT	617	HD	LK04UWZ	623	HD	LK04UXF
605	HD	LK04UWL	612	HD	LK04UWU	618	HD	LK04UXA	624	HD	LK04UXG
606	HD	LK04UWM	613	HD	LK04UWV	619	HD	LK04UXB	625	HD	LK04UXH
607	HD	LK04UWN	614	HD	LK04UWW	620	HD	LK04UXC	626	HD	LK54FWE
608	HD	LK04UWP	615	HD	LK04UWX	621	HD	LK04UXD	627	HD	LK54FWF
609	HD	LK04UWR	616	HD	LK04UWY	622	HD	LK04UXE	628	HD	LK54FWG
610	HD	LK04UWS									

VPL629-637   Volvo B7TL 10.6m   ADL President 4.4m   N43/23D   2005

629	HT	LK54FWH	632	HT	LK54FWM	634	HT	LK54FWO	636	HT	LK54FWR
630	HT	LK54FWJ	633	HT	LK54FWN	635	HT	LK54FWP	637	HT	LK54FWT
631	HT	LK54FWL									

TA638-659 — ADL Trident 9.9m — ADL ALX400 4.4m — N41/19D — 2005

638	W	LK05GFO	644	W	LK05GGE	650	W	LK05GGV	655	W	LK05GHB
639	W	LK05GFV	645	W	LK05GGF	651	W	LK05GGX	656	W	LK05GHD
640	W	LK05GFX	646	W	LK05GGJ	652	W	LK05GGY	657	W	LK05GHF
641	W	LK05GFY	647	W	LK05GGO	653	W	LK05GGZ	658	W	LK05GHG
642	W	LK05GFZ	648	W	LK05GGP	654	W	LK05GHA	659	W	LK05GHH
643	W	LK05GGA	649	W	LK05GGU						

TE665-692 — ADL Trident 2 10.1m — ADL Enviro 400 4.4m — N41/28D — 2005-06

665	HT	LK55KJV	672	HT	LK55KKD	679	HT	LK55KKM	686	HT	LK55KKV
666	HT	LK55KJX	673	HT	LK55KKE	680	HT	LK55KKO	687	HT	LK06FLA
667	HT	LK55KJY	674	HT	LK55KKF	681	HT	LK55KKP	688	HT	LK55KKY
668	HT	LK55KJZ	675	HT	LK55KKG	682	HT	LK55KKR	689	HT	LK55KKZ
669	HT	LK55KKA	676	HT	LK55KKH	683	HT	LK55KKS	690	HT	LK55KLA
670	HT	LK55KKB	677	HT	LK55KKJ	684	HT	LK55KKT	691	HT	LK06FLB
671	HT	LK55KKC	678	HT	LK55KKL	685	HT	LK55KKU	692	HT	LK06FLC

DLD693-711 — ADL Dart 10.1m — ADL Pointer — N28D — 2005-06

693	KC	LK55KLE	698	KC	LK55KLO	703	KC	LK55KLX	708	KC	LK55KMG
694	KC	LK55KLF	699	KC	LK55KLP	704	KC	LK55KLZ	709	KC	LK55KMJ
695	KC	LK55KLJ	700	KC	LK55KLS	705	KC	LK55KMA	710	KC	LK55KMM
696	KC	LK55KLL	701	KC	LK55KLU	706	KC	LK55KME	711	KC	LK55KMO
697	KC	LK55KLM	702	KC	LK55KLV	707	KC	LK55KMF			

TE712-723 — ADL Trident 2 10.1m — ADL Enviro 400 4.4m — N41/26D — 2006

712	EW	LK56FHE	715	EW	LK56FHH	718	EW	LK56FHN	721	EW	LK56FHR
713	EW	LK56FHF	716	EW	LK56FHJ	719	EW	LK56FHO	722	EW	LK56FHS
714	EW	LK56FHG	717	EW	LK56FHM	720	EW	LK56FHP	723	EW	LK56FHT

TE724-738 — ADL Trident 2 10.1m — ADL Enviro 400 4.4m — N41/26D — 2007

724	EW	LK07AYZ	728	EW	LK07AZD	732	EW	LK07AZL	736	EW	LK07AZR
725	EW	LK07AZA	729	EW	LK07AZF	733	EW	LK07AZN	737	EW	LK07AZT
726	EW	LK07AZB	730	EW	LK07AZG	734	EW	LK07AZO	738	EW	LK07AZU
727	EW	LK07AZC	731	EW	LK07AZJ	735	EW	LK07AZP			

SEL739-764 — Scania OmniDekka N230 UD — East Lancs Olympus — N45/23D — 2007

739	PA	LK07AZV	746	PA	LK07BBE	753	PA	LK07BBX	759	PA	LK07BCV
740	PA	LK07AZW	747	PA	LK07BBF	754	PA	LK07BBZ	760	PA	LK07BCX
741	PA	LK07AZX	748	PA	LK07BBJ	755	PA	LK07BCE	761	PA	LK07BCY
742	PA	LK07AZZ	749	PA	LK07BBN	756	PA	LK07BCF	762	PA	LK07BCZ
743	PA	LK07BAA	750	PA	LK07BBO	757	PA	LK07BCO	763	PA	LK07BDE
744	PA	LK07BAO	751	PA	LK07BBU	758	PA	LK07BCU	764	PA	LK57KAU
745	PA	LK07BAU	752	PA	LK07BBV						

MM771-790 — MAN 12.240 10.4m — MCV Evolution — N26D — 2007

771	AHt	LK07ELH	776	AHt	LK07AYG	781	PA	LK07AYN	786	PA	LK57EHW
772	AHt	LK07AYC	777	AHt	LK07AYH	782	PA	LK57EHS	787	PA	LK57EJA
773	AHt	LK07AYD	778	AHt	LK07AYJ	783	PA	LK57EHT	788	PA	LK57EHX
774	AHt	LK07AYE	779	PA	LK07AYL	784	PA	LK57EHU	789	PA	LK57EHY
775	AHt	LK07AYF	780	PA	LK07AYM	785	PA	LK57EHV	790	PA	LK57EHZ

DES791-802 — ADL Dart 4 8.9m — ADL Enviro 200 — N26F — 2007

791	PB	LK07BDO	794	PB	LK07BDX	797	PB	LK07BEJ	800	PB	LK07BEY
792	PB	LK07BDU	795	PB	LK07BDY	798	PB	LK07BEO	801	PB	LK07ELJ
793	PB	LK07BDV	796	PB	LK07BDZ	799	PB	LK07BEU	802	PB	LK07ELO

SEL803-809 — Scania N230 UD 10.8m — East Lancs Olympus — N45/23D — 2007-08

803	PA	LK57KAX	805	PA	LK57KBF	807	PA	LK57KBN	809	PA	LK08DVY
804	PA	LK57KBE	806	PA	LK57KBJ	808	PA	LK57KBO			

MM810-827 — MAN 12.240 10.4m — MCV Evolution — N26D — 2007

810	PA	LK57AYD	815	PA	LK57AYJ	820	PA	LK57AYP	824	PA	LK57AYV
811	PA	LK57AYE	816	PA	LK57AYL	821	PA	LK57AYS	825	PA	LK57AYW
812	PA	LK57AYF	817	PA	LK57AYM	822	PA	LK57AYT	826	PA	LK57AYX
813	PA	LK57AYG	818	PA	LK57AYN	823	PA	LK57AYU	827	PA	LK57AYY
814	PA	LK57AYH	819	PA	LK57AYO						

Thirty-eight MAN12.240s with MCV Evolution bodywork joined the fleet in 2007 and all are allocated to Perivale depot. Representing the type is MM815, LK57AYJ, seen passing through Hatton Cross en route for Feltham. The additional blue skirts on the vehicles are being phased out and white London Transport roundels applied. *Richard Godfrey*

TE828-847

			ADL Trident 2 10.1m			ADL Enviro 400 4.4m			N41/26D	2007		
828	EW	LK57AXF	833	EW	LK57AXN	838	EW	LK57AXT	843	EW	LK57AXY	
829	EW	LK57AXG	834	EW	LK57AXO	839	EW	LK57AXU	844	EW	LK57AXZ	
830	EW	LK57AXH	835	EW	LK57AXP	840	EW	LK57AXV	845	EW	LK57AYA	
831	EW	LK57AXJ	836	EW	LK57AXR	841	EW	LK57AXW	846	EW	LK57AYB	
832	EW	LK57AXM	837	EW	LK57AXS	842	EW	LK57AXX	847	EW	LK57AYC	

DEL848-858

			ADL Dart 4 10.8m			ADL Enviro 200			N37F	2008		
848	PB	LK08DVZ	851	PB	LK08DWD	854	PB	LK08DWG	857	PB	LK08DWM	
849	PB	LK08DWA	852	PB	LK08DWE	855	PB	LK08DWJ	858	PB	LK08DWN	
850	PB	LK08DWC	853	PB	LK08DWF	856	PB	LK08DWL				

DEL859-877

			ADL Dart 4 10.2m			ADL Enviro 200			N29D	2008		
859	W	LK08DWO	864	W	LK08DWX	869	W	LK08DXC	874	W	LK08DXH	
860	W	LK08DWP	865	W	LK08DWY	870	W	LK08DXD	875	W	LK58CMZ	
861	W	LK08DWU	866	W	LK08DWZ	871	W	LK08DXE	876	W	LK58CNA	
862	W	LK08DWV	867	W	LK08DXA	872	W	LK08DXF	877	W	LK58CNC	
863	W	LK08DWW	868	W	LK08DXB	873	W	LK08DXG				

TE878-914

			ADL Trident 2 10.1m			ADL Enviro 400 4.4m			N41/26D	2008		
878	EW	LK08DXO	888	EW	LK08DZA	897	HT	LK08NVN	906	HT	LK58CNX	
879	EW	LK08DXP	889	EW	LK08NVD	898	HT	LK08NVO	907	HT	LK58CNY	
880	EW	LK08DXR	890	EW	LK08NVE	899	HT	LK08NVP	908	HT	LK58CNZ	
881	EW	LK08DXS	891	EW	LK08NVF	900	HT	LK58CNE	909	HT	LK58COA	
882	EW	LK08DXU	892	W	LK08NVG	901	HT	LK58CNF	910	HT	LK58COH	
883	EW	LK08DXV	893	W	LK08NVH	902	HT	LK58CNN	911	HT	LK58COJ	
884	EW	LK08DXW	894	W	LK08NVJ	903	HT	LK58CNO	912	HT	LK58COU	
885	EW	LK08DXX	895	W	LK08NVL	904	HT	LK58CNU	913	HT	LK58CPE	
886	EW	LK08DXY	896	HT	LK08NVM	905	HT	LK58CNV	914	HT	LK58CPF	
887	EW	LK08DXZ										

TEH915-919

			ADL Trident E400H 10.1m			ADL Enviro 400 4.4m			N37/26D	2008		
915	W	SN08AAO	917	W	LK58CPO	918	W	LK58CPU	919	W	LK58CPV	
916	W	LK58CPN										

Hybrid technology continues to make advances. At the Euro Bus Expo show in 2008 a shorter hybrid version of the Tempo was exhibited and five such vehicles now operate for Metroline on route E8. Seen on that service in Boston Manor Road, Brentford, is OTH975, LK09EKH. *Mark Lyons*

TE920-951 — ADL Trident 2 10.1m — ADL Enviro 400 4.4m — N41/26D — 2009

920	HT	LK58KFW	928	HT	LK58KGJ	936	PB	LK09EKR	944	PB	LK09EHU
921	HT	LK58KFX	929	HT	LK58KGN	937	PB	LK09EKT	945	PB	LK58KHL
922	HT	LK58KFY	930	HT	LK58KGO	938	PB	LK58KHC	946	PB	LK58KHM
923	HT	LK58KFZ	931	HT	LK09EKO	939	PB	LK58KHD	947	PB	LK58KHO
924	HT	LK58KGA	932	HT	LK58KGU	940	PB	LK58KHE	948	PB	LK58KHP
925	HT	LK58KGE	933	HT	LK58KGV	941	PB	LK58KHF	949	PB	LK58KHR
926	HT	LK58KGF	934	HT	LK58KGW	942	PB	LK58KHG	950	PB	LK58KHT
927	HT	LK58KGG	935	PB	LK09EKP	943	PB	LK58KHH	951	PB	LK58KHU

DE952-960 — ADL Dart 4 10.2m — ADL Enviro 200 — N29D — 2008

952	W	LK58CSX	955	W	LK58CTE	957	W	LK58CTO	959	W	LK58CTV
953	W	LK58CSY	956	W	LK58CTF	958	W	LK58CTU	960	W	LK58CTX
954	W	LK58CSZ									

DM961-970 — ADL Dart 4 10.4m — MCV Evolution — N29D — 2009

961	AH	LK58CRF	964	AH	LK58CRV	967	AH	LK58CSF	969	AH	LK58CSU
962	AH	LK09EKJ	965	AH	LK58CRX	968	AH	LK09EKM	970	AH	LK09EKN
963	AH	LK09EKL	966	AH	LK58CRZ						

OTH971-975 — Optare Tempo X1060 Hybrid — Optare — N28D — 2009

971	AH	LK58CTY	973	AH	LK58CUA	974	AH	LK09EKG	975	AH	LK09EKH
972	AH	LK58CTZ									

TE976-992 — ADL Trident 2 10.1m — ADL Enviro 400 — N41/26D — 2009

976	EW	LK09EKV	981	EW	LK09ELC	985	EW	LK09ELU	989	EW	LK09EMF
977	EW	LK09EKW	982	EW	LK09ELH	986	EW	LK09ELV	990	EW	LK09EMJ
978	EW	LK09EKX	983	EW	LK09ELJ	987	EW	LK09ELW	991	EW	LK09EMV
979	EW	LK09EKY	984	EW	LK09ELO	988	EW	LK09ELX	992	EW	LK09EMX
980	W	LK09EKZ									

July 2013 and on Argyle Road in West Ealing VW1208, LX61BMZ, is seen working 297. It is one of a batch of forty-two Wrightbus-bodied Volvo B9TLs all allocated to Perivale depot. *Richard Godfrey*

DE993-1014 — ADL Dart 4 10.2m — ADL Enviro 200 — N29D — 2009

993	AH	LK09ENC	999	KC	LK09ENM	1005	AH	LK09ENU	1010	AH	LK09EOA
994	AH	LK09ENE	1000	AH	LK09ENN	1006	AH	LK09ENV	1011	AH	LK09EOB
995	AH	LK09ENF	1001	AH	LK09ENO	1007	AH	LK09ENW	1012	AH	LK09EOC
996	AH	LK09ENH	1002	AH	LK09ENP	1008	AH	LK09ENX	1013	AH	LK09EOD
997	AH	LK09ENJ	1003	AH	LK09ENR	1009	AH	LK09ENY	1014	AH	LK09EOE
998	AH	LK09ENL	1004	AH	LK09ENT						

DE1015-1033 — ADL Dart 4 10.2m — ADL Enviro 200 — N29D — 2009

1015	W	LK59AUW	1020	W	LK59AVF	1025	W	LK59AVN	1030	W	LK59AVU
1016	W	LK59AUY	1021	W	LK59AVG	1026	W	LK59AVO	1031	W	LK59AVV
1017	W	LK59AVB	1022	W	LK59AVJ	1027	W	LK59AVP	1032	W	LK59AVW
1018	W	LK59AVC	1023	W	LK59AVL	1028	W	LK59AVR	1033	W	LK59AVX
1019	W	LK59AVD	1024	W	LK59AVM	1029	W	LK59AVT			

VW1034-1072 — Volvo B9TL 10.4m — Wrightbus Eclipse Gemini 2 — N39/23D — 2010

1034	AH	LK59JJU	1044	AH	LK10BXN	1054	AH	LK10BXZ	1064	AH	LK60AEL
1035	AH	LK10BXC	1045	AH	LK10BXO	1055	AH	LK10BYA	1065	AH	LK60AEM
1036	AH	LK10BXD	1046	AH	LK10BXP	1056	AH	LK60AEA	1066	AH	LK60AEN
1037	AH	LK10BXE	1047	AH	LK10BXR	1057	AH	LK60AEB	1067	AH	LK60AEO
1038	AH	LK10BXF	1048	AH	LK10BXS	1058	AH	LK60AEC	1068	AH	LK60AEP
1039	AH	LK10BXG	1049	AH	LK10BXU	1059	AH	LK60AED	1069	AH	LK60AET
1040	AH	LK10BXH	1050	AH	LK10BXV	1060	AH	LK60AEE	1070	AH	LK60AEU
1041	AH	LK10BXJ	1051	AH	LK10BXW	1061	AH	LK60AEF	1071	AH	LK60AEV
1042	AH	LK10BXL	1052	AH	LK10BXX	1062	AH	LK60AEG	1072	AH	LK60AEW
1043	AH	LK10BXM	1053	AH	LK10BXY	1063	AH	LK60AEJ			

TE1073-1104 — ADL Trident 2 10.1m — ADL Enviro 400 — N41/24D* — 2010 — *1073-5 are N41/26D

1073	W	LK10BZV	1081	W	LK60AFF	1089	W	LK60AGO	1097	W	LK60AHE
1074	W	LK10BZX	1082	W	LK60AFN	1090	W	LK60AGU	1098	W	LK60AHG
1075	W	LK10BZY	1083	W	LK60AFO	1091	W	LK60AGV	1099	W	LK60AHJ
1076	W	LK60AEX	1084	W	LK60AFU	1092	W	LK60AGY	1100	W	LK60AHL
1077	W	LK60AEY	1085	W	LK60AFV	1093	W	LK60AGZ	1101	W	LK60AHN
1078	W	LK60AEZ	1086	W	LK60AFX	1094	W	LK60AHA	1102	W	LK60AHO
1079	W	LK60AFA	1087	W	LK60AFY	1095	W	LK60AHC	1103	W	LK60AHP
1080	W	LK60AFE	1088	W	LK60AFZ	1096	W	LK60AHD	1104	W	LK60AHU

TE1105-1114 ADL Trident E400H 10.1m ADL Enviro 400 N37/24D 2010

1105	W	LK60AHV	1108	W	LK60AHZ	1111	W	LK60AJV	1113	W	LK60AJY
1106	W	LK60AHX	1109	W	LK60AJO	1112	W	LK60AJX	1114	W	LK60AKF
1107	W	LK60AHY	1110	W	LK60AJU						

DE1115-1151 ADL Dart 4 10.2m ADL Enviro 200 N29D 2010

1115	W	LK10BYB	1125	W	LK10BYR	1134	W	LK10BZA	1143	W	LK10BZL
1116	W	LK10BYC	1126	W	LK10BYS	1135	W	LK10BZB	1144	W	LK10BZM
1117	W	LK10BYD	1127	W	LK10BYT	1136	W	LK10BZC	1145	W	LK10BZN
1118	W	LK10BYG	1128	W	LK10BYU	1137	W	LK10BZD	1146	W	LK10BZO
1119	W	LK10BYJ	1129	W	LK10BYV	1138	W	LK10BZE	1147	W	LK10BZP
1120	W	LK10BYL	1130	W	LK10BYW	1139	W	LK10BZF	1148	W	LK10BZR
1121	W	LK10BYM	1131	W	LK10BYX	1140	W	LK10BZG	1149	W	LK10BZS
1122	W	LK10BYN	1132	W	LK10BYY	1141	W	LK10BZH	1150	PA	LK10BZT
1123	W	LK10BYO	1133	W	LK10BYZ	1142	W	LK10BZJ	1151	PA	LK10BZU
1124	W	LK10BYP									

DE1152-1174 ADL Dart 4 10.2m ADL Enviro 200 N29D 2011

1152	KC	LK11CWF	1158	KC	LK11CWO	1164	KC	LK11CWW	1170	KC	LK11CXC
1153	KC	LK11CWG	1159	KC	LK11CWP	1165	KC	LK11CWX	1171	AH	LK11CXD
1154	KC	LK11CWJ	1160	KC	LK11CWR	1166	KC	LK11CWY	1172	AH	LK11CXE
1155	KC	LK11CWL	1161	KC	LK11CWT	1167	KC	LK11CWZ	1173	AH	LK11CXF
1156	KC	LK11CWM	1162	KC	LK11CWU	1168	KC	LK11CXA	1174	AH	LK11CXG
1157	KC	LK11CWN	1163	KC	LK11CWV	1169	KC	LK11CXB			

VW1175-1216 Volvo B9TL 10.4m* Wrightbus Eclipse Gemini 2 N39/23D 2011 *1205-16 are 10.5m

1175	PA	LK11CXJ	1186	PA	LK11CXW	1197	PA	LK11CYP	1207	PA	LK61BMY
1176	PA	LK11CXL	1187	PA	LK11CXX	1198	PA	LK11CYS	1208	PA	LK61BMZ
1177	PA	LK11CXK	1188	PA	LK11CXY	1199	PA	LK11CYT	1209	PA	LK61BNA
1178	PA	LK11CXN	1189	PA	LK11CXZ	1200	PA	LK11CYU	1210	PA	LK61BNB
1179	PA	LK11CXO	1190	PA	LK11CYA	1201	PA	LK11CYV	1211	PA	LK61BNE
1180	PA	LK11CXP	1191	PA	LK11CYE	1202	PA	LK61BJE	1212	PA	LK61BNF
1181	PA	LK11CXR	1192	PA	LK11CYF	1203	PA	LK61BJF	1213	PA	LK61BNJ
1182	PA	LK11CXS	1193	PA	LK11CYH	1204	PA	LK61BJJ	1214	PA	LK61BNL
1183	PA	LK11CXT	1194	PA	LK11CYJ	1205	PA	LK61BMU	1215	PA	LK61BNN
1184	PA	LK11CXU	1195	PA	LK11CYL	1206	PA	LK61BMV	1216	PA	LK61BNO
1185	PA	LK11CXV	1196	PA	LK11CYO						

TEH1217-1242 ADL E40H 10.2m ADL Enviro 400 N41/24D 2012

1217	W	LK61BJO	1224	W	LK61BKD	1231	W	LK61BKO	1237	W	LK61BLJ
1218	W	LK61BJU	1225	W	LK61BKE	1232	W	LK61BKU	1238	W	LK61BLN
1219	W	LK61BJV	1226	W	LK61BKF	1233	W	LK61BKV	1239	W	LK61BLV
1220	W	LK61BJX	1227	W	LK61BKG	1234	W	LK61BKY	1240	W	LK61BLX
1221	W	LK61BJY	1228	W	LK61BKJ	1235	W	LK61BKZ	1241	W	LK61BLZ
1222	W	LK61BJZ	1229	W	LK61BKL	1236	W	LK61BLF	1242	W	LK61BMO
1223	W	LK61BKA	1230	W	LK61BKN						

VW1243-1306 Volvo B9TL 10.5m Wrightbus Eclipse Gemini 2 N37/24D 2012

1243	HT	LK12AAF	1259	HT	LK12AEG	1275	HT	LK12AHZ	1291	HT	LK12APZ
1244	HT	LK12AAJ	1260	HT	LK12AET	1276	HT	LK12AJX	1292	HT	LK12ARO
1245	HT	LK12AAN	1261	HT	LK12AEU	1277	HT	LK12AKN	1293	HT	LK12ARU
1246	HT	LK12AAU	1262	HT	LK12AFO	1278	HT	LK12AKO	1294	HT	LK12ARX
1247	HT	LK12ABF	1263	HT	LK12AEW	1279	HT	LK12ALO	1295	HT	LK12ARZ
1248	HT	LK12ABO	1264	HT	LK12AEZ	1280	HT	LK12AMO	1296	HT	LK12ASZ
1249	HT	LK12ABX	1265	HT	LK12AFA	1281	HT	LK12AMV	1297	HT	LK12ATU
1250	HT	LK12ACF	1266	HT	LK12AFE	1282	HT	LK12ANF	1298	HT	LK12ATV
1251	HT	LK12ACO	1267	HT	LK12AFU	1283	HT	LK12AOA	1299	HT	LK12AUE
1252	HT	LK12ACZ	1268	HT	LK12AFV	1284	HT	LK12AOL	1300	HT	LK12AUF
1253	HT	LK12ADU	1269	HT	LK12AFX	1285	HT	LK12AOO	1301	HT	LK12AUM
1254	HT	LK12ADV	1270	HT	LK12AHA	1286	HT	LK12AOT	1302	HT	LK12AUN
1255	HT	LK12ADX	1271	HT	LK12AHC	1287	HT	LK12AOX	1303	HT	LK12AUU
1256	HT	LK12AEA	1272	HT	LK12AHD	1288	HT	LK12AOY	1304	HT	LK12AUV
1257	HT	LK12AEB	1273	HT	LK12AHO	1289	HT	LK12APF	1305	HT	LK12AUW
1258	HT	LK12AEF	1274	HT	LK12AHU	1290	HT	LK12AOV	1306	HT	LK12AUY

TE1307-1317 ADL E40D 10.2m ADL Enviro 400 N41/24D 2012

1307	W	LK12AVD	1310	W	LK12AVT	1313	W	LK12AWC	1316	W	LK12AWO
1308	W	LK12AVJ	1311	W	LK12AVU	1314	W	LK12AWJ	1317	W	LK12AWP
1309	W	LK12AVN	1312	W	LK12AWA	1315	W	LK12AWN			

Based at Cricklewood are four batches of Enviro 400 hybrid buses, all using the BAe Systems technology. Representing the type is TEH1239, LK61BLV, which is seen on Park Lane while heading for Victoria on route 16. While the initial cost of the hybrid version is much higher, the Enviro 400H offers a large fuel saving as wellas greenhouse gas reductions of circa 30%. *Richard Godfrey*

DE1318-1336

ADL E20D 10.2m   ADL Enviro 200   N29D   2012

1318	KC	LK12AWU	1323	KC	LK12AXG	1328	KC	LK12AXV	1333 KC LK12AYL
1319	KC	LK12AWX	1324	KC	LK12AXH	1329	KC	LK12AXW	1334 KC LK12AYP
1320	KC	LK12AWY	1325	KC	LK12AXP	1330	KC	LK12AXZ	1335 KC LK12AYZ
1321	KC	LK12AWZ	1326	KC	LK12AXR	1331	KC	LK12AYF	1336 KC LK12AZA
1322	KC	LK12AXA	1327	KC	LK12AXS	1332	KC	LK12AYG	

DEM1337-1359

ADL E20D 9.6m   ADL Enviro 200   N25D   2012

1337	PB	LK62DAA	1343	PB	LK62DDU	1349	PB	LK62DFP	1355 PB LK62DHE
1338	PB	LK62DAO	1344	PB	LK62DDY	1350	PB	LK62DFY	1356 PB LK62DHG
1339	PB	LK62DBZ	1345	PB	LK62DDZ	1351	PB	LK62DGF	1357 PB LK62DHP
1340	PB	LK62DCE	1346	PB	LK62DEU	1352	PB	LK62DGO	1358 PB LK62DHU
1341	PB	LK62DCF	1347	PB	LK62DFF	1353	PB	LK62DHC	1359 PB LK62DHV
1342	PB	LK62DCY	1348	PB	LK62DFJ	1354	PB	LK62DHD	

VWH1360-1364

Volvo B5LH 10.5m   Wrightbus Gemini 2   N39/21D   2012

1360	HT	LK62DHX	1362	HT	LK62DJY	1363	HT	LK62DJZ	1364 HT LK62DKE
1361	HT	LK62DHZ							

VWH1365-1407

Volvo B9TL 10.5m   Wrightbus Eclipse Gemini 2   N39/23D   2012-13

1365	ON	LK62DKN	1376	ON	LK62DNX	1387	HT	LK62DTU	1398 AC LK62DVH
1366	HT	LK62DKV	1377	ON	LK62DOH	1388	HT	LK62DTV	1399 AC LK62DVJ
1367	ON	LK62DLJ	1378	HT	LK62DPE	1389	SW	LK62DTZ	1400 AC LK62DVL
1368	HT	LK62DLO	1379	HT	LK62DPU	1390	HT	LK62DUA	1401 AC LK62DVO
1369	HT	LK62DLV	1380	HT	LK62DPY	1391	HT	LK62DUH	1402 AC LK62DVP
1370	HT	LK62DLX	1381	HT	LK62DRV	1392	HT	LK62DUJ	1403 AC LK62DVR
1371	ON	LK62DMV	1382	HT	LK62DRZ	1393	AC	LK62DUU	1404 AC LK62DVU
1372	ON	LK62DND	1383	HT	LK62DSE	1394	AC	LK62DVB	1405 AC LK13BHW
1373	HT	LK62DNE	1384	HT	LK62DSU	1395	AC	LK62DVC	1406 AC LK13BHX
1374	ON	LK62DNU	1385	HT	LK62DSV	1396	AC	LK62DVF	1407 AC LK13BHY
1375	ON	LK62DNO	1386	HT	LK62DTN	1397	AC	LK62DVG	

New arrivals with Metroline for 2013 are fifteen Wrightbus-bodied Volvo B9TLs allocated to Willesden alongside twelve of the hybrid model from the same manufacturers. Seen running alongside Kensington Gore, the name of two parallel thoroughfares on the south side of Hyde Park, is VW1405, LK13BHW.
Mark Lyons

VWH1408-1419

Volvo B5LH 10.5m — Wrightbus Eclipse Gemini 2 — N39/21D — 2013

1408	AC	LK62DWA	1411	AC	LK62DWF	1414	AC	LK62DWO	1417	AC	LK62DWY
1409	AC	LK62DWD	1412	AC	LK62DWJ	1415	AC	LK62DWU	1418	AC	LK62DXF
1410	AC	LK62DWE	1413	AC	LK13BHZ	1416	AC	LK62DWV	1419	AC	LK62DXG

TE1420-1448

ADL E40D 10.2m — ADL Enviro 400 — N41/24D — 2013

1420	PB	LK62DXM	1428	PB	LK62DYD	1435	PB	LK62DYT	1442	PB	LK13BFO
1421	PB	LK62DXP	1429	PB	LK62DYF	1436	PB	LK13BFA	1443	PB	LK13BFP
1422	PB	LK62DXS	1430	PB	LK62DYG	1437	PB	LK13BFF	1444	PB	LK13BFU
1423	PB	LK62DXT	1431	PB	LK62DYH	1438	PB	LK13BFJ	1445	PB	LK13BFV
1424	PB	LK62DXX	1432	PB	LK62DYN	1439	PB	LK13BFL	1446	PB	LK13BFX
1425	PB	LK62DXY	1433	PB	LK62DYO	1440	PB	LK13BFM	1447	PB	LK13BFY
1426	PB	LK62DYA	1434	PB	LK62DYS	1441	PB	LK13BFN	1448	W	LK13BFZ
1427	PB	LK62DYC									

TEH1449-1467

ADL E40H 10.2m — ADL Enviro 400 — N37/24D — 2013

1449	W	LK13BGE	1454	W	LK13BGX	1459	W	LK13BHE	1464	W	LK13BHO
1450	W	LK13BGF	1455	W	LK13BGY	1460	W	LK13BHF	1465	W	LK13BHP
1451	W	LK13BGO	1456	W	LK13BGZ	1461	W	LK13BHJ	1466	W	LK13BHU
1452	W	LK13BGU	1457	W	LK13BHA	1462	W	LK13BHL	1467	W	LK13BHV
1453	W	LK13BGV	1458	W	LK13BHD	1463	W	LK13BHN			

VW1468	HT	LK13BJE	Volvo B5L 10.5m	Wrightbus Eclipse Gemini 2	N39/23D	2013

TP1507	G	LT52XAD	Dennis Trident 9.9m	Plaxton President	N39/20D	2002	First, 2013

TP1508-1539

TransBus Trident 9.9m — TransBus President — N39/20D — 2003 — First, 2013

1508	G	LK03NKC	1516	G	LK03NKT	1524	G	LK03NLR	1532	UX	LK03UFP
1509	G	LK03NKD	1517	G	LK03NKU	1525	UX	LK03UFD	1533	UX	LK03UFR
1510	G	LK03NKE	1518	G	LK03NKW	1526	UX	LK03UFE	1534	UX	LK03UFS
1511	G	LK03NKF	1519	G	LK03NKX	1527	UX	LK03UFG	1535	UX	LK03UFT
1512	G	LK03NKG	1520	G	LK03NKZ	1528	UX	LK03UFJ	1536	UX	LK03UFU
1513	G	LK03NKP	1521	G	LK03NLA	1529	UX	LK03UFL	1537	UX	LK03UFV
1514	G	LK03NKR	1522	G	LK03NLC	1530	UX	LK03UFM	1538	UX	LK03UFW
1515	G	LK03NKS	1523	G	LK03NLP	1531	UX	LK03UFN	1539	UX	LK03UFX

As part of FirstGroup's strategy to reposition its UK Bus division, it announced in April 2013 that it was to sell eight of its London bus depots. Subsequently the five depots at Alperton, Greenford, Hayes, Uxbridge and Willesden Junction, along with 494 vehicles and approximately 1,700 employees, were transferred to Metroline. Metroline has allocated new fleet numbers to the acquired vehicles. DC1558, LK53FDU, shows its new number and fleet names as it works route U3 in July 2013. *Mark Lyons*

DC1540-1548

		TransBus Dart 10.1m		Caetano Nimbus			N29D	2003	First, 2013
1540	UX	LK03NLE	1543	UX	LK03NLJ	1545	UX	LK03NLM	1547	UX	LK03NFY
1541	UX	LK03NLF	1544	UX	LK03NLL	1546	UX	LK03NLT	1548	UX	LK03NFZ
1542	UX	LK03NLG									

DC1549-1559

		TransBus Dart 10.1m		Caetano Nimbus			N28D	2003	First, 2013
1549	UX	LK53FDC	1552	UX	LK53FDG	1555	UX	LK53FDN	1558	UX	LK53FDU
1550	UX	LK53FDE	1553	UX	LK53FDJ	1556	UX	LK53FDO	1559	UX	LK53FDV
1551	UX	LK53FDF	1554	UX	LK53FDM	1557	UX	LK53FDP			

VW1560-1570

		Volvo B7TL 10.4m		Wrightbus Eclipse Gemini			N41/21D	2005	First, 2013
1560	UX	LK55ACU	1563	UX	LK55AAJ	1566	UX	LK55AAV	1569	UX	LK55AAZ
1561	UX	LK55AAE	1564	UX	LK55AAN	1567	UX	LK55AAX	1570	UX	LK55ABF
1562	UX	LK55AAF	1565	UX	LK55AAU	1568	UX	LK55AAY			

TE1571-1582

		ADL Trident 2 9.9m		ADL Enviro 400			N41/26D	2008	First, 2013
1571	UX	LK08FNE	1574	UX	LK08FMP	1577	UX	LK08FMX	1580	UX	LK08FNA
1572	UX	LK08FMA	1575	UX	LK08FMU	1578	UX	LK08FMY	1581	UX	LK08FNC
1573	UX	LK08FMO	1576	UX	LK08FMV	1579	UX	LK08FMZ	1582	UX	LK08FND

DE1583-1597

		ADL Dart 4 10.2m		ADL Enviro 200			N29D	2009	First, 2013
1583	UX	LK08FNF	1587	UX	LK08FKU	1591	UX	LK08FLD	1595	UX	LK08FLV
1584	UX	LK08FNG	1588	UX	LK08FKV	1592	UX	LK08FLE	1596	UX	LK08FLW
1585	UX	LK08FNH	1589	UX	LK08FKW	1593	UX	LK08FLF	1597	UX	LK08FLZ
1586	UX	LK08FKT	1590	UX	LK08FLC	1594	UX	LK08FLG			

DE1598-1649

		ADL Dart 4 10.2m		ADL Enviro 200			N29D	2009	First, 2013
1598	ON	YX58DUA	1611	ON	YX58DWL	1624	WJ	YX58FPF	1637	WJ	YX58FOJ
1599	ON	YX58DUH	1612	ON	YX58DWM	1625	WJ	YX58FPG	1638	WJ	YX58FOK
1600	ON	YX58DUJ	1613	ON	YX58DWN	1626	WJ	YX58FPJ	1639	WJ	YX58FOM
1601	ON	YX58DUU	1614	ON	YX58DWO	1627	WJ	YX58FPK	1640	WJ	YX58FON
1602	ON	YX58DVY	1615	ON	YX58DWP	1628	WJ	YX58FPL	1641	WJ	YX58FOP
1603	ON	YX58DVZ	1616	ON	YX58DWU	1629	WJ	YX58FPN	1642	WJ	YX58FOT
1604	ON	YX58DWA	1617	ON	YX58DWV	1630	WJ	YX58FPO	1643	WJ	YX58FOU
1605	ON	YX58DWC	1618	ON	YX58DWY	1631	WJ	YX58FPT	1644	WJ	YX58FOV
1606	ON	YX58DWD	1619	ON	YX58DWZ	1632	WJ	YX58FPU	1645	WJ	YX58FRC
1607	ON	YX58DWE	1620	WJ	YX58FPA	1633	WJ	YX58FPV	1646	WJ	YX58FRD
1608	ON	YX58DWF	1621	WJ	YX58FPC	1634	WJ	YX58FPY	1647	ON	YX58HVA
1609	ON	YX58DWG	1622	WJ	YX58FPD	1635	WJ	YX58FOF	1648	WJ	YX58HVB
1610	ON	YX58DWJ	1623	WJ	YX58FPE	1636	WJ	YX58FOH	1649	WJ	YX58HVM

Twenty-eight Enviro 400s joined the Metroline fleet at Potters Bar depot during 2013 with TE1446, LK13BFX, representing the batch as it heads towards North Finchley on route 82 shortly after entering service. *Dave Heath*

DE1650-1694   ADL Dart 4 10.2m   ADL Enviro 200   N29D   2009   First, 2013

1650	WJ	YX09AEA	1662	WJ	YX09AEO	1673	ON	YX09AFJ	1684	G	YX09FLK
1651	WJ	YX09AEB	1663	WJ	YX09AEP	1674	ON	YX09AFK	1685	G	YX09FLL
1652	WJ	YX09AEC	1664	WJ	YX09AET	1675	G	YX09FLA	1686	G	YX09FNJ
1653	WJ	YX09AED	1665	ON	YX09AEU	1676	G	YX09FLB	1687	G	YX09FNK
1654	WJ	YX09AEE	1666	ON	YX09AEV	1677	G	YX09FLC	1688	G	YX09FKS
1655	WJ	YX09AEF	1667	ON	YX09AEW	1678	G	YX09FLD	1689	G	YX09FKT
1656	WJ	YX09AEG	1668	ON	YX09AEY	1679	G	YX09FLE	1690	G	YX09FKU
1657	WJ	YX09AEJ	1669	ON	YX09AEZ	1680	G	YX09FLF	1691	G	YX09FKV
1658	WJ	YX09AEK	1670	ON	YX09AFA	1681	G	YX09FLG	1692	G	YX09FKW
1659	WJ	YX09AEL	1671	ON	YX09AFE	1682	G	YX09FLH	1693	G	YX09FKY
1660	WJ	YX09AEM	1672	ON	YX09AFF	1683	G	YX09FLJ	1694	G	YX09FLM
1661	WJ	YX09AEN									

DES1695-1714   ADL Dart 4 8.9m   ADL Enviro 200   N26D   2009   First, 2013

1695	G	YX09FMA	1700	G	YX09FMG	1705	G	YX09FMO	1710	G	YX09FLV
1696	G	YX09FMC	1701	G	YX09FMJ	1706	G	YX09FMP	1711	G	YX09FLW
1697	G	YX09FMD	1702	G	YX09FMK	1707	G	YX09FLN	1712	G	YX09FLZ
1698	G	YX09FME	1703	G	YX09FML	1708	G	YX09FLP	1713	G	YX09FMU
1699	G	YX09FMF	1704	G	YX09FMM	1709	G	YX09FLR	1714	G	YX09FMV

TE1715-1751   ADL Trident 2 10.1m   ADL Enviro 400   N41/26D   2008   First, 2013

1715	G	SN09CDU	1725	G	SN09CEU	1734	G	SN09CFJ	1743	G	SN09CFY
1716	G	SN09CDV	1726	G	SN09CEV	1735	G	SN09CFK	1744	G	SN09CFZ
1717	G	SN09CDX	1727	G	SN09CEX	1736	G	SN09CFL	1745	G	SN09CGE
1718	G	SN09CDY	1728	G	SN09CEY	1737	G	SN09CFM	1746	G	SN09CGF
1719	G	SN09CDZ	1729	G	SN09CFA	1738	G	SN09CFO	1747	G	SN09CGG
1720	G	SN09CEA	1730	G	SN09CFD	1739	G	SN09CFP	1748	G	SN09CGK
1721	G	SN09CEF	1731	G	SN09CFE	1740	G	SN09CFU	1749	G	SN09CGO
1722	G	SN09CEJ	1732	G	SN09CFF	1741	G	SN09CFV	1750	G	SN09CGU
1723	G	SN09CEK	1733	G	SN09CFG	1742	G	SN09CFX	1751	G	SN09CGV
1724	G	SN09CEO									

VW1752-1782 — Volvo B9TL 10.4m — Wrightbus Eclipse Gemini — N39/23D — 2009 — First, 2013

1752	ON	LK59CWN	1760	ON	LK59CWX	1768	ON	LK59CXF	1776	ON	LK59CXP
1753	ON	LK59CWO	1761	ON	LK59CWY	1769	ON	LK59CXG	1777	ON	LK59FCO
1754	ON	LK59CWP	1762	ON	LK59CWZ	1770	ON	LK59CXH	1778	ON	LK59FCP
1755	ON	LK59CWR	1763	ON	LK59CXA	1771	ON	LK59CXJ	1779	ON	LK59FCU
1756	ON	LK59CWT	1764	ON	LK59CXB	1772	ON	LK59CXL	1780	ON	LK59FCV
1757	ON	LK59CWU	1765	ON	LK59CXC	1773	ON	LK59CXM	1781	ON	LK59FCX
1758	ON	LK59CWV	1766	ON	LK59CXD	1774	ON	LK59CXN	1782	ON	LK59FCY
1759	ON	LK59CWW	1767	ON	LK59CXE	1775	ON	LK59CXO			

DE1783-1816 — ADL Dart 4 10.2m — ADL Enviro 200 — N29D — 2010 — First, 2013

1783	HZ	YX10BCU	1792	HZ	YX10BDY	1801	UX	YX10BFJ	1809	UX	YX10BFV
1784	HZ	YX10BCV	1793	HZ	YX10BDZ	1802	UX	YX10BFK	1810	UX	YX10BFY
1785	HZ	YX10BCY	1794	HZ	YX10BEJ	1803	UX	YX10BFL	1811	UX	YX10BFZ
1786	HZ	YX10BCZ	1795	HZ	YX10BEO	1804	UX	YX10BFM	1812	UX	YX10BGE
1787	HZ	YX10BDE	1796	HZ	YX10BEU	1805	UX	YX10BFN	1813	UX	YX10BGF
1788	HZ	YX10BDF	1797	HZ	YX10BEY	1806	UX	YX10BFO	1814	UX	YX10BGK
1789	HZ	YX10BDO	1798	UX	YX10BFA	1807	UX	YX10BFP	1815	UX	YX10BGO
1790	HZ	YX10BDU	1799	UX	YX10BFE	1808	UX	YX10BFU	1816	UX	YX10BGU
1791	HZ	YX10BDV	1800	UX	YX10BFF						

VW1817-1841 — Volvo B9TL 10.4m — Wrightbus Eclipse Gemini 2 — N39/23D — 2010 — First, 2013

1817	HZ	BF10LSZ	1824	HZ	BK10MFA	1830	HZ	BF10LSU	1836	HZ	BV10WVN
1818	HZ	BF10LTA	1825	HZ	BK10MFE	1831	HZ	BF10LSV	1837	HZ	BV10WVO
1819	HZ	BV10WVP	1826	HZ	BK10MFN	1832	HZ	BF10LSX	1838	HZ	BV10WVU
1820	HZ	BV10WVR	1827	HZ	BK10MFF	1833	HZ	BF10LSY	1839	HZ	BV10WVW
1821	HZ	BV10WVS	1828	HZ	BK10MFJ	1834	HZ	BF10LTE	1840	HZ	BV10WVX
1822	HZ	BV10WVT	1829	HZ	BF10LSO	1835	HZ	BF10LTJ	1841	ON	BK10MFO
1823	HZ	BK10MEV									

VW1842-1894 — Volvo B9TL 10.4m — Wrightbus Eclipse Gemini 2 — N39/23D — 2010 — First, 2013

1842	WJ	BF60UUA	1856	WJ	BF60UUR	1869	WJ	BF60UUW	1882	WJ	BF60VJU
1843	WJ	BF60UUB	1857	WJ	BF60UUP	1870	WJ	BF60VHT	1883	WJ	BF60VJV
1844	WJ	BF60UTZ	1858	WJ	BF60UUT	1871	WJ	BF60VHX	1884	WJ	BF60UVB
1845	WJ	BF60UUD	1859	WJ	BF60UUS	1872	WJ	BF60VJA	1885	WJ	BF60UVA
1846	WJ	BF60UUC	1860	WJ	BF60UUX	1873	WJ	BF60VHY	1886	WJ	BF60UVD
1847	WJ	BF60UUE	1861	WJ	BF60UUY	1874	WJ	BF60VJC	1887	WJ	BF60UVG
1848	WJ	BF60UUJ	1862	WJ	BF60UUV	1875	WJ	BF60VJK	1888	WJ	BF60UVH
1849	WJ	BF60UUG	1863	WJ	BF60UUZ	1876	WJ	BF60VJJ	1889	WJ	BF60UVC
1850	WJ	BF60UUK	1864	WJ	BF60VHP	1877	WJ	BF60VJE	1890	WJ	BF60UVE
1851	WJ	BF60UUH	1865	WJ	BF60VHR	1878	WJ	BF60VHZ	1891	WJ	BF60VJN
1852	WJ	BF60UUL	1866	WJ	BF60VHV	1879	WJ	BF60VJG	1892	WJ	BF60VJM
1853	WJ	BF60UUN	1867	WJ	BF60VHU	1880	WJ	BF60VJD	1893	WJ	BF60VJO
1854	WJ	BF60UUM	1868	WJ	BF60CHW	1881	WJ	BF60VJL	1894	WJ	BF60VJP
1855	WJ	BF60UUO									

DE1895-1911 — ADL Dart 4 10.2m — ADL Enviro 200 — N29D — 2010-11 — First, 2013

1895	UX	YX60BZN	1900	G	YX11AEY	1904	G	YX11AFF	1908	G	YX11CNO
1896	UX	YX60BZO	1901	G	YX11AEZ	1905	G	YX11AFJ	1909	G	YX11CNU
1897	G	YX11AEU	1902	G	YX11AFA	1906	G	YX11CNK	1910	G	YX11CNV
1898	G	YX11AEV	1903	G	YX11AFE	1907	G	YX11CNN	1911	G	YX11CNY
1899	G	YX11AEW									

DEM1912-1918 — ADL Dart 4 9.6m — ADL Enviro 200 — N25D — 2011 — First, 2013

1912	ON	YX61EKR	1914	ON	YX61EKU	1916	ON	YX61EKW	1918	ON	YX61EKZ
1913	ON	YX61EKT	1915	ON	YX61EKV	1917	ON	YX61EKY			

SN1919-1957 — Scania Omnicity CN230 UD — Scania — N41/22D — 2011 — First, 2013

1919	HZ	YR61RPU	1929	HZ	YR61RRZ	1939	HZ	YR61RTX	1949	HZ	YR61RUY
1920	HZ	YR61RPV	1930	HZ	YR61RSO	1940	HZ	YR61RTZ	1950	HZ	YR61RVA
1921	HZ	YR61RPX	1931	HZ	YR61RSU	1941	HZ	YR61RUA	1951	HZ	YR61RVC
1922	HZ	YR61RPY	1932	HZ	YR61RSV	1942	HZ	YR61RUC	1952	HZ	YR61RVE
1923	HZ	YR61RPZ	1933	HZ	YR61RSX	1943	HZ	YR61RUH	1953	HZ	YR61RVF
1924	HZ	YR61RRO	1934	HZ	YR61RSY	1944	HZ	YR61RUJ	1954	HZ	YR61RVJ
1925	HZ	YR61RRU	1935	HZ	YR61RSZ	1945	HZ	YR61RUO	1955	HZ	YR61RVK
1926	HZ	YR61RRV	1936	HZ	YR61RTO	1946	HZ	YR61RUU	1956	HZ	YR61RVL
1927	HZ	YR61RRX	1937	HZ	YR61RTU	1947	HZ	YR61RUV	1957	HZ	YR61RVM
1928	HZ	YR61RRY	1938	HZ	YR61RTV	1948	HZ	YR61RUW			

Metroline is the first operator to use the New Bus for London (NBfL) on an entire service when route 24 was converted to the type on 22nd June 2013. The type will feature index plates with LTZ1 prefixing the up to 3-digit fleet number and the earlier buses will gain this feature shortly. Unusually, the vehicles are built for and retained by Transport for London and allocated to operators as required. Pictured while the rear platform was in use is LT32, LTZ1032, seen here in Parliament Square. *Mark Lyons*

DE1958-1969

			ADL Dart 4 10.2m				ADL Enviro 200		N29D	2012	First, 2013
1958	ON	YX12DKA	1961	ON	YX12DKF	1964	ON	YX12DKL	1967	ON	YX12DKU
1959	ON	YX12DKD	1962	ON	YX12DKJ	1965	ON	YX12DKN	1968	ON	YX12DKV
1960	ON	YX12DKE	1963	ON	YX12DKK	1966	ON	YX12DKO	1969	ON	YX12DKY

DEL1970-1980

			ADL Dart 4 10.8m				ADL Enviro 200		N31D	2012	First, 2013
1970	WJ	YX12AOS	1973	WJ	YX12AFK	1976	WJ	YX12AVT	1979	WJ	YX12ATF
1971	WJ	YX12AOT	1974	WJ	YX12AZG	1977	WJ	YX12AYK	1980	WJ	YX12APK
1972	WJ	YX12AFU	1975	WJ	YX12AFO	1978	WJ	YX12ATN			

TE1981-2000

			ADL E40D 9.9m				ADL Enviro 400		N37/24D	2012	First, 2013
1981	G	SN12EHD	1986	G	SN12EHJ	1991	G	SN12EHT	1996	G	SN62AAK
1982	G	SN12EHE	1987	G	SN12EHK	1992	G	SN12EHU	1997	G	SN62AAO
1983	G	SN12EHF	1988	G	SN12EHP	1993	G	SN12EHV	1998	G	SN62AAV
1984	G	SN12EHG	1989	G	SN12EHR	1994	G	SN12EHW	1999	G	SN12EGY
1985	G	SN12EHH	1990	G	SN12EHS	1995	G	SN62AAF	2000	G	SN12EGZ

LT9-40

			Wrightbus NBfL			Wrightbus			H40/22T	2013	*Owned by TfL*
9	HT	LTZ1009	17	HT	LTZ1017	25	HT	LTZ1025	33	HT	LTZ1033
10	HT	LTZ1010	18	HT	LTZ1018	26	HT	LTZ1026	34	HT	LTZ1034
11	HT	LTZ1011	19	HT	LTZ1019	27	HT	LTZ1027	35	HT	LTZ1035
12	HT	LTZ1012	20	HT	LTZ1020	28	HT	LTZ1028	36	HT	LTZ1036
13	HT	LTZ1013	21	HT	LTZ1021	29	HT	LTZ1029	37	HT	LTZ1037
14	HT	LTZ1014	22	HT	LTZ1022	30	HT	LTZ1030	38	HT	LTZ1038
15	HT	LTZ1015	23	HT	LTZ1023	31	HT	LTZ1031	39	HT	LTZ1039
16	HT	LTZ1016	24	HT	LTZ1024	32	HT	LTZ1032	40	HT	LTZ1040

Special event vehicles (with original operator's name):

RM644	HT	WLT644	AEC Routemaster RH2H	Park Royal	O36/28RD	1961	London Transport
RML903	HT	WLT903	AEC Routemaster RH2H/1	Park Royal	B40/32R	1962	London Transport

Ancillary vehicles:

DP274	PA	P674MLE	Dennis Dart 9m	Plaxton Pointer	Staff	1997	
DP275	PA	P675MLE	Dennis Dart 9m	Plaxton Pointer	Staff	1997	

London Bus Handbook

Depots and allocations:

Alperton (Ealing Road) - ON

Volvo B9TL	VWH1365	VWH1367	VWH1371	VWH1372	VWH1374	VWH1375	VWH1376	VWH1377
	VW1752	VW1753	VW1754	VW1755	VW1756	VW1757	VW1758	VW1759
	VW1760	VW1761	VW1762	VW1763	VW1764	VW1765	VW1766	VW1767
	VW1768	VW1769	VW1770	VW1771	VW1772	VW1773	VW1774	VW1775
	VW1776	VW1777	VW1778	VW1779	VW1780	VW1781	VW1782	VW1841
Enviro 200	DE1598	DE1599	DE1600	DE1601	DE1602	DE1603	DE1604	DE1605
	DE1606	DE1607	DE1608	DE1609	DE1610	DE1611	DE1612	DE1613
	DE1614	DE1615	DE1616	DE1617	DE1618	DE1619	DE1665	DE1666
	DE1667	DE1668	DE1669	DE1670	DE1671	DE1672	DE1673	DE1674
	DEM1912	DEM1913	DEM1914	DEM1915	DEM1916	DEM1917	DEM1918	DE1958
	DE1959	DE1960	DE1961	DE1962	DE1963	DE1964	DE1965	DE1966
	DE1967	DE1968	DE1969					

Brentford (Commerce Road) - AH

Enviro 200	DM961	DM962	DM963	DM964	DM965	DM966	DM967	DM968
	DM968	DM969	DM970	DE993	DE994	DE995	DE996	DE997
	DE998	DE999	DE1000	DE1001	DE1002	DE1003	DE1004	DE1005
	DE1006	DE1007	DE1008	DE1009	DE1010	DE1011	DE1012	DE1013
	DE1014							
Tempo	OTH971	OTH972	OTH973	OTH974	OTH975			
Trident	TP412	TP413	TP415	TP433				
Volvo B9TL	VW1034	VW1035	VW1036	VW1037	VW1038	VW1039	VW1040	VW1041
	VW1042	VW1043	VW1044	VW1045	VW1046	VW1047	VW1048	VW1049
	VW1050	VW1051	VW1052	VW1053	VW1054	VW1055	VW1056	VW1057
	VW1058	VW1059	VW1060	VW1061	VW1062	VW1063	VW1064	VW1065
	VW1066	VW1067	VW1068	VW1069	VW1070	VW1071	VW1072	

Cricklewood (Edgware Road) - W

Enviro 200	DE859	DE860	DE861	DE862	DE863	DE864	DE865	DE866
	DE867	DE868	DE869	DE870	DE871	DE872	DE873	DE874
	DE875	DE876	DE877	DE952	DE953	DE954	DE955	DE956
	DE957	DE958	DE959	DE960	DE1015	DE1016	DE1017	DE1018
	DE1019	DE1020	DE1021	DE1022	DE1023	DE1024	DE1025	DE1026
	DE1027	DE1028	DE1029	DE1030	DE1031	DE1032	DE1033	DE1115
	DE1116	DE1117	DE1118	DE1119	DE1120	DE1121	DE1122	DE1123
	DE1124	DE1125	DE1126	DE1127	DE1128	DE1129	DE1130	DE1131
	DE1132	DE1133	DE1134	DE1135	DE1136	DE1137	DE1138	DE1139
	DE1140	DE1141	DE1142	DE1143	DE1144	DE1145	DE1146	DE1147
	DE1148	DE1149	DE1150	DE1151				
Volvo B7tL	VPL215							
Trident	TP430	TA638	TA639	TA640	TA641	TA642	TA643	TA644
	TA645	TA646	TA647	TA648	TA649	TA650	TA651	TA652
	TA653	TA654	TA655	TA656	TA657	TA658	TA659	
Enviro 400	TE892	TE893	TE894	TE895	TE980	TE1073	TE1074	TE1075
	TE1076	TE1077	TE1078	TE1079	TE1080	TE1081	TE1082	TE1083
	TE1084	TE1085	TE1086	TE1087	TE1088	TE1089	TE1090	TE1091
	TE1092	TE1093	TE1094	TE1095	TE1096	TE1097	TE1098	TE1099
	TE1100	TE1101	TE1102	TE1103	TE1104	TE1307	TE1308	TE1309
	TE1310	TE1311	TE1312	TE1313	TE1314	TE1315	TE1316	TE1317
	TE1448							
Enviro E400 Hybrid	TEH915	TEH916	TEH917	TEH918	TEH919	TEH1105	TEH1106	TEH1107
	TEH1108	TEH1109	TEH1110	TEH1111	TEH1112	TEH1113	TEH1114	TEH1217
	TEH1218	TEH1219	TEH1220	TEH1221	TEH1222	TEH1223	TEH1224	TEH1225
	TEH1226	TEH1227	TEH1228	TEH1229	TEH1230	TEH1231	TEH1232	TEH1233
	TEH1234	TEH1235	TEH1236	TEH1237	TEH1238	TEH1239	TEH1240	TEH1241
	TEH1242	TEH1449	TEH1450	TEH1451	TEH1452	TEH1453	TEH1454	TEH1455
	TEH1456	TEH1457	TEH1458	TEH1459	TEH1460	TEH1461	TEH1462	TEH1463
	TEH1464	TEH1465	TEH1466	TEH1467				

Edgware (Station Road) - EW

Volvo B7TL	VPL157	VPL200	VPL201	VPL203	VPL205	VPL210	VPL213	VPL215
	VPL217	VPL218	VPL221	VPL236				
Enviro 400	TE712	TE713	TE714	TE716	TE717	TE718	TE719	TE720
	TE721	TE722	TE723	TE724	TE725	TE726	TE727	TE728
	TE729	TE730	TE731	TE732	TE733	TE734	TE735	TE736
	TE737	TE738	TE828	TE829	TE830	TE831	TE832	TE833
	TE834	TE835	TE836	TE837	TE838	TE839	TE840	TE841
	TE842	TE843	TE844	TE845	TE846	TE847	TE878	TE879
	TE880	TE881	TE882	TE883	TE884	TE885	TE886	TE887
	TE888	TE889	TE890	TE891	TE892			

Greenford (Greenford Road) - G

Enviro 200	DE1675	DE1676	DE1677	DE1678	DE1679	DE1680	DE1681	DE1682
	DE1683	DE1684	DE1685	DE1686	DE1687	DE1688	DE1689	DE1690
	DE1691	DE1692	DE1693	DE1694	DES1695	DES1696	DES1697	DES1698
	DES1699	DES1700	DES1701	DES1702	DES1703	DES1704	DES1705	DES1706
	DES1707	DES1708	DES1709	DES1710	DES1711	DES1712	DES1713	DES1714
	DE1795	DE1897	DE1898	DE1899	DE1900	DE1901	DE1902	DE1903
	DE1904	DE1905	DE1906	DE1907	DE1908	DE1909	DE1910	DE1911
Trident	TP1507	TP1508	TP1509	TP1510	TP1511	TP1512	TP1513	TP1514
	TP1515	TP1516	TP1517	TP1518	TP1519	TP1520	TP1521	TP1522
	TP1523	TP1524						
Enviro 400	TE1715	TE1716	TE1717	TE1718	TE1719	TE1720	TE1721	TE1722
	TE1723	TE1724	TE1725	TE1726	TE1727	TE1728	TE1729	TE1730
	TE1731	TE1732	TE1733	TE1734	TE1735	TE1736	TE1737	TE1738
	TE1739	TE1740	TE1741	TE1742	TE1743	TE1744	TE1745	TE1746
	TE1747	TE1748	TE1749	TE1750	TE1751	TE1981	TE1982	TE1983
	TE1984	TE1985	TE1986	TE1987	TE1988	TE1989	TE1990	TE1991
	TE1992	TE1993	TE1994	TE1995	TE1996	TE1997	TE1998	TE1999
	TE2000							

Harrow Weald (High Road) - HD

Volvo B7TL	VPL207	VPL222	VP317	VP318	VP319	VP320	VP321	VP322
	VP323	VP324	VP325	VP326	VP327	VP328	VP329	VP330
	VP331	VP332	VP333	VP334	VP335	VP336	VP337	VP338
	VP339	VP340	VP341	VP342	VP343	VP344	VP345	VP346
	VP347	VP466	VP467	VP468	VP469	VP470	VP471	VP484
	VP485	VP486	VP487	VP488	VP604	VP605	VP606	VP607
	VP608	VP609	VP610	VP611	VP612	VP613	VP614	VP615
	VP616	VP617	VP618	VP619	VP620	VP621	VP622	VP623
	VP624	VP625	VP626	VP627	VP628			

Hayes (Rigby Lane) - HZ

Enviro 200	DE1783	DE1784	DE1785	DE1786	DE1787	DE1788	DE1789	DE1790
	DE1791	DE1792	DE1793	DE1794	DE1796	DE1797		
Volvo B9TL	VW1817	VW1818	VW1819	VW1820	VW1821	VW1822	VW1823	VW1824
	VW1825	VW1826	VW1827	VW1828	VW1829	VW1830	VW1831	VW1832
	VW1833	VW1834	VW1835	VW1836	VW1837	VW1838	VW1839	VW1840
Scania OmniCity	SN1919	SN1920	SN1921	SN1922	SN1923	SN1924	SN1925	SN1926
	SN1927	SN1928	SN1929	SN1930	SN1931	SN1932	SN1933	SN1934
	SN1935	SN1936	SN1937	SN1938	SN1939	SN1940	SN1941	SN1942
	SN1943	SN1944	SN1945	SN1946	SN1947	SN1948	SN1949	SN1950
	SN1951	SN1952	SN1953	SN1954	SN1955	SN1956	SN1957	

Holloway (Pemberton Gardens) - HT

Trident	TPL263	TPL265	TPL267	TPL268	TPL270	TP404	TP408	TP409
	TP410	TP414	TP417	TP418	TP419	TP421	TP422	TP423
	TP426	TP427	TP428	TP432	TP451	TP452	TP453	TP454
	TP455	TP456	TP457	TP458	TP459	TP460	TP461	TP462
	TP463	TP464	TP465					
Enviro 400	TE665	TE666	TE667	TE668	TE669	TE670	TE671	TE672
	TE673	TE674	TE675	TE676	TE677	TE678	TE679	TE680
	TE681	TE682	TE683	TE684	TE685	TE686	TE687	TE688
	TE689	TE690	TE691	TE692	TE896	TE897	TE898	TE899
	TE900	TE901	TE902	TE903	TE904	TE905	TE906	TE907
	TE908	TE909	TE910	TE911	TE912	TE913	TE914	TE920
	TE921	TE922	TE923	TE924	TE925	TE926	TE927	TE928
	TE929	TE930	TE931	TE932	TE933	TE934		
Volvo B7TL	VPL224	VPL226	VPL229	VPL231	VPL232	VPL233	VPL234	VPL235
	VPL581	VPL582	VPL583	VPL584	VPL585	VPL586	VPL587	VPL588
	VPL589	VPL590	VPL591	VPL592	VPL593	VPL594	VPL595	VPL596
	VPL597	VPL598	VPL599	VPL600	VPL601	VPL602	VPL603	VPL629
	VPL630	VPL631	VPL632	VPL633	VPL634	VPL635	VPL636	VPL637
Volvo B9TL	VW1243	VW1244	VW1245	VW1246	VW1247	VW1248	VW1249	VW1250
	VW1251	VW1252	VW1253	VW1254	VW1255	VW1256	VW1257	VW1258
	VW1259	VW1260	VW1261	VW1262	VW1263	VW1264	VW1265	VW1266
	VW1267	VW1268	VW1269	VW1270	VW1271	VW1272	VW1273	VW1274
	VW1275	VW1276	VW1277	VW1278	VW1279	VW1280	VW1281	VW1282
	VW1283	VW1284	VW1285	VW1286	VW1287	VW1288	VW1289	VW1290
	VW1291	VW1292	VW1293	VW1294	VW1295	VW1296	VW1297	VW1298
	VW1299	VW1300	VW1301	VW1302	VW1303	VW1304	VW1305	VW1306
	VW1366	VW1368	VW1369	VW1370	VW1373	VW1378	VW1379	VW1380
	VW1381	VW1382	VW1383	VW1384	VW1385	VW1386	VW1387	VW1388
	VW1390	VW1391	VW1392					
Volvo B5LH	VWH1360	VWH1361	VWH1362	VWH1363	VWH1364			
Wrightbus NBfL	LT9	LT10	LT11	LT12	LT13	LT14	LT15	LT16
	LT17	LT18	LT19	LT20	LT21	LT22	LT23	LT24
	LT25	LT26	LT27	LT28	LT29	LT30	LT31	LT32
	LT33	LT34	LT35	LT36	LT37	LT38	LT39	LT40

King's Cross (York Way) - KX (Managed from Holloway)

Dart	DLD178	DLD207	DLD693	DLD694	DLD695	DLD696	DLD697	DLD698
	DLD699	DLD700	DLD701	DLD702	DLD703	DLD704	DLD705	DLD706
	DLD707	DLD708	DLD709	DLD710	DLD711			
Enviro 200	DE1152	DE1153	DE1154	DE1155	DE1156	DE1157	DE1158	DE1159
	DE1160	DE1161	DE1162	DE1163	DE1164	DE1165	DE1166	DE1167
	DE1168	DE1169	DE1170	DE1318	DE1319	DE1320	DE1321	DE1322
	DE1323	DE1324	DE1325	DE1326	DE1327	DE1328	DE1329	DE1330
	DE1331	DE1332	DE1333	DE1334	DE1335	DE1336		

Perivale (Horsenden Lane South) - PA

Dart	DP1010	DP1011	DP1012	DP1015	DP1016			
Enviro 200	DE1150	DE1151	DE1171	DE1172	DE1173	DE1174		
MAN/Evolution	MM779	MM780	MM781	MM782	MM783	MM784	MM785	MM786
	MM787	MM788	MM789	MM790	MM810	MM811	MM812	MM813
	MM814	MM815	MM816	MM817	MM818	MM819	MM820	MM821
	MM822	MM823	MM824	MM825	MM826	MM827		
OmniDekka	SEL739	SEL740	SEL741	SEL742	SEL743	SEL744	SEL745	SEL746
	SEL747	SEL748	SEL749	SEL750	SEL751	SEL752	SEL753	SEL754
	SEL755	SEL756	SEL757	SEL758	SEL759	SEL760	SEL761	SEL762
	SEL763	SEL764	SEL803	SEL804	SEL805	SEL806	SEL807	SEL808
	SEL808							
Volvo B9TL	VW1175	VW1176	VW1177	VW1178	VW1179	VW1180	VW1181	VW1182
	VW1183	VW1184	VW1185	VW1186	VW1187	VW1188	VW1189	VW1190
	VW1191	VW1192	VW1193	VW1194	VW1195	VW1196	VW1197	VW1198
	VW1199	VW1200	VW1201	VW1202	VW1203	VW1204	VW1205	VW1206
	VW1207	VW1208	VW1209	VW1210	VW1211	VW1212	VW1213	VW1214
	VW1215	VW1216						

Potters Bar (High Street) - PB

Dart	DSD209	DSD212	DSD214	DSD215	DP1009	DP1013		
Enviro 200	DES791	DES792	DES793	DES794	DES795	DES796	DES797	DES798
	DES799	DES800	DES801	DES802	DEL848	DEL849	DEL850	DEL851
	DEL852	DEL853	DEL854	DEL855	DEL856	DEL857	DEL858	DEM1337
	DEM1338	DEM1339	DEM1340	DEM1341	DEM1342	DEM1343	DEM1344	DEM1345
	DEM1346	DEM1347	DEM1348	DEM1349	DEM1350	DEM1351	DEM1352	DEM1353
	DEM1354	DEM1355	DEM1356	DEM1357	DEM1358	DEM1359		
Trident	TPL241	TPL249	TP431	TP431	TP434	TP435	TP436	TP437
	TP438	TP439	TP440	TP441	TP442	TP443	TP444	TP445
	TP446	TP447	TP448	TP449	TP450			
Enviro 400	TE935	TE936	TE937	TE938	TE939	TE940	TE941	TE942
	TE943	TE944	TE945	TE946	TE947	TE948	TE949	TE950
	TE951	TE1420	TE1421	TE1422	TE1423	TE1424	TE1425	TE1426
	TE1427	TE1428	TE1429	TE1430	TE1431	TE1432	TE1433	TE1434
	TE1435	TE1436	TE1437	TE1438	TE1439	TE1440	TE1441	TE1442
	TE1443	TE1444	TE1445	TE1446	TE1447			

Uxbridge (Bakers Road) - UX

Dart	DC1540	DC1541	DC1542	DC1543	DC1544	DC1545	DC1546	DC1547
	DC1548	DC1549	DC1550	DC1551	DC1552	DC1553	DC1554	DC1555
	DC1556	DC1557	DC1558	DC1559				
Enviro 200	DE1583	DE1584	DE1585	DE1586	DE1587	DE1588	DE1589	DE1590
	DE1591	DE1592	DE1593	DE1594	DE1595	DE1596	DE1597	DE1798
	DE1799	DE1800	DE1801	DE1802	DE1803	DE1804	DE1805	DE1806
	DE1807	DE1808	DE1809	DE1810	DE1811	DE1812	DE1813	DE1814
	DE1815	DE1816	DE1895	DE1896				
	DE1800	DE1800	DE1800	DE1800				
Trident	TP1525	TP1526	TP1527	TP1528	TP1529	TP1530	TP1531	TP1532
	TP1533	TP1534	TP1535	TP1536	TP1537	TP1538	TP1539	
Enviro 400	TE1571	TE1572	TE1573	TE1574	TE1575	TE1576	TE1577	TE1578
	TE1579	TE1580	TE1581	TE1582				
Volvo B7TL	VW1560	VW1561	VW1562	VW1563	VW1564	VW1565	VW1566	VW1567
	VW1568	VW1569	VW1570					

Willesden (High Road) - AC

Volvo B7TL	VPL191	VPL207	VP473	VP474	VP475	VP476	VP477	VP478
	VP479	VP480	VP481	VP482	VP483	VP484	VP489	VP490
	VP491	VP492	VP493	VP494	VP495	VP496	VP497	VP498
	VP499	VP500	VP501	VP502	VP503	VP504	VP505	VP506
	VP507	VP508	VP509	VP510	VP511	VP512	VP513	VP514
	VP515	VP516	VP517	VP518	VP519	VP520	VP521	VP522
	VP523	VP524	VP525	VP526	VP527	VP528	VP529	VP530
	VP531	VP532	VP533	VP534	VP535	VP536	VP537	VP538
	VP539	VP540	VP541	VP542	VP543	VP544	VP545	VP546
	VP547	VP548	VP549	VP550	VP551	VP552	VP553	VP554
	VP555	VP556	VP557	VP558	VP559	VP560	VP561	VP562
	VP563	VP564	VP565	VP566	VP567	VP568	VP569	VP570
	VP571	VP572	VP573	VP574	VP575	VP576	VP577	VP578
	VP579	VP580						
Volvo B9TL	VW1393	VW1394	VW1395	VW1396	VW1397	VW1398	VW1399	VW1400
	VW1401	VW1402	VW1403	VW1404	VW1405	VW1406	VW1407	
Volvo B5LH	VW1408	VW1409	VW1410	VW1411	VW1412	VW1413	VW1414	VW1415
	VW1416	VW1417	VW1418	VW1419	VW1468			

Willesden Junction (Station Road) - WJ

Metroline operates just one batch of Scania OmniCity double-decks and these were inherited from First and all thirty-nine are currently allocated to Hayes. Illustrating the type, complete with its new identity is SN1926, YR61RRV. *Richard Godfrey*

Enviro 200								
	DE1620	DE1621	DE1622	DE1623	DE1624	DE1625	DE1626	DE1627
	DE1628	DE1629	DE1630	DE1631	DE1632	DE1633	DE1634	DE1635
	DE1636	DE1637	DE1638	DE1639	DE1640	DE1641	DE1642	DE1643
	DE1644	DE1645	DE1646	DE1647	DE1648	DE1649	DE1650	DE1651
	DE1652	DE1653	DE1654	DE1655	DE1656	DE1657	DE1658	DE1659
	DE1660	DE1661	DE1662	DE1663	DE1664	DEL1970	DEL1971	DEL1972
	DEL1973	DEL1974	DEL1975	DEL1976	DEL1977	DEL1978	DEL1979	DEL1980
Volvo B9TL	VW1842	VW1843	VW1844	VW1845	VW1846	VW1847	VW1848	VW1849
	VW1850	VW1851	VW1852	VW1853	VW1854	VW1855	VW1856	VW1857
	VW1858	VW1859	VW1860	VW1861	VW1862	VW1863	VW1864	VW1865
	VW1866	VW1867	VW1868	VW1869	VW1870	VW1871	VW1872	VW1873
	VW1874	VW1875	VW1876	VW1877	VW1878	VW1879	VW1880	VW1881
	VW1882	VW1883	VW1884	VW1885	VW1886	VW1887	VW1888	VW1889
	VW1890	VW1891	VW1892	VW1893	VW1894			

Unallocated and reserve - u/w

Remainder

RATP GROUP

London United, Busways House, Wellington Road, Twickenham, TW2 5NX

ADE1-45
ADL E400D 10.2m | ADL Enviro 400 | N41/24D | 2012

1	AV	YX12FNG	13	AV	YX12FNU	24	AV	YX62AEW	35	AV	YX62ARZ
2	AV	YX12FNH	14	AV	YX12FNV	25	AV	YX62AGU	36	AV	YX62BXF
3	AV	YX12FNJ	15	AV	YX12FNW	26	AV	YX12FON	37	AV	YX62BXR
4	AV	YX12FNK	16	AV	YX12FNY	27	AV	YX12FOP	38	AV	YX62BXU
5	AV	YX12FNL	17	AV	YX12FNZ	28	AV	YX12GHU	39	AV	YX62BXY
6	AV	YX12FNM	18	AV	YX12FOA	29	AV	YX12GHK	40	AV	YX62BXZ
7	AV	YX12FNN	19	AV	YX12FOC	30	AV	YX12GHN	41	AV	YX62BYG
8	AV	YX12FNO	20	AV	YX12FOD	31	AV	YX12GHO	42	AV	YX62BYJ
9	AV	YX12FNP	21	AV	YX12FOF	32	AV	YX12GHU	43	AV	YX62BYK
10	AV	YX12FNR	22	AV	YX12FOH	33	AV	YX62AHE	44	AV	YX62BZE
11	AV	YX12FNS	23	AV	YX12FOJ	34	AV	YX62AOE	45	AV	YX62BZS
12	AV	YX12FNT									

ADE46-73
ADL E400D 10.2m | ADL Enviro 400 | N41/24D | 2012

46	PK	YX62BBO	53	PK	YX62BGF	60	PK	YX62BKO	67	PK	YX62BPO
47	PK	YX62BBZ	54	PK	YX62BHD	61	PK	YX62BLZ	68	PK	YX62BPU
48	PK	YX62BCK	55	PK	YX62BHW	62	PK	YX62BMV	69	PK	YX62BPZ
49	PK	YX62BCV	56	u	YX62BJF	63	PK	YX62BMY	70	PK	YX62BUA
50	PK	YX62BFL	57	PK	YX62BJU	64	PK	YX62BNO	71	PK	YX62BUE
51	PK	YX62BFU	58	PK	YX62BJZ	65	PK	YX62BNV	72	PK	YX62BVN
52	PK	YX62BGE	59	PK	YX62BKF	66	PK	YX62BPF	73	PK	YX62BWO

ADH1-22
ADL E400H 10.1m | ADL Enviro 400 | N37/24D* | 2009-10 | *seating varies

1	V	SN58EOR	7	S	SN60BYB	13	S	SN60BYJ	18	S	SN60BYP
2	V	SN58EOS	8	S	SN60BYC	14	S	SN60BYK	19	S	SN60BYR
3	S	SN60BXX	9	S	SN60BYD	15	S	SN60BYL	20	S	SN60BYS
4	S	SN60BXY	10	S	SN60BYF	16	S	SN60BYM	21	S	SN60BYT
5	S	SN60BXZ	11	S	SN60BYG	17	S	SN60BYO	22	S	SN60BYU
6	S	SN60BYA	12	S	SN60BYH						

ADH23-51
ADL E400H 10.2m | ADL Enviro 400 | N37/24D | 2013

23	V	YX62FAU	31	V	YX62FJD	38	V	YX62FMV	45	V	YX62FSS
24	V	YX62FCM	32	V	YX62FJV	39	V	YX62FNZ	46	V	YX62FTD
25	V	YX62FCO	33	V	YX62FKE	40	V	YX62FOA	47	V	YX62FTF
26	V	YX62FDY	34	V	YX62FKK	41	V	YX62FPC	48	V	YX62FTP
27	V	YX62FFB	35	V	YX62FLH	42	V	YX62FPF	49	V	YX62FTZ
28	V	YX62FFG	36	V	YX62FME	43	V	YX62FPK	50	V	YX62FUT
29	V	YX62FHA	37	V	YX62FMG	44	V	YX62FSE	51	V	YX62FUU
30	V	YX62FHO									

DE1-49
ADL Dart 4 10.2m | ADL Enviro 200 | N29D | 2008-09

1	HH	YX58DVA	14	HH	YX58DVR	26	FW	YX09HJU	38	S	YX09HKT
2	HH	YX58DVB	15	HH	YX58DVT	27	FW	YX09HJV	39	S	YX09HKH
3	HH	YX58DVC	16	HH	YX58DVU	28	FW	YX09HJY	40	S	YX09HKJ
4	HH	YX58DVF	17	HH	YX58DVV	29	FW	YX09HJZ	41	S	YX09HKK
5	HH	YX58DVG	18	HH	YX58DVW	30	FW	YX09HKZ	42	S	YX09HKL
6	HH	YX58DVH	19	HH	YX58DUV	31	FW	YX09HLA	43	S	YX09HKM
7	HH	YX58DVJ	20	HH	YX58DUY	32	S	YX09HKA	44	S	YX09HKN
8	HH	YX58DVK	21	HH	YX58DWK	33	S	YX09HKB	45	S	YX09HKO
9	HH	YX58DVL	22	HH	YX09HJJ	34	S	YX09HKC	46	S	YX09HKP
10	HH	YX58DVM	23	FW	YX09HJK	35	S	YX09HKD	47	S	YX09HKT
11	HH	YX58DVN	24	FW	YX09HJN	36	S	YX09HKE	48	S	YX09HKU
12	HH	YX58DVO	25	FW	YX09HJO	37	S	YX09HKR	49	S	YX09HKV
13	HH	YX58DVP									

London United is owned by the RATP Group, an international public transport operator owned by the government of France. In 2009, the Caisse des dépôts et consignations, the majority owner of the Transdev group, started negotiations with Veolia Environnement to merge Transdev with Veolia Transport. As part of the resulting agreement, made in May 2010, it was concuded that the RATP Group, which had a minority shareholding in Transdev, would take over ownership of some of Transdev's operations in lieu of cash payment. This had a considerable impact on Transdev's London bus operations, as it was agreed that London United would transfer to the RATP Group, whilst London Sovereign would remain with Transdev and become part of the merged Veolia Transdev group. Enviro 400 ADE70, YX62BUA, is shown outside Charing Cross Hospital. *Richard Godfrey*

DE57-92

		ADL Dart 4 10.2m			ADL Enviro 200		N29D	2008	NCP, London, 2010	
57	TV	SK07DXE	66	TV	SK07DXR	75	PK	SK07DYC	84	PK	SK07DYP
58	TV	SK07DXF	67	TV	SK07DXS	76	PK	SK07DYD	85	S	SK07DYS
59	TV	SK07DXG	68	FW	SK07DXT	77	PK	SK07DYF	86	S	SK07DYT
60	TV	SK07DXH	69	FW	SK07DXU	78	PK	SK07DYG	87	S	SK07DYU
61	TV	SK07DXJ	70	FW	SK07DXV	79	PK	SK07DYH	88	S	SK07DYV
62	TV	SK07DXL	71	FW	SK07DXW	80	PK	SK07DYJ	89	S	SK07DYW
63	TV	SK07DXM	72	TV	SK07DXX	81	PK	SK07DYM	90	S	SK07DYX
64	TV	SK07DXO	73	FW	SK07DXY	82	PK	SK07DYN	91	S	SK07DYY
65	TV	SK07DXP	74	S	SK07DXZ	83	PK	SK07DYO	92	S	VX58DXA

DE93-128

		ADL Dart 4 10.2m			ADL Enviro 200		N29D	2010		
93	S	SN10CAV	102	S	SN10CCD	111	FW	YX60CAO	120	FW	YX60CCD
94	S	SN10CAX	103	S	SN10CCE	112	FW	YX60CAU	121	FW	YX60CCE
95	S	SN10CBF	104	S	SN10CCF	113	FW	YX60CAV	122	FW	YX60CCF
96	S	SN10CBO	105	S	SN10CCJ	114	FW	YX60CBF	123	FW	YX60CCJ
97	S	SN10CBU	106	S	SN10CCK	115	FW	YX60CBO	124	FW	YX60CCK
98	S	SN10CBV	107	S	SN10CCO	116	FW	YX60CBU	125	FW	YX60CCN
99	S	SN10CBX	108	S	SN10CCU	117	FW	YX60CBV	126	FW	YX60CCO
100	S	SN10CBY	109	FW	YX60CAA	118	FW	YX60CBY	127	FW	YX60BZH
101	S	SN10CCA	110	FW	YX60CAE	119	FW	YX60CCA	128	FW	YX60BZJ

DLE1-25

		ADL Dart 4 10.8m			ADL Enviro 200		N32D	2011		
1	AV	SN60EAX	8	AV	SN60EBJ	14	HH	SN60EBU	20	AV	SN60ECD
2	AV	SN60EAY	9	AV	SN60EBK	15	HH	SN60EBV	21	AV	SN60ECE
3	AV	SN60EBA	10	HH	SN60EBL	16	HH	SN60EBX	22	AV	SN60ECF
4	AV	SN60EBC	11	AV	SN60EBM	17	HH	SN60EBZ	23	AV	SN60ECJ
5	AV	SN60EBD	12	HH	SN60EBO	18	HH	SN60ECA	24	AV	SN60ECT
6	AV	SN60EBF	13	HH	SN60EBP	19	AV	SN60ECC	25	AV	SN60ECV
7	AV	SN60EBG									

Pictured on Putney Bridge, DPS651, LG02FFV, is one of the Dart/Pointer buses built during the TransBus era. Alexander Dennis was formed as TransBus on 1 January 2001, after the merger of Mayflower Corporation-owned Dennis and Alexander, and Henlys-owned Plaxton, although the name did not appear on vehicles until late 2002. On 31 March 2004, the Mayflower Group was put into administration and by default TransBus also entered administration. Alexander Dennis was acquired from the administrators by a group of Scottish businessmen. *Dave Heath*

DP1	NC	S301MKH	Dennis Dart SLF 10.7m	Plaxton Pointer 2	N36F	1998		
DP7	Vt	S307MKH	Dennis Dart SLF 10.7m	Plaxton Pointer 2	N36F	1998		
DP10	Vt	S310MKH	Dennis Dart SLF 10.7m	Plaxton Pointer 2	N36F	1998		
DP11	NC	S311MKH	Dennis Dart SLF 10.7m	Plaxton Pointer 2	N36F	1998		

DPS579-596
Dennis Dart SLF 10.1m — Alexander ALX200 — N30D — 2001

579	w	SN51TAU	**583**	V	SN51TAV	**587**	FW	SN51TBO	**591**	TV	SN51TBU
580	w	SN51TBY	**584**	u	SN51TBZ	**588**	TV	SN51TCJ	**592**	TV	SN51TCK
581	FW	SN51TCV	**585**	u	SN51TCX	**589**	TV	SN51TCY	**595**	u	SN51TBV
582	w	SN51TDV	**586**	FW	SN51TDX	**590**	TV	SN51TDZ	**596**	u	SN51TCO

DPK624	w	SN06JPV	ADL Dart 8.8m	ADL Mini Pointer	N23F	2006
DPK625	w	SN06JPX	ADL Dart 8.8m	ADL Mini Pointer	N23F	2006

DPS624-680
TransBus Dart 10.1m — TransBus Pointer — N27D — 2002

624	u	SK02XGT	**649**	TV	LG02FFT	**660**	TV	LG02FGF	**671**	u	LG02FHA
625	u	SK02XGU	**650**	TV	LG02FFU	**661**	FW	LG02FGJ	**672**	u	LG02FHB
626	u	SK02XGV	**651**	TV	LG02FFV	**662**	TV	LG02FGK	**673**	HH	LG02FHC
641	u	LG02FFK	**652**	TV	LG02FFW	**663**	u	LG02FGM	**674**	HH	LG02FHD
642	u	LG02FFL	**653**	TV	LG02FFX	**664**	V	LG02FGN	**675**	HH	LG02FHE
643	u	LG02FFM	**654**	TV	LG02FFY	**665**	u	LG02FGO	**676**	u	LG02FHF
644	u	LG02FFN	**655**	FW	LG02FFZ	**666**	TV	LG02FGP	**677**	HH	LG02FHH
645	u	LG02FFO	**656**	TV	LG02FGA	**667**	FW	LG02FGU	**678**	HH	LG02FHJ
646	u	LG02FFP	**657**	TV	LG02FGC	**668**	u	LG02FGV	**679**	HH	LG02FHK
647	u	LG02FFR	**658**	TV	LG02FGD	**669**	u	LG02FGX	**680**	HH	LG02FHL
648	TV	LG02FFS	**659**	FW	LG02FGE	**670**	FW	LG02FGZ			

DPS681-694
TransBus Dart SLF 10.1m — TransBus Pointer — N30D* — 2003 — *seating varies

681	FW	SN03LDY	**685**	FW	SN03LEV	**689**	FW	SN03LFE	**692**	S	SN03LFH
682	FW	SN03LDZ	**686**	FW	SN03LFA	**690**	FW	SN03LFF	**693**	FW	SN03LFJ
683	FW	SN03LEF	**687**	FW	SN03LFB	**691**	FW	SN03LFG	**694**	HH	SN03LFK
684	TV	SN03LEJ	**688**	W	SN03LFD						

RATP has operated both Optare Tempo and Optare Versa buses in its London operation since 2011. Illustrating the former, OT11, YJ11EHT, arrives in Hounslow on route 203 from Staines. *Richard Godfrey*

DPS701-727

ADL Dart SLF 10.1m — ADL Pointer — N28D — 2005 — NCP, London, 2010

701	V	SN55HKD	708	HH	SN55HKL	715	HH	SN55HKW	721	TV	SN55HLA
702	V	SN55HKE	709	HH	SN55HKM	716	HH	SN55HKX	722	TV	SN55HLC
703	V	SN55HKF	710	HH	SN55HKO	717	HH	SN55HKY	724	FW	SN55DVT
704	V	SN55HKG	711	HH	SN55HKP	718	V	SN55HSD	725	FW	SN55DVU
705	V	SN55HKH	712	HH	SN55HKY	719	V	SN55HSE	726	u	SN55DVV
706	V	SN55HKJ	713	HH	SN55HKU	720	V	SN55HKZ	727	FW	SN55DVW
707	HH	SN55HKK	714	HH	SN55HKV						

HDE1-5

ADL Hybrid Dart 10.2m — ADL Enviro 200 — N29D — 2009

1	FW	SN09CHC	3	FW	SN09CHF	4	FW	SN09CHG	5	FW	SN09CHH
2	FW	SN09CHD									

MCL1-7

Mercedes-Benz Citaro O530 LE — Mercedes-Benz — N35D — 2011

1	AV	BD11LWN	3	AV	BD11LWP	6	AV	BD11LWS	7	AV	BD11LWU
2	AV	BD11LWO	4	AV	BD11LWR	5	AV	BD11LWT			

OT1-16

Optare Tempo X1200 — Optare — N34D — 2011

1	AV	YJ11EHG	5	AV	YJ11EHM	9	AV	YJ11EHR	13	AV	YJ11EHV
2	AV	YJ11EHH	6	AV	YJ11EHN	10	AV	YJ11EHS	14	AV	YJ11EHW
3	AV	YJ11EHK	7	AV	YJ11EHO	11	AV	YJ11EHT	15	AV	YJ11EHX
4	AV	YJ11EHL	8	AV	YJ11EHP	12	AV	YJ11EHU	16	AV	YJ11EHZ

OV1-19

Optare Versa V1040 — Optare — N27D — 2008-09

1	V	YJ58VBA	6	V	YJ58VBF	11	V	YJ58VBN	16	V	YJ58VBV
2	V	YJ58VBB	7	V	YJ58VBG	12	V	YJ58VBO	17	V	YJ58VBX
3	V	YJ58VBC	8	V	YJ58VBK	13	V	YJ58VBP	18	V	YJ58VBY
4	V	YJ58VBD	9	V	YJ58VBL	14	V	YJ58VBT	19	V	YJ58VBZ
5	V	YJ58VBE	10	V	YJ58VBM	15	V	YJ58VBU			

Looking splendid in the summer sunshine is London United's HDE5, SN09CHH, one of three allocated to Tolworth depot for route 371 which connects Richmond with Kingston. *Mark Lyons*

OV50-66

Optare Versa V1040 — Optare — N27D — 2009

50	PK	YJ58PHY	**55**	PK	YJ09EZF	**59**	PK	YJ09EYW	**63**	PK	YJ09EZA
51	PK	YJ58PHZ	**56**	PK	YJ09EYT	**60**	PK	YJ09EYX	**64**	PK	YJ09EZB
52	PK	YJ58PJO	**57**	PK	YJ09EYU	**61**	PK	YJ09EYY	**65**	PK	YJ09EZC
53	PK	YJ58PJU	**58**	PK	YJ09EYV	**62**	PK	YJ09EYZ	**66**	PK	YJ09EZD
54	PK	YJ09EZE									

RML880 FW WLT880 — AEC Routemaster RH2H1 — Park Royal — B40/32R — 1961

SDE1-10

ADL Dart 4 8.9m — ADL Enviro 200 — N26F — 2008

1	TV	YX08MFO	**4**	TV	YX08MDZ	**7**	TV	YX08MEV	**9**	TV	YX08MHM
2	TV	YX08MDV	**5**	TV	YX08MFN	**8**	TV	YX08MFA	**10**	TV	YX08MFK
3	TV	YX08MDY	**6**	TV	YX08MEU						

SDE11-17

ADL Dart 4 8.9m — ADL Enviro 200 — N26F — 2007 — NCP, London, 2010

11	PK	SK07HLM	**13**	PK	SK07HLO	**15**	PK	SK07HLR	**17**	PK	SK07HLV
12	PK	SK07HLN	**14**	PK	SK07HLP	**16**	PK	SK07HLU			

SLE43-64

Scania N94UD 10.6m — East Lancs OmniDekka — N45/26D — 2005

43	S	YN55NKM	**49**	FW	YN55NKU	**55**	FW	YN55NLD	**60**	FW	YN55NLL
44	S	YN55NKO	**50**	FW	YN55NKW	**56**	FW	YN55NLE	**61**	FW	YN55NLM
45	FW	YN55NKP	**51**	FW	YN55NKX	**57**	FW	YN55NLG	**62**	FW	YN55NLO
46	FW	YN55NKR	**52**	FW	YN55NKZ	**58**	FW	YN55NLJ	**63**	FW	YN55NLP
47	FW	YN55NKS	**53**	FW	YN55NLA	**59**	FW	YN55NLK	**64**	FW	YN55NLR
48	FW	YN55NKT	**54**	FW	YN55NLC						

SP1-15

Scania OmniCity CN94 UD 10.7m Scania — N41/23D — 2006-07

1	HH	YN56FCA	**5**	AV	YN56FCF	**9**	AV	YN56FBB	**13**	AV	YN56FBX
2	HH	YN56FCC	**6**	AV	YN56FCG	**10**	AV	YN56FBO	**14**	AV	YN56FBY
3	HH	YN56FCD	**7**	AV	YN56FCJ	**11**	AV	YN56FBU	**15**	AV	YN56FBZ
4	HH	YN56FCE	**8**	AV	YN56FBA	**12**	AV	YN56FBV			

RATP operates over two hundred Scania OmniCity double-deck in its London operation and these carry the SP classification. Seen at Hyde Park is SP119, YR59FZA, one of thirty-eight allocated to Shepherd's Bush depot. *Richard Godfrey*

SP16-37

Scania OmniCity CN230 UD · Scania · N41/22D · 2008

16	HH	YN08DEU	22	HH	YN08DHG	28	FW	YN08DHP	33	S	YN08DHZ
17	HH	YN08DHA	23	HH	YN08DHJ	29	S	YN08DHU	34	S	YN08MRU
18	HH	YN08DHC	24	FW	YN08DHK	30	S	YN08DHV	35	S	YN08MRV
19	HH	YN08DHD	25	AV	YN08DHL	31	S	YN08DHX	36	S	YN08MRX
20	HH	YN08DHE	26	FW	YN08DHM	32	S	YN08DHY	37	S	YN08MRY
21	HH	YN08DHF	27	FW	YN08DHO						

SP38-67

Scania OmniCity CN230 UD · Scania · N41/22D · 2009

38	AV	YP58ACF	46	AV	YT09BNA	54	FW	YT09BNN	61	FW	YT09ZCL
39	S	YP58ACJ	47	AV	YT09BNB	55	FW	YT09BJU	62	FW	YT09ZCN
40	S	YP58ACO	48	AV	YT09BND	56	FW	YT09ZCA	63	FW	YT09ZCO
41	AV	YT09BKA	49	AV	YT09BNE	57	FW	YT09ZCE	64	FW	YT09ZCU
42	AV	YT09BMO	50	AV	YT09BNF	58	FW	YT09ZCF	65	FW	YT09BJV
43	AV	YT09BMU	51	AV	YT09BNJ	59	FW	YT09ZCJ	66	FW	YT09BJX
44	AV	YT09BMY	52	FW	YT09BNK	60	FW	YT09ZCK	67	FW	YT09BJY
45	AV	YT09BMZ	53	FW	YT09BNL						

SP88-108

Scania OmniCity CN230 UD · Scania · N41/22D · 2009

88	FW	YT59SFK	94	FW	YT59SFY	99	FW	YT59SGX	104	FW	YT59SFF
89	FW	YT59SFN	95	FW	YT59SFZ	100	FW	YT59SGY	105	FW	YT59DXY
90	FW	YT59SFO	96	FW	YT59SGO	101	FW	YT59SGZ	106	FW	YT59DXZ
91	FW	YT59SFU	97	FW	YT59SGU	102	FW	YT59SHJ	107	FW	YT59DYX
92	FW	YT59SFV	98	FW	YT59SGV	103	FW	YT59SHV	108	FW	YT59DYY
93	FW	YT59SFX									

SP109-125

Scania OmniCity CN230 UD · Scania · N41/22D · 2009

109	S	YR59FYO	114	S	YR59FYV	118	S	YR59FYZ	122	S	YR59FZD
110	S	YR59FYP	115	S	YR59FYW	119	S	YR59FZA	123	S	YR59FZE
111	S	YR59FYS	116	S	YR59FYX	120	S	YR59FZB	124	S	YR59FZF
112	S	YR59FYT	117	S	YR59FYY	121	S	YR59FZC	125	S	YR59FZG
113	S	YR59FYU									

SP126-164

Scania OmniCity CN230 UD   Scania   N41/22D   2009-10

126	S	YT59PBF	136	AV	YP59ODS	146	V	YP59OEE	156	V	YP59OER
127	S	YT59PBO	137	V	YP59ODT	147	V	YP59OEF	157	V	YP59OES
128	S	YT59PBV	138	V	YP59ODU	148	V	YP59OEG	158	V	YP59OET
129	S	YT59PBX	139	V	YP59ODV	149	V	YP59OEH	159	V	YP59OEU
130	S	YT59PBY	140	V	YP59ODW	150	V	YP59OEJ	160	V	YP59OEV
131	S	YT59PBZ	141	V	YP59ODX	151	V	YP59OEK	161	V	YP59OEW
132	S	YT59PCF	142	V	YP59OEA	152	V	YP59OEL	162	V	YP59OEX
133	S	YT59PCO	143	V	YP59OEB	153	V	YP59OEM	163	V	YP59OEY
134	S	YT59PCU	144	V	YP59OEC	154	V	YP59OEN	164	V	YP59OEZ
135	S	YT59PBU	145	V	YP59OED	155	V	YP59OEO			

SP165-206

Scania OmniCity CN230 UD   Scania   N41/22D   2010

165	AV	YT10UWA	176	AV	YT10XBZ	187	AV	YT10XCL	197	HH	YR10FGD
166	AV	YT10UWB	177	AV	YT10XCA	188	AV	YT10XCM	198	HH	YR10FGE
167	AV	YT10UWD	178	AV	YT10XCB	189	AV	YT10XCN	199	HH	YR10FGF
168	AV	YT10UWF	179	AV	YT10XCC	190	AV	YT10XCO	200	HH	YR10FGG
169	AV	YT10UWG	180	AV	YT10XCD	191	HH	YR10FFW	201	HH	YR10FGJ
170	AV	YT10UWH	181	AV	YT10XCE	192	HH	YR10FFX	202	HH	YR10FGK
171	AV	YT10XBU	182	AV	YT10XCF	193	HH	YR10FFY	203	HH	YR10FGM
172	AV	YT10XBV	183	AV	YT10XCG	194	HH	YR10FFZ	204	HH	YR10FGN
173	AV	YT10XBW	184	AV	YT10XCH	195	HH	YR10FGA	205	HH	YR10FGO
174	AV	YT10XBX	185	AV	YT10XCJ	196	HH	YR10FGC	206	HH	YR10FGP
175	AV	YT10XBY	186	AV	YT10XCK						

TA204-225

Dennis Trident 9.9m   Alexander ALX400 4.4m   N43/19D   2000-01

204	FW	SN51SYA	210	FW	SN51SYJ	216	HH	SN51SYV	221	FW	SN51SZC
205	FW	SN51SYC	211	FW	SN51SYO	217	FW	SN51SYW	222	FW	SN51SZD
206	FW	SN51SYE	212	FW	SN51SYR	218	HH	SN51SYX	223	FW	SN51SZE
207	FW	SN51SYF	213	FW	SN51SYS	219	FW	SN51SYY	224	FW	SN51SZT
208	FW	SN51SYG	214	FW	SN51SYT	220	FW	SN51SYZ	225	FW	SN51SZU
209	FW	SN51SYH	215	HH	SN51SYU						

TA229-250

TransBus Trident 9.9m   TransBus ALX400 4.4m   N43/19D   2002

229	TV	LG02FAA	235	TV	LG02FAU	241	TV	LG02FBF	246	TV	LG02FBO
230	TV	LG02FAF	236	TV	LG02FBA	242	TV	LG02FBJ	247	TV	LG02FBU
231	TV	LG02FAJ	237	TV	LG02FBB	243	TV	LG02FBK	248	TV	LG02FBV
232	TV	LG02FAK	238	TV	LG02FBC	244	TV	LG02FBL	249	TV	LG02FBX
233	TV	LG02FAM	239	TV	LG02FBD	245	TV	LG02FBN	250	TV	LG02FBY
234	TV	LG02FAO	240	TV	LG02FBE						

TA281-286

TransBus Trident 9.9m   TransBus ALX400 4.4m   N43/20D   2002

281	TV	LG02FDY	283	TV	LG02FEF	285	TV	LG02FEJ	286	TV	LG02FEK
282	TV	LG02FDZ	284	TV	LG02FEH						

TA312-346

TransBus Trident 9.9m   TransBus ALX400 4.4m   N43/19D   2003

312	TV	SN03DZJ	321	FW	SN03DZX	330	FW	SN03EAW	339	FW	SN03EBL
313	FW	SN03DZK	322	FW	SN03EAA	331	FW	SN03EAX	340	FW	SN03EBM
314	FW	SN03DZM	323	FW	SN03EAC	332	FW	SN03EBA	341	FW	SN03LFL
315	FW	SN03DZP	324	FW	SN03EAE	333	FW	SN03EBC	342	FW	SN03LFM
316	FW	SN03DZR	325	FW	SN03EAF	334	FW	SN03EBD	343	FW	SN03LFP
317	FW	SN03DZS	326	FW	SN03EAG	335	FW	SN03EBF	344	FW	SN03LFR
318	FW	SN03DZT	327	FW	SN03EAJ	336	FW	SN03EBG	345	FW	SN03LFS
319	FW	SN03DZV	328	FW	SN03EAM	337	FW	SN03EBJ	346	FW	SN03LFT
320	TV	SN03DZW	329	FW	SN03EAP	338	FW	SN03EBK			

TLA1-30

TransBus Trident 10.5m   TransBus ALX400   N45/22D   2003-04

1	S	SN53EUF	7	S	SN53EUO	21	S	SN53KHW	26	S	SN53KJE
2	S	SN53EUH	8	HH	SN53EUP	22	S	SN53KHX	27	S	SN53KJF
3	FW	SN53EUJ	17	S	SN53KHR	23	S	SN53KHY	28	S	SN53KJJ
4	FW	SN53EUK	18	S	SN53KHT	24	S	SN53KHZ	29	S	SN53KJK
5	TV	SN53EUL	19	S	SN53KHU	25	S	SN53KJA	30	S	SN53KJO
6	HH	SN53EUM	20	S	SN53KHV						

VA7-10

Volvo Olympian   Alexander RH   B45/29F*   1996   *7/9 are BC45/31F

7	NC	N137YRW	8	NC	N138YRW	9	NC	N139YRW	10	NC	N140YRW

An interesting vehicle latterly used at Hounslow depot is Volvo B9TL evaluation vehicle VM1, BF62UXU and one currently seeking a new operator. Bodied by MCV the vehicle type was introduced by Volvo as an alternative body to the Wrightbus Gemini. It was pictured as it arrives in the town. *Mark Lyons*

VA46-54

Volvo Olympian — Alexander RH — B47/25D — 1998

46	FW	R946YOV	48	FW	R948YOV	49	FW	R949YOV	54	FW	R954YOV

VA62-104

Volvo B7TL 10.1m — Alexander ALX400 4.4m — N43/17D — 2000 — *Seating varies

60	Vt	V176OOE	74	AV	V190OOE	85	u	V208OOE	92	FW	W123EON
61	Vt	V177OOE	78	Vt	V201OOE	86	FW	W116EON	98	Vt	W126EON
62	S	V178OOE	80	TV	V203OOE	87	Vt	W117EON	101	u	W137EON
63	FW	V179OOE	81	NC	V204OOE	89	Vt	W121EON	102	u	W138EON
64	S	V180OOE	82	Vt	V205OOE	90	D	W122EON	103	u	W139EON
71	u	V187OOE	83	Vt	V206OOE	91	S	W124EON	104	u	W141EON
72	u	V188OOE	84	Vt	V207OOE						

VB1	FW	HF53OBG	Volvo B12M		Plaxton Paragon	C49F	1993	Yellow Buses, 2011
VB2	FW	HF53OBH	Volvo B12M		Plaxton Paragon	C49F	1993	Yellow Buses, 2011
VM1	w	BF62UXU	Volvo B9TL		MCV	N41/22D	2012	

VP105-111

Volvo B7TL 10.1m — Plaxton President 4.4m — N41/20D* — 2000 — *seating varies

105	AV	W448BCW	107	AV	W451BCW	109	TV	W453BCW	111	AV	W457BCW
106	AV	W449BCW	108	AV	W452BCW	110	AV	W454BCW			

VE1-10

Volvo B7TL 10.4m — East Lancs Myllennium Vyking N45/19D — 2004

1	S	PG04WGN	4	S	PG04WGV	7	S	PG04WGY	9	S	PG04WHA
2	S	PG04WGP	5	S	PG04WGW	8	S	PG04WGZ	10	S	PG04WHB
3	S	PG04WGU	6	S	PG04WGX						

VLE1-26

Volvo B7TL 11m — East Lancs Myllennium Vyking N47/22D — 2004

1	V	PG04WHC	8	V	PG04WHL	15	V	PG04WHU	21	V	PA04CYC
2	V	PG04WHD	9	V	PG04WHM	16	V	PG04WHV	22	V	PA04CYE
3	V	PG04WHE	10	V	PG04WHN	17	V	PG04WHW	23	V	PA04CYF
4	V	PG04WHF	11	V	PG04WHP	18	V	PG04WHX	24	V	PA04CYG
5	V	PG04WHH	12	V	PG04WHR	19	V	PG04WHY	25	w	PA04CYH
6	V	PG04WHJ	13	V	PG04WHS	20	V	PG04WJA	26	V	PA04CYJ
7	V	PG04WHK	14	V	PG04WHT						

Depots and allocations:

Fulwell (Wellington Road) - FW

Dart	DP1	DP11	DPS655	DPS659	DPS661	DPS663	DPS665	DPS667
	DPS670	DPS681	DPS682	DPS684	DPS685	DPS686	DPS687	DPS688
	DPS689	DPS690	DPS691	DPS693				
Enviro 200	DE23	DE24	DE25	DE26	DE27	DE28	DE29	DE30
	DE31	DE109	DE110	DE111	DE112	DE113	DE114	DE115
	DE116	DE117	DE118	DE119	DE120	DE121	DE122	DE123
	DE124	DE125	DE126	DE127	DE128			
Enviro 200 Hybrid	HDE1	HDE2	HDE3	HDE4	HDE5			
Volvo B12M	VB1	VB2						
Olympian	VA7	VA8	VA9	VA10	VA46	VA48	VA49	VA54
	VA63	VA71	VA81	VA85	VA689	VA92		
Trident	TA204	TA205	TA206	TA207	TA208	TA209	TA210	TA211
	TA212	TA213	TA214	TA219	TA220	TA221	TA222	TA223
	TA224	TA225	TA313	TA314	TA315	TA316	TA317	TA318
	TA319	TA320	TA321	TA322	TA323	TA324	TA325	TA326
	TA327	TA328	TA329	TA330	TA331	TA332	TA333	TA334
	TA335	TA336	TA337	TA338	TA339	TA340	TA341	TA342
	TA343	TA344	TA345	TA346	TLA3	TLA4		
Scania DD	SLE45	SLE46	SLE47	SLE48	SLE49	SLE50	SLE51	SLE53
	SLE54	SLE55	SLE58	SLE59	SLE60	SLE61	SLE62	SLE63
	SLE64	SP26	SP27	SP28	SP52	SP53	SP54	SP55
	SP56	SP57	SP58	SP59	SP60	SP61	SP62	SP63
	SP64	SP65	SP66	SP67	SP88	SP89	SP90	SP91
	SP92	SP93	SP94	SP95	SP96	SP97	SP98	SP99
	SP100	SP101	SP102	SP103	SP104	SP105	SP106	SP107
	SP108							

Hounslow (Kingsley Road) - AV

Enviro 200	DLE1	DLE2	DLE3	DLE4	DLE5	DLE6	DLE7	DLE8
	DLE9	DLE10	DLE11	DLE12	DLE13	DLE14	DLE15	DLE16
	DLE17	DLE18	DLE19	DLE20	DLE21	DLE22	DLE23	DLE24
	DLE25							
Optare Tempo	OT1	OT2	OT3	OT4	OT5	OT6	OT7	OT8
	OT9	OT10	OT11	OT12	OT13	OT14	OT15	OT16
Volvo B7TL	VA74	VA80	VM1	VP105	VP106	VP107	VP108	VP110
	VP111							
Mercedes-Benz Citaro	MCL1	MCL2	MCL3	MCL4	MCL5	MCL6	MCL7	
Scania	SP5	SP6	SP7	SP8	SP9	SP10	SP11	SP12
	SP13	SP14	SP15	SP23	SP24	SP25	SP38	SP39
	SP41	SP42	SP43	SP44	SP45	SP46	SP47	SP48
	SP49	SP50	SP51	SP136	SP165	SP166	SP167	SP168
	SP169	SP170	SP171	SP172	SP173	SP174	SP175	SP176
	SP177	SP178	SP179	SP180	SP181	SP182	SP183	SP184
	SP185	SP186	SP187	SP188	SP189	SP190		
Enviro 400	ADE1	ADE2	ADE3	ADE4	ADE5	ADE6	ADE7	ADE8
	ADE9	ADE10	ADE11	ADE12	ADE13	ADE14	ADE15	ADE16
	ADE17	ADE18	ADE19	ADE20	ADE21	ADE22	ADE23	ADE24
	ADE25	ADE26	ADE27	ADE28	ADE29	ADE30	ADE31	ADE32
	ADE33	ADE34	ADE35	ADE36	ADE37	ADE38	ADE40	ADE41
	ADE42	ADE43	ADE44	ADE45				

Hounslow Heath (Pulborough Way) - HH

Dart	DPS582	DPS673	DPS674	DPS675	DPS677	DPS678	DPS679	DPS680
	DPS694	DPS707	DPS708	DPS709	DPS710	DPS711	DPS712	DPS713
	DPS714	DPS715	DPS716	DPS717				
Enviro 200	DE1	DE2	DE3	DE4	DE5	DE6	DE7	DE8
	DE9	DE10	DE11	DE12	DE13	DE14	DE15	DE16
Trident	TA215	TA216	TA217	TA218	TLA6	TLA8		
Scania OmniCity DD	SP1	SP2	SP3	SP4	SP16	SP17	SP18	SP19
	SP20	SP21	SP22	SP23	SP191	SP192	SP193	SP194
	SP195	SP196	SP197	SP198	SP199	SP200	SP201	SP202
	SP203	SP204	SP205	SP206				

Park Royal (Atlas Road) - PK

Enviro 200	DE76	DE77	DE78	DE79	DE80	DE81	DE82	DE83
	DE84	SDE11	SDE12	SDE13	SDE14	SDE15	SDE16	SDE17
Optare Versa	OV50	OV51	OV52	OV53	OV54	OV55	OV56	OV57
	OV58	OV59	OV60	OV61	OV62	OV63	OV64	OV65
	OV66							
Enviro 400	ADE32	ADE46	ADE47	ADE48	ADE49	ADE50	ADE51	ADE52
	ADE53	ADE54	ADE55	ADE57	ADE58	ADE59	ADE60	ADE61
	ADE62	ADE63	ADE64	ADE65	ADE66	ADE67	ADE68	ADE69
	ADE70	ADE71	ADE72	ADE73	ADE75	ADE76	ADE77	ADE78
	ADE793	ADE80	ADE81	ADE82	ADE83	ADE84		

Shepherd's Bush (Wells Road) - S

Dart	DPS688							
Enviro 200	DE32	DE33	DE34	DE35	DE36	DE37	DE38	DE39
	DE40	DE41	DE42	DE43	DE44	DE45	DE46	DE47
	DE48	DE49	DE74	DE85	DE86	DE87	DE88	DE89
	DE90	DE91	DE92	DE93	DE94	DE95	DE96	DE97
	DE98	DE99	DE100	DE101	DE102	DE103	DE104	DE105
	DE106	DE107	DE108					
Trident	TLA1	TLA2	TLA3	TLA4	TLA5	TLA6	TLA7	TLA17
	TLA18	TLA19	TLA20	TLA21	TLA22	TLA23	TLA24	TLA25
	TLA26	TLA27	TLA28	TLA29	TLA30			
Volvo B7TL	VE1	VE2	VE3	VE4	VE5	VE6	VE7	VE8
	VE10	VA62	VA64					
Scania	SLE43	SLE44	SP29	SP30	SP31	SP32	SP33	SP34
	SP35	SP36	SP37	SP38	SP39	SP40	SP109	SP110
	SP111	SP112	SP113	SP114	SP115	SP116	SP117	SP118
	SP119	SP120	SP121	SP122	SP123	SP124	SP125	SP126
	SP127	SP128	SP129	SP130	SP131	SP132	SP133	SP134
	SP135							
Enviro 400	ADH3	ADH4	ADH5	ADH6	ADH7	ADH8	ADH9	ADH10
	ADH11	ADH12	ADH13	ADH14	ADH15	ADH16	ADH17	ADH18
	ADH19	ADH20	ADH21	ADH22				

Stamford Brook (Chiswick High Road, Chiswick) - V

Dart	DPS581	DPS583	DPS586	DPS587	DPS664	DPS694	DPS701	DPS702
Versa	OV1	OV2	OV3	OV4	OV5	OV6	OV7	OV8
	OV9	OV10	OV11	OV12	OV13	OV14	OV15	OV16
	OV17	OV18	OV19					
Volvo B7TL	VE9	VLE1	VLE2	VLE3	VLE4	VLE5	VLE6	VLE7
	VLE8	VLE9	VLE10	VLE11	VLE12	VLE13	VLE14	VLE15
	VLE16	VLE17	VLE18	VLE19	VLE20	VLE21	VLE22	VLE23
	VLE24	VLE26						
Scania	SP137	SP138	SP139	SP140	SP141	SP142	SP143	SP144
	SP145	SP146	SP147	SP148	SP149	SP150	SP151	SP152
	SP153	SP154	SP155	SP156	SP157	SP158	SP159	SP160
	SP161	SP162	SP163	SP164				
Enviro 400 Hybrid	ADH1	ADH2	ADH23	ADH24	ADH25	ADH26	ADH27	ADH28
	ADH29	ADH30	ADH31	ADH32	ADH33	ADH34	ADH35	ADH36
	ADH37	ADH38	ADH39	ADH40	ADH41	ADH42	ADH43	ADH44
	ADH45	ADH46	ADH47	ADH48	ADH49	ADH50	ADH51	

Tolworth (Day's Yard, Kingston Road) - TV

Dart	DPS579	DPS580	DPS588	DPS589	DPS590	DPS591	DPS592	DPK613
	DPK614	DPK615	DPK624	DPK625	DPS648	DPS649	DPS650	DPS651
	DPS652	DPS653	DPS654	DPS656	DPS657	DPS658	DPS660	DPS662
	DPS666	DPS721	DPS722					
Enviro 200	DE57	DE58	DE59	DE60	DE61	DE62	DE63	DE64
	DE65	DE66	DE67	DE72	SDE1	SDE2	SDE3	SDE4
	SDE5	SDE6	SDE7	SDE8	SDE9	SDE10		
Volvo B7TL	VP109							
Trident	TA229	TA230	TA231	TA232	TA233	TA234	TA235	TA236
	TA237	TA238	TA239	TA240	TA241	TA242	TA243	TA244
	TA245	TA246	TA247	TA248	TA249	TA250	TA281	TA282
	TA283	TA284	TA285	TA286	TA312	TLA5		

QUALITY LINE

HR Richmond Ltd, Blenheim Road, Epsom, KT19 9AF

DD1-10

						ADL Trident 2	10.1m		ADL Enviro 400			N41/26D	2007			
01	EB	SK07DZA	04	EB	SK07DZD	07	EB	SK07DZG	09	EB	SK07DZJ
02	EB	SK07DZB	05	EB	SK07DZE	08	EB	SK07DZH	10	EB	SK07DZL
03	EB	SK07DZC	06	EB	SK07DZF						

DD11	EB	SN11BVG	ADL Trident 2 10.1m	ADL Enviro 400	N41/24D	2011
DD12	EB	SN11BVH	ADL Trident 2 10.1m	ADL Enviro 400	N41/24D	2011
DD13	EB	YX61FYR	ADL E40D 10.2m	ADL Enviro 400	N41/24D	2012

EP01	EC	FJ11GLF	Volvo B9R	Caetano Levanté	C48FT	2011
EP02	EC	FJ11GMV	Volvo B9R	Caetano Levanté	C48FT	2011
EP03	EC	FJ61EYK	Volvo B9R	Caetano Levanté	C48FT	2012
EP04	EC	FJ61EYL	Volvo B9R	Caetano Levanté	C48FT	2012

MCL1	EB	BW03ZMZ	Mercedes-Benz Citaro O530	Mercedes-Benz	N38D	2003

MCL8-17

									Mercedes-Benz Citaro O530		Mercedes-Benz		N38D	2003		
08	EB	BN12EOP	11	EB	BN12EOT	14	EB	BN12EOW	16	EB	BN12EOY
09	EB	BN12EOR	12	EB	BN12EOU	15	EB	BN12EOX	17	EB	BN12EOZ
10	EB	BN12EOS	13	EB	BN12EOV						

OP04-13

									Optare Solo M850		Optare		N25F	2002-03		
04	EB	YE52FHL	07	EB	YE52FHO	10	EB	YE52FHS	12	EB	YN03ZXF
05	EB	YE52FHM	08	EB	YE52FHP	11	EB	YE52FGU	13	EB	YN53SWF
06	EB	YE52FHN	09	EB	YE52FHR						

OP14-21

									Optare Solo M850		Optare		N25F	2004		
14	EB	YN53SUF	16	EB	YN53SVL	18	EB	YN53SVP	20	EB	YN53ZXA
15	EB	YN53SVK	17	EB	YN53SVO	19	EB	YN53SVR	21	EB	YN53ZXB

OP23-30

									Optare Solo M880		Optare		N24F	2009		
23	EB	YJ09MHK	25	EB	YJ09MHM	27	EB	YJ09MHO	29	EB	YJ09MHV
24	EB	YJ09MHL	26	EB	YJ09MHN	28	EB	YJ09MHU	30	EB	YJ09MHX

Epsom Coaches was founded by the Richmond family in 1920 and in April 2012 Epsom Coaches, joined the French group RATP. Although historically known for the coach business, Epsom has expanded into bus operation under the Quality Line name. MCL9, BN12EOR, operates route 465 in Dorking. *Dave Heath*

Optare Versa OV05, YJ60KGK, is seen at Hatton Cross while operating route X26 which connects Croydon with Heathrow airport. *Dave Heath*

OP31	EB	YJ11EJA	Optare Solo M850			Optare		N23F	2011		
OP32	EB	YJ11EJC	Optare Solo M850			Optare		N23F	2011		
OP33	EB	YJ11EJD	Optare Solo M850			Optare		N23F	2011		
OP34	EB	YJ13HJN	Optare Solo M890 SR			Optare		N25F	2013		

OPL01-08			Optare Solo M970 SR			Optare		N25D	2012		
01	EB	YJ62FUD	03	EB	YJ62FVN	05	EB	YJ62FWB	07	EB	YJ62FXG
02	EB	YJ62FUG	04	EB	YJ62FVT	06	EB	YJ62FXA	08	EB	YJ62FXK

OV01-13			Optare Versa V1110			Optare		N28D*	2010-12	*9-13 are N29D	
01	EB	YJ60KGA	05	EB	YJ60KGK	08	EB	YJ60KGP	11	EB	YJ12PKY
02	EB	YJ60KGE	06	EB	YJ60KGN	09	EB	YJ12PKV	12	EB	YJ12PKZ
03	EB	YJ60KGF	07	EB	YJ60KGO	10	EB	YJ12PKX	13	EB	YJ12PLF
04	EB	YJ60KGG									

SD38-42			ADL Dart SLF 9m			East Lancs Myllennium		N26F	2005		
38	EB	PL05PLN	40	EB	PL05PLU	41	EB	PL05PLV	42	EB	PL05PLX
39	EB	PL05PLO									

SD43-51			ADL Dart 4 9.5m			East Lancs Esteem		N25D	2007		
43	EB	PE56UFH	46	EB	PE56UFL	48	EB	PE56UFN	50	EB	PE56UFR
44	EB	PE56UFJ	47	EB	PE56UFM	49	EB	PE56UFP	51	EB	PE56UFS
45	EB	PE56UFK									

SD52	EB	PN07KRZ	ADL Dart 4 9m	East Lancs Esteem	N23F	2007
SD53	EB	PN07KSE	ADL Dart 4 9m	East Lancs Esteem	N23F	2007
SD54	EB	LJ08RJY	ADL Dart 4 8.9m	ADL Enviro 200	N26F	2008

503	EC	YN08DMV	Mercedes-Benz Vario O816	Plaxton Cheetah	C25F	2008
504	EC	YN08DMX	Mercedes-Benz Vario O816	Plaxton Cheetah	C25F	2008
716	EC	BU04EXV	Setra S315 GT-HD	Setra	C53F	2004
717	EC	BU04EXW	Setra S315 GT-HD	Setra	C53F	2004
718	EC	BU04EXX	Setra S315 GT-HD	Setra	C53F	2004
719	EC	BX54ECF	Setra S315 GT-HD	Setra	C53F	2005
720	EC	BX54ECJ	Setra S315 GT-HD	Setra	C53F	2005

Optare Solo OPL08, YJ62FXK, is one of the 9.7 metre versions of the latest model. Initially introduced as an expansion of the range, the SR is now the only Solo model produced. It was pictured in Epsom during August 2013. *Mark Lyons*

813	EC	BU53ZWN	Setra S315 GT-HD	Setra	C48FT	2004	
814	EC	BU53ZWP	Setra S315 GT-HD	Setra	C48FT	2004	
815	EC	BU53ZWR	Setra S315 GT-HD	Setra	C48FT	2004	
816	EC	BU04EXT	Setra S315 GT-HD	Setra	C48FT	2004	
901	EC	BU06CSF	Setra S416 GT-HD	Setra	C49FT	2006	
902	EC	BU06CSO	Setra S416 GT-HD	Setra	C49FT	2006	
903	EC	BX56VTY	Setra S416 GT-HD	Setra	C44FT	2007	
904	EC	BX56VTZ	Setra S416 GT-HD	Setra	C44FT	2007	
905	EC	BX58URT	Setra S416 GT-HD	Setra	C53FT	2009	
906	EC	BX60OPD	Setra S416 GT-HD	Setra	C53FT	2011	
907	EC	BX60OPE	Setra S416 GT-HD	Setra	C53FT	2011	

Web: www.epsomcoaches.com

Depots and allocations:

Epsom (Blenheim Road) - EB

Solo	OP01	OP02	OP03	OP04	OP05	OP06	OP07	OP08
	OP09	OP10	OP11	OP12	OP13	OP14	OP15	OP16
	OP17	OP18	OP19	OP20	OP21	OP23	OP24	OP25
	OP26	OP27	OP29	OP30	OP31	OP32	OP33	
Dart	ET01	SD26	SD27	SD28	SD33	SD38	SD39	SD40
	SD41	SD42						
Dart 4	SD43	SD44	SD45	SD46	SD47	SD48	SD49	SD50
	SD51	SD52	SD53	SD54				
Versa	OV1	OV2	OV3	OV4	OV5	OV6	OV7	OV8
Citaro	MCL1							
Trident 2	DD01	DD02	DD03	DD04	DD05	DD06	DD07	DD08
	DD09	DD10	DD11	DD12				

Epsom coach unit (Blenheim Road) - EC

Mercedes-Benz	503	504						
Setra S315	716	717	718	719	720	811	812	813
	814	815	816					
Setra S416	901	902	903	904	905	906	907	
Volvo B9R	EP01	EP02	EP03	EP04				

STAGECOACH LONDON

East London Buses Ltd; South East London & Kent Bus Co Ltd,
Stephenson Street, Canning Town, London, E16 4SA

10101-10154 ADL E40D 10.2m / ADL Enviro 400 / N41/24D 2012

10101	WH	LX12DAU	10115	T	LX12DDE	10129	TL	LX12DFD	10142	TB	LX12DFZ
10102	WH	LX12DBO	10116	T	LX12DDF	10130	TL	LX12DFE	10143	TB	LX12DGE
10103	WH	LX12DBU	10117	T	LX12DDJ	10131	TL	LX12DFF	10144	TB	LX12DGF
10104	WH	LX12DBV	10118	T	LX12DDK	10132	TL	LX12DFG	10145	TB	LX12DGO
10105	WH	LX12DBY	10119	T	LX12DDL	10133	TL	LX12DFJ	10146	TB	LX12DGU
10106	WH	LX12DBZ	10120	T	LX12DDN	10134	TL	LX12DFK	10147	TB	LX12DGV
10107	WH	LX12DCE	10121	T	LX12DDO	10135	TL	LX12DFL	10148	TB	LX12DGY
10108	WH	LX12DCF	10122	T	LX12DDU	10136	TL	LX12DFN	10149	TB	LX12DGZ
10109	WH	LX12DCO	10123	T	LX12DDV	10137	TL	LX12DFO	10150	TB	LX12DHA
10110	WH	LX12DCU	10124	TL	LX12DDY	10138	TL	LX12DFP	10151	TB	LX12DHC
10111	WH	LX12DCV	10125	TL	LX12DDZ	10139	TB	LX12DFU	10152	TB	LX12DHD
10112	WH	LX12DCY	10126	TL	LX12DEU	10140	TB	LX12DFV	10153	TB	LX12DHE
10113	T	LX12DCZ	10127	TL	LX12DFA	10141	TB	LX12DFY	10154	TB	LX12DHF
10114	T	LX12DDA	10128	TL	LX12DFC						

10155-10163 ADL E40D 10.2m / ADL Enviro 400 / N41/24D 2012

10155	NS	EU62AXT	10158	NS	EU62AYE	10160	NS	EU62AZD	10162	NS	EU62AAO
10156	NS	EU62AXV	10159	NS	EU62AZA	10161	NS	EU62AAE	10163	NS	EU62ADZ
10157	NS	EU62AYB									

10164-10196 ADL E40D 10.2m / ADL Enviro 400 / N41/24D 2013-14

10164	TB	SN63JVM	10173	T	SN63JVY	10181	T	SN63JWJ	10189	TB	SN63NBK
10165	RM	SN63JVO	10174	T	SN63JVZ	10182	T	SN63JWK	10190	TB	SN63NBL
10166	RM	SN63JVP	10175	T	SN63JWA	10183	T	SN63JWL	10191	TB	SN63NBM
10167	RM	SN63JVR	10176	T	SN63JWC	10184	TB	SN63NBD	10192	TB	SN63NBO
10168	RM	SN63JVT	10177	T	SN63JWD	10185	TB	SN63NBE	10193	TB	SN63NBX
10169	RM	SN63JVU	10178	T	SN63JWE	10186	TB	SN63NBF	10194	TB	SN63NBY
10170	RM	SN63JVV	10179	T	SN63JWF	10187	TB	SN63NBG	10195	TB	SN63NBZ
10171	RM	SN63JVW	10180	T	SN63JWG	10188	TB	SN63NBJ	10196	PD	SN63NCA
10172	T	SN63JVX									

One of nine Enviro 400s for Stagecoach London in 2012, 10161, EU62AAE, is shown working route 175 from Romford. *Terry Longhurst*

In a move which surprised many, Stagecoach re-entered the London bus market in October 2010 when it acquired from its administrators the East London operation that it had sold to Macquarie in 2006. The business, for which Stagecoach paid just short of £60m, now operates as a stand-alone unit and, crucially, buses will be leased rather than purchased to avoid the need to cascade London specification vehicles to provincial fleets. As the efficiency of the hybrid buses increases a further order has been placed for the delivery at the end of 2013. From the 2012 intake for route 15, 12142, LX61DDV, is seen in Trafalgar Square. *Richard Godfrey*

12128-12153

ADL E40H 10.2m — ADL Enviro 400H — N37/24D — 2012

12128	BW	LX61DFD	12135	BW	LX61DFN	12142	BW	LX61DDV	12148	BW	LX61DCO
12129	BW	LX61DFE	12136	BW	LX61DFO	12143	BW	LX61DDY	12149	BW	LX61DCU
12130	BW	LX61DFF	12137	BW	LX61DFP	12144	BW	LX61DDZ	12150	BW	LX61DCV
12131	BW	LX61DFG	12138	BW	LX61DDL	12145	BW	LX61DEU	12151	BW	LX61DCY
12132	BW	LX61DFJ	12139	BW	LX61DDN	12146	BW	LX61DFA	12152	BW	LX61DCZ
12133	BW	LX61DFK	12140	BW	LX61DDO	12147	BW	LX61DFC	12153	BW	LX61DDA
12134	BW	LX61DFL	12141	BW	LX61DDU						

12261-12323

ADL E40H 10.2m — ADL Enviro 400 — N37/24D — 2013-14

12261	PD	-	12277	PD	-	12293	PD	-	12309	PD	-
12262	PD	-	12278	PD	-	12294	PD	-	12310	PD	-
12263	PD	-	12279	PD	-	12295	PD	-	12311	PD	-
12264	PD	-	12280	PD	-	12296	PD	-	12312	PD	-
12265	PD	-	12281	PD	-	12297	PD	-	12313	PD	-
12266	PD	-	12282	PD	-	12298	PD	-	12314	PD	-
12267	PD	-	12283	PD	-	12299	PD	-	12315	PD	-
12268	PD	-	12284	PD	-	12300	PD	-	12316	PD	-
12269	PD	-	12285	PD	-	12301	PD	-	12317	PD	-
12270	PD	-	12286	PD	-	12302	PD	-	12318	PD	-
12271	PD	-	12287	PD	-	12303	PD	-	12319	PD	-
12272	PD	-	12288	PD	-	12304	PD	-	12320	PD	-
12273	PD	-	12289	PD	-	12305	PD	-	12321	PD	-
12274	PD	-	12290	PD	-	12306	PD	-	12322	PD	-
12275	PD	-	12291	PD	-	12307	PD	-	12323	PD	-
12275	PD	-	12292	PD	-	12308	PD	-			

Purchased during the period when the London operations were under Australian-based Macquarie Bank ownership were 174 Scania OmniCity double-deck buses. Illustrating the model is 15078, LX09AFF, which was working route 177 in Peckham when pictured. *Richard Godfrey*

15001-15096

Scania OmniCity N230 UB 10.8m   N41/22D   2008-09

15001	RM	LX58CDV	15026	RM	LX58CFV	15050	PD	LX09ABV	15074	PD	LX09AEY
15002	RM	LX58CDY	15027	RM	LX58CFY	15051	PD	LX09ABZ	15075	PD	LX09AEZ
15003	RM	LX58CDZ	15028	RM	LX58CFZ	15052	PD	LX09ACF	15076	PD	LX09AFA
15004	RM	LX58CEA	15029	RM	LX58CGE	15053	PD	LX09ACJ	15077	PD	LX09AFE
15005	RM	LX58CEF	15030	RM	LX58CGF	15054	PD	LX09ACO	15078	PD	LX09AFF
15006	RM	LX58CEJ	15031	RM	LX58CGG	15055	PD	LX09ADZ	15079	PD	LX09AFJ
15007	RM	LX58CEK	15032	RM	LX58CGK	15056	PD	LX09AEA	15080	PD	LX09AFK
15008	RM	LX58CEN	15033	RM	LX58CGO	15057	PD	LX09AEB	15081	PD	LX09AFN
15009	RM	LX58CEO	15034	RM	LX58CGU	15058	PD	LX09AEC	15082	PD	LX09AFO
15010	RM	LX58CEU	15035	RM	LX58CGV	15059	PD	LX09AED	15083	PD	LX09AFU
15011	RM	LX58CEV	15036	PD	LX58CGY	15060	PD	LX09AEE	15084	PD	LX09AFV
15012	RM	LX58CEY	15037	PD	LX58CGZ	15061	PD	LX09AEF	15085	PD	LX09AFY
15014	RM	LX58CFD	15038	PD	LX58CHC	15062	PD	LX09AEG	15086	PD	LX09AFZ
15015	RM	LX58CFE	15039	PD	LX58CHD	15063	PD	LX09AEJ	15087	PD	LX09AGO
15016	RM	LX58CFF	15040	PD	LX09AAO	15064	PD	LX09AEK	15088	PD	LX09AGU
15017	RM	LX58CFG	15041	PD	LX09AAU	15065	PD	LX09AEL	15089	PD	LX09AGV
15018	RM	LX58CFJ	15042	PD	LX09AAV	15066	PD	LX09AEM	15090	PD	LX09AGY
15019	RM	LX58CFK	15043	PD	LX09AAY	15067	PD	LX09AEN	15091	PD	LX09AGZ
15020	RM	LX58CFL	15044	PD	LX09AAZ	15068	PD	LX09AEO	15092	PD	LX09AHA
15021	RM	LX58CFM	15045	PD	LX09ABF	15069	PD	LX09AEP	15093	PD	LX09AHC
15022	RM	LX58CFN	15046	PD	LX09ABK	15070	PD	LX09AET	15094	PD	LX09AHD
15023	RM	LX58CFO	15047	PD	LX09ABN	15071	PD	LX09AEU	15095	PD	LX09AHE
15024	RM	LX58CFP	15048	PD	LX09ABO	15072	PD	LX09AEV	15096	PD	LX09AHF
15025	RM	LX58CFU	15049	PD	LX09ABU	15073	PD	LX09AEW			

15097-15124

Scania OmniCity N230 UB 10.8m   N41/22D   2009

15097	BW	LX09FYS	15104	BW	LX09FZA	15111	BW	LX09FZH	15118	BW	LX09FZP
15098	BW	LX09FYT	15105	BW	LX09FZB	15112	BW	LX09FZJ	15119	BW	LX09FZR
15099	BW	LX09FYU	15106	BW	LX09FZC	15113	BW	LX09FZK	15120	BW	LX09FZS
15100	BW	527CLT	15107	BW	LX09FZD	15114	BW	LX09FZL	15121	BW	LX09FZT
15101	BW	LX09FYW	15108	BW	LX09FZE	15115	BW	LX09FZM	15122	BW	LX09FZU
15102	BW	LX09FYY	15109	BW	LX09FZF	15116	BW	LX09FZN	15123	BW	LX09FZV
15103	BW	LX09FYZ	15110	BW	LX09FZG	15117	BW	LX09FZO	15124	BW	LX09FZW

15125-15174   Scania OmniCity N230 UB 10.8m   N41/22D   2009-10

15125	T	LX59CLU	15138	T	LX59CNC	15151	T	LX59COJ	15163	T	LX59CRJ
15126	T	LX59CLV	15139	T	LX59CNE	15152	T	LX59COU	15164	T	LX59CRK
15127	T	LX59CLY	15140	T	LX59CNF	15153	T	LX59CPE	15165	T	LX59CRU
15128	T	LX59CLZ	15141	T	LX59CNJ	15154	T	LX59CPF	15166	T	LX59CRV
15129	T	LX59CME	15142	T	LX59CNK	15155	T	LX59CPK	15167	T	LX59CRZ
15130	T	LX59CMF	15143	T	LX59CNN	15156	T	LX59CPN	15168	T	LX59CSF
15131	T	LX59CMK	15144	T	LX59CNO	15157	T	LX59CPO	15169	T	LX59CSO
15132	T	LX59CMO	15145	T	LX59CNU	15158	T	LX59CPU	15170	T	LX10AUC
15133	T	LX59CMU	15146	T	LX59CNV	15159	T	LX59CPV	15171	T	LX10AUE
15134	T	LX59CMV	15147	T	LX59CNY	15160	T	LX59CPY	15172	T	LX10AUF
15135	T	LX59CMY	15148	T	LX59CNZ	15161	T	LX59CPZ	15173	T	LX10AUH
15136	T	LX59CMZ	15149	T	LX59COA	15162	T	LX59CRF	15174	T	LX10AUJ
15137	T	LX59CNA	15150	T	LX59COH						

17001	T	S801BWC	Dennis Trident 10.5m	Alexander ALX400 4.2m	N51/22D	1999	displays fleet number TA1
17342	w	X342NNO	Dennis Trident 10.5m	Alexander ALX400 4.4m	N45/23F	2000	

17362-17434   Dennis Trident 10.5m   Alexander ALX400 4.4m   N45/22D   2001

17362	RMt	Y362NHK	17396	TLt	LX51FHO	17407	u	Y407NHK	17426	RMt	LX51FJY
17363	RMt	Y363NHK	17397	RMt	Y367NHK	17408	u	LX51FHU	17427	PD	LX51FKA
17364	RMt	Y364NHK	17398	RMt	Y368NHK	17409	RMt	Y409NHK	17431	u	LX51FKE
17368	RMt	Y368NHK	17399	RMt	LX51FHP	17419	RMt	LX51FJJ	17432	u	LX51FKF
17370	w	Y509NHK	17401	u	Y401NHK	17423	RM	LX51FJP	17433	u	LX51FKG
17395	RMt	Y395NHK	17404	PD	Y404NHK	17425	RM	LX51FJZ	17434	RMt	Y434NHK

17440-17531   Dennis Trident 9.9m   Alexander ALX400   N43/19D   2001

17440	PD	Y522NHK	17478	TL	LX51FLP	17500	WH	LX51FNC	17518	NS	LX51FNW
17441	PD	Y441NHK	17482	T	LX51FLZ	17501	WH	LX51FND	17519	RM	LX51FNY
17444	u	LX51FKO	17484	u	LX51FMC	17503	PD	LX51FNF	17520	NS	LX51FNZ
17445	u	Y445NHK	17485	TL	LX51FMD	17504	PD	LX51FNG	17521	WH	LX51FOA
17447	u	Y447NHK	17486	PD	LX51FME	17505	PD	LX51FNH	17522	T	LX51FOC
17448	NS	Y448NHK	17487	PD	LX51FMF	17506	PD	LX51FNJ	17523	T	LX51FOD
17449	TB	Y449NHK	17488	u	LX51FMG	17507	T	LX51FNK	17524	T	LX51FOF
17450	u	Y524NHK	17489	WH	LX51FMJ	17508	PD	LX51FNL	17525	T	LX51FOH
17451	BW	LX51FKR	17490	WH	LX51FMK	17509	WH	LX51FNM	17526	BK	LX51FOJ
17452	WH	Y452NHK	17493	WH	LX51FMO	17510	u	LX51FNN	17527	WH	LX51FOK
17453	u	Y453NHK	17494	WH	LX51FMP	17511	PD	LX51FNO	17528	WH	LX51FOM
17454	WH	Y454NHK	17495	WH	LX51FMU	17512	PD	LX51FNP	17529	WH	LX51FON
17460	WH	Y529NHK	17497	WH	LX51FMY	17515	WH	LX51FNT	17529	WH	LX51FON
17466	PD	LX51FLC	17498	WH	LX51FMZ	17516	RM	LX51FNU	17531	TB	LX51FOT
17467	RM	LX51FLD	17499	WH	LX51FNA	17517	T	LX51FNV			

Many of the early Tridents used in London have been withdrawn in a change of policy that has seen fewer vehicles being converted to single door for provincial use. Stratford is the location for this view of 17865. LX03NFK, working route 241.
Dave Heath

17535-17591 — Dennis Trident 9.9m — Alexander ALX400 — N43/20D — 2002

No.		Reg	No.		Reg	No.		Reg	No.		Reg
17535	WH	LY02OAA	17552	WH	LY02OBD	17566	PD	LV52HDZ	17578	NS	LV52HFL
17536	WH	LY02OAB	17553	WH	LY02OBE	17567	PD	LV52HEJ	17580	WH	LV52HFN
17537	PD	LY02OAC	17554	WH	LY02OBF	17568	T	LV52HFU	17581	BK	LV52HFO
17538	PD	LY02OAD	17555	WH	LY02OBG	17569	NS	LV52HFA	17582	BK	LV52HFP
17540	PD	LY02OAG	17556	WH	LY02OBH	17570	PD	LV52HFB	17583	BK	LV52HFR
17541	T	LY02OAN	17557	WH	LY02OBJ	17571	PD	LV52HFC	17585	BK	LV52HFT
17543	T	LY02OAP	17559	NS	LY02OBL	17572	PD	LV52HFD	17586	WH	LV52HFU
17545	WH	LY02OAU	17560	PD	LY02OBM	17573	PD	LV52HFE	17587	BK	LV52HFW
17546	WH	LY02OAV	17561	PD	LV52USV	17574	NS	LV52HFF	17588	WH	LV52HFX
17547	WH	LY02OAW	17562	NS	LV52HDO	17575	T	LV52HFH	17589	WH	LV52HFY
17549	WH	LY02OAZ	17563	PD	LV52HDU	17576	WH	LV52HFJ	17590	PD	LV52HFZ
17550	WH	LY02OBB	17564	NS	LV52HDX	17577	NS	LV52HFK	17591	PD	LV52HGA
17551	WH	LY02OBC	17565	NS	LV52HDY						

17740-17853 — TransBus Trident 10.5m — TransBus ALX400 4.4m — N45/22D — 2003

No.		Reg	No.		Reg	No.		Reg	No.		Reg
17740	BW	LY52ZDX	17770	NS	LX03BVF	17798	T	LX03BWM	17826	T	LX03BXZ
17741	BW	LY52ZDZ	17771	NS	LX03BVG	17799	T	LX03BWN	17827	T	LX03BYA
17742	BW	LY52ZFA	17772	NS	LX03BVH	17800	T	LX03BWP	17828	T	LX03BYB
17743	BW	LY52ZFB	17773	NS	LX03BVJ	17801	T	LX03BWU	17829	NS	LX03BYC
17744	BW	LY52ZFC	17774	NS	LX03BVK	17802	T	LX03BWV	17830	NS	LX03BYD
17745	T	LY52ZFD	17775	NS	LX03BVL	17803	T	LX03BWW	17831	TB	LX03BYF
17746	T	LY52ZFE	17776	NS	LX03BVM	17804	T	LX03BWY	17832	TB	LX03BYG
17747	T	LY52ZFF	17777	NS	LX03BVN	17805	T	LX03BWZ	17833	TB	LX03BYH
17748	NS	LY52ZFG	17778	NS	LX03BVP	17806	T	LX03BXA	17834	WH	LX03BYJ
17749	T	LY52ZFH	17779	TB	LX03BVR	17807	T	LX03BXB	17835	NS	LX03BYL
17750	BW	LX03BTE	17780	TB	LX03BVS	17808	T	LX03BXC	17836	PD	LX03BYM
17751	BW	LX03BTF	17781	BW	LX03BVT	17809	T	LX03BXD	17837	PD	LX03BYN
17752	BW	LX03BTU	17782	BW	LX03BVU	17810	T	LX03BXE	17838	PD	LX03BYP
17753	BW	LX03BTV	17783	BW	LX03BVV	17811	T	LX03BXF	17839	PD	LX03BYR
17754	BW	LX03BTY	17784	BW	LX03BVW	17812	T	LX03BXG	17840	PD	LX03BYS
17755	BW	LX03BTZ	17785	BW	LX03BVY	17813	T	LX03BXH	17841	T	LX03BYT
17756	BW	LX03BUA	17786	BW	LX03BVZ	17814	T	LX03BXJ	17842	TB	LX03BYU
17757	BW	LX03BUE	17787	BW	LX03BWA	17815	WH	LX03BXK	17843	TB	LX03BYV
17759	NS	LX03BUH	17788	TB	LX03BWB	17816	WH	LX03BXL	17844	TB	LX03BYW
17760	NS	LX03BUJ	17789	PD	LX03BWC	17817	WH	LX03BXM	17845	T	LX03BYY
17761	NS	LX03BUP	17790	PD	LX03BWD	17818	BW	LX03BXN	17846	BW	LX03BYZ
17762	NS	LX03BUU	17791	NS	LX03BWE	17819	BW	LX03BXP	17847	WH	LX03BZA
17763	NS	LX03BUV	17792	NS	LX03BWF	17820	WH	LX03BXR	17848	WH	LX03BZB
17764	NS	LX03BUW	17793	NS	LX03BWG	17821	WH	LX03BXS	17849	WH	LX03BZC
17765	NS	LX03BVA	17794	TB	LX03BWH	17822	WH	LX03BXU	17850	WH	LX03BZD
17766	NS	LX03BVB	17795	TB	LX03BWJ	17823	WH	LX03BXV	17851	T	LX03BZE
17767	NS	LX03BVC	17796	T	LX03BWK	17824	WH	LX03BXW	17852	T	LX03BZF
17768	NS	LX03BVD	17797	T	LX03BWL	17825	WH	LX03BXY	17853	T	LX03BZG
17769	NS	LX03BVE									

17854	NS	LX03BZH	TransBus Trident 9.9m		TransBus ALX400 4.4m	N43/21D	2003

Dalson Lane in April 2013 and Stagecoach 2-axle Trident 1 17751, LX03BTF heads for Canary Wharf. It is one of sixty of the type allocated to Bow depot. *Dave Heath*

17855-17933 — TransBus Trident 10.5m — TransBus ALX400 4.4m — N45/22D — 2003

17855	BW	LX03NEU	17876	T	LX03NGE	17896	BK	LX03ORJ	17915	WH	LX03OSL
17856	BK	LX03NEY	17877	T	LX03NGF	17897	BK	LX03ORK	17916	WH	LX03OSM
17857	BK	LX03NFA	17878	BW	LX03NGJ	17898	BK	LX03ORN	17917	WH	LX03OSN
17858	BK	LX03NFC	17879	BK	LX03NGN	17899	BK	LX03ORP	17918	WH	LX03OSP
17859	BK	LX03NFD	17880	BK	LX03NGU	17900	BK	LX03ORS	17919	WH	LX03OSR
17860	BK	LX03NFE	17881	BK	LX03NGV	17901	BK	LX03ORT	17920	WH	LX03OSU
17861	BK	LX03NFF	17882	BK	LX03NGY	17902	BK	LX03ORU	17921	WH	LX03OSV
17862	BK	LX03NFG	17883	BK	LX03NGZ	17903	WH	LX03ORV	17922	WH	LX03OSW
17863	BK	LX03NFH	17884	BK	LX03NHA	17904	BK	LX03ORW	17923	WH	LX03OSY
17864	TB	LX03NFJ	17885	BK	LX03OPT	17905	T	LX03ORY	17924	WH	LX03OSZ
17865	WH	LX03NFK	17886	BK	LX03OPU	17906	T	LX03ORZ	17925	WH	LX03OTA
17866	TB	LX03NFL	17887	BK	LX03OPV	17907	T	LX03OSA	17926	WH	LX03OTB
17867	NS	LX03NFM	17888	BK	LX03OPW	17908	T	LX03OSB	17927	WH	LX03OTC
17868	NS	LX03NFN	17889	WH	LX03OPY	17909	WH	LX03OSC	17928	WH	LX03OTD
17869	NS	LX03NFP	17890	WH	LX03OPZ	17910	WH	LX03OSD	17929	WH	LX03OTE
17870	NS	LX03NFR	17891	WH	LX03ORA	17911	WH	LX03OSE	17930	WH	LX03OTF
17871	T	LX03NFT	17892	T	LX03ORC	17912	WH	LX03OSG	17931	WH	LX03OTG
17873	WH	LX03NFV	17893	BK	LX03ORF	17913	WH	LX03OSJ	17932	WH	LX03OTH
17874	NS	LX03NFY	17894	BK	LX03ORG	17914	WH	LX03OSK	17933	WH	LX03OTJ
17875	T	LX03NFZ	17895	BK	LX03ORH						

17934-17975 — TransBus Trident 10.5m — TransBus ALX400 — N45/22D — 2003

17934	WH	LX53JXU	17945	PD	LX53JYH	17956	PD	LX53JYW	17966	TB	LX53JZJ
17935	WH	LX53JXV	17946	PD	LX53JYJ	17957	PD	LX53JYY	17967	TB	LX53JZK
17936	WH	LX53JXW	17947	PD	LX53JYK	17958	PD	LX53JYZ	17968	TB	LX53JZL
17937	WH	LX53JXY	17948	PD	LX53JYL	17959	PD	LX53JZA	17969	TB	LX53JZM
17938	WH	LX53JYA	17949	PD	LX53JYN	17960	PD	LX53JZC	17970	TB	LX53JZN
17939	WH	LX53JYB	17950	PD	LX53JYO	17961	PD	LX53JZD	17971	TB	LX53JZO
17940	WH	LX53JYC	17951	PD	LX53JYP	17962	PD	LX53JZE	17972	TB	LX53JZP
17941	WH	LX53JYD	17952	PD	LX53JYR	17963	PD	LX53JZF	17973	TB	LX53JZR
17942	WH	LX53JYE	17953	PD	LX53JYT	17964	PD	LX53JZG	17974	TB	LX53JZT
17943	WH	LX53JYF	17954	PD	LX53JYU	17965	TB	LX53JZH	17975	TB	LX53JZU
17944	WH	LX53JYG	17955	PD	LX53JYV						

17976-17999 — TransBus Trident 9.9m — TransBus ALX400 — N43/20D — 2004

17976	NS	LX53JZV	17982	NS	LX53KAU	17988	NS	LX53KBO	17994	NS	LX53KCC
17977	NS	LX53JZW	17983	NS	LX53KBE	17989	NS	LX53KBP	17995	NS	LX53KCE
17978	NS	LX53KAE	17984	NS	LX53KBF	17990	NS	LX53KBV	17996	NS	LX53KCF
17979	NS	LX53KAJ	17985	NS	LX53KBJ	17991	NS	LX53KBW	17997	NS	LX53KCG
17980	NS	LX53KAK	17986	NS	LX53KBK	17992	NS	LX53KBZ	17998	NS	LX53KCJ
17981	NS	LX53KAO	17987	NS	LX53KBN	17993	NS	LX53KCA	17999	NS	LX53KCK

At the end of July 2013 the number of Trident buses with Stagecoach London stood at 519 with a further 235 Trident 2s. 17846, LX03BYZ, was pictured working route 15 from West Ham, though it has subsequently moved to Bow.
Terry Longhurst

18201-18265   TransBus Trident 10.5m   TransBus ALX400   N45/22D   2004

18201	BW	LX04FWL	18218	BW	LX04FXF	18234	BW	LX04FYA	18250	WH	LX04FYT
18202	BW	LX04FWM	18219	BW	LX04FXG	18235	BW	LX04FYB	18251	WH	LX04FYU
18203	BW	LX04FWN	18220	BW	LX04FXH	18236	WH	LX04FYC	18252	WH	LX04FYV
18204	BW	LX04FWP	18221	BW	LX04FXJ	18237	WH	LX04FYD	18253	WH	LX04FYW
18205	BW	LX04FWR	18222	BW	LX04FXK	18238	WH	LX04FYE	18254	WH	LX04FYY
18206	BW	LX04FWS	18223	BW	LX04FXL	18239	WH	LX04FYF	18255	WH	LX04FYZ
18207	BW	LX04FWT	18224	BW	LX04FXM	18240	WH	LX04FYG	18256	WH	LX04FZA
18208	BW	LX04FWU	18225	BW	LX04FXP	18241	WH	LX04FYH	18257	WH	LX04FZB
18209	BW	LX04FWV	18226	BW	LX04FXR	18242	WH	LX04FYK	18258	WH	LX04FZC
18210	BW	LX04FWW	18227	BW	LX04FXS	18243	WH	LX04FYL	18259	WH	LX04FZD
18211	BW	LX04FWY	18228	BW	LX04FXT	18244	WH	LX04FYM	18260	WH	LX04FZE
18212	BW	LX04FWZ	18229	BW	LX04FXU	18245	WH	LX04FYN	18261	WH	LX04FZF
18213	BW	LX04FXA	18230	BW	LX04FXV	18246	WH	LX04FYP	18262	WH	LX04FZG
18214	BW	LX04FXB	18231	BW	LX04FXW	18247	WH	LX04FYR	18263	WH	LX04FZH
18215	BW	LX04FXC	18232	WH	LX04FXY	18248	WH	LX04FYS	18264	WH	LX04FZJ
18216	BW	LX04FXD	18233	WH	LX04FXZ	18249	WH	LX04FYT	18265	WH	LX04FZK
18217	BW	LX04FXE									

18266-18277   ADL Trident 10.5m   ADL ALX400   N45/23D   2005

18266	WH	LX05BVY	18269	WH	LX05BWB	18272	WH	LX05BWE	18275	WH	LX05BWH
18267	WH	LX05BVZ	18270	WH	LX05BWC	18273	WH	LX05BWF	18276	WH	LX05BWJ
18268	WH	LX05BWA	18271	WH	LX05BWD	18274	WH	LX05BWG	18277	WH	LX05BWK

18451-18499   ADL Trident 10.5m   ADL ALX400   N45/22D*   2005-06   *18451-80 are N45/23D

18451	NS	LX05LLM	18464	TL	LX55EPO	18476	NS	LX55ERZ	18488	TL	LX06AFY
18452	NS	LX05LLN	18465	NS	LX55EPP	18477	NS	LX55ESF	18489	TL	LX06AFZ
18453	NS	LX05LLO	18466	NS	LX55EPU	18478	NS	LX55ESG	18490	TL	LX06AGO
18454	WH	LX05LLP	18467	NS	LX55EPV	18479	NS	LX55ESN	18491	TL	LX06AGU
18455	TL	LX55EPA	18468	NS	LX55EPY	18480	NS	LX55ESO	18492	TL	LX06AGV
18456	WH	LX55EPC	18469	NS	LX55EPZ	18481	TL	LX06AFF	18493	TL	LX06AGY
18457	WH	LX55EPD	18470	NS	LX55ERJ	18482	TL	LX06AFJ	18494	TL	LX06AGZ
18458	WH	LX55EPE	18471	NS	LX55ERK	18483	TL	LX06AFK	18495	TL	LX06AHA
18459	WH	LX55EPF	18472	NS	LX55ERO	18484	TL	LX06AFN	18496	TL	LX06AHC
18460	WH	LX55EPJ	18473	NS	LX55ERU	18485	TL	LX06AFO	18497	TL	LX06AHD
18461	WH	LX55EPK	18474	NS	LX55ERV	18486	TL	LX06AFU	18498	TL	LX06AHE
18462	WH	LX55EPL	18475	NS	LX55ERY	18487	TL	LX06AFV	18499	TL	LX06AHF
18463	TL	LX55EPN									

19000   T   LX55HGC   ADL Trident 2 10.8m   ADL Enviro 400   N51/30D   2006   *Spirit of London*

19131-19140   ADL Trident 2 10.8m   ADL Enviro 400   N45/30D   2006

19131	TB	LX56EAF	19134	TB	LX56EAK	19137	TB	LX56EAP	19139	TB	LX56EAY
19132	TB	LX56EAG	19135	TB	LX56EAM	19138	TB	LX56EAW	19140	TB	LX56EBA
19133	TB	LX56EAJ	19136	TB	LX56EAO						

19711-19741   ADL Trident 2 10.2m   ADL Enviro 400   N41/24D   2011

19711	RM	LX11AYS	19719	RM	LX11AZB	19727	RM	LX11AZO	19735	NS	LX11BAA
19712	RM	LX11AYT	19720	RM	LX11AZC	19728	RM	LX11AZP	19736	NS	LX11BAO
19713	RM	LX11AYU	19721	RM	LX11AZD	19729	RM	LX11AZR	19737	NS	LX11BAU
19714	RM	LX11AYV	19722	RM	LX11AZF	19730	RM	LX11AZT	19738	NS	LX11BAV
19715	RM	LX11AYW	19723	RM	LX11AZG	19731	RM	LX11AZU	19739	NS	LX11BBE
19716	RM	LX11AYY	19724	RM	LX11AZJ	19732	RM	LX11AZV	19740	NS	LX11BBF
19717	RM	LX11AYZ	19725	RM	LX11AZL	19733	RM	LX11AZW	19741	NS	LX11BBJ
19718	RM	LX11AZA	19726	RM	LX11AZN	19734	NS	LX11AZZ			

19742-19755   ADL Trident 2 10.2m   ADL Enviro 400   N41/24D   2011

19742	PD	LX11BBK	19746	PD	LX11BBZ	19750	PD	LX11BCO	19753	PD	LX11BCY
19743	PD	LX11BBN	19747	PD	LX11BCE	19751	PD	LX11BCU	19754	PD	LX11BCZ
19744	PD	LX11BBO	19748	PD	LX11BCF	19752	PD	LX11BCV	19755	PD	LX11BDE
19745	PD	LX11BBV	19749	PD	LX11BCK						

Turning from Beckenham High Street is Mercedes-Benz Citaro 23104, LX12DKO, one of thirteen supplied in 2012. *Richard Godfrey*

Fourteen of the shorter Versa model operate on London routes approved in 2009 and these are fitted with dual doorways to TfL requirements. Seen in Chadwell Heath is 25313, LX09AAF. *Dave Heath*

19756-19805   ADL Trident 2 10.2m   ADL Enviro 400   N41/24D   2011

19756	BK	LX11BDF	19769	BK	LX11BFK	19782	BK	LX11BGO	19794	BK	LX11BHN
19757	BK	LX11BDO	19770	BK	LX11BFL	19783	BK	LX11BGU	19795	BK	LX11BHO
19758	BK	LX11BDU	19771	BK	LX11BFM	19784	BK	LX11BGV	19796	BK	LX11BHP
19759	BK	LX11BDV	19772	BK	LX11BFN	19785	BK	LX11BGY	19797	BK	LX11BHU
19760	BK	LX11BDY	19773	BK	LX11BFO	19786	RM	LX11BGZ	19798	BK	LX11BHV
19761	BK	LX11BDZ	19774	BK	LX11BFP	19787	RM	LX11BHA	19799	BK	LX11BHW
19762	BK	LX11BEJ	19775	BK	LX11BFU	19788	RM	LX11BHD	19800	BK	LX11BHY
19763	BK	LX11BEO	19776	BK	LX11BFV	19789	RM	LX11BHE	19801	BK	LX11BHZ
19764	BK	LX11BEU	19777	BK	LX11BFY	19790	RM	LX11BHF	19802	BK	LX11BJE
19765	BK	LX11BEY	19778	BK	LX11BFZ	19791	RM	LX11BHJ	19803	BK	LX11BJF
19766	BK	LX11BFA	19779	BK	LX11BGE	19792	RM	LX11BHK	19804	BK	LX11BJJ
19767	BK	LX11BFF	19780	BK	LX11BGF	19793	RM	LX11BHL	19805	BK	LX11BJK
19768	BK	LX11BFJ	19781	BK	LX11BGK						

19806-19834   ADL Trident 2 10.2m   ADL Enviro 400   N45/30D   2011

19806	PD	LX11BJO	19814	PD	LX11BKF	19821	PD	LX11BKU	19828	PD	LX11BLN
19807	PD	LX11BJU	19815	PD	LX11BKG	19822	PD	LX11BKV	19829	PD	LX11BLV
19808	PD	LX11BJV	19816	PD	LX11BKJ	19823	PD	LX11BKY	19830	PD	LX11BLZ
19809	PD	LX11BJY	19817	PD	LX11BKK	19824	PD	LX11BKZ	19831	PD	LX11BMO
19810	PD	LX11BJZ	19818	PD	LX11BKL	19825	PD	LX11BLF	19832	PD	LX11BMU
19811	PD	LX11BKA	19819	PD	LX11BKN	19826	PD	LX11BLJ	19833	PD	LX11BMV
19812	PD	LX11BKD	19820	PD	LX11BKO	19827	PD	LX11BLK	19834	PD	LX11BMY
19813	PD	LX11BKE									

19835-19871   ADL E40D 10.2m   ADL Enviro 400   N45/30D   2011-12

19835	TB	LX61DDE	19845	TL	LX61DBY	19854	BK	LX12CZH	19863	WH	LX12CZS
19836	TL	LX61DDF	19846	TL	LX61DBZ	19855	BK	LX12CZJ	19864	WH	LX12CZT
19837	TL	LX61DDJ	19847	BK	LX12CZA	19856	BK	LX12CZK	19865	WH	LX12CZU
19838	TL	LX61DDK	19848	BK	LX12CZB	19857	BK	LX12CZL	19866	WH	LX12CZV
19839	TL	LX61DAA	19849	BK	LX12CZC	19858	BK	LX12CZM	19867	WH	LX12CZW
19840	TL	LX61DAO	19850	BK	LX12CZD	19859	WH	LX12CZN	19868	WH	LX12CZY
19841	TL	LX61DAU	19851	BK	LX12CZE	19860	WH	LX12CZO	19869	WH	LX12CZZ
19842	TL	LX61DBO	19852	BK	LX12CZF	19861	WH	LX12CZP	19870	WH	LX12DAA
19843	TL	LX61DBU	19853	BK	LX12CZG	19862	WH	LX12CZR	19871	WH	LX12DAO
19844	TL	LX61DBV									

19960	LNp	SMK760F	AEC Routemaster R2RH/1	Park Royal		B40/32R	1968	*on loan to Brooklands Museum*
19961	WH	WLT324	AEC Routemaster R2RH	Park Royal		B36/28R	1960	*carries RM324 fleetnumber*
19962	WH	WLT652	AEC Routemaster R2RH	Park Royal		B36/28R	1961	*carries RM652 fleetnumber*
19963	WH	WLT871	AEC Routemaster R2RH	Park Royal		B36/28R	1962	*carries RM871 fleetnumber*
19964	WH	ALD933B	AEC Routemaster 2R2RH	Park Royal		B36/28R	1964	*carries RM1933 fleetnumber*
19965	WH	ALD941B	AEC Routemaster 2R2RH	Park Royal		B36/28R	1964	*carries RM1941 fleetnumber*
19966	WH	ALD968B	AEC Routemaster 2R2RH	Park Royal		B36/28R	1964	*carries RM1968 fleetnumber*
19967	WH	ALD50B	AEC Routemaster 2R2RH	Park Royal		B36/28R	1965	*carries RM2050 fleetnumber*
19968	WH	ALD60B	AEC Routemaster 2R2RH	Park Royal		B36/28R	1965	*carries RM2060 fleetnumber*
19969	WH	ALD71B	AEC Routemaster 2R2RH	Park Royal		B36/28R	1965	*carries RM2071 fleetnumber*
19970	WH	ALD89B	AEC Routemaster 2R2RH	Park Royal		B36/28R	1964	*carries RM2089 fleetnumber*

23101-23113   Mercedes-Benz Citaro O530 LE   Mercedes-Benz   N35D   2012

23101	TB	LX12DKK	23105	TB	LX12DKU	23108	TB	LX12DLD	23111	TB	LX12DLJ
23102	TB	LX12DKL	23106	TB	LX12DKV	23109	TB	LX12DLE	23112	TB	LX12DLK
23103	TB	LX12DKN	23107	TB	LX12DKY	23110	TB	LX12DLF	23113	TB	LX12DLN
23104	TB	LX12DKO									

25111-25115   Optare Tempo X1060H   Optare   N28D   2009

25111	TL	YJ08PGO	25113	TL	LX09BGK	25114	TL	LX09BGU	25115	TL	LX09BGV
25112	TL	WLT461									

25301-25314   Optare Versa V1040   Optare   N27D   2009

25301	BK	LX58CHF	25305	BK	LX58CHK	25309	BK	LX58CHV	25312	BK	LX09AAJ
25302	BK	LX58CHG	25306	BK	LX58CHL	25310	BK	LX09AAE	25313	BK	LX09AAF
25303	BK	LX58CHH	25307	BK	LX58CHN	25311	BK	LX09AAK	25314	BK	LX09AAN
25304	BK	LX58CHJ	25308	BK	LX58CHO						

34353-34365   Dennis Dart SLF 10.1m   TransBus Pointer   N27D   2002

34353	TL	LV52HKE	34357	TL	LV52HKJ	34360	TL	LV52HKM	34363	TL	LV52HKP
34355	TL	LV52HKG	34358	TL	LV52HKK	34361	TL	LV52HKN	34364	TL	LV52HKT
34356	TL	LV52HKH	34359	TL	LV52HKL	34362	TB	LV52HKO	34365	TL	LV52HKU

Delivered in the period when the London operation was under Australian-based Macquarie Bank, Enviro 200 36351, LX59AOB, is one of ten 10.2 metre dual-doored examples. It is seen working route D3 through Bethnal Green. *Richard Godfrey*

34366-34376

TransBus Dart 8.8m   TransBus Pointer   N23D   2003

34366	PD	LV52HGC	34372	TL	LV52HGK	34374	PD	LV52HGM	34376	TL	LV52HGO
34370	TL	LV52HGG									

34377-34386

TransBus Dart 9.3m   TransBus Pointer   N31F   2003

34377	PD	LX03BZJ	34380	PD	LX03BZM	34383	PD	LX03BZR	34385	PD	LX03BZT
34378	PD	LX03BZK	34381	PD	LX03BZN	34384	PD	LX03BZS	34386	PD	LX03BZU
34379	PD	LX03BZL	34382	PD	LX03BZP						

34387-34397

TransBus Dart 10.1m   TransBus Pointer   N31D   2003

34387	TL	LX03BZV	34390	TL	LX03CAA	34393	TL	LX03CAV	34396	TL	LX03CBV
34388	TL	LX03BZW	34391	TL	LX03CAE	34394	TL	LX03CBF	34397	TL	LX03CBY
34389	TL	LX03BZY	34392	TL	LX03CAU	34395	TL	LX03CBU			

34551-34560

TransBus Dart 10.1m   TransBus Pointer   N31D   2003

34551	TL	LX53LGF	34554	TL	LX53LGK	34557	TL	LX53LGO	34559	TL	LX53LGV
34552	TL	LX53LGG	34555	TL	LX53LGL	34558	TL	LX53LGU	34560	TL	LX53LGW
34553	TL	LX53LGJ	34556	TL	LX53LGN						

36261-36299

ADL Dart 4 10.2m   ADL Enviro 200   N29D   2011

36261	NS	LX11AVP	36271	PD	LX11AWG	36281	BK	LX11AWW	36291	BK	LX11AXJ
36262	NS	LX11AVR	36272	PD	LX11AWH	36282	BK	LX11AWY	36292	BK	LX11AXK
36263	NS	LX11AVT	36273	PD	LX11AWJ	36283	BK	LX11AWZ	36293	BK	LX11AXM
36264	NS	LX11AVU	36274	PD	LX11AWM	36284	BK	LX11AXA	36294	BK	LX11AXN
36265	NS	LX11AVV	36275	PD	LX11AWN	36285	BK	LX11AXB	36295	BK	LX11AXO
36266	NS	LX11AVW	36276	BK	LX11AWO	36286	BK	LX11AXC	36296	BK	LX11AXP
36267	NS	LX11AVY	36277	BK	LX11AWP	36287	BK	LX11AXD	36297	BK	LX11AXR
36268	PD	LX11AVZ	36278	BK	LX11AWR	36288	BK	LX11AXF	36298	BK	LX11AXS
36269	PD	LX11AWC	36279	BK	LX11AWU	36289	BK	LX11AXG	36299	BK	LX11AXT
36270	PD	LX11AWF	36280	BK	LX11AWV	36290	BK	LX11AXH			

36301-36308

ADL Dart 4 8.9m   ADL Enviro 200   N26F   2006

36301	TL	LX56DZU	36303	TL	LX56DZW	36305	TL	LX56DZZ	36307	TL	LX56EAC
36302	TL	LX56DZV	36304	TL	LX56DZY	36306	TL	LX56EAA	36308	TL	LX56EAE

36309-36313

ADL Dart 4 10.8m   ADL Enviro 200   N32D   2008

36309	TB	LX58BZW	36311	TB	LX58CAA	36312	TB	LX58CAE	36313	TB	LX58CAO
36310	TB	LX58BZY									

36314-36326

ADL Dart 4 8.9m   ADL Enviro 200   N26F   2008

36314	TL	LX58CAU	36318	TL	LX58CBU	36321	TL	LX58CCA	36324	TL	LX58CCF
36315	TL	LX58CAV	36319	TL	LX58CBV	36322	TL	LX58CCD	36325	TL	LX58CCJ
36316	TL	LX58CBF	36320	TL	LX58CBY	36323	TL	LX58CCE	36326	TL	LX58CCK
36317	TL	LX58CBO									

36327-36337 — ADL Dart 4 9.3m — ADL Enviro 200 — N24D — 2008

36327	PD	LX58CCN	36330	PD	LX58CCV	36333	PD	LX58CDF	36336	PD	LX58CDO
36328	PD	LX58CCO	36331	PD	LX58CCY	36334	PD	LX58CDK	36337	PD	LX58CDU
36329	PD	LX58CCU	36332	PD	LX58CDE	36335	TL	LX58CDN			

36338-36344 — ADL Dart 4 10.8m — ADL Enviro 200 — N32D — 2009

36338	RM	LX09ACU	36340	WH	LX09ACY	36342	RM	LX09ADO	36344	WH	LX09ADV
36339	RM	LX09ACV	36341	RM	LX09ACZ	36343	RM	LX09ADU			

36345-36375 — ADL Dart 4 10.2m — ADL Enviro 200 — N29D — 2009-10

36345	WH	LX59ANF	36353	WH	LX59AOD	36361	WH	LX59AOM	36369	WH	LX59ECZ
36346	WH	LX59ANP	36354	WH	LX59AOE	36362	WH	LX59ECF	36370	WH	LX59EDC
36347	WH	LX59ANR	36355	WH	LX59AOF	36363	WH	LX59ECJ	36371	WH	LX59EDF
36348	WH	LX59ANU	36356	WH	LX59AOG	36364	WH	LX59ECN	36372	WH	LX59EDJ
36349	WH	LX59ANV	36357	WH	LX59AOH	36365	WH	LX59ECT	36373	WH	LX59EDK
36350	WH	LX59AOA	36358	WH	LX59AOJ	36366	WH	LX59ECV	36374	WH	LX59EDL
36351	WH	LX59AOB	36359	WH	LX59AOK	36367	WH	LX59ECW	36375	WH	LX59EDO
36352	WH	LX59AOC	36360	WH	LX59AOL	36368	WH	LX59ECY			

36528-36540 — ADL E20D 8.9m — ADL Enviro 200 — N25F — 2012

36528	TL	LX12DHG	36532	TL	LX12DHM	36535	TL	LX12DHP	36538	TL	LX12DHY
36529	TL	LX12DHJ	36533	TL	LX12DHN	36536	TL	LX12DHU	36539	TL	LX12DHZ
36530	TL	LX12DHK	36534	TL	LX12DHO	36537	TL	LX12DHV	36540	TL	LX12DJD
36531	TL	LX12DHL									

36541-36554 — ADL E20D 10.2m — ADL Enviro 200 — N29D — 2012

36541	TB	LX12DJE	36545	TB	LX12DJO	36549	TB	LX12DJZ	36552	TB	LX12DKE
36542	TB	LX12DJF	36546	TB	LX12DJU	36550	TB	LX12DKA	36553	TB	LX12DKF
36543	TB	LX12DJJ	36547	TB	LX12DJV	36551	TB	LX12DKD	36554	TB	LX12DKJ
36544	TB	LX12DJK	36548	TB	LX12DJY						

36555	PD	LX13CYW	ADL E20D 9.6m	ADL Enviro 200	N25D	2013

36556-36580 — ADL E20D 10.9m — ADL Enviro 200 — N31D — 2013

36556	RM	LX13CYY	36563	RM	LX13CZF	36569	RM	LX13CZM	36575	RM	LX13CZT
36557	RM	LX13CYZ	36564	RM	LX13CZG	36570	RM	LX13CZN	36576	RM	LX13CZU
36558	RM	LX13CZA	36565	RM	LX13CZH	36571	RM	LX13CZO	36577	RM	LX13CZV
36559	RM	LX13CZB	36566	RM	LX13CZJ	36572	RM	LX13CZP	36578	RM	LX13CZW
36560	RM	LX13CZC	36567	RM	LX13CZK	36573	RM	LX13CZR	36579	RM	LX13CZY
36561	RM	LX13CZD	36568	RM	LX13CZL	36574	RM	LX13CZS	36580	RM	LX13CZZ
36562	RM	LX13CZE									

36581	TB	SN63	ADL E20D 8.6m	ADL Enviro 200	N26F	2013
36582	TB	SN63	ADL E20D 8.6m	ADL Enviro 200	N26F	2013
36583	TB	SN63	ADL E20D 8.6m	ADL Enviro 200	N26F	2013

Previous registrations:

527CLT	LX09FYN		WLT461	LX09BGF
LX03NGN	527CLT			

Lakeside is the location for this view of Enviro 200 36344, LX09ADV from West Ham depot. *Mark Lyons*

Depots and allocations:

Barking (Longbridge Road, IG11 8UE) - BK

Trident	17526	17581	17582	17583	17585	17587	17856	17857
	17858	17859	17860	17861	17862	17863	17878	17879
	17880	17881	17882	17883	17884	17885	17886	17887
	17888	17893	17894	17895	17896	17897	17898	17899
	17900	17901	17902	17904				
Enviro 400	19756	19757	19758	19759	19760	19761	19762	19763
	19764	19765	19766	19767	19768	19769	19770	19771
	19772	19773	19774	19775	19776	19777	19778	19779
	19780	19781	19782	19783	19784	19785	19794	19795
	19796	19797	19798	19799	19800	19801	19802	19803
	19804	19805	19847	19848	19849	19850	19851	19852
	19853	19854	19855	19856	19857	19858		
Optare Versa	25301	25302	25303	25304	25305	25306	25307	25308
	25309	25310	25311	25312	25313	25314		
Enviro 200	36276	36277	36278	36279	36280	36281	36282	36283
	36284	36285	36286	36287	36288	36289	36290	36291
	36292	36293	36294	36295	36296	36297	36298	36299

Bow (Fairfield Road, E3 2QP) - BW

Enviro 400 Hybrid	12128	12129	12130	12131	12132	12133	12134	12135
	12136	12137	12138	12139	12140	12141	12142	12143
	12144	12145	12146	12147	12148	12149	12150	12151
	12152	12153						
Scania CN230	15097	15098	15099	15100	15101	15102	15103	15104
	15105	15106	15107	15108	15109	15110	15111	15112
	15113	15114	15115	15116	15117	15118	15119	15120
	15121	15122	15123	15124				
Trident	17451	17516	17740	17741	17742	17743	17744	17750
	17751	17752	17753	17754	17755	17756	17757	17781
	17782	17783	17784	17785	17786	17787	17818	17819
	17846	17855	17879	18201	18202	18203	18204	18205
	18206	18207	18208	18209	18210	18211	18212	18213
	18214	18215	18216	18217	18218	18219	18220	18221
	18222	18223	18224	18225	18226	18227	18228	18229
	18230	18231	18234	18235				

Bromley (Hastings Road, BR2 8NH) - TB

Trident	17531	17561	17779	17780	17780	17788	17794	17795
	17831	17832	17833	17841	17842	17843	17844	17845
	17864	17965	17966	17967	17968	17969	17970	17971
	17972	17973	17974	17975				
Enviro 400	10139	10140	10141	10142	10143	10144	10145	10146
	10147	10148	10149	10150	10151	10152	10153	10154
	19131	19132	19133	19134	19135	19136	19137	19138
	19139	19140	19835					
Citaro	23101	23102	23103	23104	23105	23106	23107	23108
	23109	23110	23111	23112	23113			
Dart SLF	34362	34366						
Enviro 200	36309	36310	36311	36312	36313	36541	36542	36543
	36544	36545	36546	36547	36548	36549	36550	36551
	36552	36553	36554					

Catford (Bromley Road, SE6 2XA) - TL

Trident	17478	17485	18455	18463	18464	18481	18482	18483
	18484	18485	18486	18487	18488	18489	18490	18491
	18492	18493	18494	18495	18496	18497	18498	18499
Enviro 400	10124	10125	10126	10127	10128	10129	10130	10131
	10132	10133	10134	10135	10136	10137	10138	19836
	19837	19838	19839	19840	19841	19842	19843	19844
	19845	19846						
Tempo	25111	25112	25113	25114	25115			

Dart SLF	34353	34355	34356	34357	34358	34359	34360	34361
	34363	34364	34365	34370	34372	34376	34387	34388
	34389	34390	34391	34392	34393	34394	34395	34396
	34397	34551	34552	34553	34554	34555	34556	34557
	34558	34559	34560					
Enviro 200	36301	36302	36303	36304	36305	36306	36307	36308
	36314	36316	36317	36318	36319	36320	36321	36322
	36323	36324	36325	36326	36343	36528	36529	36530
	36531	36532	36533	36534	36535	36536	36537	36538
	36539	36540						

Leyton (High Road, E10 6AD) - T

Enviro 400	10113	10115	10116	10117	10118	10119	10120	10121
	10122	10123						
Scania CN230	15125	15126	15127	15128	15129	15130	15131	15132
	15133	15134	15135	15136	15137	15138	15139	15140
	15141	15142	15143	15144	15145	15146	15147	15148
	15149	15150	15151	15152	15153	15154	15155	15156
	15157	15158	15159	15160	15161	15162	15163	15164
	15165	15166	15167	15168	15169	15170	15171	15172
	15173	15174						
Trident	17504	17505	17506	17507	17522	17523	17524	17525
	17541	17543	17568	17575	17745	17746	17747	17749
	17796	17797	17798	17799	17800	17801	17802	17803
	17804	17805	17806	17807	17808	17809	17810	17811
	17812	17813	17814	17826	17827	17828	17851	17852
	17853	17871	17873	17875	17876	17877	17892	17905
	17906	17907	17908					
Enviro 400	19000							

Plumstead (Pettman Crescent, SE28 0BJ) - PD

Scania CN230	15036	15037	15038	15039	15040	15041	15042	15043
	15044	15045	15046	15047	15048	15049	15050	15051
	15052	15053	15054	15055	15056	15057	15058	15059
	15060	15061	15062	15063	15064	15065	15066	15067
	15068	15069	15070	15071	15072	15073	15074	15075
	15076	15077	15078	15079	15080	15081	15082	15083
	15084	15085	15086	15087	15088	15089	15090	15091
	15092	15093	15094	15095	15096			
Trident	17404	17427	17440	17441	17503	17508	17511	17512
	17537	17538	17540	17560	17561	17563	17567	17570
	17571	17572	17573	17590	17591	17789	17790	17836
	17837	17838	17839	17866	17945	17946	17947	17948
	17949	17950	17951	17952	17953	17954	17955	17956
	17957	17958	17959	17960	17961	17962	17963	17964
Enviro 400	19742	19743	19744	19745	19746	19747	19748	19749
	19750	19751	19752	19753	19754	19755	19806	19807
	19808	19809	19810	19811	19812	19813	19814	19815
	19816	19817	19818	19819	19820	19821	19822	19823
	19824	19825	19826	19827	19828	19829	19830	19831
	19832	19833	19834					
Dart SLF	34374	34377	34378	34379	34380	34381	34382	34383
	34384	34385	34386					
Enviro 200	36268	36269	36270	36271	36272	36273	36274	36275
	36327	36328	36329	36330	36331	36332	36333	36334
	36335	36336	36337	36555				

Rainham (Albright Industrial Estate, RM13 9BU) - RM

Scania CN230	15001	15002	15003	15004	15005	15006	15007	15008
	15009	15010	15011	15012	15014	15015	15016	15017
	15018	15019	15020	15021	15022	15023	15024	15025
	15026	15027	15028	15029	15030	15031	15032	15033
	15034	15035						
Trident	17425	17467	17519					
Enviro 400	19711	19712	19713	19714	19715	19716	19717	19718
	19719	19720	19721	19722	19723	19724	19725	19726
	19727	19728	19729	19730	19731	19732	19733	19786
	19787	19788	19789	19790	19791	19792	19793	

Enviro 200	36338	36339	36341	36342	36556	36557	36558	36559
	36560	36561	36562	36563	36564	36565	36566	36567
	36568	36569	36570	36571	36572	36573	36574	36575
	36576	36577	36578	36579	36580			
Ancillary	*17363*	*17364*	*17368*	*17395*	*17396*	*17397*	*17398*	*17399*
	17409	*17419*	*17426*	*17434*				

Romford (North Street, RM1 1DS) - NS

Trident	17448	17518	17520	17559	17562	17564	17565	17566
	17569	17574	17577	17578	17748	17759	17760	17761
	17762	17763	17764	17765	17766	17767	17768	17769
	17770	17771	17772	17773	17774	17775	17776	17777
	17778	17791	17792	17793	17829	17830	17835	17854
	17867	17868	17869	17870	17874	17976	17977	17978
	17979	17980	17981	17982	17983	17984	17985	17986
	17987	17988	17989	17990	17991	17992	17993	17994
	17995	17996	17997	17998	17999	18451	18452	18453
	18454	18465	18466	18467	18468	18469	18470	18471
	18472	18473	18474	18475	18476	18477	18478	18479
	18480							
Enviro 400	10155	10156	10157	10158	10159	10160	10161	10162
	10163	19734	19735	19736	19737	19738	19739	19740
	19741							
Enviro 200	36261	36262	36263	36264	36265	36266	36267	

West Ham (Stephenson Street, Canning Town, E16 4SA) - WH

Enviro 400	10101	10102	10103	10104	10105	10106	10107	10108
	10109	10110	10111	10112	19000	19859	19860	19861
	19862	19863	19864	19865	19866	19867	19868	19869
	19870	19871						
Trident	17452	17454	17460	17489	17493	17494	17495	17497
	17498	17499	17500	17501	17509	17515	17521	17527
	17528	17529	17530	17535	17536	17545	17546	17547
	17549	17550	17551	17552	17553	17554	17555	17556
	17557	17576	17580	17586	17588	17589	17815	17816
	17817	17820	17821	17822	17823	17824	17825	17834
	17847	17848	17849	17850	17865	17889	17890	17891
	17903	17909	17910	17911	17912	17913	17914	17915
	17916	17917	17918	17919	17920	17921	17922	17923
	17924	17925	17926	17927	17928	17929	17930	17931
	17932	17933	17934	17935	17936	17937	17938	17939
	17940	17941	17942	17943	17944	18232	18233	18236
	18237	18238	18239	18240	18241	18242	18243	18244
	18245	18246	18247	18248	18249	18250	18251	18252
	18253	18254	18255	18256	18257	18258	18259	18260
	18261	18262	18263	18264	18265	18266	18267	18268
	18269	18270	18271	18272	18273	18274	18275	18276
	18277	18454	18456	18457	18458	18459	18460	18461
	18462							
Enviro 400	19859	19860	19861	19862	19863	19864	19865	19866
	19867	19868	19869	19870	19871			
Routemaster	19961	19962	19963	19964	19965	19966	19967	19968
	19969							
Enviro 200	36340	36344	36345	36346	36347	36348	36349	36350
	36351	36352	36353	36354	36355	36356	36357	36358
	36359	36360	36361	36362	36363	36364	36365	36366
	36367	36368	36369	36370	36371	36372	36373	36374
	36375							

unallocated and stored - u

Remainder

TOWER TRANSIT

Tower Transit Operations Ltd, 19 Eastbourne Terrace, London W2 6LG

VNW32361-32370 — Volvo B7TL 10.1m — Wrightbus Eclipse Gemini — N38/21D — 2004

32361	AS	LK04HYN	32364	AS	LK04HYT	32367	AS	LK04HYA	32369	AS	LK04HYU
32362	AS	LK04HYM	32365	AS	LK04HYX	32368	AS	LK04HYS	32370	AS	LK04HYV
32363	AS	LK04HYW	32366	AS	LK04HYY						

VNW32371-32430 — Volvo B7TL 10.1m — Wrightbus Eclipse Gemini — N41/21D — 2004

32371	AS	LK04HZA	32386	AS	LK04HZU	32401	AS	LK04HXL	32416	AS	LK04JBY
32372	AS	LK04HZB	32387	AS	LK04HZV	32402	AS	LK04HXM	32417	AS	LK04JBZ
32373	AS	LK04HZC	32388	AS	LK04HZW	32403	AS	LK04HXN	32418	AS	LK04JCJ
32374	AS	LK04HZD	32389	AS	LK04HZX	32404	AS	LK04HXP	32419	AS	LK04JCU
32375	AS	LK04HZE	32390	AS	LK04HZY	32405	AS	LK04HXR	32420	AS	LK04JCV
32376	AS	LK04HZF	32391	AS	LK04HZZ	32406	AS	LK04HXS	32421	AS	LK04JCX
32377	AS	LK04HZG	32392	AS	LK04HXA	32407	AS	LK04HXT	32422	AS	LK04HYZ
32378	AS	LK04HZH	32393	AS	LK04HXB	32408	AS	LK04HXU	32423	AS	LK04JCZ
32379	AS	LK04HZJ	32394	AS	LK04HXC	32409	AS	LK04HXV	32424	AS	LK04HYB
32380	AS	LK04HZL	32395	AS	LK04HXD	32410	AS	LK04HXW	32425	AS	LK04HYC
32381	AS	LK04HZM	32396	AS	LK04HXE	32411	AS	LK04HXX	32426	AS	LK04HYF
32382	AS	LK04HZN	32397	AS	LK54FNO	32412	AS	LK04JBE	32427	AS	LK04HYG
32383	AS	LK04JBU	32398	AS	LK54FNP	32413	AS	LK04HZP	32428	AS	LK04HYH
32384	AS	LK04HZS	32399	AS	LK04HXH	32414	AS	LK04JBV	32429	AS	LK04HYJ
32385	AS	LK04HZT	32400	AS	LK04HXJ	32415	AS	LK04JBX	32430	AS	LK04HYL

VNZ32495-32502 — Volvo B7TL 10.6m — Wrightbus Eclipse Gemini — N41/24D — 2004

32495	AS	LK54FLA	32497	AS	LK54FLC	32499	AS	LK54FLE	32501	AS	LK54FLG
32496	AS	LK54FLB	32498	AS	LK54FLD	32500	AS	LK54FLF	32502	AS	LK54FLH

TN32822	ASt	T822LLC	Dennis Trident 9.9m	Plaxton President 4.4m	N39/20D	1999
TNL33036	AS	LK51UYE	Dennis Trident 10.5m	Plaxton President 4.4m	N42/23D	2001
TN33197	AS	LT52XAH	TransBus Trident 9.9m	TransBus President 4.4m	N39/20D	2002
TN33198	AS	LT52XAJ	TransBus Trident 9.9m	TransBus President 4.4m	N39/20D	2002
TN33199	AS	LT52XAK	TransBus Trident 9.9m	TransBus President 4.4m	N39/20D	2002

In April 2013 FirstGroup announced the sale of eight of its London bus depots. Three of these depots, at Atlas Road, Lea Interchange and Westbourne Park, along with approximately 400 vehicles and 1,500 employees, were subsequently transferred to Transit Systems Group, an Australian transport operator. While the former First fleetnumbers have been retained the name and logo have been changed to Tower Transit as shown here on Volvo B7TL 32372, LK04HZB. *Mark Lyons*

DN33612-33655 ADL Trident 2 / ADL Enviro 400 / N41/24D / 2011

33612	L	SN11BMU	33623	L	SN11BNL	33634	L	SN11BOV	33645	L	SN11BRV
33613	L	SN11BMV	33624	L	SN11BNO	33635	L	SN11BPE	33646	L	SN11BRZ
33614	L	SN11BMY	33625	L	SN11BNU	33636	L	SN11BPF	33647	L	SN11BSO
33615	L	SN11BMZ	33626	L	SN11BNV	33637	L	SN11BPK	33648	L	SN11BSU
33616	L	SN11BNA	33627	L	SN11BNX	33638	L	SN11BPO	33649	L	SN11BSV
33617	L	SN11BNB	33628	L	SN11BNY	33639	L	SN11BPU	33650	L	SN11BSX
33618	L	SN11BND	33629	L	SN11BNZ	33640	L	SN11BPV	33651	L	SN11BSY
33619	L	SN11BNE	33630	L	SN11BOF	33641	L	SN11BPX	33652	L	SN11BSZ
33620	L	SN11BNF	33631	L	SN11BOH	33642	L	SN11BPY	33653	L	SN11BTE
33621	L	SN11BNJ	33632	L	SN11BOJ	33643	L	SN11BPZ	33654	L	SN11BTO
33622	L	SN11BNK	33633	L	SN11BOU	33644	L	SN11BRF	33655	L	SN11BTU

DN33776-33787 ADL E40D / ADL Enviro 400 / N41/24D / 2012

33776	X	SN12AVR	33779	X	SN12AVV	33782	X	SN12AVY	33785	X	SN12AWC
33777	X	SN12AVT	33780	X	SN12AVW	33783	X	SN12AVZ	33786	X	SN12EHB
33778	X	SN12AVU	33781	X	SN12AVX	33784	X	SN12AWA	33787	X	SN12EHC

DN33789-33798 ADL E40D / ADL Enviro 400 / N41/26D / 2013

33789	L	SN13CGH	33792	L	SN13CHD	33795	L	SN13CHH	33797	L	SN13CHK
33790	L	SN13CGZ	33793	L	SN13CHF	33796	L	SN13CHJ	33798	L	SN13CHL
33791	L	SN13CHC	33794	L	SN13CHG						

WN35001-35004 Wrightbus DB300 10.4m / Wrightbus Pulsar Gemini 2 / N41/24D / 2009

35001	AS	LK58EDO	35002	AS	LK58EDP	35003	AS	LK58EDR	35004	AS	LK09CZS

VN36101-36165 Volvo B9TL 10.4m / Wrightbus Eclipse Gemini 2 / N39/23D / 2011

36101	L	BJ11DSE	36118	L	BJ11DVC	36134	L	BJ11DTZ	36150	L	BJ11EBD
36102	L	BJ11DSZ	36119	L	BJ11DSY	36135	L	BJ11DUH	36151	L	BJ11EBC
36103	L	BJ11DSU	36120	L	BJ11DRZ	36136	L	BJ11DVV	36152	L	BJ11EAE
36104	L	BJ11DTF	36121	L	BJ11DSO	36137	L	BJ11DVW	36153	L	BJ11DVX
36105	L	BJ11DSV	36122	L	BJ11DTK	36138	L	BJ11DVT	36154	L	BJ11EAA
36106	L	BJ11DTV	36123	L	BJ11DTX	36139	L	BJ11DVU	36155	L	BJ11DZZ
36107	L	BJ11DTY	36124	L	BJ11DTU	36140	L	BJ11DZX	36156	L	BJ11DZY
36108	L	BJ11DTO	36125	L	BJ11DVG	36141	L	BJ11EBP	36157	L	BJ11EAC
36109	L	BJ11DUV	36126	L	BJ11DUY	36142	L	BJ11EAM	36158	L	BJ11EAG
36110	L	BJ11DUA	36127	L	BJ11DVA	36143	L	BJ11EAF	36159	L	BJ11EAP
36111	L	BJ11DVH	36128	L	BJ11DVB	36144	L	BJ11EAX	36160	L	BJ11EAY
36112	L	BJ11DVF	36129	L	BJ11DVO	36145	L	BJ11EBG	36161	L	BJ11EBA
36113	L	BJ11DVP	36130	L	BJ11DVN	36146	L	BJ11EBL	36162	L	BJ11EBK
36114	L	BJ11DVM	36131	L	BJ11DVR	36147	L	BJ11EAK	36163	L	BJ11EBM
36115	L	BJ11DVL	36132	L	BJ11DSX	36148	L	BJ11EAW	36164	L	BJ11EBO
36116	L	BJ11DUU	36133	L	BJ11DTN	36149	L	BJ11EAO	36165	L	BJ11EBN
36117	L	BJ11DVK									

VN36291-36295 Volvo B9TL 10.4m / Wrightbus Eclipse Gemini 2 / N39/23D / 2012

36291	AS	BX12CVO	36293	AS	BX12CVK	36294	AS	BX12CVL	36295	AS	BX12CVP
36292	AS	BX12CVM									

VN37842-37864 Volvo B9TL / Wrightbus Eclipse Gemini 2 / N39/23D / 2010

37842	L	BV10WVM	37850	L	BV10WWH	37854	L	BV10WWM	37861	L	BV10WWU
37844	L	BV10WWT	37851	L	BV10WWJ	37855	L	BV10WWN	37862	L	BV10WWX
37847	L	BV10WWE	37852	L	BV10WWK	37859	L	BV10WWS	37863	L	BV10WWY
37849	L	BV10WWG	37853	L	BV10WWL	37860	L	BV10WWB	37864	L	BV10WWZ

37943	X	BK10MFZ	Volvo B9TL 10.4m	Wrightbus Eclipse Gemini 2	N39/23D	2010

Another view of an Enviro 400 Hybrid, this time showing its off-side as 39126, SN13ATU passes St Paul's Cathedral. *Mark Lyons.*

VN37952-37984 — Volvo B9TL 10.5m — Wrightbus Eclipse Gemini 2 — N39/23D — 2012

37952	X	BN61MWZ	37961	X	BN61MXL	37969	AS	BN61MXT	37977	AS	BN61MYB
37953	X	BN61MXB	37962	X	BN61MXK	37970	AS	BN61MXU	37978	AS	BG61SXJ
37954	X	BN61MXA	37963	AS	BN61MXJ	37971	AS	BN61MXY	37979	AS	BG61SXM
37955	X	BN61MXE	37964	X	BN61MXP	37972	AS	BN61MXX	37980	AS	BG61SXL
37956	X	BN61MXD	37965	AS	BN61MXM	37973	AS	BN61MXW	37981	AS	BG61SXN
37957	X	BN61MXH	37966	AS	BN61MXO	37974	AS	BN61MXV	37982	AS	BG61SXO
37958	X	BN61MXC	37967	AS	BN61MXR	37975	AS	BG61SXK	37983	AS	BG61SXP
37959	X	BN61MXF	37968	AS	BN61MXS	37976	AS	BN61MYA	37984	AS	BG61SXR
37960	AS	BN61MXG									

VN37988-37996 — Volvo B9TL 10.5m — Wrightbus Eclipse Gemini 2 — N39/23D — 2012

37988	X	BF62UYB	37991	X	BF62UYE	37993	X	BF62UYD	37995	X	BF62UYJ
37989	X	BF62UYA	37992	X	BF62UYG	37994	X	BF62UYH	37996	X	BF62UYK
37990	X	BF62UYC									

DNH39111-39132 — ADL E40H 10.2m — ADL Enviro 400 — N37/24D — 2012

39111	X	SN12APY	39117	X	SN12ARZ	39123	X	SN12ATF	39128	X	SN12AYX
39112	X	SN12APZ	39118	X	SN12ASO	39124	X	SN12ATK	39129	X	SN12ATY
39113	X	SN12ARF	39119	X	SN12ASU	39125	X	SN12ATO	39130	X	SN12ATZ
39114	X	SN12ARO	39120	X	SN12ASV	39126	X	SN12ATU	39131	X	SN12AUA
39115	X	SN12ARU	39121	X	SN12ASX	39127	X	SN12ATV	39132	X	SN12AUC
39116	X	SN12ARX	39122	X	SN12ASZ						

39804	X	204CLT	AEC Routemaster R2RH	Park Royal/Marshall	B36/28R	1962	*carries RM1204 fleetnumber*
39813	X	ALD913B	AEC Routemaster R2RH	Park Royal/Marshall	B36/28R	1964	*carries RM1913 fleetnumber*
39818	X	218CLT	AEC Routemaster R2RH	Park Royal/Marshall	B36/28R	1962	*carries RM1218 fleetnumber*
39827	X	627DYE	AEC Routemaster R2RH	Park Royal/Marshall	B36/28R	1963	*carries RM1627 fleetnumber*
39835	X	735DYE	AEC Routemaster R2RH	Park Royal/Marshall	B36/28R	1963	*carries RM1735 fleetnumber*
39840	X	640DYE	AEC Routemaster R2RH	Park Royal/Marshall	B36/28R	1962	*carries RM1640 fleetnumber*
39862	X	562CLT	AEC Routemaster R2RH	Park Royal/Marshall	B36/28R	1962	*carries RM1562 fleetnumber*
39876	X	776DYE	AEC Routemaster R2RH	Park Royal/Marshall	B36/28R	1962	*carries RM1776 fleetnumber*
39880	u	280CLT	AEC Routemaster R2RH	Park Royal/Marshall	B36/28R	1962	*carries RM1280 fleetnumber*
39950	X	650DYE	AEC Routemaster R2RH	Park Royal/Marshall	B36/28R	1963	*carries SRM3 fleetnumber*
41444	L	LN51DUA	Dennis Dart SLF 9.3m	Marshall Capital	N24D	2002	
41445	L	LN51DUH	Dennis Dart SLF 9.3m	Marshall Capital	N24D	2002	

DMC42515-42519   TransBus Dart 10.5m   Caetano Nimbus   N28D   2003

42515	L	LK03NKH	42517	L	LK03NKL	42518	L	LK03NKM	42519	w	LK03NKN
42516	L	LK03NKJ						

44073	L	YX58HVC	ADL Dart 4 10.2m	ADL Enviro 200	N29D	2009
44074	L	YX58HVD	ADL Dart 4 10.2m	ADL Enviro 200	N29D	2009
44075	L	YX58HVE	ADL Dart 4 10.2m	ADL Enviro 200	N29D	2009
44163	L	YX10BGV	ADL Dart 4 10.2m	ADL Enviro 200	N29D	2010
44164	L	YX10BGY	ADL Dart 4 10.2m	ADL Enviro 200	N29D	2010

DM44167-44170   ADL Dart 4 9.3m   ADL Enviro 200   N24D   2010

44167	L	YX60DXL	44168	L	YX60DXM	44169	L	YX60DXO	44170	L	YX60DXP

DML44171-44178   ADL Dart 4 10.2m   ADL Enviro 200   N29D   2011

44171	L	YX11AFK	44173	L	YX11AFO	44175	L	YX11AFV	44177	L	YX11AFZ
44172	L	YX11AFN	44174	L	YX11AFU	44176	L	YX11AFY	44178	L	YX11AFZ

DMV44221-44236   ADL E20D 10.8m   ADL Enviro 200   N31D   2012

44221	L	YX12AYZ	44225	L	YX12AEW	44229	L	YX12AUA	44233	L	YX12AZN
44222	L	YX12AZA	44226	L	YX12AEY	44230	L	YX12AGY	44234	L	YX12AJY
44223	L	YX12AKK	44227	L	YX12AEO	44231	L	YX12AXV	44235	L	YX12AGZ
44224	L	YX12AKN	44228	L	YX12AEP	44232	L	YX12AFZ	44236	L	YX12AON

DMV44250-44259   ADL E20D 10.8m   ADL Enviro 200   N31D   2012

44250	L	YX12AKP	44253	L	YX12AKY	44256	L	YX12AHK	44258	L	YX12ABK
44251	L	YX12AKU	44254	L	YX12AKZ	44257	L	YX12ABF	44259	L	YX12AWU
44252	L	YX12AKV	44255	L	YX12AHJ						

DM44260-44270   ADL E20D 9.6m   ADL Enviro 200   N25D   2012

44260	L	YX61FZC	44263	L	YX61FZF	44266	L	YX61FZJ	44269	L	YX61FZM
44261	L	YX61FZD	44264	L	YX61FZG	44267	L	YX61FZK	44270	L	YX61FZN
44262	L	YX61FZE	44265	L	YX61FZH	44268	L	YX61FZL			

DML44279-44292   ADL E20D 10.2m   ADL Enviro 200   N29D   2012

44279	L	YX61FYB	44283	L	YX61FYF	44286	L	YX61FYJ	44290	L	YX61FYN
44280	L	YX61FYC	44284	L	YX61FYG	44287	L	YX61FYK	44291	L	YX61FYO
44281	L	YX61FYD	44285	L	YX61FYH	44288	L	YX61FYL	44292	L	YX61FYP
44282	L	YX61FYE	44290	L	YX61FYN	44289	L	YX61FYM			

DML44313-44328   ADL E20D 10.2m   ADL Enviro 200   N29D   2012

44313	X	YX12AAJ	44317	X	YX12AEU	44321	X	YX12ARZ	44325	X	YX12AZW
44314	X	YX12AEA	44318	X	YX12AOF	44322	X	YX12AXU	44326	X	YX12DHZ
44315	X	YX12AED	44319	X	YX12AFV	44323	X	YX12AVJ	44327	X	YX12DJD
44316	X	YX12AEF	44320	X	YX12AMK	44324	X	YX12AYF	44328	X	YX12DJE

WSH62991-62998   VDL Bus SB200 LF Fuelcell   Wrightbus Pulsar 2   N35D   2010-13   *Owned by TfL*

62991	L	LK60HPE	62993	L	LK60HPJ	62995	L	LK60HPN	62997	L	LJ13JZP
62992	Lu	LK60HPF	62994	L	LK60HPL	62996	L	LJ13JNP	62998	L	LJ13JZO

Depots and allocations:

Atlas Road (Ealing Road) - AS

Volvo B7TL	32361	32362	32363	32364	32365	32366	32367	32368
	32369	32370	32371	32372	32373	32374	32375	32376
	32377	32378	32379	32380	32381	32382	32383	32384
	32385	32386	32387	32388	32389	32390	32391	32392
	32393	32394	32395	32396	32397	32398	32399	32400
	32401	32402	32403	32404	32405	32406	32407	32408
	32409	32410	32411	32412	32413	32414	32415	32416
	32417	32418	32419	32420	32421	32422	32423	32424
	32425	32426	32427	32428	32429	32430	32495	32496
	32497	32498	32499	32500	32501	32502		
Wrightbus DB300	35001	35002	35003	35004				
Volvo B9TL	36291	36292	36293	36294	36295	37960	37962	37963
	37964	37965	37966	37967	37968	37969	37970	37971
	37972	37973	37974	37975	37976	37977	37978	37979
	37980	37981	37982	37983	37984			

Heading for South Kensington with a background of Regency properties in Queen's Gate is Enviro 200 44325, YX12AZW, one of eighty-three now operated by Tower Transit. *Mark Lyons*

Leyton (Lea Interchange) - L

Dart	41444	41445	42515	42516	42517	42518	42519	44073
	44074	44075	44163	44164	44171	44172	44173	44174
	44175	44176	44177	44178				
Enviro 200	44167	44168	44169	44170	44221	44222	44223	44224
	44225	44226	44227	44228	44229	44230	44231	44232
	44233	44234	44235	44236	44250	44251	44252	44253
	44254	44255	44256	44257	44258	44259	44260	44261
	44262	44263	44264	44265	44266	44267	44268	44269
	44270	44279	44280	44281	44282	44283	44284	44285
	44286	44287	44288	44289	44290	44291	44292	
VDL SB200 Fuelcell	62991	62993	62994	62995				
Trident	33036							
Volvo B9TL	36101	36102	36103	36104	36105	36106	36107	36108
	36109	36110	36111	36112	36113	36114	36115	36116
	36117	36118	36119	36120	36121	36122	36123	36124
	36125	36126	36127	36128	36129	36130	36131	36132
	36133	36134	36135	36136	36137	36138	36139	36140
	36141	36142	36143	36144	36145	36146	36147	36148
	36149	36150	36151	36152	36153	36154	36155	36156
	36157	36158	36159	36160	36161	36162	36163	36164
	36165	37842	37844	37847	37849	37850	37851	37852
	37853	37854	37855	37859	37860	37861	37862	37863
	37864							
Enviro 400	33612	33613	33614	33615	33616	33617	33618	33619
	33620	33621	33622	33623	33624	33625	33626	33627
	33628	33629	33630	33631	33632	33633	33634	33635
	33636	33637	33638	33639	33640	33641	33642	33643
	33644	33645	33646	33647	33648	33649	33650	33651
	33652	33653	33654	33655	33789	33790	33791	33792
	33793	33794	33795	33796	33797	33798		
VDL Fuelcell	62991	62992	62993	62994	62995	62996	62997	62998

Pictured at Mile End is Enviro 200 44269, YX61FZM, one of the shorter 9.3 metre dual-doored examples, all of which operate from Leyton depot. Route 339 has a peak vehicle requirement of six of this type.
Mark Lyons

Westbourne Park (Great Western Road, W9 3NW) - X

Enviro 200	44313	44314	44315	44316	44317	44318	44319	44320
	44322	44323	44324	44325	44326	44327	44328	
Trident	33036	33197	33198	33199				
Enviro 400	33776	33777	33778	33779	33780	33781	33782	33783
	33784	33785	33786	33787				
Enviro 400 Hybrid	39111	39112	39113	39114	39115	39116	39117	39118
	39119	39120	39121	39122	39123	39124	39125	39126
	39127	39128	39129	39130	39131	39132		
Routemaster	39804	39813	39818	39827	39835	39840	39862	39880
	39876	39950						
Volvo B9TL	37943	37952	37953	37954	37955	37956	37957	37958
	37959	37961	37988	37989	37990	37991	37992	37993
	37994	37995	37996					

Unallocated and reserves - u/t/w

Remainder

TRANSDEV LONDON

London Sovereign Ltd, Approach Road, Edgware, HA8 7AN

DE50-56

						ADL Dart 4 10.2m		ADL Enviro 200		N29D	2008-09		
50	SO	YX59BYA	52	SO	YX59BYC	54	SO	YX59BYF	56	SO	YX59BYH
51	SO	YX59BYB	53	SO	YX59BYD	55	SO	YX59BYG			

DE57-99

						ADL Dart 4 10.2m		ADL Enviro 200		N29D	2011		
57	BT	YX11GBE	68	BT	YX11GCV	79	SO	YX11FZF	90	SO	YX11FZS
58	BT	YX11GBF	69	BT	YX11GCY	80	SO	YX11FZG	91	SO	YX11FZT
59	BT	YX11GBO	70	BT	YX11GCZ	81	SO	YX11FZH	92	SO	YX11FZU
60	BT	YX11GBU	71	SO	YX11GDA	82	SO	YX11FZJ	93	SO	YX11FZV
61	BT	YX11GBV	72	SO	YX11GDE	83	SO	YX11FZK	94	SO	YX11FZW
62	BT	YX11GBY	73	SO	YX11GDF	84	SO	YX11FZL	95	SO	YX11FZY
63	BT	YX11GBZ	74	SO	YX11FZA	85	SO	YX11FZM	96	SO	YX11FZZ
64	BT	YX11GCF	75	SO	YX11FZB	86	SO	YX11FZN	97	SO	YX11COH
65	BT	YX11GCK	76	SO	YX11FZC	87	SO	YX11FZO	98	SO	YX11COJ
66	BT	YX11GCO	77	SO	YX11FZD	88	SO	YX11FZP	99	SO	YX11ENJ
67	BT	YX11GCU	78	SO	YX11FZE	89	SO	YX11FZR			

DPS599	SO	SN51TBX	Dennis Dart SLF 10.1m		Alexander ALX200		N30D	2001		

DPS627-640

						TransBus Dart 10.1m		TransBus Pointer		N27D*	2002	*627 is N27F	
627	SO	SK02XGW	632	SO	SK02XHG	635	SO	SK02XHL	638	SO	SK02XHO
628	SO	SK02XGX	633	SO	SK02XHH	636	SO	SK02XHM	639	SO	SK02XHP
629	SO	SK02XHD	634	SO	SK02XHJ	637	SO	SK02XHN	640	SO	SK02XHR
630	SO	SK02XHE									

Transdev is a major international public transport group based in Issy-les-Moulineaux near Paris, and acquired London Sovereign and London United in 2002 but in 2010 London United was transferred to the RATP Group leaving Transdev with just two depots in London. Allocated to Edgware is SDE23, YX60BZF, seen on route 324 from Stanmore. *Dave Heath*

Following on from two batches of Scania N94UDs with East Lancs OmniDekka bodywork, a batch of the integral Scania OmniCity CN230 arrived in 2009. Illustrating the East Lancs product is SLE28, TN55NJF.
Terry Longhurst

VH1-23
Volvo B5LH 10.5m   Wrightbus Gemini 2   N39/21D   2013

1	BT	BD13OHU	7	BT	BD13OJA	13	BT	BD13YWL	19	BT	BD13YWR
2	BT	BD13OHV	8	BT	BD13OJB	14	BT	BD13YWN	20	BT	BD13YWS
3	BT	BD13OHW	9	BT	BD13OJC	15	BT	BD13YWJ	21	BT	BD13YWW
4	BT	BD13OHX	10	BT	BD13OJE	16	BT	BD13YWM	22	BT	BD13YWU
5	BT	BD13OHY	11	BT	BD13OHJ	17	BT	BD13YWP	23	BT	BD13YWV
6	BT	BD13OHZ	12	BT	BD13YWK	18	BT	BD13YWO			

SDE18-24
ADL Dart 4 8.9m   ADL Enviro 200   N26F   2010

18	BT	YX60BZA	20	BT	YX60BZC	22	BT	YX60BZE	24	BT	YX60BZG
19	BT	YX60BZB	21	BT	YX60BZD	23	BT	YX60BZF			

SLE1-6
Scania N94UD 10.6m   East Lancs OmniDekka   N49/27D   2004

1	BT	YN54OAA	3	BT	YN54OAC	5	BT	YN54OAG	6	BT	YN54OAH
2	BT	YN54OAB	4	BT	YN54OAE						

SLE21-42
Scania N94UD 10.6m   East Lancs OmniDekka   N45/27D   2005

21	BT	YN55NHT	27	BT	YN55NJE	33	BT	YN55NKA	38	BT	YN55NKG
22	BT	YN55NHU	28	BT	YN55NJF	34	BT	YN55NKC	39	BT	YN55NKH
23	BT	YN55NHV	29	BT	YN55NJJ	35	BT	YN55NKD	40	BT	YN55NKJ
24	BT	YN55NHX	30	BT	YN55NJK	36	BT	YN55NKE	41	BT	YN55NKK
25	BT	YN55NHY	31	BT	YN55NJU	37	BT	YN55NKF	42	BT	YN55NKL
26	BT	YN55NHZ	32	BT	YN55NJV						

SP68-87
Scania OmniCity CN230 UD   Scania   N41/22D   2009

68	BT	YT59RXR	73	BT	YT59RXX	78	BT	YT59RYC	83	BT	YT59RYJ
69	BT	YT59RXS	74	BT	YT59RXY	79	BT	YT59RYD	84	BT	YT59RYK
70	BT	YT59RXU	75	BT	YT59RXZ	80	BT	YT59RYF	85	BT	YT59RYM
71	BT	YT59RXV	76	BT	YT59RYA	81	BT	YT59RYG	86	BT	YT59RYN
72	BT	YT59RXW	77	BT	YT59RYB	82	BT	YT59RYH	87	BT	YT59RYO

VA17	BTt	XDZ5917	Volvo Olympian	Alexander RH	B47/25D	1997

VLE27-39 — Volvo B7TL 11m — East Lancs Mylennium Vyking N47/22D — 2004

27	BT	PA04CYK	31	BT	PA04CYT	34	BT	PO54ACJ	37	BT	PO54ACX
28	BT	PA04CYL	32	BT	PO54ABZ	35	BT	PO54ACU	38	BT	PO54ACY
29	BT	PA04CYP	33	BT	PO54ACF	36	BT	PO54ACV	39	BT	PO54ACZ
30	BT	PA04CYS									

VLP18-27 — Volvo B7TL 10.6m — TransBus President 4.4m — N45/23D — 2003

18	BT	PJ53OUN	21	BT	PJ53OUU	24	BT	PJ53OUX	26	BT	PJ53OVA
19	BT	PJ53OUO	22	BT	PJ53OUV	25	BT	PJ53OUY	27	BT	PJ53OVB
20	BT	PJ53OUP	23	u	PJ53OUW						

VLP220 BT LK51XGP Volvo B7TL 10.6m Plaxton President N43/24D 2001 Metroline, 2012

Depots and allocations:

Edgware (Station Road) - BT

Enviro 200	SDE18	SDE19	SDE20	SDE21	SDE22	SDE23	SDE24	DE57
	DE58	DE59	DE60	DE61	DE62	DE63	DE64	DE65
	DE66	DE67	DE68	DE69	DE70			
Scania DD	SLE1	SLE2	SLE3	SLE4	SLE5	SLE6	SLE21	SLE22
	SLE23	SLE24	SLE25	SLE26	SLE27	SLE28	SLE29	SLE30
	SLE31	SLE32	SLE33	SLE34	SLE35	SLE36	SLE37	SLE38
	SLE39	SLE40	SLE41	SLE42	SP68	SP69	SP70	SP71
	SP72	SP73	SP74	SP75	SP76	SP77	SP78	SP79
	SP80	SP81	SP82	SP83	SP84	SP85	SP86	SP87
Volvo B7TL	VLE27	VLE28	VLE29	VLE30	VLE31	VLE32	VLE33	VLE34
	VLE35	VLE36	VLE37	VLE38	VLE39	VLP18	VLP19	VLP20
	VLP21	VLP22	VLP23	VLP24	VLP25	VLP26	VLP27	VLP220
Volvo B5LH	HWW1	HWW2	HWW3	HWW4	HWW5	HWW6	HWW7	HWW8
	HWW8	HWW10	HWW11	HWW12	HWW13	HWW14	HWW15	HWW16
	HWW17	HWW18	HWW19	HWW20	HWW21	HWW22	HWW23	

Ancillary   VA17

Harrow (Pinner Road) - SO

Dart	DPS599	DPS627	DPS628	DPS629	DPS630	DPS631	DPS632	DPS633
	DPS634	DPS635	DPS636	DPS637	DPS638	DPS639	DPS640	
Enviro 200	DE50	DE51	DE52	DE53	DE54	DE55	DE56	DE71
	DE72	DE73	DE74	DE75	DE76	DE77	DE78	DE79
	DE80	DE81	DE82	DE83	DE84	DE85	DE86	DE87
	DE88	DE89	DE90	DE91	DE92	DE93	DE95	DE96
	DE97	DE98	DE99					

All of Sovereign's double-decks are allocated to Edgware depot. East Lancs-bodied VLE34, PO54ACJ, illustrates the type as it operates route 114 in Harrow town centre.
Terry Longhurst

LONDON TRAMLINK

First Tram Operations Ltd, Tramlink Depot, Coomber Way, Croydon, CR0 4TQ

2530-2553	Bombardier Eurorail CR-4000		Bombardier		AB70T	1998-99		
2530	2533	2536	2539	2542	2544	2546	2548	2550	2552
2531	2534	2537	2540	2543	2545	2547	2549	2551	2553
2532	2535	2538	2541						

2554-2559	Stadler Variobahn		Stadler		AB72T	2012
2554	2555	2556	2557	2558	2559	

Depot: Coomer Way, Croydon

London Tramlink began operation in May 2000 and features Croydon as its central point. A division of the First Group currently operates the system on behalf of London Tramlink with a fleet now painted into the lime blue and white scheme. Seen at Addiscombe Road is Bombardier Eurorail type 2538 while further along the road is 2558, one of the six Stadler Variobahn trams which arrived in 2012. *Mark Lyons*

Vehicle index

Reg	Operator	Reg	Operator	Reg	Operator	Reg	Operator
3CLT	Arriva	ALM89B	Stagecoach	BF59NHJ	Go-Ahead		
70CLT	Arriva	B14BUS	Big Bus Company	BF60OFD	RATP - Quality Line		
185CLT	Arriva	BD09ZPR	Go-Ahead	BF60OFE	RATP - Quality Line		
201KYD	Original Tour	BD09ZPS	Go-Ahead	BF60UTZ	Metroline		
202UXJ	Go-Ahead	BD09ZPT	Go-Ahead	BF60UUA	Metroline		
204CLT	Tower Transit	BD09ZPU	Go-Ahead	BF60UUB	Metroline		
205CLT	Arriva	BD09ZPV	Go-Ahead	BF60UUC	Metroline		
217CLT	Arriva	BD09ZPW	Go-Ahead	BF60UUD	Metroline		
218CLT	Tower Transit	BD09ZPX	Go-Ahead	BF60UUE	Metroline		
280CLT	Tower Transit	BD09ZPY	Go-Ahead	BF60UUG	Metroline		
319CLT	Arriva	BD09ZPZ	Go-Ahead	BF60UUH	Metroline		
324CLT	Arriva	BD09ZRA	Go-Ahead	BF60UUJ	Metroline		
330CLT	Arriva	BD09ZRC	Go-Ahead	BF60UUK	Metroline		
398CLT	Arriva	BD09ZRE	Go-Ahead	BF60UUL	Metroline		
519CLT	Arriva	BD09ZRF	Go-Ahead	BF60UUM	Metroline		
527CLT	Stagecoach	BD09ZRG	Go-Ahead	BF60UUN	Metroline		
562CLT	Tower Transit	BD09ZRJ	Go-Ahead	BF60UUO	Metroline		
593CLT	Arriva	BD09ZRK	Go-Ahead	BF60UUP	Metroline		
627DYE	Tower Transit	BD09ZVT	Go-Ahead	BF60UUR	Metroline		
640DYE	Tower Transit	BD09ZVU	Go-Ahead	BF60UUS	Metroline		
650DYE	Tower Transit	BD09ZVV	Go-Ahead	BF60UUT	Metroline		
656DYE	Arriva	BD09ZVW	Go-Ahead	BF60UUV	Metroline		
725DYE	Arriva	BD09ZVX	Go-Ahead	BF60UUW	Metroline		
734DYE	Arriva	BD09ZVY	Go-Ahead	BF60UUX	Metroline		
735DYE	Tower Transit	BD09ZVZ	Go-Ahead	BF60UUY	Metroline		
776DYE	Tower Transit	BD09ZWA	Go-Ahead	BF60UUZ	Metroline		
801DYE	Arriva	BD09ZWB	Go-Ahead	BF60UVA	Metroline		
822DYE	Arriva	BD09ZWC	Go-Ahead	BF60UVB	Metroline		
A737WEV	Original Tour	BD09ZWE	Go-Ahead	BF60UVC	Metroline		
A749WEV	Original Tour	BD09ZWF	Go-Ahead	BF60UVD	Metroline		
A750WEV	Original Tour	BD09ZWG	Go-Ahead	BF60UVE	Metroline		
A755WEV	Original Tour	BD09ZWH	Go-Ahead	BF60UVG	Metroline		
AE06HCA	Go-Ahead	BD11LWN	RATP - London	BF60UVH	Metroline		
AE06HCC	Go-Ahead	BD11LWO	RATP - London	BF60VHP	Metroline		
AE06HCD	Go-Ahead	BD11LWP	RATP - London	BF60VHR	Metroline		
AE06HCF	Go-Ahead	BD11LWR	RATP - London	BF60VHT	Metroline		
AE06HCG	Go-Ahead	BD11LWS	RATP - London	BF60VHU	Metroline		
AE06HCH	Go-Ahead	BD11LWT	RATP - London	BF60VHV	Metroline		
AE06HCJ	Go-Ahead	BD11LWU	RATP - London	BF60VHW	Metroline		
AE06HCK	Go-Ahead	BD13OHJ	Transdev	BF60VHX	Metroline		
AE09DHG	Metrobus	BD13OHU	Transdev	BF60VHY	Metroline		
AE09DHJ	Metrobus	BD13OHV	Transdev	BF60VHZ	Metroline		
AE09DHK	Metrobus	BD13OHW	Transdev	BF60VJA	Metroline		
AE09DHL	Metrobus	BD13OHX	Transdev	BF60VJC	Metroline		
AE09DHM	Metrobus	BD13OHY	Transdev	BF60VJD	Metroline		
AE09DHN	Metrobus	BD13OHZ	Transdev	BF60VJE	Metroline		
AE09DHO	Metrobus	BD13OJA	Transdev	BF60VJG	Metroline		
AE09DHP	Metrobus	BD13OJB	Transdev	BF60VJJ	Metroline		
AE09DHU	Metrobus	BD13OJC	Transdev	BF60VJK	Metroline		
AE09DHV	Metrobus	BD13OJE	Transdev	BF60VJL	Metroline		
AE56OUH	Go-Ahead	BD13YWJ	Transdev	BF60VJM	Metroline		
AE56OUJ	Go-Ahead	BD13YWK	Transdev	BF60VJN	Metroline		
AE56OUK	Go-Ahead	BD13YWL	Transdev	BF60VJO	Metroline		
AE56OUL	Go-Ahead	BD13YWM	Transdev	BF60VJP	Metroline		
AE56OUM	Go-Ahead	BD13YWN	Transdev	BF60VJU	Metroline		
AE56OUN	Go-Ahead	BD13YWO	Transdev	BF60VJV	Metroline		
AE56OUO	Go-Ahead	BD13YWP	Transdev	BF62UXU	RATP - London		
AE56OUP	Go-Ahead	BD13YWR	Transdev	BF62UYA	Tower Transit		
AE56OUS	Go-Ahead	BD13YWS	Transdev	BF62UYB	Tower Transit		
AJ58WBD	Metrobus	BD13YWU	Transdev	BF62UYC	Tower Transit		
AJ58WBE	Metrobus	BD13YWV	Transdev	BF62UYD	Tower Transit		
AJ58WBF	Metrobus	BD13YWW	Transdev	BF62UYE	Tower Transit		
AJ58WBG	Metrobus	BF10LSO	Metroline	BF62UYG	Tower Transit		
AJ58WBK	Metrobus	BF10LSU	Metroline	BF62UYH	Tower Transit		
ALD913B	Tower Transit	BF10LSV	Metroline	BF62UYJ	Tower Transit		
ALD933B	Stagecoach	BF10LSX	Metroline	BF62UYK	Tower Transit		
ALD941B	Stagecoach	BF10LSY	Metroline	BG09JJK	Go-Ahead		
ALD968B	Stagecoach	BF10LSZ	Metroline	BG09JJL	Go-Ahead		
ALM50B	Stagecoach	BF10LTA	Metroline	BG09JJU	Go-Ahead		
ALM60B	Stagecoach	BF10LTE	Metroline	BG09JJV	Go-Ahead		
ALM71B	Stagecoach	BF10LTJ	Metroline	BG09JJX	Go-Ahead		

Reg	Operator	Reg	Operator	Reg	Operator
BG09JJY	Go-Ahead	BJ11EBD	Tower Transit	BU05HDY	Abellio
BG09JJZ	Go-Ahead	BJ11EBG	Tower Transit	BU05HEJ	Abellio
BG09JKE	Go-Ahead	BJ11EBK	Tower Transit	BU05HFA	Abellio
BG09JKF	Go-Ahead	BJ11EBL	Tower Transit	BU05HFB	Abellio
BG09JKJ	Go-Ahead	BJ11EBM	Tower Transit	BU05HFC	Abellio
BG59FXA	Go-Ahead	BJ11EBN	Tower Transit	BU05HFD	Abellio
BG59FXB	Go-Ahead	BJ11EBO	Tower Transit	BU05HFG	HCT - CT Plus
BG59FXC	Go-Ahead	BJ11EBP	Tower Transit	BU05HFK	Abellio
BG59FXD	Go-Ahead	BJ11XGZ	Go-Ahead	BU05HFN	Abellio
BG59FXE	Go-Ahead	BK10MEV	Metroline	BU05HFV	Abellio
BG59FXF	Go-Ahead	BK10MFA	Metroline	BU05HFW	Abellio
BG59FXH	Go-Ahead	BK10MFE	Metroline	BU05HFX	Abellio
BG61SXJ	Tower Transit	BK10MFF	Metroline	BU06CSF	RATP - Quality Line
BG61SXL	Tower Transit	BK10MFJ	Metroline	BU06CSO	RATP - Quality Line
BG61SXM	Tower Transit	BK10MFN	Metroline	BU53ZWN	RATP - Quality Line
BG61SXN	Tower Transit	BK10MFO	Metroline	BU53ZWP	RATP - Quality Line
BG61SXO	Tower Transit	BK10MFZ	Tower Transit	BU53ZWR	RATP - Quality Line
BG61SXP	Tower Transit	BK58URT	RATP - Quality Line	BV10WVD	Go-Ahead
BG61SXR	Tower Transit	BL61ACX	Go-Ahead	BV10WVE	Go-Ahead
BJ11DRZ	Tower Transit	BL61ACY	Go-Ahead	BV10WVF	Go-Ahead
BJ11DSE	Tower Transit	BL61ACZ	Go-Ahead	BV10WVG	Go-Ahead
BJ11DSO	Tower Transit	BL61ADO	Go-Ahead	BV10WVH	Go-Ahead
BJ11DSU	Tower Transit	BL61ADU	Go-Ahead	BV10WVJ	Go-Ahead
BJ11DSV	Tower Transit	BL61ADV	Go-Ahead	BV10WVK	Go-Ahead
BJ11DSX	Tower Transit	BL61ADX	Go-Ahead	BV10WVL	Go-Ahead
BJ11DSY	Tower Transit	BL61ADZ	Go-Ahead	BV10WVM	Tower Transit
BJ11DSZ	Tower Transit	BN12EOP	RATP - Quality Line	BV10WVN	Metroline
BJ11DTF	Tower Transit	BN12EOR	RATP - Quality Line	BV10WVO	Metroline
BJ11DTK	Tower Transit	BN12EOS	RATP - Quality Line	BV10WVP	Metroline
BJ11DTN	Tower Transit	BN12EOT	RATP - Quality Line	BV10WVR	Metroline
BJ11DTO	Tower Transit	BN12EOU	RATP - Quality Line	BV10WVS	Metroline
BJ11DTU	Tower Transit	BN12EOV	RATP - Quality Line	BV10WVT	Metroline
BJ11DTV	Tower Transit	BN12EOW	RATP - Quality Line	BV10WVU	Metroline
BJ11DTX	Tower Transit	BN12EOX	RATP - Quality Line	BV10WVW	Metroline
BJ11DTY	Tower Transit	BN12EOY	RATP - Quality Line	BV10WVX	Metroline
BJ11DTZ	Tower Transit	BN12EOZ	RATP - Quality Line	BV10WVY	Tower Transit
BJ11DUA	Tower Transit	BN61MWZ	Tower Transit	BV10WVZ	Tower Transit
BJ11DUH	Tower Transit	BN61MXA	Tower Transit	BV10WWA	Go-Ahead
BJ11DUU	Tower Transit	BN61MXB	Tower Transit	BV10WWB	Tower Transit
BJ11DUV	Tower Transit	BN61MXC	Tower Transit	BV10WWC	Go-Ahead
BJ11DUY	Tower Transit	BN61MXD	Tower Transit	BV10WWD	Go-Ahead
BJ11DVA	Tower Transit	BN61MXE	Tower Transit	BV10WWE	Tower Transit
BJ11DVB	Tower Transit	BN61MXF	Tower Transit	BV10WWF	Go-Ahead
BJ11DVC	Tower Transit	BN61MXG	Tower Transit	BV10WWG	Tower Transit
BJ11DVF	Tower Transit	BN61MXH	Tower Transit	BV10WWH	Tower Transit
BJ11DVG	Tower Transit	BN61MXJ	Tower Transit	BV10WWJ	Tower Transit
BJ11DVH	Tower Transit	BN61MXK	Tower Transit	BV10WWK	Tower Transit
BJ11DVK	Tower Transit	BN61MXL	Tower Transit	BV10WWL	Tower Transit
BJ11DVL	Tower Transit	BN61MXM	Tower Transit	BV10WWM	Tower Transit
BJ11DVM	Tower Transit	BN61MXO	Tower Transit	BV10WWN	Tower Transit
BJ11DVN	Tower Transit	BN61MXP	Tower Transit	BV10WWO	Go-Ahead
BJ11DVO	Tower Transit	BN61MXR	Tower Transit	BV10WWP	Go-Ahead
BJ11DVP	Tower Transit	BN61MXS	Tower Transit	BV10WWR	Go-Ahead
BJ11DVR	Tower Transit	BN61MXT	Tower Transit	BV10WWS	Tower Transit
BJ11DVT	Tower Transit	BN61MXU	Tower Transit	BV10WWT	Tower Transit
BJ11DVU	Tower Transit	BN61MXV	Tower Transit	BV10WWU	Tower Transit
BJ11DVV	Tower Transit	BN61MXW	Tower Transit	BV10WWX	Tower Transit
BJ11DVW	Tower Transit	BN61MXX	Tower Transit	BV55UCT	Go-Ahead
BJ11DVX	Tower Transit	BN61MXY	Tower Transit	BV55UCU	Go-Ahead
BJ11DZX	Tower Transit	BN61MYA	Tower Transit	BV55UCW	Go-Ahead
BJ11DZY	Tower Transit	BN61MYB	Tower Transit	BV55UCX	Go-Ahead
BJ11DZZ	Tower Transit	BN61SXK	Tower Transit	BV55UCY	Go-Ahead
BJ11EAA	Tower Transit	BT04BUS	Go-Ahead	BW03ZMZ	RATP - Quality Line
BJ11EAC	Tower Transit	BT09GOH	Go-Ahead	BX02CMO	RATP - Quality Line
BJ11EAE	Tower Transit	BT09GOJ	Go-Ahead	BX02CMU	RATP - Quality Line
BJ11EAF	Tower Transit	BT09GOK	Go-Ahead	BX04AZU	Go-Ahead
BJ11EAG	Tower Transit	BT09GOP	Go-Ahead	BX04AZV	Go-Ahead
BJ11EAK	Tower Transit	BT09GOU	Go-Ahead	BX04AZW	Go-Ahead
BJ11EAM	Tower Transit	BT09GOX	Go-Ahead	BX04AZZ	Go-Ahead
BJ11EAO	Tower Transit	BT09GPE	Go-Ahead	BX04BAA	Go-Ahead
BJ11EAP	Tower Transit	BT09GPF	Go-Ahead	BX04BAU	Go-Ahead
BJ11EAW	Tower Transit	BT09GPJ	Go-Ahead	BX04BAV	Go-Ahead
BJ11EAX	Tower Transit	BU04EXT	RATP - Quality Line	BX04BBE	Go-Ahead
BJ11EAY	Tower Transit	BU04EXV	RATP - Quality Line	BX04BBF	Go-Ahead
BJ11EBA	Tower Transit	BU04EXW	RATP - Quality Line	BX04BBJ	Go-Ahead
BJ11EBC	Tower Transit	BU04EXX	RATP - Quality Line	BX04BKJ	Go-Ahead

BX04BKK	Go-Ahead	BX55XMW	Abellio	FJ61EYK	RATP - Quality Line
BX04BKL	Go-Ahead	BX55XMZ	Abellio	FJ61EYL	RATP - Quality Line
BX04BXM	Go-Ahead	BX55XNA	Abellio	G32FWC	Big Bus Company
BX04BXN	Go-Ahead	BX55XNB	Abellio	G34FWC	Big Bus Company
BX12CVK	Tower Transit	BX55XNC	Abellio	G42FWC	Big Bus Company
BX12CVL	Tower Transit	BX55XND	Abellio	G59SYE	Big Bus Company
BX12CVM	Tower Transit	BX55XNE	Abellio	G67SYE	Big Bus Company
BX12CVO	Tower Transit	BX55XNF	Abellio	G96SGO	Big Bus Company
BX12CVP	Tower Transit	BX55XNG	Abellio	G159FWC	Big Bus Company
BX54DHJ	Abellio	BX55XNJ	Abellio	G938FVX	Big Bus Company
BX54DHK	Abellio	BX55XNK	Abellio	G939FVX	Big Bus Company
BX54DHL	Abellio	BX55XNL	Abellio	G943FVX	Big Bus Company
BX54DHM	Abellio	BX55XNM	Abellio	G952FVX	Big Bus Company
BX54DHN	Abellio	BX55XNN	Abellio	G953FVX	Big Bus Company
BX54DHO	Abellio	BX55XNO	Abellio	G954FVX	Big Bus Company
BX54DHP	Abellio	BX55XNP	Abellio	G956FVX	Big Bus Company
BX54DHV	Abellio	BX55XNR	Abellio	G963FVX	Big Bus Company
BX54DHY	Abellio	BX55XNS	Abellio	G969FVX	Big Bus Company
BX54DHZ	Abellio	BX55XNT	Abellio	G991FVX	Big Bus Company
BX54DJD	Abellio	BX55XNU	Abellio	GK53AOA	Arriva Southern Cs
BX54DJE	Abellio	BX55XNV	Abellio	GK53AOB	Arriva Southern Cs
BX54DJF	Abellio	BX55XNW	Abellio	GK53AOC	Arriva Southern Cs
BX54DJJ	Abellio	BX55XNY	Abellio	GK53AOD	Arriva Southern Cs
BX54DJK	Abellio	BX55XNZ	Abellio	GK53AOE	Arriva Southern Cs
BX54DJO	Abellio	BX56VTY	RATP - Quality Line	GK53AOF	Arriva Southern Cs
BX54DJU	Abellio	BX56VTZ	RATP - Quality Line	GK53AOG	Arriva Southern Cs
BX54DJV	Abellio	CUV318C	Go-Ahead	GK53AOH	Arriva Southern Cs
BX54DJY	Abellio	D512UGT	Big Bus Company	GK53AOJ	Arriva Southern Cs
BX54DJZ	Abellio	D519UGT	Big Bus Company	GK53AOL	Arriva Southern Cs
BX54DKA	Abellio	D527UGT	Big Bus Company	GK53AON	Arriva Southern Cs
BX54DKD	Abellio	D553YNO	Original Tour	GK53AOO	Arriva Southern Cs
BX54DKE	Abellio	D692UGT	Big Bus Company	GK53AOP	Arriva Southern Cs
BX54DKF	Abellio	DK04SUU	Abellio	GK53AOU	Arriva Southern Cs
BX54DKJ	Abellio	E8NJB	HCT - CT Plus	GK53AOV	Arriva Southern Cs
BX54DKK	Abellio	E354NUV	Big Bus Company	GK53AOW	Arriva Southern Cs
BX54DKL	Abellio	E356NUV	Big Bus Company	GK53AOX	Arriva Southern Cs
BX54DKO	Abellio	E358NUV	Big Bus Company	GK53AOY	Arriva Southern Cs
BX54DKU	Abellio	E949JAR	Big Bus Company	GM03TGM	Abellio
BX54DKV	Abellio	EJ52WXF	Go-Ahead	GN07AUY	Metrobus
BX54DLK	HCT - CT Plus	EU05DVW	Original Tour	GN07AVR	Metrobus
BX54DLU	Abellio	EU05DVX	Original Tour	GN07AVT	Metrobus
BX54DLZ	Abellio	EU53PXY	Go-Ahead	GN07AVU	Metrobus
BX54DME	Abellio	EU53PXZ	Go-Ahead	GN07AVV	Metrobus
BX54DMF	Abellio	EU53PYA	Go-Ahead	GN07AVW	Metrobus
BX54DMO	Abellio	EU53PYB	Go-Ahead	GN07DLE	Arriva Southern Cs
BX54DMU	Abellio	EU53PYD	Go-Ahead	GN07DLF	Arriva Southern Cs
BX54DMV	Abellio	EU53PYF	Go-Ahead	GN07DLJ	Arriva Southern Cs
BX54DMY	Abellio	EU53PYG	Go-Ahead	GN07DLK	Arriva Southern Cs
BX54DMZ	Abellio	EU53PYH	Go-Ahead	GN07DLO	Arriva Southern Cs
BX54ECF	RATP - Quality Line	EU53PYJ	Go-Ahead	GN07DLU	Arriva Southern Cs
BX54ECJ	RATP - Quality Line	EU53PYL	Go-Ahead	GN07DLV	Arriva Southern Cs
BX55XLS	Abellio	EU53PYO	Go-Ahead	GN07DLX	Arriva Southern Cs
BX55XLT	Abellio	EU53PYP	Go-Ahead	GN07DLY	Arriva Southern Cs
BX55XLU	Abellio	EU62AAE	Stagecoach	GN07DLZ	Arriva Southern Cs
BX55XLV	Abellio	EU62AAO	Stagecoach	GN07DME	Arriva Southern Cs
BX55XLW	Abellio	EU62ADZ	Stagecoach	GN07DMF	Arriva Southern Cs
BX55XLY	Abellio	EU62AXT	Stagecoach	GN07DMO	Arriva Southern Cs
BX55XLZ	Abellio	EU62AXV	Stagecoach	GN07DMU	Arriva Southern Cs
BX55XMA	Abellio	EU62AYB	Stagecoach	GN07DMV	Arriva Southern Cs
BX55XMB	Abellio	EU62AYE	Stagecoach	GN08CGO	Arriva Southern Cs
BX55XMC	Abellio	EU62AZA	Stagecoach	GN08CGU	Arriva Southern Cs
BX55XMD	Abellio	EU62AZO	Stagecoach	GN08CGV	Arriva Southern Cs
BX55XME	Abellio	F418UJN	Big Bus Company	GN08CGX	Arriva Southern Cs
BX55XMG	Abellio	FJ11GLF	RATP - Quality Line	GN08CGY	Arriva Southern Cs
BX55XMH	Abellio	FJ11GMV	RATP - Quality Line	GN08CGZ	Arriva Southern Cs
BX55XMJ	Abellio	FJ54ZDC	Go-Ahead	GN09AVV	Arriva Southern Cs
BX55XMK	Abellio	FJ54ZDP	Go-Ahead	GN09AVW	Arriva Southern Cs
BX55XML	Abellio	FJ54ZDR	Go-Ahead	GN09AVX	Arriva Southern Cs
BX55XMM	Abellio	FJ54ZDR	Go-Ahead	GN09AVY	Arriva Southern Cs
BX55XMO	Abellio	FJ54ZDV	Go-Ahead	GN09AVZ	Arriva Southern Cs
BX55XMP	Abellio	FJ54ZDW	Go-Ahead	GN09AWA	Arriva Southern Cs
BX55XMR	Abellio	FJ54ZFA	Go-Ahead	GN09AWB	Arriva Southern Cs
BX55XMS	Abellio	FJ54ZTV	Go-Ahead	GN09AWC	Arriva Southern Cs
BX55XMT	Abellio	FJ54ZTZ	Go-Ahead	GN10KWE	Arriva Southern Cs
BX55XMU	Abellio	FJ54ZUA	Go-Ahead	GN10KWF	Arriva Southern Cs
BX55XMV	Abellio	FJ54ZVB	Go-Ahead	GN10KWG	Arriva Southern Cs

Reg	Operator	Reg	Operator	Reg	Operator
GN10KWH	Arriva Southern Cs	J347BSH	Original Tour	KX06LYS	Abellio
GN10KWJ	Arriva Southern Cs	J348BSH	Original Tour	KX06LYT	Abellio
GN10KWK	Arriva Southern Cs	J349BSH	Original Tour	KX56HCZ	Abellio
GN57BOU	Arriva Southern Cs	J350BSH	Original Tour	KX59AEE	Arriva The Shires
GN57BOV	Arriva Southern Cs	J351BSH	Original Tour	KX59AEF	Arriva The Shires
GN57BPE	Arriva Southern Cs	J352BSH	Original Tour	KX61LDL	Arriva Southern Cs
GN57BPF	Arriva	J433BSH	Original Tour	KX61LDN	Arriva Southern Cs
GN57BPK	Arriva	JJD427D	Go-Ahead	KX61LDO	Arriva Southern Cs
GN57BPO	Arriva	KE51PUA	Arriva Southern Cs	KX61LDU	Arriva Southern Cs
GN57BPU	Arriva	KL52CWZ	Arriva The Shires	KX61LDV	Arriva Southern Cs
GN57BPV	Arriva	KL52CXB	Arriva The Shires	LB02XYA	Go-Ahead
GN57BPX	Arriva	KL52CXC	Arriva The Shires	LB02YWX	Go-Ahead
GN57BPY	Arriva	KL52CXG	Arriva The Shires	LB02YWY	Go-Ahead
GN58BUP	Arriva Southern Cs	KL52CXH	Arriva The Shires	LB02YWZ	Go-Ahead
GN58BUU	Arriva Southern Cs	KL52CXJ	Arriva The Shires	LB02YXD	Go-Ahead
GN58BUV	Arriva Southern Cs	KL52CXK	Arriva The Shires	LB02YXE	Go-Ahead
GN58LVA	Arriva Southern Cs	KL52CXM	Arriva The Shires	LB02YXF	Go-Ahead
GN58LVB	Arriva Southern Cs	KL52CXN	Arriva The Shires	LB02YXG	Go-Ahead
GN61JGV	Arriva Southern Cs	KL52CXO	Arriva The Shires	LB02YXH	Go-Ahead
GN61JPY	Arriva Southern Cs	KL52CXP	Arriva The Shires	LB02YXJ	Go-Ahead
GN61JRO	Arriva Southern Cs	KL52CXR	Arriva The Shires	LB02YXK	Go-Ahead
GN61JRU	Arriva Southern Cs	KL52CXS	Arriva The Shires	LB02YXL	Go-Ahead
GN61JRV	Arriva Southern Cs	KM02HFP	Abellio	LB02YXM	Go-Ahead
GN61JRX	Arriva Southern Cs	KM02HFR	Abellio	LB02YXN	Go-Ahead
GN61JRZ	Arriva Southern Cs	KM02HFS	Abellio	LF02PKA	Arriva
GN61JSU	Arriva Southern Cs	KM02HFT	Abellio	LF02PKC	Arriva
GO58CHC	Arriva Southern Cs	KM02HFU	Abellio	LF02PKE	Arriva
GO58CHD	Arriva Southern Cs	KM02HFV	Abellio	LF02PKJ	Arriva
GO58CHF	Arriva Southern Cs	KM02HGE	Abellio	LF02PKO	Arriva
GO58CHG	Arriva Southern Cs	KM02HGF	Abellio	LF02PKU	Arriva
GO58CHH	Arriva Southern Cs	KN52NCE	Abellio	LF02PKV	Arriva
HF53OBG	RATP - London	KN52NDD	Abellio	LF02PKX	Arriva
HF53OBH	RATP - London	KN52NDE	Abellio	LF02PKY	Arriva
HV52WSZ	RATP - Quality Line	KN52NDG	Abellio	LF02PKZ	Arriva
HX03MGJ	HCT - CT Plus	KN52NDJ	Abellio	LF02PLJ	Arriva
HX03MGV	HCT - CT Plus	KN52NDO	Abellio	LF02PLN	Arriva
HX03MGX	HCT - CT Plus	KN52NDY	Abellio	LF02PLO	Arriva
HX03MGY	HCT - CT Plus	KN52NDZ	Abellio	LF02POA	Arriva
HX03MGZ	HCT - CT Plus	KN52NEJ	Abellio	LF02POH	Arriva
HX04HTP	Abellio	KN52NEO	Abellio	LF02PSO	Arriva
HX04HTT	Abellio	KN52NEU	Abellio	LF02PSU	Arriva
HX04HTU	Abellio	KN52NEY	Abellio	LF02PSY	Arriva
HX04HTV	Abellio	KN52NFA	Abellio	LF02PSZ	Arriva
HX04HTY	Abellio	KP02PUJ	Abellio	LF02PTO	Arriva
HX04HTZ	Abellio	KP02PUK	Abellio	LF02PTU	Arriva
J315BSH	Original Tour	KP02PVE	Abellio	LF02PTX	Arriva
J316BSH	Original Tour	KP02PVU	Abellio	LF02PTY	Arriva
J317BSH	Original Tour	KP02PWV	Abellio	LF02PVE	Arriva
J318BSH	Original Tour	KU52YKO	Abellio	LF02PVJ	Arriva
J319BSH	Original Tour	KU52YKR	Abellio	LF02PVK	Arriva
J320BSH	Original Tour	KU52YKS	Abellio	LF02PVL	Arriva
J321BSH	Original Tour	KV03ZFF	HCT - CT Plus	LF02PVN	Arriva
J322BSH	Original Tour	KV03ZFG	HCT - CT Plus	LF02PVO	Arriva
J323BSH	Original Tour	KV03ZFH	HCT - CT Plus	LF06YRC	Abellio
J324BSH	Original Tour	KV03ZFM	Abellio	LF06YRD	Abellio
J325BSH	Original Tour	KV03ZFN	Abellio	LF06YRE	Abellio
J326BSH	Original Tour	KV03ZFP	Abellio	LF06YRG	Abellio
J327BSH	Original Tour	KV03ZFR	Abellio	LF06YRJ	Abellio
J328BSH	Original Tour	KV03ZFS	Abellio	LF06YRK	Abellio
J329BSH	Original Tour	KV03ZFT	Abellio	LF06YRL	Abellio
J330BSH	Original Tour	KV03ZFU	Abellio	LF06YRM	Abellio
J331BSH	Original Tour	KV03ZFW	Abellio	LF06YRN	Abellio
J332BSH	Original Tour	KV03ZFX	Abellio	LF12ACZ	Big Bus Company
J334BSH	Original Tour	KV03ZFY	Abellio	LF12ADU	Big Bus Company
J335BSH	Original Tour	KX03HZF	Abellio	LF12LHE	Big Bus Company
J336BSH	Original Tour	KX03HZR	Abellio	LF52TGN	Go-Ahead
J337BSH	Original Tour	KX03HZS	Abellio	LF52TGO	Go-Ahead
J338BSH	Original Tour	KX03HZT	Abellio	LF52TGU	Go-Ahead
J339BSH	Original Tour	KX03HZV	Abellio	LF52TGV	Go-Ahead
J340BSH	Original Tour	KX03HZY	Abellio	LF52TGX	Go-Ahead
J341BSH	Original Tour	KX03HZZ	Abellio	LF52TGY	Go-Ahead
J342BSH	Original Tour	KX04HRD	Abellio	LF52TGZ	Go-Ahead
J343BSH	Original Tour	KX04HRE	Abellio	LF52THG	Go-Ahead
J344BSH	Original Tour	KX04HRF	Abellio	LF52THK	Go-Ahead
J345BSH	Original Tour	KX04HRG	Abellio	LF52THN	Go-Ahead
J346BSH	Original Tour	KX05HFW	Abellio	LF52THU	Go-Ahead

LF52THV	Go-Ahead	LF52USH	Arriva	LF52ZRV	Go-Ahead
LF52THX	Go-Ahead	LF52USJ	Arriva	LF52ZRX	Go-Ahead
LF52THZ	Go-Ahead	LF52USL	Arriva	LF52ZRY	Go-Ahead
LF52TJO	Go-Ahead	LF52USM	Arriva	LF52ZRZ	Go-Ahead
LF52TJU	Go-Ahead	LF52USN	Arriva	LF52ZSD	Go-Ahead
LF52TJV	Go-Ahead	LF52USO	Arriva	LF52ZSO	Go-Ahead
LF52TJX	Go-Ahead	LF52USS	Arriva	LF52ZSP	Go-Ahead
LF52TJY	Go-Ahead	LF52UST	Arriva	LF52ZSR	Go-Ahead
LF52TKA	Go-Ahead	LF52USU	Arriva	LF52ZST	Go-Ahead
LF52TKC	Go-Ahead	LF52USV	Arriva	LF52ZTG	Go-Ahead
LF52TKD	Go-Ahead	LF52USW	Arriva	LF52ZTH	Go-Ahead
LF52TKJ	Go-Ahead	LF52USX	Arriva	LF52ZTJ	Go-Ahead
LF52TKK	Go-Ahead	LF52USY	Arriva	LF52ZTK	Go-Ahead
LF52TKN	Go-Ahead	LF52UTC	Arriva	LF52ZTL	Go-Ahead
LF52TKO	Go-Ahead	LF52UTE	Arriva	LF52ZTM	Go-Ahead
LF52TKT	Go-Ahead	LF52UTG	Arriva	LF52ZTN	Go-Ahead
LF52UNV	Arriva	LF52UTH	Arriva	LF52ZTO	Go-Ahead
LF52UNW	Arriva	LF52UTL	Arriva	LF52ZTP	Go-Ahead
LF52UNX	Arriva	LF52UTM	Arriva	LF52ZTR	Go-Ahead
LF52UNY	Arriva	LF52ZLZ	Go-Ahead	LF59XDZ	Abellio
LF52UNZ	Arriva	LF52ZMO	Go-Ahead	LG02FAA	RATP - London
LF52UOA	Arriva	LF52ZMU	Go-Ahead	LG02FAF	RATP - London
LF52UOC	Arriva	LF52ZND	Go-Ahead	LG02FAJ	RATP - London
LF52UOR	Arriva	LF52ZNE	Go-Ahead	LG02FAK	RATP - London
LF52UOS	Arriva	LF52ZNG	Go-Ahead	LG02FAM	RATP - London
LF52UOT	Arriva	LF52ZNH	Go-Ahead	LG02FAO	RATP - London
LF52UOU	Arriva	LF52ZNJ	Go-Ahead	LG02FAU	RATP - London
LF52UOV	Arriva	LF52ZNK	Go-Ahead	LG02FBA	RATP - London
LF52UOW	Arriva	LF52ZNL	Go-Ahead	LG02FBB	RATP - London
LF52UOX	Arriva	LF52ZNM	Go-Ahead	LG02FBC	RATP - London
LF52UOY	Arriva	LF52ZNN	Go-Ahead	LG02FBD	RATP - London
LF52UPA	Arriva	LF52ZNO	Go-Ahead	LG02FBE	RATP - London
LF52UPB	Arriva	LF52ZNP	Go-Ahead	LG02FBF	RATP - London
LF52UPC	Arriva	LF52ZNR	Go-Ahead	LG02FBJ	RATP - London
LF52UPD	Arriva	LF52ZNS	Go-Ahead	LG02FBK	RATP - London
LF52UPG	Arriva	LF52ZNT	Go-Ahead	LG02FBL	RATP - London
LF52UPH	Arriva	LF52ZNU	Go-Ahead	LG02FBN	RATP - London
LF52UPK	Arriva	LF52ZNV	Go-Ahead	LG02FBO	RATP - London
LF52UPL	Arriva	LF52ZNW	Go-Ahead	LG02FBU	RATP - London
LF52UPN	Arriva	LF52ZNX	Go-Ahead	LG02FBV	RATP - London
LF52UPN	Arriva	LF52ZNY	Go-Ahead	LG02FBX	RATP - London
LF52UPO	Arriva	LF52ZNZ	Go-Ahead	LG02FBY	RATP - London
LF52UPP	Arriva	LF52ZPB	Go-Ahead	LG02FDY	RATP - London
LF52UPR	Arriva	LF52ZPC	Go-Ahead	LG02FDZ	RATP - London
LF52UPS	Arriva	LF52ZPD	Go-Ahead	LG02FEF	RATP - London
LF52UPT	Arriva	LF52ZPE	Go-Ahead	LG02FEH	RATP - London
LF52UPV	Arriva	LF52ZPG	Go-Ahead	LG02FEJ	RATP - London
LF52UPW	Arriva	LF52ZPH	Go-Ahead	LG02FEK	RATP - London
LF52UPX	Arriva	LF52ZPJ	Go-Ahead	LG02FFK	RATP - London
LF52UPZ	Arriva	LF52ZPK	Go-Ahead	LG02FFL	RATP - London
LF52URA	Arriva	LF52ZPL	Go-Ahead	LG02FFM	RATP - London
LF52URB	Arriva	LF52ZPM	Go-Ahead	LG02FFN	RATP - London
LF52URC	Arriva	LF52ZPN	Go-Ahead	LG02FFO	RATP - London
LF52URD	Arriva	LF52ZPO	Go-Ahead	LG02FFP	RATP - London
LF52URE	Arriva	LF52ZPP	Go-Ahead	LG02FFR	RATP - London
LF52URG	Arriva	LF52ZPR	Go-Ahead	LG02FFS	RATP - London
LF52URH	Arriva	LF52ZPS	Go-Ahead	LG02FFT	RATP - London
LF52URJ	Arriva	LF52ZPU	Go-Ahead	LG02FFU	RATP - London
LF52URK	Arriva	LF52ZPV	Go-Ahead	LG02FFV	RATP - London
LF52URL	Arriva	LF52ZPW	Go-Ahead	LG02FFW	RATP - London
LF52URM	Arriva	LF52ZPY	Go-Ahead	LG02FFX	RATP - London
LF52URN	Arriva	LF52ZPZ	Go-Ahead	LG02FFY	RATP - London
LF52URO	Arriva	LF52ZRA	Go-Ahead	LG02FFZ	RATP - London
LF52URP	Arriva	LF52ZRC	Go-Ahead	LG02FGA	RATP - London
LF52URR	Arriva	LF52ZRD	Go-Ahead	LG02FGC	RATP - London
LF52URS	Arriva	LF52ZRE	Go-Ahead	LG02FGD	RATP - London
LF52URT	Arriva	LF52ZRG	Go-Ahead	LG02FGE	RATP - London
LF52URU	Arriva	LF52ZRJ	Go-Ahead	LG02FGF	RATP - London
LF52URV	Arriva	LF52ZRK	Go-Ahead	LG02FGJ	RATP - London
LF52URW	Arriva	LF52ZRL	Go-Ahead	LG02FGK	RATP - London
LF52URX	Arriva	LF52ZRN	Go-Ahead	LG02FGM	RATP - London
LF52URY	Arriva	LF52ZRO	Go-Ahead	LG02FGN	RATP - London
LF52URZ	Arriva	LF52ZRP	Go-Ahead	LG02FGO	RATP - London
LF52USB	Arriva	LF52ZRR	Go-Ahead	LG02FGP	RATP - London
LF52USD	Arriva	LF52ZRT	Go-Ahead	LG02FGU	RATP - London
LF52USE	Arriva	LF52ZRU	Go-Ahead	LG02FGV	RATP - London

Reg	Operator	Reg	Operator	Reg	Operator
LG02FGX	RATP - London	LG52XZS	Abellio	LJ03MLY	Arriva
LG02FGZ	RATP - London	LG52XZT	Abellio	LJ03MLY	Arriva
LG02FHA	RATP - London	LJ03MBF	Arriva	LJ03MMA	Arriva
LG02FHB	RATP - London	LJ03MBU	Arriva	LJ03MME	Arriva
LG02FHC	RATP - London	LJ03MBV	Arriva	LJ03MMF	Arriva
LG02FHD	RATP - London	LJ03MBX	Arriva	LJ03MMK	Arriva
LG02FHE	RATP - London	LJ03MBY	Arriva	LJ03MMU	Arriva
LG02FHH	RATP - London	LJ03MDE	Arriva	LJ03MMV	Arriva
LG02FHJ	RATP - London	LJ03MDF	Arriva	LJ03MMX	Arriva
LG02FHK	RATP - London	LJ03MDK	Arriva	LJ03MOA	Arriva
LG02FHL	RATP - London	LJ03MDN	Arriva	LJ03MOF	Arriva
LG02KGP	Go-Ahead	LJ03MDU	Arriva	LJ03MOV	Arriva
LG02KGU	Go-Ahead	LJ03MDV	Arriva	LJ03MPF	Arriva
LG02KGV	Go-Ahead	LJ03MDX	Arriva	LJ03MPU	Arriva
LG02KGX	Go-Ahead	LJ03MDY	Arriva	LJ03MPV	Arriva
LG02KGY	Go-Ahead	LJ03MDZ	Arriva	LJ03MPX	Arriva
LG02KGZ	Go-Ahead	LJ03MEU	Arriva	LJ03MPY	Arriva
LG02KHA	Go-Ahead	LJ03MEV	Arriva	LJ03MPZ	Arriva
LG02KHE	Go-Ahead	LJ03MFA	Arriva	LJ03MRU	Arriva
LG02KHF	Go-Ahead	LJ03MFE	Arriva	LJ03MRV	Arriva
LG02KHH	Go-Ahead	LJ03MFF	Arriva	LJ03MRX	Arriva
LG02KHJ	Go-Ahead	LJ03MFK	Arriva	LJ03MRY	Arriva
LG02KHK	Go-Ahead	LJ03MFN	Arriva	LJ03MSU	Arriva
LG02KHL	Go-Ahead	LJ03MFP	Arriva	LJ03MSV	Arriva
LG02KHM	Go-Ahead	LJ03MFU	Arriva	LJ03MSX	Arriva
LG02KHO	Go-Ahead	LJ03MFV	Arriva	LJ03MSY	Arriva
LG02KHP	Go-Ahead	LJ03MFX	Arriva	LJ03MTE	Arriva
LG02KHR	Go-Ahead	LJ03MFY	Arriva	LJ03MTF	Arriva
LG02KHT	Go-Ahead	LJ03MFZ	Arriva	LJ03MTK	Arriva
LG02KHU	Go-Ahead	LJ03MGE	Arriva	LJ03MTU	Arriva
LG02KHV	Go-Ahead	LJ03MGU	Arriva	LJ03MTV	Arriva
LG02KHW	Go-Ahead	LJ03MGV	Arriva	LJ03MTY	Arriva
LG02KHX	Go-Ahead	LJ03MGX	Arriva	LJ03MTZ	Arriva
LG02KHY	Go-Ahead	LJ03MGY	Arriva	LJ03MUA	Arriva
LG02KHZ	Go-Ahead	LJ03MGZ	Arriva	LJ03MUB	Arriva
LG02KJA	Go-Ahead	LJ03MHA	Arriva	LJ03MUW	Arriva The Shires
LG02KJE	Go-Ahead	LJ03MHE	Arriva	LJ03MUY	Arriva
LG02KJF	Go-Ahead	LJ03MHF	Arriva	LJ03MVC	Arriva
LG52DAA	Arriva	LJ03MHK	Arriva	LJ03MVD	Arriva
LG52DAO	Arriva	LJ03MHL	Arriva	LJ03MVE	Arriva
LG52DAU	Arriva	LJ03MHN	Arriva	LJ03MVF	Arriva
LG52DBO	Arriva	LJ03MHN	Arriva	LJ03MVG	Arriva
LG52DBU	Arriva	LJ03MHU	Arriva	LJ03MVT	Arriva
LG52DBV	Arriva	LJ03MHV	Arriva	LJ03MVV	Arriva
LG52DBY	Arriva	LJ03MHX	Arriva	LJ03MVW	Arriva
LG52DBZ	Arriva	LJ03MHY	Arriva	LJ03MVX	Arriva
LG52DCE	Arriva	LJ03MHZ	Arriva	LJ03MVY	Arriva
LG52DCF	Arriva	LJ03MJE	Arriva	LJ03MVZ	Arriva
LG52DCO	Arriva	LJ03MJF	Arriva	LJ03MWA	Arriva
LG52DCU	Arriva	LJ03MJK	Arriva	LJ03MWC	Arriva
LG52DCV	Arriva	LJ03MJU	Arriva	LJ03MWD	Arriva
LG52DCX	Arriva	LJ03MJV	Arriva	LJ03MWE	Arriva
LG52DCY	Arriva	LJ03MJX	Arriva	LJ03MWF	Arriva
LG52DCZ	Arriva	LJ03MJY	Arriva	LJ03MWG	Arriva
LG52DDA	Arriva	LJ03MKA	Arriva	LJ03MWK	Arriva
LG52DDE	Arriva	LJ03MKC	Arriva	LJ03MWL	Arriva
LG52DDF	Arriva	LJ03MKD	Arriva	LJ03MWN	Arriva
LG52DDJ	Arriva	LJ03MKE	Arriva	LJ03MWP	Arriva
LG52DDK	Arriva	LJ03MKF	Arriva	LJ03MWU	Arriva
LG52DDL	Arriva	LJ03MKG	Arriva	LJ03MWV	Arriva
LG52HWN	Abellio	LJ03MKK	Arriva	LJ03MWX	Arriva
LG52URZ	Abellio	LJ03MKL	Arriva	LJ03MXH	Arriva
LG52XWD	Abellio	LJ03MKM	Arriva	LJ03MXK	Arriva
LG52XWE	Abellio	LJ03MKN	Arriva	LJ03MXL	Arriva
LG52XYJ	Abellio	LJ03MKP	Arriva	LJ03MXM	Arriva
LG52XYK	Abellio	LJ03MKU	Arriva	LJ03MXN	Arriva
LG52XYL	Abellio	LJ03MKV	Arriva	LJ03MXP	Arriva
LG52XYM	Abellio	LJ03MKX	Arriva	LJ03MXR	Arriva
LG52XYN	Abellio	LJ03MKZ	Arriva	LJ03MXS	Arriva
LG52XYO	Abellio	LJ03MLE	Arriva	LJ03MXT	Arriva
LG52XYP	Abellio	LJ03MLF	Arriva	LJ03MXU	Arriva
LG52XYY	Abellio	LJ03MLK	Arriva	LJ03MXV	Arriva
LG52XYZ	Abellio	LJ03MLL	Arriva	LJ03MXW	Arriva
LG52XZA	Abellio	LJ03MLN	Arriva	LJ03MXX	Arriva
LG52XZB	Abellio	LJ03MLV	Arriva	LJ03MXY	Arriva
LG52XZR	Abellio	LJ03MLX	Arriva	LJ03MXZ	Arriva

LJ03MYA	Arriva	LJ05BHV	Arriva	LJ07ECT	Arriva
LJ03MYB	Arriva	LJ05BHW	Arriva	LJ07ECV	Arriva
LJ03MYC	Arriva	LJ05BHX	Arriva	LJ07ECW	Arriva
LJ03MYD	Arriva	LJ05BHY	Arriva	LJ07ECX	Arriva
LJ03MYF	Arriva	LJ05BHZ	Arriva	LJ07ECY	Arriva
LJ03MYP	Arriva	LJ05BJE	Arriva	LJ07ECZ	Arriva
LJ03MYR	Arriva	LJ05BJF	Arriva	LJ07EDC	Arriva
LJ03MYS	Arriva	LJ05BJK	Arriva	LJ07EDD	Arriva
LJ03MYT	Arriva	LJ05BJO	Arriva	LJ07EDK	Arriva
LJ03MYU	Arriva	LJ05BJU	Arriva	LJ07EDL	Arriva
LJ03MYV	Arriva	LJ05BJV	Arriva	LJ07EDO	Arriva
LJ03MYX	Arriva	LJ05BJX	Arriva	LJ07EDP	Arriva
LJ03MYY	Arriva	LJ05BJY	Arriva	LJ07EDR	Arriva
LJ03MYZ	Arriva	LJ05BJZ	Arriva	LJ07EDU	Arriva
LJ03MZD	Arriva	LJ05BKA	Arriva	LJ07EDV	Arriva
LJ03MZE	Arriva Southern Cs	LJ05BKD	Arriva Southern Cs	LJ07EDX	Arriva
LJ04LDA	Arriva	LJ05BKF	Arriva Southern Cs	LJ07EEA	Arriva
LJ04LDC	Arriva	LJ05BKG	Arriva Southern Cs	LJ07EEB	Arriva
LJ04LDD	Arriva	LJ05BKK	Arriva Southern Cs	LJ07OPE	Abellio
LJ04LDF	Arriva	LJ05BKL	Arriva Southern Cs	LJ07OPF	Abellio
LJ04LDK	Arriva	LJ05BKN	Arriva Southern Cs	LJ07OPG	Abellio
LJ04LDN	Arriva	LJ05BKO	Arriva Southern Cs	LJ07OPH	Abellio
LJ04LDU	Arriva	LJ05BKU	Arriva Southern Cs	LJ07OPK	Abellio
LJ04LDX	Arriva	LJ05BKV	Arriva Southern Cs	LJ07OPL	Abellio
LJ04LDY	Arriva	LJ05BKX	Arriva The Shires	LJ07OPM	Abellio
LJ04LDZ	Arriva	LJ05BKY	Arriva	LJ07UDD	Original Tour
LJ04LEF	Arriva	LJ05BKZ	Arriva	LJ07XEN	Original Tour
LJ04LEU	Arriva	LJ05BLF	Arriva	LJ07XEO	Original Tour
LJ04LFB	Arriva	LJ05BLK	Arriva	LJ07XEP	Original Tour
LJ04LFD	Arriva	LJ05BLN	Arriva	LJ07XER	Original Tour
LJ04LFE	Arriva	LJ05BLV	Arriva The Shires	LJ07XES	Original Tour
LJ04LFF	Arriva	LJ05BLX	Arriva Southern Cs	LJ07XET	Original Tour
LJ04LFG	Arriva	LJ05BLZ	Arriva Southern Cs	LJ07XEU	Original Tour
LJ04LFH	Arriva	LJ05BMO	Arriva Southern Cs	LJ07XEV	Original Tour
LJ04LFK	Arriva	LJ05BMU	Arriva Southern Cs	LJ07XEW	Original Tour
LJ04LFL	Arriva	LJ05BMV	Arriva	LJ08CSO	Arriva
LJ04LFM	Arriva	LJ05BMZ	Arriva	LJ08CSU	Arriva
LJ04LFN	Arriva	LJ05BNA	Arriva	LJ08CSV	Arriva
LJ04LFP	Arriva	LJ05BNB	Arriva	LJ08CSX	Arriva
LJ04LFR	Arriva	LJ05BND	Arriva	LJ08CSY	Arriva
LJ04LFS	Arriva	LJ05BNE	Arriva	LJ08CSZ	Arriva
LJ04LFT	Arriva	LJ05BNF	Arriva	LJ08CTE	Arriva
LJ04LFV	Arriva	LJ05BNK	Arriva	LJ08CTF	Arriva
LJ04LFW	Arriva	LJ05BNL	Arriva	LJ08CTK	Arriva
LJ04LFX	Arriva	LJ05GKX	Arriva	LJ08CTO	Arriva
LJ04LFY	Arriva	LJ05GKY	Arriva	LJ08CTV	Arriva
LJ04LFZ	Arriva	LJ05GKZ	Arriva	LJ08CTX	Arriva
LJ04LGA	Arriva	LJ05GLF	Arriva	LJ08CTY	Arriva
LJ04LGC	Arriva	LJ05GLK	Arriva	LJ08CTZ	Arriva
LJ04LGD	Arriva	LJ05GLV	Arriva	LJ08CUA	Arriva
LJ04LGE	Arriva	LJ05GLY	Arriva The Shires	LJ08CUC	Arriva
LJ04LGF	Arriva	LJ05GLZ	Arriva	LJ08CUG	Arriva
LJ04LGG	Arriva	LJ05GME	Arriva	LJ08CUH	Arriva
LJ04LGK	Arriva	LJ05GMF	Arriva	LJ08CUK	Arriva
LJ04LGL	Arriva	LJ05GOP	Arriva	LJ08CUO	Arriva
LJ04LGN	Arriva	LJ05GOU	Arriva	LJ08CUU	Arriva
LJ04LGV	Arriva	LJ05GOX	Arriva	LJ08CUV	Arriva
LJ04LGW	Arriva	LJ05GPF	Arriva	LJ08CUW	Arriva
LJ04LGX	Arriva	LJ05GPK	Arriva	LJ08CUY	Arriva
LJ04LGY	Arriva	LJ05GPO	Arriva	LJ08CVA	Arriva
LJ04YWE	Arriva	LJ05GPU	Arriva	LJ08CVB	Arriva
LJ04YWS	Arriva	LJ05GPX	Arriva	LJ08CVC	Arriva
LJ04YWT	Arriva	LJ05GPY	Arriva	LJ08CVD	Arriva
LJ04YWU	Arriva	LJ05GPZ	Arriva	LJ08CVF	Arriva
LJ04YWV	Arriva	LJ05GRF	Arriva	LJ08CVG	Arriva
LJ04YWW	Arriva	LJ05GRK	Arriva	LJ08CVH	Arriva
LJ04YWX	Arriva	LJ05GRU	Arriva	LJ08CVK	Arriva
LJ04YWY	Arriva	LJ05GRX	Arriva	LJ08CVL	Arriva
LJ04YWZ	Arriva	LJ05GRZ	Arriva	LJ08CVM	Arriva
LJ04YXA	Arriva	LJ05GSO	Arriva	LJ08CVO	Arriva
LJ04YXB	Arriva	LJ05GSU	Arriva	LJ08CVR	Arriva
LJ05BHL	Arriva	LJ07EBO	Arriva	LJ08CVS	Arriva
LJ05BHN	Arriva	LJ07EBP	Arriva	LJ08CVT	Arriva
LJ05BHO	Arriva	LJ07EBU	Arriva	LJ08CVV	Arriva
LJ05BHP	Arriva	LJ07ECF	Arriva	LJ08CVX	Arriva
LJ05BHU	Arriva	LJ07ECN	Arriva	LJ08CVY	Arriva

LJ08CVZ	Arriva	LJ09KPG	Arriva	LJ09SVF	Arriva
LJ08CWA	Arriva	LJ09KPK	Arriva	LJ10CSF	Arriva
LJ08CWC	Arriva	LJ09KPL	Arriva	LJ10CSO	Arriva
LJ08CXR	Arriva	LJ09KPN	Arriva	LJ10CSU	Arriva
LJ08CXS	Arriva	LJ09KPO	Arriva	LJ10CSV	Arriva
LJ08CXT	Arriva	LJ09KPR	Arriva	LJ10CSX	Arriva
LJ08CXU	Arriva	LJ09KPT	Arriva	LJ10CSY	Arriva
LJ08CXV	Arriva	LJ09KPU	Arriva	LJ10CSZ	Arriva
LJ08CYC	Arriva	LJ09KPV	Arriva	LJ10CTE	Arriva
LJ08CYE	Arriva	LJ09KPX	Arriva	LJ10CTF	Arriva
LJ08CYF	Arriva	LJ09KPY	Arriva	LJ10CTK	Arriva
LJ08CYG	Arriva	LJ09KPZ	Arriva	LJ10CUH	Arriva
LJ08CYH	Arriva	LJ09KRD	Arriva	LJ10CUK	Arriva
LJ08CYK	Arriva	LJ09KRE	Arriva	LJ10CUO	Arriva
LJ08CYL	Arriva	LJ09KRF	Arriva	LJ10CUU	Arriva
LJ08CYO	Arriva	LJ09KRG	Arriva	LJ10CUV	Arriva
LJ08CYP	Arriva	LJ09KRK	Arriva	LJ10CUW	Arriva
LJ08CYS	Arriva	LJ09KRN	Arriva	LJ10CUX	Arriva
LJ08CZP	Abellio	LJ09KRO	Arriva	LJ10CUY	Arriva
LJ08CZR	Abellio	LJ09KRU	Arriva	LJ10CVA	Arriva
LJ08CZS	Abellio	LJ09OJZ	Abellio	LJ10CVB	Arriva
LJ08CZT	Abellio	LJ09OKA	Abellio	LJ10CVC	Arriva
LJ08CZU	Abellio	LJ09OKB	Abellio	LJ10CVD	Arriva
LJ08CZV	Abellio	LJ09OKC	Abellio	LJ10CVE	Arriva
LJ08CZX	Abellio	LJ09OKD	Abellio	LJ10CVF	Arriva
LJ08CZY	Abellio	LJ09OKE	Abellio	LJ10CVG	Arriva
LJ08CZZ	Abellio	LJ09OKF	Abellio	LJ10CVH	Arriva
LJ08RJY	RATP - Quality Line	LJ09OKG	Abellio	LJ10CVK	Arriva
LJ09CAA	Abellio	LJ09OKH	Abellio	LJ10CVL	Arriva
LJ09CAE	Abellio	LJ09OKK	Abellio	LJ10CVM	Arriva
LJ09CAO	Abellio	LJ09OKL	Abellio	LJ10CVN	Arriva
LJ09CAU	Abellio	LJ09OKM	Abellio	LJ10CVO	Arriva
LJ09CAV	Abellio	LJ09OKN	Abellio	LJ10CVP	Arriva
LJ09CAX	Abellio	LJ09OKO	Abellio	LJ10HTT	Arriva
LJ09CBF	Abellio	LJ09OKP	Abellio	LJ10HTU	Arriva
LJ09CBO	Abellio	LJ09OKR	Abellio	LJ10HTV	Arriva
LJ09CBU	Abellio	LJ09OKS	Abellio	LJ10HTX	Arriva
LJ09CBV	Abellio	LJ09OKT	Abellio	LJ10HTZ	Arriva
LJ09CBX	Abellio	LJ09OKU	Abellio	LJ10HUA	Arriva
LJ09CBY	Abellio	LJ09OKV	Abellio	LJ10HUH	Arriva
LJ09CCA	Abellio	LJ09OKW	Abellio	LJ10HUK	Arriva
LJ09CCD	Abellio	LJ09OKX	Abellio	LJ10HUO	Arriva
LJ09CCE	Abellio	LJ09OKZ	Abellio	LJ10HUP	Arriva
LJ09CCF	Abellio	LJ09OLA	Abellio	LJ10HUU	Arriva
LJ09CCK	Abellio	LJ09OLB	Abellio	LJ10HUV	Arriva
LJ09CCN	Abellio	LJ09OLC	Abellio	LJ10HUY	Arriva
LJ09CCO	Abellio	LJ09OLE	Abellio	LJ10HUZ	Arriva
LJ09CCU	Abellio	LJ09OLG	Abellio	LJ10HVA	Arriva
LJ09CCX	Abellio	LJ09OLH	Abellio	LJ10HVB	Arriva
LJ09CCY	Abellio	LJ09OLK	Abellio	LJ10HVC	Arriva
LJ09CCZ	Abellio	LJ09OLM	Abellio	LJ10HVD	Arriva
LJ09CDE	Abellio	LJ09OLN	Abellio	LJ10HVE	Arriva
LJ09CDF	Abellio	LJ09OLO	Abellio	LJ10HVF	Arriva
LJ09CDK	Abellio	LJ09OLP	Abellio	LJ10HVG	Arriva
LJ09CDN	Abellio	LJ09OLR	Abellio	LJ10HVH	Arriva
LJ09CDO	Abellio	LJ09OLT	Abellio	LJ10HVK	Arriva
LJ09CDU	Abellio	LJ09OLU	Abellio	LJ10HVL	Arriva
LJ09CDV	Abellio	LJ09SSO	Arriva	LJ10HVO	Arriva
LJ09CDX	Abellio	LJ09SSU	Arriva	LJ10HVP	Arriva
LJ09CDY	Abellio	LJ09SSV	Arriva	LJ10HVR	Arriva
LJ09CDZ	Abellio	LJ09SSX	Arriva	LJ11AAE	Arriva
LJ09CEA	Abellio	LJ09SSZ	Arriva	LJ11AAF	Arriva
LJ09CEF	Abellio	LJ09STX	Arriva	LJ11AAX	Arriva
LJ09CEK	Abellio	LJ09STZ	Arriva	LJ11AAY	Arriva
LJ09CEN	Abellio	LJ09SUA	Arriva	LJ11ABK	Arriva
LJ09CEO	Abellio	LJ09SUF	Arriva	LJ11ABN	Arriva
LJ09CEU	Abellio	LJ09SUH	Arriva	LJ11ABO	Arriva
LJ09KOE	Arriva	LJ09SUO	Arriva	LJ11ABU	Arriva
LJ09KOH	Arriva	LJ09SUU	Arriva	LJ11ABV	Arriva
LJ09KOU	Arriva	LJ09SUV	Arriva	LJ11ABX	Arriva
LJ09KOV	Arriva	LJ09SUX	Arriva	LJ11ABZ	Arriva
LJ09KOW	Arriva	LJ09SUY	Arriva	LJ11ACF	Arriva
LJ09KOX	Arriva	LJ09SVA	Arriva	LJ11ACO	Arriva
LJ09KPA	Arriva	LJ09SVC	Arriva	LJ11ACU	Arriva
LJ09KPE	Arriva	LJ09SVD	Arriva	LJ11ACV	Arriva
LJ09KPF	Arriva	LJ09SVE	Arriva	LJ11ACX	Arriva

LJ11ACY	Arriva	LJ12CGG	Go-Ahead	LJ13CJO	Arriva
LJ11ACZ	Arriva	LJ12CGK	Go-Ahead	LJ13CJU	Arriva
LJ11ADO	Arriva	LJ12CGO	Go-Ahead	LJ13CJV	Arriva
LJ11ADU	Arriva	LJ12CGU	Go-Ahead	LJ13CKC	Arriva
LJ11ADV	Arriva	LJ12CGV	Go-Ahead	LJ13CKD	Arriva
LJ11ADX	Arriva	LJ12CGX	Go-Ahead	LJ13CKE	Arriva
LJ11ADZ	Arriva	LJ12CGY	Go-Ahead	LJ13CKF	Arriva
LJ11AEA	Arriva	LJ12CGZ	Go-Ahead	LJ13CKG	Arriva
LJ11AEB	Arriva	LJ12CHC	Go-Ahead	LJ13CKK	Arriva
LJ11AEC	Arriva	LJ12CHD	Go-Ahead	LJ13CKL	Arriva
LJ11AED	Arriva	LJ12CHF	Go-Ahead	LJ13CKN	Arriva
LJ11AEE	Arriva	LJ12CHG	Go-Ahead	LJ13CKO	Arriva
LJ11AEF	Arriva	LJ12CHH	Go-Ahead	LJ13CKP	Arriva
LJ11AEG	Arriva	LJ12CHK	Go-Ahead	LJ13CKU	Arriva
LJ11AEK	Arriva	LJ12GKL	Big Bus Company	LJ13CKV	Arriva
LJ11AEL	Arriva	LJ12GSZ	Big Bus Company	LJ13CKX	Arriva
LJ11AEM	Arriva	LJ12GTZ	Big Bus Company	LJ13CKY	Arriva
LJ11AEN	Arriva	LJ12JSX	Big Bus Company	LJ13CLF	Arriva
LJ11AEO	Arriva	LJ12JSY	Big Bus Company	LJ13CLN	Arriva
LJ11AEP	Arriva	LJ12JUO	Big Bus Company	LJ13CLO	Arriva
LJ11AET	Arriva	LJ12JUT	Big Bus Company	LJ13CLV	Arriva
LJ11AEU	Arriva	LJ12JVK	Big Bus Company	LJ13CLX	Arriva
LJ11AEV	Arriva	LJ12JVL	Big Bus Company	LJ13CLY	Arriva
LJ11AEW	Arriva	LJ12JVZ	Big Bus Company	LJ13CLZ	Arriva
LJ11AEX	Arriva	LJ12JWA	Big Bus Company	LJ13CME	Arriva
LJ11AEY	Arriva	LJ12LJL	Big Bus Company	LJ13CMF	Arriva
LJ11AEZ	Arriva	LJ12MYG	Big Bus Company	LJ13CMK	Arriva
LJ11AFA	Arriva	LJ12MYH	Big Bus Company	LJ13FAM	Arriva
LJ11EEU	Arriva	LJ13CCE	Arriva	LJ13FAO	Arriva
LJ11EFE	Arriva	LJ13CCF	Arriva	LJ13FAU	Arriva
LJ11EFF	Arriva	LJ13CCK	Arriva	LJ13FBA	Arriva
LJ11EFG	Arriva	LJ13CCL	Arriva	LJ13FBB	Arriva
LJ11EFK	Arriva	LJ13CCO	Arriva	LJ13FBC	Arriva
LJ11EFL	Arriva	LJ13CCU	Arriva	LJ13FBD	Arriva
LJ11EFM	Arriva	LJ13CCV	Arriva	LJ13FBE	Arriva
LJ11EFN	Arriva	LJ13CCX	Arriva	LJ13FBF	Arriva
LJ11EFO	Arriva	LJ13CCY	Arriva	LJ13FBG	Arriva
LJ11EFP	Arriva	LJ13CCZ	Arriva	LJ13FBK	Arriva
LJ11EFR	Arriva	LJ13CDE	Arriva	LJ13FBL	Arriva
LJ11EFT	Arriva	LJ13CDF	Arriva	LJ13FBN	Arriva
LJ11EFU	Arriva	LJ13CDK	Arriva	LJ13FBO	Arriva
LJ11EFV	Arriva	LJ13CDN	Arriva	LJ13FBU	Arriva
LJ11EFW	Arriva	LJ13CDO	Arriva	LJ13FBV	Arriva
LJ11EFX	Arriva	LJ13CDU	Arriva	LJ13FBX	Arriva
LJ11EFY	Arriva	LJ13CDV	Arriva	LJ13FBY	Arriva
LJ11EFZ	Arriva	LJ13CDX	Arriva	LJ13FBZ	Arriva
LJ11EGC	Arriva	LJ13CDY	Arriva	LJ13FCA	Arriva
LJ11EGD	Arriva	LJ13CDZ	Arriva	LJ13FCC	Arriva
LJ12BXY	Arriva	LJ13CEA	Arriva	LJ13FCD	Arriva
LJ12BXZ	Arriva	LJ13CEF	Arriva	LJ13FCE	Arriva
LJ12BYA	Arriva	LJ13CEK	Arriva	LJ13FCF	Arriva
LJ12BYB	Arriva	LJ13CEN	Arriva	LJ13FCG	Arriva
LJ12BYC	Arriva	LJ13CEO	Arriva	LJ13FCL	Arriva
LJ12BYD	Arriva	LJ13CEU	Arriva	LJ13FCM	Arriva
LJ12BYF	Arriva	LJ13CEV	Arriva	LJ13FCN	Arriva
LJ12BYL	Arriva	LJ13CEX	Arriva	LJ13FCO	Arriva
LJ12BYM	Arriva	LJ13CFA	Arriva	LJ13FCP	Arriva
LJ12BYN	Arriva	LJ13CFD	Arriva	LJ13FCU	Arriva
LJ12BYO	Arriva	LJ13CFE	Arriva	LJ13FCV	Arriva
LJ12BYP	Arriva	LJ13CFF	Arriva	LJ13FCX	Arriva
LJ12BYR	Arriva	LJ13CFG	Arriva	LJ13FCY	Arriva
LJ12BYS	Arriva	LJ13CFK	Arriva	LJ13FCZ	Arriva
LJ12BYT	Arriva	LJ13CFL	Arriva	LJ13FDA	Arriva
LJ12BYU	Arriva	LJ13CFM	Arriva	LJ13FDC	Arriva
LJ12BYV	Arriva	LJ13CGG	Arriva	LJ13FDD	Arriva
LJ12BYW	Arriva	LJ13CGK	Arriva	LJ13FDE	Arriva
LJ12BYX	Arriva	LJ13CGO	Arriva	LJ13FDF	Arriva
LJ12BYY	Arriva	LJ13CHL	Arriva	LJ13FDG	Arriva
LJ12BYZ	Arriva	LJ13CHN	Arriva	LJ13FDK	Arriva
LJ12BZA	Arriva	LJ13CHO	Arriva	LJ13FDL	Arriva
LJ12BZB	Arriva	LJ13CHV	Arriva	LJ13FDM	Arriva
LJ12BZC	Arriva	LJ13CHX	Arriva	LJ13FDN	Arriva
LJ12BZD	Arriva	LJ13CHY	Arriva	LJ13FDO	Arriva
LJ12BZE	Arriva	LJ13CHZ	Arriva	LJ13FDP	Arriva
LJ12BZF	Arriva	LJ13CJE	Arriva	LJ13FEO	Arriva
LJ12CGF	Go-Ahead	LJ13CJF	Arriva	LJ13FEP	Arriva

Reg	Operator	Reg	Operator	Reg	Operator
LJ13FET	Arriva	LJ51ORL	Arriva	LJ53NHK	Arriva
LJ13GJU	Go-Ahead	LJ51OSK	Arriva	LJ53NHL	Arriva
LJ13GJV	Go-Ahead	LJ51OSX	Arriva	LJ53NHM	Arriva
LJ13GJX	Go-Ahead	LJ51OSY	Arriva	LJ53NHN	Arriva
LJ13GJY	Go-Ahead	LJ51OSZ	Arriva	LJ53NHO	Arriva
LJ13GJZ	Go-Ahead	LJ53BAA	Arriva	LJ53NHP	Arriva
LJ13GKA	Go-Ahead	LJ53BAO	Arriva	LJ53NHT	Arriva
LJ13GKC	Go-Ahead	LJ53BAU	Arriva	LJ53NHT	Arriva
LJ13GKD	Go-Ahead	LJ53BAV	Arriva	LJ53NHV	Arriva
LJ13GKE	Go-Ahead	LJ53BBE	Arriva	LJ53NHX	Arriva
LJ13GKF	Go-Ahead	LJ53BBF	Arriva	LJ53NHY	Arriva
LJ13GKG	Go-Ahead	LJ53BBK	Arriva	LJ53NHZ	Arriva
LJ13GKK	Go-Ahead	LJ53BBN	Arriva	LJ53NJF	Arriva
LJ13GKL	Go-Ahead	LJ53BBO	Arriva	LJ53NJK	Arriva
LJ13GKN	Go-Ahead	LJ53BBU	Arriva	LJ53NJN	Arriva
LJ13GKO	Go-Ahead	LJ53BBV	Arriva	LJ54BAA	Arriva Southern Cs
LJ13GKP	Go-Ahead	LJ53BBX	Arriva	LJ54BAO	Arriva
LJ13GKU	Go-Ahead	LJ53BBZ	Arriva	LJ54BAU	Arriva
LJ13GKV	Go-Ahead	LJ53BBZ	Arriva	LJ54BAV	Arriva
LJ13GKX	Go-Ahead	LJ53BCF	Arriva	LJ54BBE	Arriva
LJ13GKY	Go-Ahead	LJ53BCK	Arriva	LJ54BBF	Arriva
LJ13GKZ	Go-Ahead	LJ53BCO	Arriva	LJ54BBK	Arriva
LJ13GLF	Go-Ahead	LJ53BCU	Arriva	LJ54BBN	Arriva
LJ13GLK	Go-Ahead	LJ53BCV	Arriva	LJ54BBO	Arriva
LJ13JWP	Tower Transit	LJ53BCX	Arriva	LJ54BBU	Arriva
LJ13JZO	Tower Transit	LJ53BCY	Arriva	LJ54BBV	Arriva
LJ51DDK	Arriva	LJ53BCZ	Arriva	LJ54BBX	Arriva
LJ51DDL	Arriva	LJ53BDE	Arriva	LJ54BBZ	Arriva
LJ51DDN	Arriva	LJ53BDE	Arriva	LJ54BCE	Arriva
LJ51DDO	Arriva	LJ53BDE	Arriva	LJ54BCF	Arriva
LJ51DDU	Arriva	LJ53BDU	Arriva	LJ54BCK	Arriva
LJ51DDV	Arriva Southern Cs	LJ53BDV	Arriva	LJ54BCO	Arriva
LJ51DDX	Arriva Southern Cs	LJ53BDX	Arriva	LJ54BCU	Arriva
LJ51DGX	Arriva	LJ53BDY	Arriva	LJ54BCV	Arriva
LJ51DGY	Arriva	LJ53BEO	Arriva	LJ54BCX	Arriva Southern Cs
LJ51DGZ	Arriva	LJ53BEU	Arriva	LJ54BCY	Arriva
LJ51DHA	Arriva	LJ53BEY	Arriva	LJ54BCZ	Arriva
LJ51DHC	Arriva	LJ53BFA	Arriva	LJ54BDE	Arriva
LJ51DHD	Arriva	LJ53BFE	Arriva	LJ54BDF	Arriva
LJ51DHE	Arriva	LJ53BFF	Arriva	LJ54BDO	Arriva
LJ51DHF	Arriva	LJ53BFK	Arriva	LJ54BDU	Arriva
LJ51DHG	Arriva	LJ53BFL	Arriva	LJ54BDV	Arriva
LJ51DHK	Arriva	LJ53BFM	Arriva	LJ54BDX	Arriva
LJ51DHL	Arriva	LJ53BFN	Arriva	LJ54BDY	Arriva
LJ51DHO	Arriva	LJ53BFO	Arriva	LJ54BDZ	Arriva
LJ51DHP	Arriva	LJ53BFP	Arriva	LJ54BEO	Arriva
LJ51DHV	Arriva	LJ53BFU	Arriva	LJ54BEU	Arriva
LJ51DHX	Arriva	LJ53BFX	Arriva	LJ54BFA	Arriva
LJ51DHY	Arriva	LJ53BFY	Arriva	LJ54BFE	Arriva
LJ51DHZ	Arriva	LJ53BGF	Arriva	LJ54BFF	Arriva
LJ51DJD	Arriva	LJ53BGK	Arriva	LJ54BFK	Arriva
LJ51DJE	Arriva	LJ53BGO	Arriva	LJ54BFL	Arriva
LJ51DJU	Original Tour	LJ53BGU	Arriva	LJ54BFM	Arriva
LJ51DJV	Original Tour	LJ53NFE	Arriva	LJ54BFN	Arriva
LJ51DJX	Original Tour	LJ53NFF	Arriva	LJ54BFO	Arriva
LJ51DJY	Original Tour	LJ53NFG	Arriva	LJ54BFP	Arriva
LJ51DJZ	Original Tour	LJ53NFU	Arriva	LJ54BFV	Arriva
LJ51DKA	Original Tour	LJ53NFV	Arriva	LJ54BFY	Arriva
LJ51DKD	Original Tour	LJ53NFX	Arriva	LJ54BFZ	Arriva
LJ51DKE	Original Tour	LJ53NFY	Arriva	LJ54BGE	Arriva
LJ51DKF	Original Tour	LJ53NFZ	Arriva	LJ54BGF	Arriva
LJ51DKK	Original Tour	LJ53NGE	Arriva	LJ54BGK	Arriva
LJ51DKL	Original Tour	LJ53NGF	Arriva	LJ54BGO	Arriva
LJ51DKN	Original Tour	LJ53NGG	Arriva	LJ54LGV	Arriva
LJ51DKO	Original Tour	LJ53NGN	Arriva	LJ54LHF	Arriva
LJ51DKU	Original Tour	LJ53NGU	Arriva	LJ54LHG	Arriva
LJ51DKV	Original Tour	LJ53NGV	Arriva	LJ54LHH	Arriva
LJ51DKX	Original Tour	LJ53NGZ	Arriva	LJ54LHK	Arriva
LJ51DLF	Arriva	LJ53NHA	Arriva	LJ54LHL	Arriva
LJ51DLV	Arriva	LJ53NHB	Arriva	LJ54LHM	Arriva
LJ51DLY	Arriva	LJ53NHC	Arriva	LJ54LHN	Arriva
LJ51ORA	Arriva	LJ53NHD	Arriva	LJ54LHO	Arriva
LJ51ORC	Arriva	LJ53NHE	Arriva	LJ54LHP	Arriva
LJ51ORF	Arriva	LJ53NHF	Arriva	LJ54LHR	Arriva
LJ51ORG	Arriva	LJ53NHG	Arriva	LJ55BPZ	Arriva
LJ51ORK	Arriva	LJ53NHH	Arriva	LJ55BRV	Arriva

Reg	Operator	Reg	Operator	Reg	Operator
LJ55BRX	Arriva	LJ56VTO	Abellio	LJ59AEC	Arriva
LJ55BRZ	Arriva	LJ56VTP	Abellio	LJ59AED	Arriva
LJ55BSO	Arriva	LJ56VTT	Abellio	LJ59AEE	Arriva
LJ55BSU	Arriva	LJ56VTU	Abellio	LJ59AEF	Arriva
LJ55BSV	Arriva	LJ56VTV	Abellio	LJ59AEG	Arriva
LJ55BSX	Arriva	LJ56VTW	Abellio	LJ59AEK	Arriva
LJ55BSY	Arriva	LJ56VTY	Abellio	LJ59AEL	Arriva
LJ55BSZ	Arriva	LJ56VUD	Abellio	LJ59AEM	Arriva
LJ55BTE	Arriva	LJ56VUF	Abellio	LJ59AEN	Arriva
LJ55BTF	Arriva	LJ57USS	Arriva	LJ59AEO	Arriva
LJ55BTO	Arriva	LJ57UST	Arriva	LJ59AEP	Arriva
LJ55BTU	Arriva	LJ57USU	Arriva	LJ59AET	Arriva
LJ55BTV	Arriva	LJ57USV	Arriva	LJ59AEU	Arriva
LJ55BTX	Arriva	LJ57USW	Arriva	LJ59AEV	Arriva
LJ55BTY	Arriva	LJ57USX	Arriva	LJ59AEW	Arriva
LJ55BTZ	Arriva	LJ57USY	Arriva	LJ59AEX	Arriva
LJ55BUA	Arriva	LJ57USZ	Arriva	LJ59AEY	Arriva
LJ55BUE	Arriva	LJ57UTA	Arriva	LJ59AEZ	Arriva
LJ55BVD	Arriva The Shires	LJ57UTB	Arriva	LJ59AFA	Arriva
LJ55BVE	Arriva The Shires	LJ57UTC	Arriva	LJ59GTF	Arriva
LJ55BVF	Arriva The Shires	LJ57UTE	Arriva	LJ59GTU	Arriva
LJ55BVG	Arriva The Shires	LJ57UTF	Arriva	LJ59GTZ	Arriva
LJ55BVH	Arriva The Shires	LJ58AUC	Arriva	LJ59GUA	Arriva
LJ55BVK	Arriva The Shires	LJ58AUE	Arriva	LJ59GVC	Arriva
LJ55BVL	Arriva The Shires	LJ58AUV	Arriva	LJ59GVE	Arriva
LJ55BVM	Arriva The Shires	LJ58AUW	Arriva	LJ59GVF	Arriva
LJ55BVP	Arriva	LJ58AUX	Arriva	LJ59GVG	Arriva
LJ55BVR	Arriva	LJ58AUY	Arriva	LJ59GVK	Arriva
LJ55BVS	Arriva The Shires	LJ58AVB	Arriva	LJ59LVL	Arriva
LJ55BVT	Arriva The Shires	LJ58AVC	Arriva	LJ59LVM	Arriva
LJ55BVU	Arriva The Shires	LJ58AVD	Arriva	LJ59LVN	Arriva
LJ55BVV	Arriva The Shires	LJ58AVE	Arriva	LJ59LVU	Arriva
LJ55BVW	Arriva The Shires	LJ58AVG	Arriva	LJ59LVV	Arriva
LJ55BVX	Arriva The Shires	LJ58AVK	Arriva	LJ59LVW	Arriva
LJ55BVY	Arriva The Shires	LJ58AVT	Arriva	LJ59LVX	Arriva
LJ55BVZ	Arriva The Shires	LJ58AVU	Arriva The Shires	LJ59LVY	Arriva
LJ56AOW	Arriva	LJ58AVV	Arriva The Shires	LJ59LVZ	Arriva
LJ56AOX	Arriva	LJ58AVX	Arriva The Shires	LJ59LWA	Arriva
LJ56AOY	Arriva	LJ58AVY	Arriva The Shires	LJ59LWF	Arriva
LJ56APZ	Arriva	LJ58AVZ	Arriva The Shires	LJ59LWG	Arriva
LJ56ARF	Arriva	LJ58AWA	Arriva The Shires	LJ59LWH	Arriva
LJ56ARO	Arriva	LJ58AWC	Arriva The Shires	LJ59LWK	Arriva
LJ56ARU	Arriva	LJ58AWF	Arriva The Shires	LJ59LWL	Arriva
LJ56ARX	Arriva	LJ58AWF	Arriva	LJ59LWM	Arriva
LJ56ARZ	Arriva	LJ58AWG	Arriva The Shires	LJ59LWN	Arriva
LJ56ASO	Arriva	LJ58AWG	Arriva	LJ59LWO	Arriva
LJ56ASU	Arriva	LJ59AAE	Arriva	LJ59LWP	Arriva
LJ56ASV	Arriva	LJ59AAF	Arriva	LJ59LWR	Arriva
LJ56ASX	Arriva	LJ59AAK	Arriva	LJ59LWS	Arriva
LJ56ONH	Abellio	LJ59AAN	Arriva	LJ59LWT	Arriva
LJ56ONK	Abellio	LJ59AAO	Arriva	LJ59LWU	Arriva
LJ56ONL	Abellio	LJ59AAU	Arriva	LJ59LWV	Arriva
LJ56ONM	Abellio	LJ59AAV	Arriva	LJ59LWW	Arriva
LJ56ONN	Abellio	LJ59AAX	Arriva	LJ59LWX	Arriva
LJ56ONO	Abellio	LJ59AAY	Arriva	LJ59LWY	Arriva
LJ56ONP	Abellio	LJ59AAZ	Arriva	LJ59LWZ	Arriva
LJ56ONR	Abellio	LJ59ABF	Arriva	LJ59LXA	Arriva
LJ56ONS	Abellio	LJ59ABK	Arriva	LJ59LXB	Arriva
LJ56ONT	Abellio	LJ59ABN	Arriva	LJ59LXP	Arriva
LJ56VSP	Abellio	LJ59ABO	Arriva	LJ59LXR	Arriva
LJ56VST	Abellio	LJ59ABU	Arriva	LJ59LXS	Arriva
LJ56VSU	Abellio	LJ59ABV	Arriva	LJ59LXT	Arriva
LJ56VSV	Abellio	LJ59ABX	Arriva	LJ59LXU	Arriva
LJ56VSX	Abellio	LJ59ABZ	Arriva	LJ59LXV	Arriva
LJ56VSY	Abellio	LJ59ACF	Arriva	LJ59LXW	Arriva
LJ56VSZ	Abellio	LJ59ACO	Arriva	LJ59LXX	Arriva
LJ56VTA	Abellio	LJ59ACU	Arriva	LJ59LXY	Arriva
LJ56VTC	Abellio	LJ59ACV	Arriva	LJ59LXZ	Arriva
LJ56VTD	Abellio	LJ59ACX	Arriva	LJ59LYA	Arriva
LJ56VTE	Abellio	LJ59ACY	Arriva	LJ59LYC	Arriva
LJ56VTF	Abellio	LJ59ACZ	Arriva	LJ59LYD	Arriva
LJ56VTG	Abellio	LJ59ADO	Arriva	LJ59LYF	Arriva
LJ56VTK	Abellio	LJ59ADV	Arriva	LJ59LYG	Arriva
LJ56VTL	Abellio	LJ59ADZ	Arriva	LJ59LYH	Arriva
LJ56VTM	Abellio	LJ59AEA	Arriva	LJ59LYK	Arriva
LJ56VTN	Abellio	LJ59AEB	Arriva	LJ59LYO	Arriva

LJ59LYP	Arriva	LJ60AWR	Arriva	LJ61CDY	Arriva
LJ59LYS	Arriva	LJ60AWS	Arriva	LJ61CDZ	Arriva
LJ59LYT	Arriva	LJ60AWV	Arriva	LJ61CEA	Arriva
LJ59LYU	Arriva	LJ60AWW	Arriva	LJ61CEF	Arriva
LJ59LYV	Arriva	LJ60AWY	Arriva	LJ61CEK	Arriva
LJ59LYW	Arriva	LJ60AWZ	Arriva	LJ61CEN	Arriva
LJ59LYY	Arriva	LJ60AXA	Arriva	LJ61CEO	Arriva
LJ59LYZ	Arriva	LJ60AXB	Arriva	LJ61CEU	Arriva
LJ59LZA	Arriva	LJ60AXC	Arriva	LJ61CEV	Arriva
LJ59LZB	Arriva	LJ60AXD	Arriva	LJ61CEX	Arriva
LJ59LZC	Arriva	LJ60AXF	Arriva	LJ61CEY	Arriva
LJ59LZD	Arriva	LJ60AXG	Arriva	LJ61CFA	Arriva
LJ59LZF	Arriva	LJ60AXH	Arriva	LJ61CFD	Arriva
LJ59LZG	Arriva	LJ60AXK	Arriva	LJ61CFE	Arriva
LJ59LZH	Arriva	LJ60AXM	Arriva	LJ61CFF	Arriva
LJ59LZK	Arriva	LJ60AXN	Arriva	LJ61CFG	Arriva
LJ59LZL	Arriva	LJ60AXO	Arriva	LJ61CFK	Arriva
LJ59LZM	Arriva	LJ60AXP	Arriva	LJ61CFL	Arriva
LJ59LZN	Arriva	LJ60AXR	Arriva	LJ61CFM	Arriva
LJ60ASX	Arriva	LJ60AXS	Arriva	LJ61CFN	Arriva
LJ60ASZ	Arriva	LJ60AXT	Arriva	LJ61CFO	Arriva
LJ60ATF	Arriva	LJ60AXU	Arriva	LJ61CFP	Arriva
LJ60ATK	Arriva	LJ60AXV	Arriva	LJ61CFU	Arriva
LJ60ATN	Arriva	LJ60AXW	Arriva	LJ61CFV	Arriva
LJ60ATO	Arriva	LJ60AXX	Arriva	LJ61CFX	Arriva
LJ60ATU	Arriva	LJ60AXY	Arriva	LJ61CFY	Arriva
LJ60ATV	Arriva	LJ60AXZ	Arriva	LJ61CFZ	Arriva
LJ60ATX	Arriva	LJ60AYA	Arriva	LJ61CGE	Arriva
LJ60ATY	Arriva	LJ60AYB	Arriva	LJ61CGF	Arriva
LJ60ATZ	Arriva	LJ60AYC	Arriva	LJ61CGG	Arriva
LJ60AUA	Arriva	LJ60AYD	Arriva	LJ61CGK	Arriva
LJ60AUC	Arriva	LJ60AYE	Arriva	LJ61CGO	Arriva
LJ60AUE	Arriva	LJ60AYF	Arriva	LJ61CGU	Arriva
LJ60AUF	Arriva	LJ60AYG	Arriva	LJ61CGV	Arriva
LJ60AUH	Arriva	LJ60AYH	Arriva	LJ61CGX	Arriva
LJ60AUK	Arriva	LJ60AYK	Arriva	LJ61CGY	Arriva
LJ60AUL	Arriva	LJ60AYL	Arriva	LJ61CGZ	Arriva
LJ60AUM	Arriva	LJ60AYM	Arriva	LJ61CHC	Arriva
LJ60AUN	Arriva	LJ60AYN	Arriva	LJ61CHD	Arriva
LJ60AUO	Arriva	LJ60AYO	Arriva	LJ61CHF	Arriva
LJ60AUP	Arriva	LJ60AYP	Arriva	LJ61CHG	Arriva
LJ60AUR	Arriva	LJ60AYS	Arriva	LJ61CHH	Arriva
LJ60AUT	Arriva	LJ60JGY	Arriva	LJ61CHK	Arriva
LJ60AUU	Arriva	LJ60JGZ	Arriva	LJ61CHL	Arriva
LJ60AUV	Arriva	LJ61CAA	Arriva	LJ61CHN	Arriva
LJ60AUW	Arriva	LJ61CAE	Arriva	LJ61CHO	Arriva
LJ60AUX	Arriva	LJ61CAO	Arriva	LJ61CHV	Arriva
LJ60AUY	Arriva	LJ61CAU	Arriva	LJ61CHX	Arriva
LJ60AVB	Arriva	LJ61CAV	Arriva	LJ61CHY	Arriva
LJ60AVC	Arriva	LJ61CAX	Arriva	LJ61CHZ	Arriva
LJ60AVD	Arriva	LJ61CBF	Arriva	LJ61CKA	Arriva
LJ60AVE	Arriva	LJ61CBO	Arriva	LJ61CKC	Arriva
LJ60AVF	Arriva	LJ61CBU	Arriva	LJ61CKD	Arriva
LJ60AVG	Arriva	LJ61CBV	Arriva	LJ61CKE	Arriva
LJ60AVK	Arriva	LJ61CBX	Arriva	LJ61CKF	Arriva
LJ60AVM	Arriva	LJ61CBY	Arriva	LJ61CKG	Arriva
LJ60AVN	Arriva	LJ61CCA	Arriva	LJ61CKK	Arriva
LJ60AVO	Arriva	LJ61CCD	Arriva	LJ61CKL	Arriva
LJ60AVP	Arriva	LJ61CCE	Arriva	LJ61CKN	Arriva
LJ60AVR	Arriva	LJ61CCF	Arriva	LJ61CKO	Arriva
LJ60AVT	Arriva	LJ61CCK	Arriva	LJ61GVP	Go-Ahead
LJ60AVU	Arriva	LJ61CCN	Arriva	LJ61GVT	Go-Ahead
LJ60AVV	Arriva	LJ61CCO	Arriva	LJ61GVW	Go-Ahead
LJ60AVW	Arriva	LJ61CCU	Arriva	LJ61GVX	Go-Ahead
LJ60AVX	Arriva	LJ61CCV	Arriva	LJ61GVY	Go-Ahead
LJ60AVY	Arriva	LJ61CCX	Arriva	LJ61GVZ	Go-Ahead
LJ60AVZ	Arriva	LJ61CCY	Arriva	LJ61GWA	Go-Ahead
LJ60AWA	Arriva	LJ61CCZ	Arriva	LJ61GWC	Go-Ahead
LJ60AWC	Arriva	LJ61CDE	Arriva	LJ61GWD	Go-Ahead
LJ60AWF	Arriva	LJ61CDF	Arriva	LJ61GWE	Go-Ahead
LJ60AWG	Arriva	LJ61CDK	Arriva	LJ61GWF	Go-Ahead
LJ60AWH	Arriva	LJ61CDN	Arriva	LJ61GWG	Go-Ahead
LJ60AWM	Arriva	LJ61CDO	Arriva	LJ61GWK	Go-Ahead
LJ60AWN	Arriva	LJ61CDU	Arriva	LJ61GWL	Go-Ahead
LJ60AWO	Arriva	LJ61CDV	Arriva	LJ61GWM	Go-Ahead
LJ60AWP	Arriva	LJ61CDX	Arriva	LJ61GWN	Go-Ahead

LJ61GWO	Go-Ahead	LJ61NUX	Go-Ahead	LJ62BVY	Arriva		
LJ61GWP	Go-Ahead	LJ61NUY	Go-Ahead	LJ62BWF	Arriva		
LJ61GWU	Go-Ahead	LJ61NVA	Go-Ahead	LJ62BWP	Arriva		
LJ61GWV	Go-Ahead	LJ61NVB	Go-Ahead	LJ62BXD	Arriva		
LJ61GWW	Go-Ahead	LJ61NVC	Go-Ahead	LJ62BXF	Arriva		
LJ61GWX	Go-Ahead	LJ61NVD	Go-Ahead	LJ62BYT	Arriva		
LJ61GWY	Go-Ahead	LJ61NVE	Go-Ahead	LJ62BYU	Arriva		
LJ61GWZ	Go-Ahead	LJ61NVF	Go-Ahead	LJ62BZH	Arriva		
LJ61GXA	Go-Ahead	LJ61NVG	Go-Ahead	LJ62BZR	Arriva		
LJ61GXB	Go-Ahead	LJ61NVH	Go-Ahead	LJ62BZV	Arriva		
LJ61GXC	Go-Ahead	LJ61NVK	Go-Ahead	LJ62BZY	Arriva		
LJ61GXD	Go-Ahead	LJ61NVL	Go-Ahead	LJ62FNF	Arriva		
LJ61GXE	Go-Ahead	LJ61NVM	Go-Ahead	LJ62FNG	Arriva		
LJ61GXF	Go-Ahead	LJ61NVN	Go-Ahead	LJ62FNR	Arriva		
LJ61GXG	Go-Ahead	LJ61NVP	Go-Ahead	LJ62FOD	Arriva		
LJ61GXH	Go-Ahead	LJ61NVR	Go-Ahead	LJ62KBY	Go-Ahead		
LJ61GXK	Go-Ahead	LJ61NVS	Go-Ahead	LJ62KCU	Go-Ahead		
LJ61GXL	Go-Ahead	LJ61NVZ	Go-Ahead	LJ62KDV	Go-Ahead		
LJ61GXM	Go-Ahead	LJ61NWA	Go-Ahead	LJ62KDZ	Go-Ahead		
LJ61GXN	Go-Ahead	LJ61NWB	Go-Ahead	LJ62KFD	Go-Ahead		
LJ61GXO	Go-Ahead	LJ61NWC	Go-Ahead	LJ62KFF	Go-Ahead		
LJ61GXP	Go-Ahead	LJ61NWD	Go-Ahead	LJ62KFU	Go-Ahead		
LJ61LHP	Arriva	LJ61NWE	Go-Ahead	LJ62KGF	Go-Ahead		
LJ61LHR	Arriva	LJ61NWF	Go-Ahead	LJ62KGG	Go-Ahead		
LJ61LHT	Arriva	LJ61NWG	Go-Ahead	LJ62KGN	Go-Ahead		
LJ61LHU	Arriva	LJ61NWH	Go-Ahead	LJ62KGY	Go-Ahead		
LJ61LHV	Arriva	LJ61NWL	Go-Ahead	LJ62KHF	Go-Ahead		
LJ61LHW	Arriva	LJ61NWM	Go-Ahead	LJ62KHV	Go-Ahead		
LJ61LHX	Arriva	LJ61NWN	Go-Ahead	LJ62KKP	Go-Ahead		
LJ61LHY	Arriva	LJ61NWO	Go-Ahead	LJ62KLC	Go-Ahead		
LJ61LJC	Arriva	LJ61NWR	Go-Ahead	LJ62KLS	Go-Ahead		
LJ61LJE	Arriva	LJ61NWU	Go-Ahead	LJ62KOX	Go-Ahead		
LJ61LJF	Arriva	LJ61NWV	Go-Ahead	LJ62KXX	Go-Ahead		
LJ61LJK	Arriva	LJ61NWW	Go-Ahead	LJ62KXZ	Go-Ahead		
LJ61LJL	Arriva	LJ61NWX	Go-Ahead	LJ62KYA	Go-Ahead		
LJ61LJN	Arriva	LJ61NWZ	Go-Ahead	LJ62KYG	Go-Ahead		
LJ61LJO	Arriva	LJ61NXA	Go-Ahead	LJ62KZD	Go-Ahead		
LJ61LJU	Arriva	LJ61NXB	Go-Ahead	LJ62KZP	Go-Ahead		
LJ61LJV	Arriva	LJ61NXC	Go-Ahead	LJ63...	Arriva		
LJ61LJX	Arriva	LJ61NXD	Go-Ahead	LJ63...	Arriva		
LJ61LJY	Arriva	LJ61NXE	Go-Ahead	LJ63...	Arriva		
LJ61LJZ	Arriva	LJ61NXF	Go-Ahead	LJ63...	Arriva		
LJ61LKA	Arriva	LJ62BAA	Arriva	LJ63...	Arriva		
LJ61LKC	Arriva	LJ62BAO	Arriva	LJ63...	Arriva		
LJ61LKD	Arriva	LJ62BAU	Arriva	LJ63...	Arriva		
LJ61LKE	Arriva	LJ62BBZ	Arriva	LJ63...	Arriva		
LJ61LKF	Arriva	LJ62BCU	Arriva	LJ63...	Arriva		
LJ61LKG	Arriva	LJ62BDF	Arriva	LJ63...	Arriva		
LJ61LKK	Arriva	LJ62BDO	Arriva	LJ63...	Arriva		
LJ61LKL	Arriva	LJ62BEO	Arriva	LJ63...	Arriva		
LJ61LKM	Arriva	LJ62BFZ	Arriva	LJ63...	Arriva		
LJ61LKN	Arriva	LJ62BGK	Arriva	LJ63...	Arriva		
LJ61LKO	Arriva	LJ62BGX	Arriva	LJ63...	Arriva		
LJ61LKP	Arriva	LJ62BGZ	Arriva	LJ63...	Arriva		
LJ61LKU	Arriva	LJ62BHF	Arriva	LJ63...	Arriva		
LJ61LKV	Arriva	LJ62BHY	Arriva	LJ63...	Arriva		
LJ61LKX	Arriva	LJ62BJK	Arriva	LJ63...	Arriva		
LJ61LKY	Arriva	LJ62BJX	Arriva	LJ63...	Arriva		
LJ61LKZ	Arriva	LJ62BKD	Arriva	LJ63...	Arriva		
LJ61LLA	Arriva	LJ62BKG	Arriva	LJ63...	Arriva		
LJ61LLC	Arriva	LJ62BKN	Arriva	LJ63...	Arriva		
LJ61LLD	Arriva	LJ62BKU	Arriva	LJ63...	Arriva		
LJ61LLE	Arriva	LJ62BKX	Arriva	LJ63...	Arriva		
LJ61LLF	Arriva	LJ62BMO	Arriva	LJ63...	Arriva		
LJ61LLG	Arriva	LJ62BMZ	Arriva	LJ63...	Arriva		
LJ61LLK	Arriva	LJ62BNA	Arriva	LJ63...	Arriva		
LJ61LLM	Arriva	LJ62BND	Arriva	LJ63...	Arriva		
LJ61LLN	Arriva	LJ62BNE	Arriva	LK03CEN	Metroline		
LJ61LLO	Arriva	LJ62BNL	Arriva	LK03CEX	Metroline		
LJ61LLP	Arriva	LJ62BNU	Arriva	LK03CEY	Metroline		
LJ61NUM	Go-Ahead	LJ62BPV	Arriva	LK03CFA	Metroline		
LJ61NUO	Go-Ahead	LJ62BSO	Arriva	LK03CFD	Metroline		
LJ61NUP	Go-Ahead	LJ62BTO	Arriva	LK03CFF	Metroline		
LJ61NUU	Go-Ahead	LJ62BTY	Arriva	LK03CFG	Metroline		
LJ61NUV	Go-Ahead	LJ62BVE	Arriva	LK03CFJ	Metroline		
LJ61NUW	Go-Ahead	LJ62BVP	Arriva	LK03CFL	Metroline		

LK03CFN	Metroline	LK03NHT	Go-Ahead	LK04CTZ	Metroline
LK03CFP	Metroline	LK03NHV	Go-Ahead	LK04CUA	Metroline
LK03CFU	Metroline	LK03NHX	Go-Ahead	LK04CUC	Metroline
LK03CFX	Metroline	LK03NHY	Go-Ahead	LK04CUG	Metroline
LK03CFY	Metroline	LK03NHZ	Go-Ahead	LK04CUH	Metroline
LK03CFZ	Metroline	LK03NJE	Go-Ahead	LK04CUJ	Metroline
LK03CGG	Metroline	LK03NJF	Go-Ahead	LK04CUU	Metroline
LK03CGU	Metroline	LK03NJJ	Go-Ahead	LK04CUW	Metroline
LK03FJZ	Metroline	LK03NJN	Go-Ahead	LK04CUX	Metroline
LK03GFV	Metroline	LK03NJV	Go-Ahead	LK04CUY	Metroline
LK03GFX	Metroline	LK03NJX	Go-Ahead	LK04CVA	Metroline
LK03GFY	Metroline	LK03NJY	Go-Ahead	LK04CVB	Metroline
LK03GFZ	Metroline	LK03NJZ	Go-Ahead	LK04CVC	Metroline
LK03GGF	Metroline	LK03NKA	Go-Ahead	LK04CVD	Metroline
LK03GGJ	Metroline	LK03NKC	Metroline	LK04CVE	Metroline
LK03GGP	Metroline	LK03NKD	Metroline	LK04CVF	Metroline
LK03GGU	Metroline	LK03NKE	Metroline	LK04CVG	Metroline
LK03GGV	Metroline	LK03NKF	Metroline	LK04CVH	Metroline
LK03GGX	Metroline	LK03NKG	Metroline	LK04CVJ	Metroline
LK03GGY	Metroline	LK03NKH	Tower Transit	LK04CVL	Metroline
LK03GGZ	Metroline	LK03NKJ	Tower Transit	LK04CVM	Metroline
LK03GHA	Metroline	LK03NKL	Tower Transit	LK04CVN	Metroline
LK03GHB	Metroline	LK03NKM	Tower Transit	LK04CVP	Metroline
LK03GHD	Metroline	LK03NKN	Tower Transit	LK04CVR	Metroline
LK03GHF	Metroline	LK03NKP	Metroline	LK04CVS	Metroline
LK03GHG	Metroline	LK03NKR	Metroline	LK04CVT	Metroline
LK03GHH	Metroline	LK03NKS	Metroline	LK04CVU	Metroline
LK03GHJ	Metroline	LK03NKT	Metroline	LK04CVV	Metroline
LK03GHN	Metroline	LK03NKU	Metroline	LK04CVW	Metroline
LK03GHV	Metroline	LK03NKW	Metroline	LK04CVX	Metroline
LK03GHX	Metroline	LK03NKX	Metroline	LK04EKU	Metroline
LK03GHY	Metroline	LK03NKZ	Metroline	LK04EKV	Metroline
LK03GHZ	Metroline	LK03NLA	Metroline	LK04EKW	Metroline
LK03GJF	Metroline	LK03NLC	Metroline	LK04EKX	Metroline
LK03GJG	Metroline	LK03NLE	Metroline	LK04EKY	Metroline
LK03GJU	Metroline	LK03NLF	Metroline	LK04EKZ	Metroline
LK03GJV	Metroline	LK03NLG	Metroline	LK04ELC	Metroline
LK03GJX	Metroline	LK03NLJ	Metroline	LK04ELH	Metroline
LK03GJY	Metroline	LK03NLL	Metroline	LK04ELJ	Metroline
LK03GKA	Metroline	LK03NLM	Metroline	LK04ELU	Metroline
LK03GKC	Metroline	LK03NLP	Metroline	LK04ELV	Metroline
LK03GKD	Metroline	LK03NLR	Metroline	LK04ELW	Metroline
LK03GKF	Metroline	LK03NLT	Metroline	LK04ELX	Metroline
LK03GKG	Metroline	LK03UFD	Metroline	LK04EMF	Metroline
LK03GKJ	Metroline	LK03UFE	Metroline	LK04EMJ	Metroline
LK03GKL	Metroline	LK03UFG	Metroline	LK04EMV	Metroline
LK03GKN	Metroline	LK03UFJ	Metroline	LK04EMX	Metroline
LK03GKP	Metroline	LK03UFL	Metroline	LK04ENE	Metroline
LK03GKU	Metroline	LK03UFM	Metroline	LK04ENF	Metroline
LK03GKV	Metroline	LK03UFN	Metroline	LK04ENH	Metroline
LK03GKW	Metroline	LK03UFP	Metroline	LK04ENJ	Metroline
LK03GKX	Metroline	LK03UFR	Metroline	LK04HXA	Tower Transit
LK03GKY	Metroline	LK03UFS	Metroline	LK04HXB	Tower Transit
LK03GKZ	Metroline	LK03UFT	Metroline	LK04HXC	Tower Transit
LK03GLF	Metroline	LK03UFU	Metroline	LK04HXD	Tower Transit
LK03GLJ	Metroline	LK03UFV	Metroline	LK04HXE	Tower Transit
LK03GLV	Metroline	LK03UFW	Metroline	LK04HXH	Tower Transit
LK03GLY	Metroline	LK03UFX	Metroline	LK04HXJ	Tower Transit
LK03GLZ	Metroline	LK04CPY	Metroline	LK04HXL	Tower Transit
LK03GME	Metroline	LK04CPZ	Metroline	LK04HXM	Tower Transit
LK03GMF	Metroline	LK04CRF	Metroline	LK04HXN	Tower Transit
LK03GMG	Metroline	LK04CRJ	Metroline	LK04HXP	Tower Transit
LK03GMU	Metroline	LK04CRU	Metroline	LK04HXR	Tower Transit
LK03GMV	Metroline	LK04CRV	Metroline	LK04HXS	Tower Transit
LK03GMX	Metroline	LK04CRZ	Metroline	LK04HXT	Tower Transit
LK03GMY	Metroline	LK04CSF	Metroline	LK04HXU	Tower Transit
LK03GMZ	Metroline	LK04CSU	Metroline	LK04HXV	Tower Transit
LK03GNF	Metroline	LK04CSV	Metroline	LK04HXW	Tower Transit
LK03GNJ	Metroline	LK04CSX	Metroline	LK04HXX	Tower Transit
LK03GNN	Metroline	LK04CSY	Metroline	LK04HYA	Tower Transit
LK03GNP	Metroline	LK04CSZ	Metroline	LK04HYB	Tower Transit
LK03NFY	Metroline	LK04CTE	Metroline	LK04HYC	Tower Transit
LK03NFZ	Metroline	LK04CTF	Metroline	LK04HYF	Tower Transit
LK03NHF	Go-Ahead	LK04CTU	Metroline	LK04HYG	Tower Transit
LK03NHG	Go-Ahead	LK04CTV	Metroline	LK04HYH	Tower Transit
LK03NHP	Go-Ahead	LK04CTX	Metroline	LK04HYJ	Tower Transit

LK04HYL	Tower Transit	LK04UWW	Metroline	LK07BBU	Metroline
LK04HYM	Tower Transit	LK04UWX	Metroline	LK07BBV	Metroline
LK04HYN	Tower Transit	LK04UWY	Metroline	LK07BBX	Metroline
LK04HYS	Tower Transit	LK04UWZ	Metroline	LK07BBZ	Metroline
LK04HYT	Tower Transit	LK04UXA	Metroline	LK07BCE	Metroline
LK04HYU	Tower Transit	LK04UXB	Metroline	LK07BCF	Metroline
LK04HYV	Tower Transit	LK04UXC	Metroline	LK07BCO	Metroline
LK04HYW	Tower Transit	LK04UXD	Metroline	LK07BCU	Metroline
LK04HYX	Tower Transit	LK04UXE	Metroline	LK07BCV	Metroline
LK04HYY	Tower Transit	LK04UXF	Metroline	LK07BCX	Metroline
LK04HYZ	Tower Transit	LK04UXG	Metroline	LK07BCY	Metroline
LK04HZA	Tower Transit	LK04UXH	Metroline	LK07BCZ	Metroline
LK04HZB	Tower Transit	LK05GFO	Metroline	LK07BDE	Metroline
LK04HZC	Tower Transit	LK05GFV	Metroline	LK07BDF	Metroline
LK04HZD	Tower Transit	LK05GFX	Metroline	LK07BDO	Metroline
LK04HZE	Tower Transit	LK05GFY	Metroline	LK07BDU	Metroline
LK04HZF	Tower Transit	LK05GFZ	Metroline	LK07BDV	Metroline
LK04HZG	Tower Transit	LK05GGA	Metroline	LK07BDX	Metroline
LK04HZH	Tower Transit	LK05GGE	Metroline	LK07BDY	Metroline
LK04HZJ	Tower Transit	LK05GGF	Metroline	LK07BDZ	Metroline
LK04HZL	Tower Transit	LK05GGJ	Metroline	LK07BEJ	Metroline
LK04HZM	Tower Transit	LK05GGO	Metroline	LK07BEO	Metroline
LK04HZN	Tower Transit	LK05GGP	Metroline	LK07BEU	Metroline
LK04HZP	Tower Transit	LK05GGU	Metroline	LK07BEY	Metroline
LK04HZS	Tower Transit	LK05GGV	Metroline	LK07CBF	Abellio
LK04HZT	Tower Transit	LK05GGX	Metroline	LK07CBV	Abellio
LK04HZU	Tower Transit	LK05GGY	Metroline	LK07CBX	Abellio
LK04HZV	Tower Transit	LK05GGZ	Metroline	LK07ELH	Metroline
LK04HZW	Tower Transit	LK05GHA	Metroline	LK07ELJ	Metroline
LK04HZX	Tower Transit	LK05GHB	Metroline	LK07ELO	Metroline
LK04HZY	Tower Transit	LK05GHD	Metroline	LK08DVY	Metroline
LK04HZZ	Tower Transit	LK05GHF	Metroline	LK08DVZ	Metroline
LK04JBE	Tower Transit	LK05GHG	Metroline	LK08DWA	Metroline
LK04JBU	Tower Transit	LK05GHH	Metroline	LK08DWC	Metroline
LK04JBV	Tower Transit	LK06BWC	Abellio	LK08DWD	Metroline
LK04JBX	Tower Transit	LK06BWD	Abellio	LK08DWE	Metroline
LK04JBY	Tower Transit	LK06FLA	Metroline	LK08DWF	Metroline
LK04JBZ	Tower Transit	LK06FLB	Metroline	LK08DWG	Metroline
LK04JCJ	Tower Transit	LK06FLC	Metroline	LK08DWJ	Metroline
LK04JCU	Tower Transit	LK07AYC	Metroline	LK08DWL	Metroline
LK04JCV	Tower Transit	LK07AYD	Metroline	LK08DWM	Metroline
LK04JCX	Tower Transit	LK07AYE	Metroline	LK08DWN	Metroline
LK04JCZ	Tower Transit	LK07AYF	Metroline	LK08DWO	Metroline
LK04NLZ	Metroline	LK07AYG	Metroline	LK08DWP	Metroline
LK04NMA	Metroline	LK07AYH	Metroline	LK08DWU	Metroline
LK04NME	Metroline	LK07AYK	Metroline	LK08DWV	Metroline
LK04NMF	Metroline	LK07AYL	Metroline	LK08DWW	Metroline
LK04NMJ	Metroline	LK07AYM	Metroline	LK08DWX	Metroline
LK04NMM	Metroline	LK07AYN	Metroline	LK08DWY	Metroline
LK04NMU	Metroline	LK07AYZ	Metroline	LK08DWZ	Metroline
LK04NMV	Metroline	LK07AZA	Metroline	LK08DXA	Metroline
LK04NMX	Metroline	LK07AZB	Metroline	LK08DXB	Metroline
LK04NMY	Metroline	LK07AZC	Metroline	LK08DXO	Metroline
LK04NMZ	Metroline	LK07AZD	Metroline	LK08DXP	Metroline
LK04NNA	Metroline	LK07AZF	Metroline	LK08DXR	Metroline
LK04NNB	Metroline	LK07AZG	Metroline	LK08DXS	Metroline
LK04NNC	Metroline	LK07AZJ	Metroline	LK08DXU	Metroline
LK04NND	Metroline	LK07AZL	Metroline	LK08DXV	Metroline
LK04NNE	Metroline	LK07AZN	Metroline	LK08DXW	Metroline
LK04NNF	Metroline	LK07AZO	Metroline	LK08DXX	Metroline
LK04NNG	Metroline	LK07AZP	Metroline	LK08DXY	Metroline
LK04NNH	Metroline	LK07AZR	Metroline	LK08DXZ	Metroline
LK04NNJ	Metroline	LK07AZT	Metroline	LK08DYA	Metroline
LK04NNL	Metroline	LK07AZU	Metroline	LK08FKT	Metroline
LK04NNM	Metroline	LK07AZV	Metroline	LK08FKU	Metroline
LK04NNP	Metroline	LK07AZW	Metroline	LK08FKV	Metroline
LK04UWJ	Metroline	LK07AZX	Metroline	LK08FKW	Metroline
LK04UWL	Metroline	LK07AZZ	Metroline	LK08FLC	Metroline
LK04UWM	Metroline	LK07BAA	Metroline	LK08FLD	Metroline
LK04UWN	Metroline	LK07BAO	Metroline	LK08FLE	Metroline
LK04UWP	Metroline	LK07BAU	Metroline	LK08FLF	Metroline
LK04UWR	Metroline	LK07BBE	Metroline	LK08FLG	Metroline
LK04UWS	Metroline	LK07BBF	Metroline	LK08FLH	Go-Ahead
LK04UWT	Metroline	LK07BBJ	Metroline	LK08FLJ	Go-Ahead
LK04UWU	Metroline	LK07BBN	Metroline	LK08FLL	Go-Ahead
LK04UWV	Metroline	LK07BBO	Metroline	LK08FLM	Go-Ahead

Reg	Operator	Reg	Operator	Reg	Operator	Reg	Operator
LK08FLN	Go-Ahead	LK10BXW	Metroline	LK11CXT	Metroline		Metroline
LK08FLP	Go-Ahead	LK10BXX	Metroline	LK11CXU	Metroline		Metroline
LK08FLR	Go-Ahead	LK10BXY	Metroline	LK11CXV	Metroline		Metroline
LK08FLV	Metroline	LK10BXZ	Metroline	LK11CXW	Metroline		Metroline
LK08FLW	Metroline	LK10BYA	Metroline	LK11CXX	Metroline		Metroline
LK08FLX	Go-Ahead	LK10BYB	Metroline	LK11CXY	Metroline		Metroline
LK08FLZ	Metroline	LK10BYC	Metroline	LK11CXZ	Metroline		Metroline
LK08FMA	Metroline	LK10BYD	Metroline	LK11CYA	Metroline		Metroline
LK08FMO	Metroline	LK10BYG	Metroline	LK11CYE	Metroline		Metroline
LK08FMP	Metroline	LK10BYJ	Metroline	LK11CYF	Metroline		Metroline
LK08FMU	Metroline	LK10BYL	Metroline	LK11CYH	Metroline		Metroline
LK08FMV	Metroline	LK10BYM	Metroline	LK11CYJ	Metroline		Metroline
LK08FMX	Metroline	LK10BYN	Metroline	LK11CYL	Metroline		Metroline
LK08FMY	Metroline	LK10BYO	Metroline	LK11CYO	Metroline		Metroline
LK08FMZ	Metroline	LK10BYP	Metroline	LK11CYP	Metroline		Metroline
LK08FNA	Metroline	LK10BYR	Metroline	LK11CYS	Metroline		Metroline
LK08FNC	Metroline	LK10BYS	Metroline	LK11CYT	Metroline		Metroline
LK08FND	Metroline	LK10BYT	Metroline	LK11CYU	Metroline		Metroline
LK08FNE	Metroline	LK10BYU	Metroline	LK11CYV	Metroline		Metroline
LK08FNF	Metroline	LK10BYV	Metroline	LK12AAF	Metroline		Metroline
LK08FNG	Metroline	LK10BYW	Metroline	LK12AAJ	Metroline		Metroline
LK08FNH	Metroline	LK10BYX	Metroline	LK12AAN	Metroline		Metroline
LK08NVD	Metroline	LK10BYY	Metroline	LK12AAU	Metroline		Metroline
LK08NVE	Metroline	LK10BYZ	Metroline	LK12ABF	Metroline		Metroline
LK08NVF	Metroline	LK10BZA	Metroline	LK12ABO	Metroline		Metroline
LK08NVG	Metroline	LK10BZB	Metroline	LK12ABX	Metroline		Metroline
LK08NVH	Metroline	LK10BZC	Metroline	LK12ACF	Metroline		Metroline
LK08NVJ	Metroline	LK10BZD	Metroline	LK12ACO	Metroline		Metroline
LK08NVL	Metroline	LK10BZE	Metroline	LK12ACZ	Metroline		Metroline
LK08NVM	Metroline	LK10BZF	Metroline	LK12ADU	Metroline		Metroline
LK08NVN	Metroline	LK10BZG	Metroline	LK12ADV	Metroline		Metroline
LK08NVO	Metroline	LK10BZH	Metroline	LK12ADX	Metroline		Metroline
LK08NVP	Metroline	LK10BZJ	Metroline	LK12AEA	Metroline		Metroline
LK09CZS	Tower Transit	LK10BZL	Metroline	LK12AEB	Metroline		Metroline
LK09EKG	Metroline	LK10BZM	Metroline	LK12AEF	Metroline		Metroline
LK09EKH	Metroline	LK10BZN	Metroline	LK12AEG	Metroline		Metroline
LK09EKM	Metroline	LK10BZO	Metroline	LK12AET	Metroline		Metroline
LK09EKN	Metroline	LK10BZP	Metroline	LK12AEU	Metroline		Metroline
LK09ENC	Metroline	LK10BZR	Metroline	LK12AEW	Metroline		Metroline
LK09ENE	Metroline	LK10BZS	Metroline	LK12AEZ	Metroline		Metroline
LK09ENF	Metroline	LK10BZT	Metroline	LK12AFA	Metroline		Metroline
LK09ENH	Metroline	LK10BZU	Metroline	LK12AFE	Metroline		Metroline
LK09ENJ	Metroline	LK10BZV	Metroline	LK12AFO	Metroline		Metroline
LK09ENL	Metroline	LK10BZX	Metroline	LK12AFU	Metroline		Metroline
LK09ENM	Metroline	LK10BZY	Metroline	LK12AFV	Metroline		Metroline
LK09ENN	Metroline	LK11CWF	Metroline	LK12AFX	Metroline		Metroline
LK09ENO	Metroline	LK11CWG	Metroline	LK12AHA	Metroline		Metroline
LK09ENP	Metroline	LK11CWJ	Metroline	LK12AHC	Metroline		Metroline
LK09ENR	Metroline	LK11CWL	Metroline	LK12AHD	Metroline		Metroline
LK09ENT	Metroline	LK11CWM	Metroline	LK12AHO	Metroline		Metroline
LK09ENU	Metroline	LK11CWN	Metroline	LK12AHU	Metroline		Metroline
LK09ENV	Metroline	LK11CWO	Metroline	LK12AHZ	Metroline		Metroline
LK09ENW	Metroline	LK11CWP	Metroline	LK12AJX	Metroline		Metroline
LK09ENX	Metroline	LK11CWR	Metroline	LK12AKN	Metroline		Metroline
LK09ENY	Metroline	LK11CWT	Metroline	LK12AKO	Metroline		Metroline
LK09EOA	Metroline	LK11CWU	Metroline	LK12ALO	Metroline		Metroline
LK09EOB	Metroline	LK11CWV	Metroline	LK12AMO	Metroline		Metroline
LK09EOC	Metroline	LK11CWW	Metroline	LK12AMV	Metroline		Metroline
LK09EOD	Metroline	LK11CWX	Metroline	LK12ANF	Metroline		Metroline
LK09EOE	Metroline	LK11CWY	Metroline	LK12AOA	Metroline		Metroline
LK10BXC	Metroline	LK11CWZ	Metroline	LK12AOL	Metroline		Metroline
LK10BXD	Metroline	LK11CXA	Metroline	LK12AOO	Metroline		Metroline
LK10BXE	Metroline	LK11CXB	Metroline	LK12AOT	Metroline		Metroline
LK10BXF	Metroline	LK11CXC	Metroline	LK12AOV	Metroline		Metroline
LK10BXG	Metroline	LK11CXD	Metroline	LK12AOX	Metroline		Metroline
LK10BXH	Metroline	LK11CXE	Metroline	LK12AOY	Metroline		Metroline
LK10BXJ	Metroline	LK11CXF	Metroline	LK12APF	Metroline		Metroline
LK10BXL	Metroline	LK11CXG	Metroline	LK12APZ	Metroline		Metroline
LK10BXM	Metroline	LK11CXJ	Metroline	LK12ARO	Metroline		Metroline
LK10BXN	Metroline	LK11CXL	Metroline	LK12ARU	Metroline		Metroline
LK10BXO	Metroline	LK11CXM	Metroline	LK12ARX	Metroline		Metroline
LK10BXP	Metroline	LK11CXN	Metroline	LK12ARZ	Metroline		Metroline
LK10BXR	Metroline	LK11CXO	Metroline	LK12ASZ	Metroline		Metroline
LK10BXS	Metroline	LK11CXP	Metroline	LK12ATU	Metroline		Metroline
LK10BXU	Metroline	LK11CXR	Metroline	LK12ATV	Metroline		Metroline
LK10BXV	Metroline	LK11CXS	Metroline	LK12AUE	Metroline		Metroline

LK12AUF	Metroline	LK51JYN	Metrobus	LK55ACX	Abellio
LK12AUM	Metroline	LK51UYE	Tower Transit	LK55ADU	Abellio
LK12AUN	Metroline	LK51XGB	Metroline	LK55ADV	Abellio
LK12AUU	Metroline	LK51XGC	Metroline	LK55KJV	Metroline
LK12AUV	Metroline	LK51XGG	Metroline	LK55KJX	Metroline
LK12AUW	Metroline	LK51XGJ	Metroline	LK55KJY	Metroline
LK12AUY	Metroline	LK51XGL	Metroline	LK55KJZ	Metroline
LK12AVD	Metroline	LK51XGN	Metroline	LK55KKA	Metroline
LK12AVJ	Metroline	LK51XGO	Metroline	LK55KKB	Metroline
LK12AVN	Metroline	LK51XGP	Transdev	LK55KKC	Metroline
LK12AVT	Metroline	LK51XGR	Metroline	LK55KKD	Metroline
LK12AVU	Metroline	LK51XGU	Metroline	LK55KKE	Metroline
LK12AWA	Metroline	LK51XGW	Metroline	LK55KKF	Metroline
LK12AWC	Metroline	LK51XGZ	Metroline	LK55KKG	Metroline
LK12AWJ	Metroline	LK51XHB	Metroline	LK55KKH	Metroline
LK12AWN	Metroline	LK53FDC	Metroline	LK55KKJ	Metroline
LK12AWO	Metroline	LK53FDE	Metroline	LK55KKL	Metroline
LK12AWP	Metroline	LK53FDF	Metroline	LK55KKM	Metroline
LK12AWU	Metroline	LK53FDG	Metroline	LK55KKO	Metroline
LK12AWX	Metroline	LK53FDJ	Metroline	LK55KKP	Metroline
LK12AWY	Metroline	LK53FDM	Metroline	LK55KKR	Metroline
LK12AWZ	Metroline	LK53FDN	Metroline	LK55KKS	Metroline
LK12AXA	Metroline	LK53FDO	Metroline	LK55KKT	Metroline
LK12AXG	Metroline	LK53FDP	Metroline	LK55KKU	Metroline
LK12AXH	Metroline	LK53FDU	Metroline	LK55KKV	Metroline
LK12AXP	Metroline	LK53FDV	Metroline	LK55KKY	Metroline
LK12AXR	Metroline	LK53LXM	Metroline	LK55KKZ	Metroline
LK12AXS	Metroline	LK53LXN	Metroline	LK55KLA	Metroline
LK12AXV	Metroline	LK53LXO	Metroline	LK55KLE	Metroline
LK12AXW	Metroline	LK53LXP	Metroline	LK55KLF	Metroline
LK12AXZ	Metroline	LK53LXR	Metroline	LK55KLJ	Metroline
LK12AYF	Metroline	LK53LXT	Metroline	LK55KLL	Metroline
LK12AYG	Metroline	LK53LXU	Metroline	LK55KLL	Metroline
LK12AYL	Metroline	LK53LXV	Metroline	LK55KLM	Metroline
LK12AYP	Metroline	LK53LXW	Metroline	LK55KLO	Metroline
LK12AYZ	Metroline	LK53LXX	Metroline	LK55KLP	Metroline
LK12AZA	Metroline	LK53LXY	Metroline	LK55KLS	Metroline
LK13BFA	Metroline	LK53LXZ	Metroline	LK55KLV	Metroline
LK13BFF	Metroline	LK53LYA	Metroline	LK55KLX	Metroline
LK13BFJ	Metroline	LK53LYC	Metroline	LK55KLZ	Metroline
LK13BFL	Metroline	LK53LYD	Metroline	LK55KMA	Metroline
LK13BFM	Metroline	LK53LYF	Metroline	LK55KME	Metroline
LK13BFN	Metroline	LK53LYG	Metroline	LK55KMF	Metroline
LK13BFO	Metroline	LK54FLA	Tower Transit	LK55KMG	Metroline
LK13BFP	Metroline	LK54FLB	Tower Transit	LK55KMJ	Metroline
LK13BFU	Metroline	LK54FLC	Tower Transit	LK55KMM	Metroline
LK13BFV	Metroline	LK54FLD	Tower Transit	LK55KMO	Metroline
LK13BFX	Metroline	LK54FLE	Tower Transit	LK56FHE	Metroline
LK13BFY	Metroline	LK54FLF	Tower Transit	LK56FHF	Metroline
LK13BFZ	Metroline	LK54FLG	Tower Transit	LK56FHG	Metroline
LK13BGE	Metroline	LK54FLH	Tower Transit	LK56FHJ	Metroline
LK13BGF	Metroline	LK54FNO	Tower Transit	LK56FHM	Metroline
LK13BGO	Metroline	LK54FNP	Tower Transit	LK56FHN	Metroline
LK13BGU	Metroline	LK54FWE	Metroline	LK56FHO	Metroline
LK13BGV	Metroline	LK54FWF	Metroline	LK56FHP	Metroline
LK13BGX	Metroline	LK54FWG	Metroline	LK56FHR	Metroline
LK13BGY	Metroline	LK54FWH	Metroline	LK56FHS	Metroline
LK13BGZ	Metroline	LK54FWJ	Metroline	LK56FHT	Metroline
LK13BHA	Metroline	LK54FWL	Metroline	LK56JKE	Abellio
LK13BHD	Metroline	LK54FWM	Metroline	LK56JKF	Abellio
LK13BHE	Metroline	LK54FWN	Metroline	LK56JKJ	Abellio
LK13BHF	Metroline	LK54FWO	Metroline	LK56JKN	Abellio
LK13BHJ	Metroline	LK54FWP	Metroline	LK56JKO	Abellio
LK13BHL	Metroline	LK54FWR	Metroline	LK56JKV	Abellio
LK13BHN	Metroline	LK54FWT	Metroline	LK57AXF	Metroline
LK13BHO	Metroline	LK55AAE	Metroline	LK57AXG	Metroline
LK13BHP	Metroline	LK55AAF	Metroline	LK57AXH	Metroline
LK13BHU	Metroline	LK55AAJ	Metroline	LK57AXJ	Metroline
LK13BHV	Metroline	LK55AAN	Metroline	LK57AXM	Metroline
LK13BHW	Metroline	LK55AAU	Metroline	LK57AXN	Metroline
LK13BHX	Metroline	LK55AAV	Metroline	LK57AXO	Metroline
LK13BHY	Metroline	LK55AAX	Metroline	LK57AXP	Metroline
LK13BHZ	Metroline	LK55AAY	Metroline	LK57AXR	Metroline
LK13BJE	Metroline	LK55AAZ	Metroline	LK57AXS	Metroline
LK51JYJ	Metrobus	LK55ABF	Metroline	LK57AXT	Metroline
LK51JYL	Metrobus	LK55ACU	Metroline	LK57AXU	Metroline

Reg	Operator	Reg	Operator	Reg	Operator
LK57AXV	Metroline	LK58CRZ	Metroline	LK59CWW	Metroline
LK57AXW	Metroline	LK58CSF	Metroline	LK59CWX	Metroline
LK57AXX	Metroline	LK58CSU	Metroline	LK59CWY	Metroline
LK57AXY	Metroline	LK58CSX	Metroline	LK59CWZ	Metroline
LK57AXZ	Metroline	LK58CSY	Metroline	LK59CXA	Metroline
LK57AYA	Metroline	LK58CSZ	Metroline	LK59CXB	Metroline
LK57AYB	Metroline	LK58CTE	Metroline	LK59CXC	Metroline
LK57AYC	Metroline	LK58CTF	Metroline	LK59CXD	Metroline
LK57AYD	Metroline	LK58CTO	Metroline	LK59CXE	Metroline
LK57AYE	Metroline	LK58CTU	Metroline	LK59CXF	Metroline
LK57AYF	Metroline	LK58CTV	Metroline	LK59CXG	Metroline
LK57AYG	Metroline	LK58CTX	Metroline	LK59CXH	Metroline
LK57AYH	Metroline	LK58CTY	Metroline	LK59CXJ	Metroline
LK57AYJ	Metroline	LK58CTZ	Metroline	LK59CXL	Metroline
LK57AYL	Metroline	LK58CUA	Metroline	LK59CXM	Metroline
LK57AYM	Metroline	LK58EDO	Tower Transit	LK59CXN	Metroline
LK57AYN	Metroline	LK58EDP	Tower Transit	LK59CXO	Metroline
LK57AYO	Metroline	LK58EDR	Tower Transit	LK59CXP	Metroline
LK57AYP	Metroline	LK58KFW	Metroline	LK59DYY	Metroline
LK57AYS	Metroline	LK58KFX	Metroline	LK59DZA	Metroline
LK57AYT	Metroline	LK58KFY	Metroline	LK59DZB	Metroline
LK57AYU	Metroline	LK58KFZ	Metroline	LK59DZC	Metroline
LK57AYV	Metroline	LK58KGA	Metroline	LK59DZD	Metroline
LK57AYW	Metroline	LK58KGE	Metroline	LK59DZE	Metroline
LK57AYX	Metroline	LK58KGF	Metroline	LK59DZF	Metroline
LK57AYY	Metroline	LK58KGG	Metroline	LK59DZG	Metroline
LK57EHS	Metroline	LK58KGJ	Metroline	LK59DZH	Metroline
LK57EHT	Metroline	LK58KGN	Metroline	LK59DZJ	Metroline
LK57EHU	Metroline	LK58KGO	Metroline	LK59DZL	Metroline
LK57EHV	Metroline	LK58KGP	Metroline	LK59DZM	Metroline
LK57EHW	Metroline	LK58KGU	Metroline	LK59DZN	Metroline
LK57EHX	Metroline	LK58KGV	Metroline	LK59DZO	Metroline
LK57EHY	Metroline	LK58KGY	Metroline	LK59DZP	Metroline
LK57EHZ	Metroline	LK58KGZ	Metroline	LK59DZR	Metroline
LK57EJA	Metroline	LK58KHA	Metroline	LK59DZS	Metroline
LK57EJN	Go-Ahead	LK58KHB	Metroline	LK59FCO	Metroline
LK57EJO	Go-Ahead	LK58KHC	Metroline	LK59FCP	Metroline
LK57KAX	Metroline	LK58KHD	Metroline	LK59FCU	Metroline
LK57KBE	Metroline	LK58KHE	Metroline	LK59FCV	Metroline
LK57KBF	Metroline	LK58KHF	Metroline	LK59FCX	Metroline
LK57KBJ	Metroline	LK58KHG	Metroline	LK59FCY	Metroline
LK57KBN	Metroline	LK58KHH	Metroline	LK59FDE	Go-Ahead
LK57KBO	Metroline	LK58KHJ	Metroline	LK59FDF	Go-Ahead
LK58CAN	Metroline	LK58KHL	Metroline	LK59FDG	Go-Ahead
LK58CMY	Metroline	LK58KHM	Metroline	LK59FDJ	Go-Ahead
LK58CMZ	Metroline	LK58KHO	Metroline	LK59FDL	Go-Ahead
LK58CNC	Metroline	LK58KHP	Metroline	LK59FDM	Go-Ahead
LK58CNE	Metroline	LK58KHR	Metroline	LK59FDN	Go-Ahead
LK58CNF	Metroline	LK58KHT	Metroline	LK59FDO	Go-Ahead
LK58CNN	Metroline	LK58KHU	Metroline	LK59FDP	Go-Ahead
LK58CNO	Metroline	LK59AUW	Metroline	LK59FDU	Go-Ahead
LK58CNU	Metroline	LK59AUY	Metroline	LK59FDV	Go-Ahead
LK58CNV	Metroline	LK59AVB	Metroline	LK59FDX	Go-Ahead
LK58CNX	Metroline	LK59AVC	Metroline	LK59FDY	Go-Ahead
LK58CNY	Metroline	LK59AVD	Metroline	LK59FDZ	Go-Ahead
LK58CNZ	Metroline	LK59AVF	Metroline	LK59FEF	Go-Ahead
LK58COA	Metroline	LK59AVG	Metroline	LK59FEG	Go-Ahead
LK58COH	Metroline	LK59AVJ	Metroline	LK59FEH	Go-Ahead
LK58COJ	Metroline	LK59AVL	Metroline	LK59FEJ	Go-Ahead
LK58COU	Metroline	LK59AVM	Metroline	LK59FEM	Go-Ahead
LK58CPE	Metroline	LK59AVN	Metroline	LK59FEO	Go-Ahead
LK58CPF	Metroline	LK59AVO	Metroline	LK59FEP	Go-Ahead
LK58CPN	Metroline	LK59AVP	Metroline	LK59FET	Go-Ahead
LK58CPO	Metroline	LK59AVR	Metroline	LK59FEU	Go-Ahead
LK58CPU	Metroline	LK59AVT	Metroline	LK59JJU	Metroline
LK58CPV	Metroline	LK59AVU	Metroline	LK60AEA	Metroline
LK58CPV	Metroline	LK59AVV	Metroline	LK60AEB	Metroline
LK58CPW	Metroline	LK59AVW	Metroline	LK60AEC	Metroline
LK58CPX	Metroline	LK59AVX	Metroline	LK60AED	Metroline
LK58CPY	Metroline	LK59CWN	Metroline	LK60AEE	Metroline
LK58CPZ	Metroline	LK59CWO	Metroline	LK60AEF	Metroline
LK58CRF	Metroline	LK59CWP	Metroline	LK60AEG	Metroline
LK58CRJ	Metroline	LK59CWR	Metroline	LK60AEJ	Metroline
LK58CRU	Metroline	LK59CWT	Metroline	LK60AEL	Metroline
LK58CRV	Metroline	LK59CWU	Metroline	LK60AEM	Metroline
LK58CRX	Metroline	LK59CWV	Metroline	LK60AEN	Metroline

LK60AEO	Metroline	LK61BLX	Metroline	LK62DVH	Metroline
LK60AEP	Metroline	LK61BLZ	Metroline	LK62DVJ	Metroline
LK60AET	Metroline	LK61BMO	Metroline	LK62DVL	Metroline
LK60AEU	Metroline	LK61BMU	Metroline	LK62DVO	Metroline
LK60AEV	Metroline	LK61BMV	Metroline	LK62DVP	Metroline
LK60AEW	Metroline	LK61BMY	Metroline	LK62DVR	Metroline
LK60AEX	Metroline	LK61BMZ	Metroline	LK62DVU	Metroline
LK60AEY	Metroline	LK61BNA	Metroline	LK62DWA	Metroline
LK60AEZ	Metroline	LK61BNB	Metroline	LK62DWD	Metroline
LK60AFA	Metroline	LK61BNE	Metroline	LK62DWE	Metroline
LK60AFE	Metroline	LK61BNF	Metroline	LK62DWF	Metroline
LK60AFF	Metroline	LK61BNJ	Metroline	LK62DWJ	Metroline
LK60AFN	Metroline	LK61BNL	Metroline	LK62DWO	Metroline
LK60AFO	Metroline	LK61BNN	Metroline	LK62DWU	Metroline
LK60AFU	Metroline	LK61BNO	Metroline	LK62DWV	Metroline
LK60AFV	Metroline	LK62DAA	Metroline	LK62DWY	Metroline
LK60AFX	Metroline	LK62DAO	Metroline	LK62DXF	Metroline
LK60AFY	Metroline	LK62DBZ	Metroline	LK62DXG	Metroline
LK60AFZ	Metroline	LK62DCE	Metroline	LK62DXM	Metroline
LK60AGO	Metroline	LK62DCF	Metroline	LK62DXP	Metroline
LK60AGU	Metroline	LK62DCY	Metroline	LK62DXS	Metroline
LK60AGV	Metroline	LK62DDU	Metroline	LK62DXT	Metroline
LK60AGY	Metroline	LK62DDY	Metroline	LK62DXX	Metroline
LK60AGZ	Metroline	LK62DDZ	Metroline	LK62DXY	Metroline
LK60AHA	Metroline	LK62DEU	Metroline	LK62DYA	Metroline
LK60AHC	Metroline	LK62DFF	Metroline	LK62DYC	Metroline
LK60AHD	Metroline	LK62DFJ	Metroline	LK62DYD	Metroline
LK60AHE	Metroline	LK62DFP	Metroline	LK62DYF	Metroline
LK60AHG	Metroline	LK62DFY	Metroline	LK62DYG	Metroline
LK60AHJ	Metroline	LK62DGF	Metroline	LK62DYH	Metroline
LK60AHL	Metroline	LK62DGO	Metroline	LK62DYN	Metroline
LK60AHN	Metroline	LK62DHC	Metroline	LK62DYO	Metroline
LK60AHO	Metroline	LK62DHD	Metroline	LK62DYS	Metroline
LK60AHP	Metroline	LK62DHE	Metroline	LK62DYT	Metroline
LK60AHU	Metroline	LK62DHG	Metroline	LN51DUA	Tower Transit
LK60AHV	Metroline	LK62DHP	Metroline	LN51DUH	Tower Transit
LK60AHX	Metroline	LK62DHU	Metroline	LN51DWJ	Tower Transit
LK60AHY	Metroline	LK62DHV	Metroline	LN51DWL	Go-Ahead
LK60AHZ	Metroline	LK62DHX	Metroline	LN51DWM	Go-Ahead
LK60AJO	Metroline	LK62DHZ	Metroline	LN51DWO	Go-Ahead
LK60AJU	Metroline	LK62DJY	Metroline	LN51DWP	Go-Ahead
LK60AJV	Metroline	LK62DJZ	Metroline	LN51DWU	Go-Ahead
LK60AJX	Metroline	LK62DKE	Metroline	LN51DXH	Tower Transit
LK60AJY	Metroline	LK62DKN	Metroline	LN51GKD	Go-Ahead
LK60AKF	Metroline	LK62DKV	Metroline	LN51GKE	Go-Ahead
LK60HPE	Tower Transit	LK62DLJ	Metroline	LN51GKG	Go-Ahead
LK60HPF	Tower Transit	LK62DLO	Metroline	LN51GOJ	Go-Ahead
LK60HPJ	Tower Transit	LK62DLV	Metroline	LN51GOK	Go-Ahead
LK60HPL	Tower Transit	LK62DLX	Metroline	LN51KXD	Metroline
LK60HPN	Tower Transit	LK62DMV	Metroline	LN51KXE	Metroline
LK61BJE	Metroline	LK62DND	Metroline	LN51KXF	Metroline
LK61BJF	Metroline	LK62DNE	Metroline	LN51KXG	Metroline
LK61BJJ	Metroline	LK62DNO	Metroline	LN51KXH	Metroline
LK61BJO	Metroline	LK62DNU	Metroline	LN51KXJ	Metroline
LK61BJU	Metroline	LK62DNX	Metroline	LN51KXK	Metroline
LK61BJV	Metroline	LK62DOH	Metroline	LN51KXL	Metroline
LK61BJX	Metroline	LK62DPE	Metroline	LN51KXM	Metroline
LK61BJY	Metroline	LK62DPU	Metroline	LN51KXO	Metroline
LK61BJZ	Metroline	LK62DPY	Metroline	LN51KXU	Metroline
LK61BKA	Metroline	LK62DRV	Metroline	LN51KYE	Metroline
LK61BKD	Metroline	LK62DRZ	Metroline	LN51KYX	Metroline
LK61BKE	Metroline	LK62DSE	Metroline	LN51KYZ	Metroline
LK61BKF	Metroline	LK62DSU	Metroline	LN51KZB	Metroline
LK61BKG	Metroline	LK62DSV	Metroline	LN51KZC	Metroline
LK61BKJ	Metroline	LK62DTN	Metroline	LR02BAA	Metroline
LK61BKL	Metroline	LK62DTU	Metroline	LR02BDX	Metroline
LK61BKN	Metroline	LK62DTV	Metroline	LR02BEJ	Metroline
LK61BKO	Metroline	LK62DTZ	Metroline	LR02BEU	Metroline
LK61BKU	Metroline	LK62DUA	Metroline	LR02BEY	Metroline
LK61BKV	Metroline	LK62DUH	Metroline	LR52BLK	Metroline
LK61BKY	Metroline	LK62DUJ	Metroline	LR52BLN	Metroline
LK61BKZ	Metroline	LK62DUU	Metroline	LR52BLV	Metroline
LK61BLF	Metroline	LK62DVB	Metroline	LR52BLX	Metroline
LK61BLJ	Metroline	LK62DVC	Metroline	LR52BLZ	Metroline
LK61BLN	Metroline	LK62DVF	Metroline	LR52BMO	Metroline
LK61BLV	Metroline	LK62DVG	Metroline	LR52BMU	Metroline

Reg	Operator	Reg	Operator	Reg	Operator
LR52BMV	Metroline	LTZ1022	Metroline	LV52USF	Stagecoach
LR52BMY	Metroline	LTZ1023	Metroline	LX03BTE	Stagecoach
LR52BMZ	Metroline	LTZ1024	Metroline	LX03BTF	Stagecoach
LR52BNA	Metroline	LTZ1025	Metroline	LX03BTU	Stagecoach
LR52BNB	Metroline	LTZ1026	Metroline	LX03BTV	Stagecoach
LR52BND	Metroline	LTZ1027	Metroline	LX03BTY	Stagecoach
LR52BNE	Metroline	LTZ1028	Metroline	LX03BTZ	Stagecoach
LR52BNF	Metroline	LTZ1029	Metroline	LX03BUA	Stagecoach
LR52BNJ	Metroline	LTZ1030	Metroline	LX03BUE	Stagecoach
LR52BNK	Metroline	LTZ1031	Metroline	LX03BUH	Stagecoach
LR52BNL	Metroline	LTZ1032	Metroline	LX03BUJ	Stagecoach
LR52BNN	Metroline	LTZ1033	Metroline	LX03BUP	Stagecoach
LR52BNO	Metroline	LTZ1034	Metroline	LX03BUU	Stagecoach
LR52BNU	Metroline	LTZ1035	Metroline	LX03BUV	Stagecoach
LR52BNV	Metroline	LTZ1036	Metroline	LX03BUW	Stagecoach
LR52BNX	Metroline	LTZ1037	Metroline	LX03BVA	Stagecoach
LR52BNY	Metroline	LTZ1038	Metroline	LX03BVB	Stagecoach
LR52BNZ	Metroline	LTZ1039	Metroline	LX03BVC	Stagecoach
LR52BOF	Metroline	LTZ1040	Metroline	LX03BVD	Stagecoach
LR52BOH	Metroline	LV51YCC	Big Bus Company	LX03BVE	Stagecoach
LR52BOJ	Metroline	LV51YCD	Big Bus Company	LX03BVF	Stagecoach
LR52BOU	Metroline	LV51YCE	Big Bus Company	LX03BVG	Stagecoach
LR52BOV	Metroline	LV51YCF	Big Bus Company	LX03BVH	Stagecoach
LR52BPE	Metroline	LV51YCG	Big Bus Company	LX03BVJ	Stagecoach
LR52LTF	HCT - CT Plus	LV51YCH	Big Bus Company	LX03BVK	Stagecoach
LR52LTJ	HCT - CT Plus	LV51YCJ	Big Bus Company	LX03BVL	Stagecoach
LR52LTK	HCT - CT Plus	LV51YCK	Big Bus Company	LX03BVM	Stagecoach
LR52LTN	HCT - CT Plus	LV51YCL	Big Bus Company	LX03BVN	Stagecoach
LR52LTO	HCT - CT Plus	LV51YCM	Big Bus Company	LX03BVP	Stagecoach
LR52LWE	HCT - CT Plus	LV51YCN	Big Bus Company	LX03BVR	Stagecoach
LR52LWF	HCT - CT Plus	LV51YCO	Big Bus Company	LX03BVS	Stagecoach
LR52LWH	HCT - CT Plus	LV52HDO	Stagecoach	LX03BVT	Stagecoach
LR52LWJ	HCT - CT Plus	LV52HDU	Stagecoach	LX03BVU	Stagecoach
LR52LYC	HCT - CT Plus	LV52HDX	Stagecoach	LX03BVV	Stagecoach
LR52LYJ	HCT - CT Plus	LV52HDY	Stagecoach	LX03BVW	Stagecoach
LT02NUK	Go-Ahead	LV52HDZ	Stagecoach	LX03BVY	Stagecoach
LT02NUM	Go-Ahead	LV52HEJ	Stagecoach	LX03BVZ	Stagecoach
LT02NUO	Go-Ahead	LV52HEU	Stagecoach	LX03BWA	Stagecoach
LT02NUP	Go-Ahead	LV52HFA	Stagecoach	LX03BWB	Stagecoach
LT02NUU	Go-Ahead	LV52HFB	Stagecoach	LX03BWC	Stagecoach
LT02NUV	Go-Ahead	LV52HFC	Stagecoach	LX03BWD	Stagecoach
LT02NVE	Go-Ahead	LV52HFD	Stagecoach	LX03BWE	Stagecoach
LT02NVH	Go-Ahead	LV52HFE	Stagecoach	LX03BWF	Stagecoach
LT02NVJ	Go-Ahead	LV52HFF	Stagecoach	LX03BWG	Stagecoach
LT02ZDR	Metrobus	LV52HFH	Stagecoach	LX03BWH	Stagecoach
LT02ZDS	Metrobus	LV52HFJ	Stagecoach	LX03BWJ	Stagecoach
LT52WUM	Go-Ahead	LV52HFK	Stagecoach	LX03BWK	Stagecoach
LT52WUO	Go-Ahead	LV52HFL	Stagecoach	LX03BWL	Stagecoach
LT52WUP	Go-Ahead	LV52HFN	Stagecoach	LX03BWM	Stagecoach
LT52WUR	Go-Ahead	LV52HFO	Stagecoach	LX03BWN	Stagecoach
LT52WXJ	Go-Ahead	LV52HFP	Stagecoach	LX03BWP	Stagecoach
LT52XAD	Metroline	LV52HFR	Stagecoach	LX03BWU	Stagecoach
LT52XAH	Tower Transit	LV52HFT	Stagecoach	LX03BWV	Stagecoach
LT52XAJ	Tower Transit	LV52HFU	Stagecoach	LX03BWW	Stagecoach
LT52XAK	Tower Transit	LV52HFW	Stagecoach	LX03BWY	Stagecoach
LTZ1001	Arriva	LV52HFX	Stagecoach	LX03BWZ	Stagecoach
LTZ1002	Arriva	LV52HFY	Stagecoach	LX03BXA	Stagecoach
LTZ1003	Arriva	LV52HFZ	Stagecoach	LX03BXB	Stagecoach
LTZ1004	Arriva	LV52HGA	Stagecoach	LX03BXC	Stagecoach
LTZ1005	Arriva	LV52HGC	Stagecoach	LX03BXD	Stagecoach
LTZ1006	Arriva	LV52HGG	Stagecoach	LX03BXE	Stagecoach
LTZ1007	Arriva	LV52HGK	Stagecoach	LX03BXF	Stagecoach
LTZ1008	Arriva	LV52HGM	Stagecoach	LX03BXG	Stagecoach
LTZ1009	Metroline	LV52HGO	Stagecoach	LX03BXH	Stagecoach
LTZ1010	Metroline	LV52HKE	Stagecoach	LX03BXJ	Stagecoach
LTZ1011	Metroline	LV52HKG	Stagecoach	LX03BXK	Stagecoach
LTZ1012	Metroline	LV52HKH	Stagecoach	LX03BXL	Stagecoach
LTZ1013	Metroline	LV52HKJ	Stagecoach	LX03BXM	Stagecoach
LTZ1014	Metroline	LV52HKK	Stagecoach	LX03BXN	Stagecoach
LTZ1015	Metroline	LV52HKL	Stagecoach	LX03BXP	Stagecoach
LTZ1016	Metroline	LV52HKM	Stagecoach	LX03BXR	Stagecoach
LTZ1017	Metroline	LV52HKN	Stagecoach	LX03BXS	Stagecoach
LTZ1018	Metroline	LV52HKO	Stagecoach	LX03BXU	Stagecoach
LTZ1019	Metroline	LV52HKP	Stagecoach	LX03BXV	Stagecoach
LTZ1020	Metroline	LV52HKT	Stagecoach	LX03BXW	Stagecoach
LTZ1021	Metroline	LV52HKU	Stagecoach	LX03BXY	Stagecoach

LX03BXZ	Stagecoach	LX03NFJ	Stagecoach	LX04FWS	Stagecoach
LX03BYA	Stagecoach	LX03NFK	Stagecoach	LX04FWT	Stagecoach
LX03BYB	Stagecoach	LX03NFL	Stagecoach	LX04FWU	Stagecoach
LX03BYC	Stagecoach	LX03NFM	Stagecoach	LX04FWV	Stagecoach
LX03BYD	Stagecoach	LX03NFN	Stagecoach	LX04FWW	Stagecoach
LX03BYF	Stagecoach	LX03NFP	Stagecoach	LX04FWY	Stagecoach
LX03BYG	Stagecoach	LX03NFR	Stagecoach	LX04FWZ	Stagecoach
LX03BYH	Stagecoach	LX03NFT	Stagecoach	LX04FXA	Stagecoach
LX03BYJ	Stagecoach	LX03NFV	Stagecoach	LX04FXB	Stagecoach
LX03BYL	Stagecoach	LX03NFY	Stagecoach	LX04FXC	Stagecoach
LX03BYM	Stagecoach	LX03NFZ	Stagecoach	LX04FXD	Stagecoach
LX03BYN	Stagecoach	LX03NGE	Stagecoach	LX04FXE	Stagecoach
LX03BYP	Stagecoach	LX03NGF	Stagecoach	LX04FXF	Stagecoach
LX03BYR	Stagecoach	LX03NGJ	Stagecoach	LX04FXG	Stagecoach
LX03BYS	Stagecoach	LX03NGN	Stagecoach	LX04FXH	Stagecoach
LX03BYT	Stagecoach	LX03NGU	Stagecoach	LX04FXJ	Stagecoach
LX03BYU	Stagecoach	LX03NGV	Stagecoach	LX04FXK	Stagecoach
LX03BYV	Stagecoach	LX03NGY	Stagecoach	LX04FXL	Stagecoach
LX03BYW	Stagecoach	LX03NGZ	Stagecoach	LX04FXM	Stagecoach
LX03BYY	Stagecoach	LX03NHA	Stagecoach	LX04FXP	Stagecoach
LX03BYZ	Stagecoach	LX03OJN	Metrobus	LX04FXR	Stagecoach
LX03BZA	Stagecoach	LX03OJP	Metrobus	LX04FXS	Stagecoach
LX03BZB	Stagecoach	LX03OPT	Stagecoach	LX04FXT	Stagecoach
LX03BZC	Stagecoach	LX03OPU	Stagecoach	LX04FXU	Stagecoach
LX03BZD	Stagecoach	LX03OPV	Stagecoach	LX04FXV	Stagecoach
LX03BZE	Stagecoach	LX03OPW	Stagecoach	LX04FXW	Stagecoach
LX03BZF	Stagecoach	LX03OPY	Stagecoach	LX04FXY	Stagecoach
LX03BZG	Stagecoach	LX03OPZ	Stagecoach	LX04FXZ	Stagecoach
LX03BZH	Stagecoach	LX03ORA	Stagecoach	LX04FYA	Stagecoach
LX03BZJ	Stagecoach	LX03ORC	Stagecoach	LX04FYB	Stagecoach
LX03BZK	Stagecoach	LX03ORF	Stagecoach	LX04FYC	Stagecoach
LX03BZL	Stagecoach	LX03ORG	Stagecoach	LX04FYD	Stagecoach
LX03BZM	Stagecoach	LX03ORH	Stagecoach	LX04FYE	Stagecoach
LX03BZN	Stagecoach	LX03ORJ	Stagecoach	LX04FYF	Stagecoach
LX03BZP	Stagecoach	LX03ORK	Stagecoach	LX04FYG	Stagecoach
LX03BZR	Stagecoach	LX03ORN	Stagecoach	LX04FYH	Stagecoach
LX03BZS	Stagecoach	LX03ORP	Stagecoach	LX04FYJ	Stagecoach
LX03BZT	Stagecoach	LX03ORS	Stagecoach	LX04FYK	Stagecoach
LX03BZU	Stagecoach	LX03ORT	Stagecoach	LX04FYL	Stagecoach
LX03BZV	Stagecoach	LX03ORU	Stagecoach	LX04FYM	Stagecoach
LX03BZW	Stagecoach	LX03ORV	Stagecoach	LX04FYN	Stagecoach
LX03BZY	Stagecoach	LX03ORW	Stagecoach	LX04FYP	Stagecoach
LX03CAA	Stagecoach	LX03ORY	Stagecoach	LX04FYR	Stagecoach
LX03CAE	Stagecoach	LX03ORZ	Stagecoach	LX04FYS	Stagecoach
LX03CAU	Stagecoach	LX03OSA	Stagecoach	LX04FYT	Stagecoach
LX03CAV	Stagecoach	LX03OSB	Stagecoach	LX04FYU	Stagecoach
LX03CBF	Stagecoach	LX03OSC	Stagecoach	LX04FYV	Stagecoach
LX03CBU	Stagecoach	LX03OSD	Stagecoach	LX04FYW	Stagecoach
LX03CBV	Stagecoach	LX03OSE	Stagecoach	LX04FYY	Stagecoach
LX03CBY	Stagecoach	LX03OSG	Stagecoach	LX04FYZ	Stagecoach
LX03ECV	Go-Ahead	LX03OSJ	Stagecoach	LX04FZA	Stagecoach
LX03ECW	Go-Ahead	LX03OSK	Stagecoach	LX04FZB	Stagecoach
LX03ECY	Go-Ahead	LX03OSL	Stagecoach	LX04FZC	Stagecoach
LX03EDR	Go-Ahead	LX03OSM	Stagecoach	LX04FZD	Stagecoach
LX03EDU	Go-Ahead	LX03OSN	Stagecoach	LX04FZE	Stagecoach
LX03EDV	Go-Ahead	LX03OSP	Stagecoach	LX04FZF	Stagecoach
LX03EEA	Go-Ahead	LX03OSR	Stagecoach	LX04FZG	Stagecoach
LX03EEB	Go-Ahead	LX03OSU	Stagecoach	LX04FZH	Stagecoach
LX03EEF	Go-Ahead	LX03OSV	Stagecoach	LX04FZJ	Stagecoach
LX03EEG	Go-Ahead	LX03OSW	Stagecoach	LX04FZK	Stagecoach
LX03EEH	Go-Ahead	LX03OSY	Stagecoach	LX04GCU	Stagecoach
LX03EEJ	Go-Ahead	LX03OSZ	Stagecoach	LX05BVY	Stagecoach
LX03EEM	Go-Ahead	LX03OTA	Stagecoach	LX05BVZ	Stagecoach
LX03EXU	Go-Ahead	LX03OTB	Stagecoach	LX05BWA	Stagecoach
LX03EXV	Go-Ahead	LX03OTC	Stagecoach	LX05BWB	Stagecoach
LX03EXW	Go-Ahead	LX03OTD	Stagecoach	LX05BWC	Stagecoach
LX03EXZ	Go-Ahead	LX03OTE	Stagecoach	LX05BWD	Stagecoach
LX03NEU	Stagecoach	LX03OTF	Stagecoach	LX05BWE	Stagecoach
LX03NEY	Stagecoach	LX03OTG	Stagecoach	LX05BWF	Stagecoach
LX03NFA	Stagecoach	LX03OTH	Stagecoach	LX05BWG	Stagecoach
LX03NFC	Stagecoach	LX03OTJ	Stagecoach	LX05BWH	Stagecoach
LX03NFD	Stagecoach	LX04FWL	Stagecoach	LX05BWJ	Stagecoach
LX03NFE	Stagecoach	LX04FWM	Stagecoach	LX05BWK	Stagecoach
LX03NFF	Stagecoach	LX04FWN	Stagecoach	LX05EXZ	Go-Ahead
LX03NFG	Stagecoach	LX04FWP	Stagecoach	LX05EYA	Go-Ahead
LX03NFH	Stagecoach	LX04FWR	Stagecoach	LX05EYM	Go-Ahead

Reg	Operator	Reg	Operator	Reg	Operator
LX05EYO	Go-Ahead	LX06AGZ	Stagecoach	LX06EZA	Go-Ahead
LX05EYP	Go-Ahead	LX06AHA	Stagecoach	LX06EZB	Go-Ahead
LX05EYR	Go-Ahead	LX06AHC	Stagecoach	LX06EZC	Go-Ahead
LX05EYS	Go-Ahead	LX06AHD	Stagecoach	LX06EZD	Go-Ahead
LX05EYT	Go-Ahead	LX06AHE	Stagecoach	LX06EZE	Go-Ahead
LX05EYU	Go-Ahead	LX06AHF	Stagecoach	LX06EZF	Go-Ahead
LX05EYV	Go-Ahead	LX06DYS	Go-Ahead	LX06EZG	Go-Ahead
LX05EYW	Go-Ahead	LX06DYT	Go-Ahead	LX06EZH	Go-Ahead
LX05EYY	Go-Ahead	LX06DYU	Go-Ahead	LX06EZJ	Go-Ahead
LX05EYZ	Go-Ahead	LX06DYV	Go-Ahead	LX06EZK	Go-Ahead
LX05EZA	Go-Ahead	LX06DYX	Go-Ahead	LX06EZL	Go-Ahead
LX05EZB	Go-Ahead	LX06DYY	Go-Ahead	LX06EZM	Go-Ahead
LX05EZC	Go-Ahead	LX06DZA	Go-Ahead	LX06EZN	Go-Ahead
LX05EZD	Go-Ahead	LX06DZB	Go-Ahead	LX06EZO	Go-Ahead
LX05EZE	Go-Ahead	LX06DZC	Go-Ahead	LX06EZP	Go-Ahead
LX05EZF	Go-Ahead	LX06DZE	Go-Ahead	LX06EZR	Go-Ahead
LX05EZG	Go-Ahead	LX06DZF	Go-Ahead	LX06EZS	Go-Ahead
LX05EZH	Go-Ahead	LX06DZG	Go-Ahead	LX06EZT	Go-Ahead
LX05EZJ	Go-Ahead	LX06DZH	Go-Ahead	LX06EZU	Go-Ahead
LX05EZK	Go-Ahead	LX06DZJ	Go-Ahead	LX06EZV	Go-Ahead
LX05EZL	Go-Ahead	LX06DZK	Go-Ahead	LX06EZW	Go-Ahead
LX05EZM	Go-Ahead	LX06DZL	Go-Ahead	LX06EZZ	Go-Ahead
LX05EZN	Go-Ahead	LX06DZM	Go-Ahead	LX06FAA	Go-Ahead
LX05EZO	Go-Ahead	LX06DZN	Go-Ahead	LX06FAF	Go-Ahead
LX05EZP	Go-Ahead	LX06DZO	Go-Ahead	LX06FAJ	Go-Ahead
LX05EZR	Go-Ahead	LX06DZP	Go-Ahead	LX06FAK	Go-Ahead
LX05EZS	Go-Ahead	LX06DZR	Go-Ahead	LX06FAM	Go-Ahead
LX05EZT	Go-Ahead	LX06DZS	Go-Ahead	LX06FAO	Go-Ahead
LX05EZU	Go-Ahead	LX06DZT	Go-Ahead	LX06FAU	Go-Ahead
LX05EZV	Go-Ahead	LX06DZU	Go-Ahead	LX06FBA	Go-Ahead
LX05EZW	Go-Ahead	LX06DZV	Go-Ahead	LX06FBB	Go-Ahead
LX05EZZ	Go-Ahead	LX06DZW	Go-Ahead	LX06FBC	Go-Ahead
LX05FAA	Go-Ahead	LX06DZY	Go-Ahead	LX06FBD	Go-Ahead
LX05FAF	Go-Ahead	LX06DZZ	Go-Ahead	LX06FBE	Go-Ahead
LX05FAJ	Go-Ahead	LX06EAA	Go-Ahead	LX06FKL	Go-Ahead
LX05FAK	Go-Ahead	LX06EAC	Go-Ahead	LX06FKM	Go-Ahead
LX05FAM	Go-Ahead	LX06EAE	Go-Ahead	LX06FKN	Go-Ahead
LX05FAO	Go-Ahead	LX06EAF	Go-Ahead	LX06FKO	Go-Ahead
LX05FAU	Go-Ahead	LX06EAG	Go-Ahead	LX07BXH	Go-Ahead
LX05FBA	Go-Ahead	LX06EAJ	Go-Ahead	LX07BXJ	Go-Ahead
LX05FBB	Go-Ahead	LX06EAK	Go-Ahead	LX07BXK	Go-Ahead
LX05FBC	Go-Ahead	LX06EAM	Go-Ahead	LX07BXL	Go-Ahead
LX05FBD	Go-Ahead	LX06EAO	Go-Ahead	LX07BXM	Go-Ahead
LX05FBE	Go-Ahead	LX06EAP	Go-Ahead	LX07BXN	Go-Ahead
LX05FBF	Go-Ahead	LX06EAW	Go-Ahead	LX07BXO	Go-Ahead
LX05FBJ	Go-Ahead	LX06EAY	Go-Ahead	LX07BXP	Go-Ahead
LX05FBK	Go-Ahead	LX06EBA	Go-Ahead	LX07BXR	Go-Ahead
LX05FBL	Go-Ahead	LX06EBC	Go-Ahead	LX07BXS	Go-Ahead
LX05FBN	Go-Ahead	LX06EBD	Go-Ahead	LX07BXU	Go-Ahead
LX05FBO	Go-Ahead	LX06EBF	Go-Ahead	LX07BXV	Go-Ahead
LX05FBU	Go-Ahead	LX06EBG	Go-Ahead	LX07BXW	Go-Ahead
LX05FBV	Go-Ahead	LX06EBJ	Go-Ahead	LX07BXY	Go-Ahead
LX05FBY	Go-Ahead	LX06EBK	Go-Ahead	LX07BXZ	Go-Ahead
LX05FBZ	Go-Ahead	LX06EBL	Go-Ahead	LX07BYA	Go-Ahead
LX05FCA	Go-Ahead	LX06EBM	Go-Ahead	LX07BYB	Go-Ahead
LX05FCC	Go-Ahead	LX06EBN	Go-Ahead	LX07BYC	Go-Ahead
LX05FCD	Go-Ahead	LX06EBO	Go-Ahead	LX07BYD	Go-Ahead
LX05FCE	Go-Ahead	LX06EBP	Go-Ahead	LX07BYF	Go-Ahead
LX05FCF	Go-Ahead	LX06EBU	Go-Ahead	LX07BYG	Go-Ahead
LX05GDV	Original Tour	LX06EBV	Go-Ahead	LX07BYH	Go-Ahead
LX05GDY	Original Tour	LX06EBZ	Go-Ahead	LX07BYJ	Go-Ahead
LX05GDZ	Original Tour	LX06ECA	Go-Ahead	LX07BYK	Go-Ahead
LX05GEJ	Original Tour	LX06ECC	Go-Ahead	LX07BYL	Go-Ahead
LX05HRO	Original Tour	LX06ECD	Go-Ahead	LX07BYM	Go-Ahead
LX05HSC	Original Tour	LX06ECE	Go-Ahead	LX07BYN	Go-Ahead
LX05KNZ	Original Tour	LX06ECF	Go-Ahead	LX07BYO	Go-Ahead
LX05KOA	Original Tour	LX06ECJ	Go-Ahead	LX07BYP	Go-Ahead
LX05LLM	Stagecoach	LX06ECN	Go-Ahead	LX07BYR	Go-Ahead
LX05LLN	Stagecoach	LX06ECT	Go-Ahead	LX07BYS	Go-Ahead
LX05LLO	Stagecoach	LX06ECV	Go-Ahead	LX07BYT	Go-Ahead
LX05LLP	Stagecoach	LX06EYT	Go-Ahead	LX07BYU	Go-Ahead
LX06AFZ	Stagecoach	LX06EYU	Go-Ahead	LX08EBP	Go-Ahead
LX06AGO	Stagecoach	LX06EYV	Go-Ahead	LX08EBU	Go-Ahead
LX06AGU	Stagecoach	LX06EYW	Go-Ahead	LX08EBV	Go-Ahead
LX06AGV	Stagecoach	LX06EYY	Go-Ahead	LX08EBZ	Go-Ahead
LX06AGY	Stagecoach	LX06EYZ	Go-Ahead	LX08ECA	Go-Ahead

LX08ECC	Go-Ahead	LX09AHD	Stagecoach	LX09FBD	Go-Ahead
LX08ECD	Go-Ahead	LX09AHE	Stagecoach	LX09FBE	Go-Ahead
LX08ECE	Go-Ahead	LX09AHF	Stagecoach	LX09FBF	Go-Ahead
LX08ECF	Go-Ahead	LX09AXU	Go-Ahead	LX09FBG	Go-Ahead
LX08ECJ	Go-Ahead	LX09AXV	Go-Ahead	LX09FBJ	Go-Ahead
LX08ECN	Go-Ahead	LX09AXW	Go-Ahead	LX09FBK	Go-Ahead
LX08ECT	Go-Ahead	LX09AXY	Go-Ahead	LX09FBN	Go-Ahead
LX08ECV	Go-Ahead	LX09AXZ	Go-Ahead	LX09FBO	Go-Ahead
LX08ECW	Go-Ahead	LX09AYA	Go-Ahead	LX09FBU	Go-Ahead
LX08ECY	Go-Ahead	LX09AYB	Go-Ahead	LX09FBV	Go-Ahead
LX09AAE	Stagecoach	LX09AYC	Go-Ahead	LX09FBX	Go-Ahead
LX09AAF	Stagecoach	LX09AYD	Go-Ahead	LX09FBY	Go-Ahead
LX09AAJ	Stagecoach	LX09AYE	Go-Ahead	LX09FCA	Go-Ahead
LX09AAK	Stagecoach	LX09AYF	Go-Ahead	LX09FCC	Go-Ahead
LX09AAN	Stagecoach	LX09AYG	Go-Ahead	LX09FCD	Go-Ahead
LX09AAO	Stagecoach	LX09AYH	Go-Ahead	LX09FCE	Go-Ahead
LX09AAU	Stagecoach	LX09AYJ	Go-Ahead	LX09FYS	Stagecoach
LX09AAV	Stagecoach	LX09AYK	Go-Ahead	LX09FYT	Stagecoach
LX09AAY	Stagecoach	LX09AYL	Go-Ahead	LX09FYU	Stagecoach
LX09AAZ	Stagecoach	LX09AYM	Go-Ahead	LX09FYW	Stagecoach
LX09ABF	Stagecoach	LX09AYN	Go-Ahead	LX09FYY	Stagecoach
LX09ABK	Stagecoach	LX09AYO	Go-Ahead	LX09FYZ	Stagecoach
LX09ABN	Stagecoach	LX09AYP	Go-Ahead	LX09FZA	Stagecoach
LX09ABO	Stagecoach	LX09AYS	Go-Ahead	LX09FZB	Stagecoach
LX09ABU	Stagecoach	LX09AYT	Go-Ahead	LX09FZC	Stagecoach
LX09ABV	Stagecoach	LX09AYU	Go-Ahead	LX09FZD	Stagecoach
LX09ABZ	Stagecoach	LX09AYV	Go-Ahead	LX09FZE	Stagecoach
LX09ACF	Stagecoach	LX09AYW	Go-Ahead	LX09FZF	Stagecoach
LX09ACJ	Stagecoach	LX09AYY	Go-Ahead	LX09FZG	Stagecoach
LX09ACO	Stagecoach	LX09AYZ	Go-Ahead	LX09FZH	Stagecoach
LX09ACU	Stagecoach	LX09AZA	Go-Ahead	LX09FZJ	Stagecoach
LX09ACV	Stagecoach	LX09AZB	Go-Ahead	LX09FZK	Stagecoach
LX09ACY	Stagecoach	LX09AZC	Go-Ahead	LX09FZL	Stagecoach
LX09ACZ	Stagecoach	LX09AZD	Go-Ahead	LX09FZM	Stagecoach
LX09ADO	Stagecoach	LX09AZF	Go-Ahead	LX09FZN	Stagecoach
LX09ADU	Stagecoach	LX09AZG	Go-Ahead	LX09FZO	Stagecoach
LX09ADV	Stagecoach	LX09AZJ	Go-Ahead	LX09FZP	Stagecoach
LX09ADZ	Stagecoach	LX09AZL	Go-Ahead	LX09FZR	Stagecoach
LX09AEA	Stagecoach	LX09AZN	Go-Ahead	LX09FZS	Stagecoach
LX09AEB	Stagecoach	LX09AZO	Go-Ahead	LX09FZT	Stagecoach
LX09AEC	Stagecoach	LX09AZP	Go-Ahead	LX09FZU	Stagecoach
LX09AED	Stagecoach	LX09AZR	Go-Ahead	LX09FZV	Stagecoach
LX09AEE	Stagecoach	LX09AZT	Go-Ahead	LX09FZW	Stagecoach
LX09AEF	Stagecoach	LX09BGK	Stagecoach	LX10AUC	Stagecoach
LX09AEG	Stagecoach	LX09BGU	Stagecoach	LX10AUE	Stagecoach
LX09AEJ	Stagecoach	LX09BGV	Stagecoach	LX10AUF	Stagecoach
LX09AEK	Stagecoach	LX09BXG	Go-Ahead	LX10AUH	Stagecoach
LX09AEL	Stagecoach	LX09BXH	Go-Ahead	LX10AUJ	Stagecoach
LX09AEM	Stagecoach	LX09BXJ	Go-Ahead	LX10AUP	Go-Ahead
LX09AEN	Stagecoach	LX09BXK	Go-Ahead	LX10AUR	Go-Ahead
LX09AEO	Stagecoach	LX09BXL	Go-Ahead	LX10AUT	Go-Ahead
LX09AEP	Stagecoach	LX09BXM	Go-Ahead	LX10AUU	Go-Ahead
LX09AET	Stagecoach	LX09BXO	Go-Ahead	LX10AUV	Go-Ahead
LX09AEU	Stagecoach	LX09BXP	Go-Ahead	LX10AUW	Go-Ahead
LX09AEV	Stagecoach	LX09BXR	Go-Ahead	LX10AUY	Go-Ahead
LX09AEW	Stagecoach	LX09BXS	Go-Ahead	LX10AVB	Go-Ahead
LX09AEY	Stagecoach	LX09EVB	Go-Ahead	LX10AVC	Go-Ahead
LX09AEZ	Stagecoach	LX09EVC	Go-Ahead	LX10AVD	Go-Ahead
LX09AFA	Stagecoach	LX09EVD	Go-Ahead	LX11AVP	Stagecoach
LX09AFE	Stagecoach	LX09EVF	Go-Ahead	LX11AVR	Stagecoach
LX09AFF	Stagecoach	LX09EVG	Go-Ahead	LX11AVT	Stagecoach
LX09AFJ	Stagecoach	LX09EVH	Go-Ahead	LX11AVU	Stagecoach
LX09AFK	Stagecoach	LX09EVJ	Go-Ahead	LX11AVV	Stagecoach
LX09AFN	Stagecoach	LX09EZU	Go-Ahead	LX11AVW	Stagecoach
LX09AFO	Stagecoach	LX09EZV	Go-Ahead	LX11AVY	Stagecoach
LX09AFU	Stagecoach	LX09EZW	Go-Ahead	LX11AVZ	Stagecoach
LX09AFV	Stagecoach	LX09EZZ	Go-Ahead	LX11AWC	Stagecoach
LX09AFY	Stagecoach	LX09FAF	Go-Ahead	LX11AWF	Stagecoach
LX09AFZ	Stagecoach	LX09FAJ	Go-Ahead	LX11AWG	Stagecoach
LX09AGO	Stagecoach	LX09FAK	Go-Ahead	LX11AWH	Stagecoach
LX09AGU	Stagecoach	LX09FAM	Go-Ahead	LX11AWJ	Stagecoach
LX09AGV	Stagecoach	LX09FAO	Go-Ahead	LX11AWM	Stagecoach
LX09AGY	Stagecoach	LX09FAU	Go-Ahead	LX11AWN	Stagecoach
LX09AGZ	Stagecoach	LX09FBA	Go-Ahead	LX11AWO	Stagecoach
LX09AHA	Stagecoach	LX09FBB	Go-Ahead	LX11AWP	Stagecoach
LX09AHC	Stagecoach	LX09FBC	Go-Ahead	LX11AWR	Stagecoach

LX11AWU	Stagecoach	LX11BFA	Stagecoach	LX11CVT	Go-Ahead
LX11AWV	Stagecoach	LX11BFF	Stagecoach	LX11CVU	Go-Ahead
LX11AWW	Stagecoach	LX11BFJ	Stagecoach	LX11CVV	Go-Ahead
LX11AWY	Stagecoach	LX11BFK	Stagecoach	LX11CVW	Go-Ahead
LX11AWZ	Stagecoach	LX11BFL	Stagecoach	LX11CVY	Go-Ahead
LX11AXA	Stagecoach	LX11BFM	Stagecoach	LX11CVZ	Go-Ahead
LX11AXB	Stagecoach	LX11BFN	Stagecoach	LX11CWA	Go-Ahead
LX11AXC	Stagecoach	LX11BFO	Stagecoach	LX11CWC	Go-Ahead
LX11AXD	Stagecoach	LX11BFP	Stagecoach	LX11CWD	Go-Ahead
LX11AXF	Stagecoach	LX11BFU	Stagecoach	LX11CWE	Go-Ahead
LX11AXG	Stagecoach	LX11BFV	Stagecoach	LX11CWG	Go-Ahead
LX11AXH	Stagecoach	LX11BFY	Stagecoach	LX11CWJ	Go-Ahead
LX11AXJ	Stagecoach	LX11BFZ	Stagecoach	LX11CWK	Go-Ahead
LX11AXK	Stagecoach	LX11BGE	Stagecoach	LX11CWL	Go-Ahead
LX11AXM	Stagecoach	LX11BGF	Stagecoach	LX11CWM	Go-Ahead
LX11AXN	Stagecoach	LX11BGK	Stagecoach	LX11CWN	Go-Ahead
LX11AXO	Stagecoach	LX11BGO	Stagecoach	LX11CWO	Go-Ahead
LX11AXP	Stagecoach	LX11BGU	Stagecoach	LX11CWP	Go-Ahead
LX11AXR	Stagecoach	LX11BGV	Stagecoach	LX11CWR	Go-Ahead
LX11AXS	Stagecoach	LX11BGY	Stagecoach	LX11CWT	Go-Ahead
LX11AXT	Stagecoach	LX11BGZ	Stagecoach	LX11CWU	Go-Ahead
LX11AYS	Stagecoach	LX11BHA	Stagecoach	LX11CWV	Go-Ahead
LX11AYT	Stagecoach	LX11BHD	Stagecoach	LX11CWW	Go-Ahead
LX11AYU	Stagecoach	LX11BHE	Stagecoach	LX11CWY	Go-Ahead
LX11AYV	Stagecoach	LX11BHF	Stagecoach	LX11CWZ	Go-Ahead
LX11AYW	Stagecoach	LX11BHJ	Stagecoach	LX11CXA	Go-Ahead
LX11AYY	Stagecoach	LX11BHK	Stagecoach	LX11CXB	Go-Ahead
LX11AYZ	Stagecoach	LX11BHL	Stagecoach	LX11CXC	Go-Ahead
LX11AZA	Stagecoach	LX11BHN	Stagecoach	LX11CXD	Go-Ahead
LX11AZB	Stagecoach	LX11BHO	Stagecoach	LX11DVA	Go-Ahead
LX11AZC	Stagecoach	LX11BHP	Stagecoach	LX11DVB	Go-Ahead
LX11AZD	Stagecoach	LX11BHU	Stagecoach	LX11DVC	Go-Ahead
LX11AZF	Stagecoach	LX11BHV	Stagecoach	LX11DVE	Go-Ahead
LX11AZG	Stagecoach	LX11BHW	Stagecoach	LX11DVG	Go-Ahead
LX11AZJ	Stagecoach	LX11BHY	Stagecoach	LX11DVH	Go-Ahead
LX11AZL	Stagecoach	LX11BHZ	Stagecoach	LX11FHV	Go-Ahead
LX11AZN	Stagecoach	LX11BJE	Stagecoach	LX11FHW	Go-Ahead
LX11AZO	Stagecoach	LX11BJF	Stagecoach	LX11FHY	Go-Ahead
LX11AZP	Stagecoach	LX11BJJ	Stagecoach	LX11FHZ	Go-Ahead
LX11AZR	Stagecoach	LX11BJK	Stagecoach	LX11FJA	Go-Ahead
LX11AZT	Stagecoach	LX11BJO	Stagecoach	LX11FJC	Go-Ahead
LX11AZU	Stagecoach	LX11BJU	Stagecoach	LX11FJD	Go-Ahead
LX11AZV	Stagecoach	LX11BJV	Stagecoach	LX11FJE	Go-Ahead
LX11AZW	Stagecoach	LX11BJY	Stagecoach	LX11FJF	Go-Ahead
LX11AZZ	Stagecoach	LX11BJZ	Stagecoach	LX11FJJ	Go-Ahead
LX11BAA	Stagecoach	LX11BKA	Stagecoach	LX11FJK	Go-Ahead
LX11BAO	Stagecoach	LX11BKD	Stagecoach	LX11FJN	Go-Ahead
LX11BAU	Stagecoach	LX11BKE	Stagecoach	LX11FJO	Go-Ahead
LX11BAV	Stagecoach	LX11BKF	Stagecoach	LX12AYN	Big Bus Company
LX11BBE	Stagecoach	LX11BKG	Stagecoach	LX12AZF	Big Bus Company
LX11BBF	Stagecoach	LX11BKJ	Stagecoach	LX12AZL	Big Bus Company
LX11BBJ	Stagecoach	LX11BKK	Stagecoach	LX12CZA	Stagecoach
LX11BBK	Stagecoach	LX11BKL	Stagecoach	LX12CZB	Stagecoach
LX11BBN	Stagecoach	LX11BKN	Stagecoach	LX12CZC	Stagecoach
LX11BBO	Stagecoach	LX11BKO	Stagecoach	LX12CZD	Stagecoach
LX11BBV	Stagecoach	LX11BKU	Stagecoach	LX12CZE	Stagecoach
LX11BBZ	Stagecoach	LX11BKV	Stagecoach	LX12CZF	Stagecoach
LX11BCE	Stagecoach	LX11BKY	Stagecoach	LX12CZG	Stagecoach
LX11BCF	Stagecoach	LX11BKZ	Stagecoach	LX12CZH	Stagecoach
LX11BCK	Stagecoach	LX11BLF	Stagecoach	LX12CZJ	Stagecoach
LX11BCO	Stagecoach	LX11BLJ	Stagecoach	LX12CZK	Stagecoach
LX11BCU	Stagecoach	LX11BLK	Stagecoach	LX12CZL	Stagecoach
LX11BCV	Stagecoach	LX11BLN	Stagecoach	LX12CZM	Stagecoach
LX11BCY	Stagecoach	LX11BLV	Stagecoach	LX12CZN	Stagecoach
LX11BCZ	Stagecoach	LX11BLZ	Stagecoach	LX12CZO	Stagecoach
LX11BDE	Stagecoach	LX11BMO	Stagecoach	LX12CZP	Stagecoach
LX11BDF	Stagecoach	LX11BMU	Stagecoach	LX12CZR	Stagecoach
LX11BDO	Stagecoach	LX11BMV	Stagecoach	LX12CZS	Stagecoach
LX11BDU	Stagecoach	LX11BMY	Stagecoach	LX12CZT	Stagecoach
LX11BDV	Stagecoach	LX11CVL	Go-Ahead	LX12CZU	Stagecoach
LX11BDY	Stagecoach	LX11CVM	Go-Ahead	LX12CZV	Stagecoach
LX11BDZ	Stagecoach	LX11CVN	Go-Ahead	LX12CZW	Stagecoach
LX11BEJ	Stagecoach	LX11CVO	Go-Ahead	LX12CZY	Stagecoach
LX11BEO	Stagecoach	LX11CVP	Go-Ahead	LX12CZZ	Stagecoach
LX11BEU	Stagecoach	LX11CVR	Go-Ahead	LX12DAA	Stagecoach
LX11BEY	Stagecoach	LX11CVS	Go-Ahead	LX12DAO	Stagecoach

Reg	Operator	Reg	Operator	Reg	Operator
LX12DAU	Stagecoach	LX12DKA	Stagecoach	LX51FNF	Stagecoach
LX12DBO	Stagecoach	LX12DKD	Stagecoach	LX51FNG	Stagecoach
LX12DBU	Stagecoach	LX12DKE	Stagecoach	LX51FNH	Stagecoach
LX12DBV	Stagecoach	LX12DKF	Stagecoach	LX51FNJ	Stagecoach
LX12DBY	Stagecoach	LX12DKJ	Stagecoach	LX51FNK	Stagecoach
LX12DBZ	Stagecoach	LX12DKK	Stagecoach	LX51FNL	Stagecoach
LX12DCE	Stagecoach	LX12DKL	Stagecoach	LX51FNM	Stagecoach
LX12DCF	Stagecoach	LX12DKN	Stagecoach	LX51FNN	Stagecoach
LX12DCO	Stagecoach	LX12DKO	Stagecoach	LX51FNO	Stagecoach
LX12DCU	Stagecoach	LX12DKU	Stagecoach	LX51FNP	Stagecoach
LX12DCV	Stagecoach	LX12DKV	Stagecoach	LX51FNT	Stagecoach
LX12DCY	Stagecoach	LX12DKY	Stagecoach	LX51FNU	Stagecoach
LX12DCZ	Stagecoach	LX12DLD	Stagecoach	LX51FNV	Stagecoach
LX12DDA	Stagecoach	LX12DLE	Stagecoach	LX51FNW	Stagecoach
LX12DDE	Stagecoach	LX12DLF	Stagecoach	LX51FNY	Stagecoach
LX12DDF	Stagecoach	LX12DLJ	Stagecoach	LX51FNZ	Stagecoach
LX12DDJ	Stagecoach	LX12DLK	Stagecoach	LX51FOA	Stagecoach
LX12DDK	Stagecoach	LX12DLN	Stagecoach	LX51FOC	Stagecoach
LX12DDL	Stagecoach	LX13CYW	Stagecoach	LX51FOD	Stagecoach
LX12DDN	Stagecoach	LX13CYY	Stagecoach	LX51FOF	Stagecoach
LX12DDO	Stagecoach	LX13CYZ	Stagecoach	LX51FOH	Stagecoach
LX12DDU	Stagecoach	LX13CZA	Stagecoach	LX51FOJ	Stagecoach
LX12DDV	Stagecoach	LX13CZB	Stagecoach	LX51FOK	Stagecoach
LX12DDY	Stagecoach	LX13CZC	Stagecoach	LX51FOM	Stagecoach
LX12DDZ	Stagecoach	LX13CZD	Stagecoach	LX51FON	Stagecoach
LX12DEU	Stagecoach	LX13CZE	Stagecoach	LX51FOP	Stagecoach
LX12DFA	Stagecoach	LX13CZF	Stagecoach	LX51FOT	Stagecoach
LX12DFC	Stagecoach	LX13CZG	Stagecoach	LX53AYM	Go-Ahead
LX12DFD	Stagecoach	LX13CZH	Stagecoach	LX53AYN	Go-Ahead
LX12DFE	Stagecoach	LX13CZJ	Stagecoach	LX53AYO	Go-Ahead
LX12DFF	Stagecoach	LX13CZK	Stagecoach	LX53AYP	Go-Ahead
LX12DFG	Stagecoach	LX13CZL	Stagecoach	LX53AYT	Go-Ahead
LX12DFJ	Stagecoach	LX13CZM	Stagecoach	LX53AYU	Go-Ahead
LX12DFK	Stagecoach	LX13CZN	Stagecoach	LX53AYV	Go-Ahead
LX12DFL	Stagecoach	LX13CZO	Stagecoach	LX53AYW	Go-Ahead
LX12DFN	Stagecoach	LX13CZP	Stagecoach	LX53AYY	Go-Ahead
LX12DFO	Stagecoach	LX13CZR	Stagecoach	LX53AYZ	Go-Ahead
LX12DFP	Stagecoach	LX13CZS	Stagecoach	LX53AZA	Go-Ahead
LX12DFU	Stagecoach	LX13CZT	Stagecoach	LX53AZB	Go-Ahead
LX12DFV	Stagecoach	LX13CZU	Stagecoach	LX53AZC	Go-Ahead
LX12DFY	Stagecoach	LX13CZV	Stagecoach	LX53AZD	Go-Ahead
LX12DFZ	Stagecoach	LX13CZW	Stagecoach	LX53AZF	Go-Ahead
LX12DGE	Stagecoach	LX13CZY	Stagecoach	LX53AZG	Go-Ahead
LX12DGF	Stagecoach	LX13CZZ	Stagecoach	LX53AZJ	Go-Ahead
LX12DGO	Stagecoach	LX51FHO	Stagecoach	LX53AZL	Go-Ahead
LX12DGU	Stagecoach	LX51FHP	Stagecoach	LX53AZN	Go-Ahead
LX12DGV	Stagecoach	LX51FHU	Stagecoach	LX53AZO	Go-Ahead
LX12DGY	Stagecoach	LX51FJJ	Stagecoach	LX53AZP	Go-Ahead
LX12DGZ	Stagecoach	LX51FJP	Stagecoach	LX53AZR	Go-Ahead
LX12DHA	Stagecoach	LX51FJY	Stagecoach	LX53AZT	Go-Ahead
LX12DHC	Stagecoach	LX51FJZ	Stagecoach	LX53AZU	Go-Ahead
LX12DHD	Stagecoach	LX51FKA	Stagecoach	LX53AZV	Go-Ahead
LX12DHE	Stagecoach	LX51FKE	Stagecoach	LX53BAA	Go-Ahead
LX12DHF	Stagecoach	LX51FKF	Stagecoach	LX53BAO	Go-Ahead
LX12DHG	Stagecoach	LX51FKG	Stagecoach	LX53BBZ	Go-Ahead
LX12DHJ	Stagecoach	LX51FKO	Stagecoach	LX53BDO	Go-Ahead
LX12DHK	Stagecoach	LX51FKR	Stagecoach	LX53BDY	Go-Ahead
LX12DHL	Stagecoach	LX51FLC	Stagecoach	LX53BEY	Go-Ahead
LX12DHM	Stagecoach	LX51FLD	Stagecoach	LX53BFK	Go-Ahead
LX12DHN	Stagecoach	LX51FLP	Stagecoach	LX53BGE	Go-Ahead
LX12DHO	Stagecoach	LX51FLZ	Stagecoach	LX53BJK	Go-Ahead
LX12DHP	Stagecoach	LX51FMC	Stagecoach	LX53BJO	Go-Ahead
LX12DHU	Stagecoach	LX51FMD	Stagecoach	LX53BJU	Go-Ahead
LX12DHV	Stagecoach	LX51FME	Stagecoach	LX53JXU	Stagecoach
LX12DHY	Stagecoach	LX51FMF	Stagecoach	LX53JXV	Stagecoach
LX12DHZ	Stagecoach	LX51FMG	Stagecoach	LX53JXW	Stagecoach
LX12DJD	Stagecoach	LX51FMJ	Stagecoach	LX53JXY	Stagecoach
LX12DJE	Stagecoach	LX51FMK	Stagecoach	LX53JYA	Stagecoach
LX12DJF	Stagecoach	LX51FMO	Stagecoach	LX53JYB	Stagecoach
LX12DJJ	Stagecoach	LX51FMP	Stagecoach	LX53JYC	Stagecoach
LX12DJK	Stagecoach	LX51FMU	Stagecoach	LX53JYD	Stagecoach
LX12DJO	Stagecoach	LX51FMY	Stagecoach	LX53JYE	Stagecoach
LX12DJU	Stagecoach	LX51FMZ	Stagecoach	LX53JYF	Stagecoach
LX12DJV	Stagecoach	LX51FNA	Stagecoach	LX53JYG	Stagecoach
LX12DJY	Stagecoach	LX51FNC	Stagecoach	LX53JYH	Stagecoach
LX12DJZ	Stagecoach	LX51FND	Stagecoach	LX53JYJ	Stagecoach

LX53JYK	Stagecoach	LX54GZO	Go-Ahead	LX56ETJ	Go-Ahead
LX53JYL	Stagecoach	LX54GZP	Go-Ahead	LX56ETK	Go-Ahead
LX53JYN	Stagecoach	LX54GZR	Go-Ahead	LX56ETL	Go-Ahead
LX53JYO	Stagecoach	LX54GZT	Go-Ahead	LX56ETO	Go-Ahead
LX53JYP	Stagecoach	LX54GZU	Go-Ahead	LX56ETR	Go-Ahead
LX53JYR	Stagecoach	LX54GZV	Go-Ahead	LX56ETT	Go-Ahead
LX53JYT	Stagecoach	LX54GZW	Go-Ahead	LX56ETU	Go-Ahead
LX53JYU	Stagecoach	LX54GZY	Go-Ahead	LX56ETV	Go-Ahead
LX53JYV	Stagecoach	LX54GZZ	Go-Ahead	LX56ETY	Go-Ahead
LX53JYW	Stagecoach	LX54HAA	Go-Ahead	LX56ETZ	Go-Ahead
LX53JYY	Stagecoach	LX54HAE	Go-Ahead	LX56EUA	Go-Ahead
LX53JYZ	Stagecoach	LX54HAO	Go-Ahead	LX56EUB	Go-Ahead
LX53JZA	Stagecoach	LX54HAU	Go-Ahead	LX56EUC	Go-Ahead
LX53JZC	Stagecoach	LX54HBA	Go-Ahead	LX56EUD	Go-Ahead
LX53JZD	Stagecoach	LX54HBB	Go-Ahead	LX57CHV	Go-Ahead
LX53JZE	Stagecoach	LX55BDY	Stagecoach	LX57CHY	Go-Ahead
LX53JZF	Stagecoach	LX55BDZ	Stagecoach	LX57CHZ	Go-Ahead
LX53JZG	Stagecoach	LX55BEJ	Stagecoach	LX57CJE	Go-Ahead
LX53JZH	Stagecoach	LX55BEO	Stagecoach	LX57CJF	Go-Ahead
LX53JZJ	Stagecoach	LX55BEY	Stagecoach	LX57CJJ	Go-Ahead
LX53JZK	Stagecoach	LX55BFA	Stagecoach	LX57CJO	Go-Ahead
LX53JZL	Stagecoach	LX55BFE	Stagecoach	LX57CJU	Go-Ahead
LX53JZM	Stagecoach	LX55BFF	Stagecoach	LX57CJV	Go-Ahead
LX53JZN	Stagecoach	LX55EAC	Go-Ahead	LX57CJY	Go-Ahead
LX53JZO	Stagecoach	LX55EAE	Go-Ahead	LX57CJZ	Go-Ahead
LX53JZP	Stagecoach	LX55EAF	Go-Ahead	LX57CKA	Go-Ahead
LX53JZR	Stagecoach	LX55EAG	Go-Ahead	LX57CKC	Go-Ahead
LX53JZT	Stagecoach	LX55EAJ	Go-Ahead	LX57CKD	Go-Ahead
LX53JZU	Stagecoach	LX55EPA	Stagecoach	LX57CKE	Go-Ahead
LX53JZV	Stagecoach	LX55EPC	Stagecoach	LX57CKF	Go-Ahead
LX53JZW	Stagecoach	LX55EPD	Stagecoach	LX57CKG	Go-Ahead
LX53KAE	Stagecoach	LX55EPE	Stagecoach	LX57CKJ	Go-Ahead
LX53KAJ	Stagecoach	LX55EPF	Stagecoach	LX57CKK	Go-Ahead
LX53KAK	Stagecoach	LX55EPJ	Stagecoach	LX57CKL	Go-Ahead
LX53KAO	Stagecoach	LX55EPK	Stagecoach	LX57CKN	Go-Ahead
LX53KAU	Stagecoach	LX55EPL	Stagecoach	LX57CKO	Go-Ahead
LX53KBE	Stagecoach	LX55EPN	Stagecoach	LX57CKP	Go-Ahead
LX53KBF	Stagecoach	LX55EPO	Stagecoach	LX57CKU	Go-Ahead
LX53KBJ	Stagecoach	LX55EPP	Stagecoach	LX57CKV	Go-Ahead
LX53KBK	Stagecoach	LX55EPU	Stagecoach	LX57CKY	Go-Ahead
LX53KBN	Stagecoach	LX55EPV	Stagecoach	LX57CLF	Go-Ahead
LX53KBO	Stagecoach	LX55EPY	Stagecoach	LX57CLJ	Go-Ahead
LX53KBP	Stagecoach	LX55EPZ	Stagecoach	LX57CLN	Go-Ahead
LX53KBV	Stagecoach	LX55ERJ	Stagecoach	LX57CLO	Go-Ahead
LX53KBY	Stagecoach	LX55ERK	Stagecoach	LX57CLV	Go-Ahead
LX53KBZ	Stagecoach	LX55ERO	Stagecoach	LX57CLY	Go-Ahead
LX53KCA	Stagecoach	LX55ERU	Stagecoach	LX57CLZ	Go-Ahead
LX53KCC	Stagecoach	LX55ERV	Stagecoach	LX58BZW	Stagecoach
LX53KCE	Stagecoach	LX55ERY	Stagecoach	LX58BZY	Stagecoach
LX53KCF	Stagecoach	LX55ERZ	Stagecoach	LX58CAA	Stagecoach
LX53KCG	Stagecoach	LX55ESF	Stagecoach	LX58CAE	Stagecoach
LX53KCJ	Stagecoach	LX55ESG	Stagecoach	LX58CAO	Stagecoach
LX53LGF	Stagecoach	LX55ESN	Stagecoach	LX58CAU	Stagecoach
LX53LGG	Stagecoach	LX55ESO	Stagecoach	LX58CAV	Stagecoach
LX53LGJ	Stagecoach	LX55HGC	Stagecoach	LX58CBF	Stagecoach
LX53LGK	Stagecoach	LX56DZU	Stagecoach	LX58CBO	Stagecoach
LX53LGN	Stagecoach	LX56DZV	Stagecoach	LX58CBU	Stagecoach
LX53LGO	Stagecoach	LX56DZW	Stagecoach	LX58CBV	Stagecoach
LX53LGU	Stagecoach	LX56DZY	Stagecoach	LX58CBY	Stagecoach
LX53LGV	Stagecoach	LX56DZZ	Stagecoach	LX58CCA	Stagecoach
LX53LGW	Stagecoach	LX56EAA	Stagecoach	LX58CCD	Stagecoach
LX54GYV	Go-Ahead	LX56EAC	Stagecoach	LX58CCE	Stagecoach
LX54GYW	Go-Ahead	LX56EAE	Stagecoach	LX58CCF	Stagecoach
LX54GYY	Go-Ahead	LX56EAF	Stagecoach	LX58CCJ	Stagecoach
LX54GYZ	Go-Ahead	LX56EAG	Stagecoach	LX58CCK	Stagecoach
LX54GZB	Go-Ahead	LX56EAJ	Stagecoach	LX58CCN	Stagecoach
LX54GZC	Go-Ahead	LX56EAK	Stagecoach	LX58CCO	Stagecoach
LX54GZD	Go-Ahead	LX56EAM	Stagecoach	LX58CCU	Stagecoach
LX54GZE	Go-Ahead	LX56EAO	Stagecoach	LX58CCV	Stagecoach
LX54GZF	Go-Ahead	LX56EAP	Stagecoach	LX58CCY	Stagecoach
LX54GZG	Go-Ahead	LX56EAW	Stagecoach	LX58CDE	Stagecoach
LX54GZH	Go-Ahead	LX56EAY	Stagecoach	LX58CDF	Stagecoach
LX54GZK	Go-Ahead	LX56EBA	Stagecoach	LX58CDK	Stagecoach
LX54GZL	Go-Ahead	LX56ETD	Go-Ahead	LX58CDN	Stagecoach
LX54GZM	Go-Ahead	LX56ETE	Go-Ahead	LX58CDO	Stagecoach
LX54GZN	Go-Ahead	LX56ETF	Go-Ahead	LX58CDU	Stagecoach

LX58CDV	Stagecoach	LX58CXS	Go-Ahead	LX59CRZ	Stagecoach
LX58CDY	Stagecoach	LX58CXT	Go-Ahead	LX59CSF	Stagecoach
LX58CDZ	Stagecoach	LX58CXU	Go-Ahead	LX59CSO	Stagecoach
LX58CEA	Stagecoach	LX58CXV	Go-Ahead	LX59CYA	Go-Ahead
LX58CEF	Stagecoach	LX58CXW	Go-Ahead	LX59CYC	Go-Ahead
LX58CEJ	Stagecoach	LX58CXY	Go-Ahead	LX59CYE	Go-Ahead
LX58CEK	Stagecoach	LX58CXZ	Go-Ahead	LX59CYF	Go-Ahead
LX58CEN	Stagecoach	LX58CYA	Go-Ahead	LX59CYG	Go-Ahead
LX58CEO	Stagecoach	LX58CYC	Go-Ahead	LX59CYH	Go-Ahead
LX58CEU	Stagecoach	LX58CYE	Go-Ahead	LX59CYJ	Go-Ahead
LX58CEV	Stagecoach	LX58CYF	Go-Ahead	LX59CYK	Go-Ahead
LX58CEY	Stagecoach	LX58CYG	Go-Ahead	LX59CYL	Go-Ahead
LX58CFD	Stagecoach	LX58DDJ	Go-Ahead	LX59CYO	Go-Ahead
LX58CFE	Stagecoach	LX58DDK	Go-Ahead	LX59CYP	Go-Ahead
LX58CFF	Stagecoach	LX58DDL	Go-Ahead	LX59CYS	Go-Ahead
LX58CFG	Stagecoach	LX58DDN	Go-Ahead	LX59CYT	Go-Ahead
LX58CFJ	Stagecoach	LX58DDO	Go-Ahead	LX59CYU	Go-Ahead
LX58CFK	Stagecoach	LX59ANF	Stagecoach	LX59CYV	Go-Ahead
LX58CFL	Stagecoach	LX59ANP	Stagecoach	LX59CYW	Go-Ahead
LX58CFM	Stagecoach	LX59ANR	Stagecoach	LX59CYY	Go-Ahead
LX58CFN	Stagecoach	LX59ANU	Stagecoach	LX59CYZ	Go-Ahead
LX58CFO	Stagecoach	LX59ANV	Stagecoach	LX59CZA	Go-Ahead
LX58CFP	Stagecoach	LX59AOA	Stagecoach	LX59CZB	Go-Ahead
LX58CFU	Stagecoach	LX59AOB	Stagecoach	LX59CZC	Go-Ahead
LX58CFV	Stagecoach	LX59AOC	Stagecoach	LX59CZD	Go-Ahead
LX58CFY	Stagecoach	LX59AOD	Stagecoach	LX59CZF	Go-Ahead
LX58CFZ	Stagecoach	LX59AOE	Stagecoach	LX59CZG	Go-Ahead
LX58CGE	Stagecoach	LX59AOF	Stagecoach	LX59CZH	Go-Ahead
LX58CGF	Stagecoach	LX59AOG	Stagecoach	LX59CZJ	Go-Ahead
LX58CGG	Stagecoach	LX59AOH	Stagecoach	LX59CZK	Go-Ahead
LX58CGK	Stagecoach	LX59AOJ	Stagecoach	LX59CZL	Go-Ahead
LX58CGO	Stagecoach	LX59AOK	Stagecoach	LX59CZM	Go-Ahead
LX58CGU	Stagecoach	LX59AOL	Stagecoach	LX59CZN	Go-Ahead
LX58CGV	Stagecoach	LX59AOM	Stagecoach	LX59CZO	Go-Ahead
LX58CGY	Stagecoach	LX59CLU	Stagecoach	LX59CZP	Go-Ahead
LX58CGZ	Stagecoach	LX59CLV	Stagecoach	LX59CZR	Go-Ahead
LX58CHC	Stagecoach	LX59CLY	Stagecoach	LX59CZS	Go-Ahead
LX58CHD	Stagecoach	LX59CLZ	Stagecoach	LX59CZT	Go-Ahead
LX58CHF	Stagecoach	LX59CME	Stagecoach	LX59CZU	Go-Ahead
LX58CHG	Stagecoach	LX59CMF	Stagecoach	LX59CZV	Go-Ahead
LX58CHH	Stagecoach	LX59CMK	Stagecoach	LX59CZW	Go-Ahead
LX58CHJ	Stagecoach	LX59CMO	Stagecoach	LX59CZY	Go-Ahead
LX58CHK	Stagecoach	LX59CMU	Stagecoach	LX59CZZ	Go-Ahead
LX58CHL	Stagecoach	LX59CMV	Stagecoach	LX59DAA	Go-Ahead
LX58CHN	Stagecoach	LX59CMY	Stagecoach	LX59DAO	Go-Ahead
LX58CHO	Stagecoach	LX59CMZ	Stagecoach	LX59DAU	Go-Ahead
LX58CHV	Stagecoach	LX59CNA	Stagecoach	LX59DBO	Go-Ahead
LX58CWG	Go-Ahead	LX59CNC	Stagecoach	LX59DBU	Go-Ahead
LX58CWK	Go-Ahead	LX59CNE	Stagecoach	LX59DBV	Go-Ahead
LX58CWL	Go-Ahead	LX59CNF	Stagecoach	LX59DBY	Go-Ahead
LX58CWM	Go-Ahead	LX59CNJ	Stagecoach	LX59DBZ	Go-Ahead
LX58CWN	Go-Ahead	LX59CNK	Stagecoach	LX59DCE	Go-Ahead
LX58CWO	Go-Ahead	LX59CNN	Stagecoach	LX59DCF	Go-Ahead
LX58CWP	Go-Ahead	LX59CNO	Stagecoach	LX59DCO	Go-Ahead
LX58CWR	Go-Ahead	LX59CNU	Stagecoach	LX59DCU	Go-Ahead
LX58CWT	Go-Ahead	LX59CNV	Stagecoach	LX59DCV	Go-Ahead
LX58CWU	Go-Ahead	LX59CNY	Stagecoach	LX59DCY	Go-Ahead
LX58CWV	Go-Ahead	LX59CNZ	Stagecoach	LX59DCZ	Go-Ahead
LX58CWW	Go-Ahead	LX59COA	Stagecoach	LX59DDA	Go-Ahead
LX58CWX	Go-Ahead	LX59COH	Stagecoach	LX59DDE	Go-Ahead
LX58CWY	Go-Ahead	LX59COJ	Stagecoach	LX59DDF	Go-Ahead
LX58CWZ	Go-Ahead	LX59COU	Stagecoach	LX59DDJ	Go-Ahead
LX58CXA	Go-Ahead	LX59CPE	Stagecoach	LX59DDK	Go-Ahead
LX58CXB	Go-Ahead	LX59CPF	Stagecoach	LX59DDL	Go-Ahead
LX58CXD	Go-Ahead	LX59CPK	Stagecoach	LX59DDN	Go-Ahead
LX58CXE	Go-Ahead	LX59CPN	Stagecoach	LX59DDO	Go-Ahead
LX58CXF	Go-Ahead	LX59CPO	Stagecoach	LX59DDU	Go-Ahead
LX58CXG	Go-Ahead	LX59CPU	Stagecoach	LX59DDV	Go-Ahead
LX58CXH	Go-Ahead	LX59CPV	Stagecoach	LX59DDY	Go-Ahead
LX58CXJ	Go-Ahead	LX59CPY	Stagecoach	LX59DDZ	Go-Ahead
LX58CXK	Go-Ahead	LX59CPZ	Stagecoach	LX59DEU	Go-Ahead
LX58CXL	Go-Ahead	LX59CRF	Stagecoach	LX59DFA	Go-Ahead
LX58CXN	Go-Ahead	LX59CRJ	Stagecoach	LX59DFC	Go-Ahead
LX58CXO	Go-Ahead	LX59CRK	Stagecoach	LX59DFD	Go-Ahead
LX58CXP	Go-Ahead	LX59CRU	Stagecoach	LX59DFE	Go-Ahead
LX58CXR	Go-Ahead	LX59CRV	Stagecoach	LX59DFF	Go-Ahead

Reg	Operator	Reg	Operator	Reg	Operator
LX59DFG	Go-Ahead	LX61DDY	Stagecoach	PE56UFK	RATP - Quality Line
LX59DFJ	Go-Ahead	LX61DDZ	Stagecoach	PE56UFL	RATP - Quality Line
LX59DFK	Go-Ahead	LX61DEU	Stagecoach	PE56UFM	RATP - Quality Line
LX59ECF	Stagecoach	LX61DFA	Stagecoach	PE56UFN	RATP - Quality Line
LX59ECJ	Stagecoach	LX61DFC	Stagecoach	PE56UFP	RATP - Quality Line
LX59ECN	Stagecoach	LX61DFD	Stagecoach	PE56UFR	RATP - Quality Line
LX59ECT	Stagecoach	LX61DFE	Stagecoach	PE56UFS	RATP - Quality Line
LX59ECV	Stagecoach	LX61DFF	Stagecoach	PF08URP	Big Bus Company
LX59ECW	Stagecoach	LX61DFG	Stagecoach	PF08URR	Big Bus Company
LX59ECY	Stagecoach	LX61DFJ	Stagecoach	PF08URS	Big Bus Company
LX59ECZ	Stagecoach	LX61DFK	Stagecoach	PF08URU	Big Bus Company
LX59EDC	Stagecoach	LX61DFL	Stagecoach	PF08URV	Big Bus Company
LX59EDF	Stagecoach	LX61DFN	Stagecoach	PF08URW	Big Bus Company
LX59EDJ	Stagecoach	LX61DFO	Stagecoach	PF08URX	Big Bus Company
LX59EDK	Stagecoach	LX61DFP	Stagecoach	PF08URZ	Big Bus Company
LX59EDL	Stagecoach	LY02OAA	Stagecoach	PF08USB	Big Bus Company
LX59EDO	Stagecoach	LY02OAB	Stagecoach	PF08USC	Big Bus Company
LX60DVY	Go-Ahead	LY02OAC	Stagecoach	PF52WPT	Go-Ahead
LX60DVZ	Go-Ahead	LY02OAD	Stagecoach	PF52WPU	Go-Ahead
LX60DWA	Go-Ahead	LY02OAG	Stagecoach	PF52WPV	Go-Ahead
LX60DWC	Go-Ahead	LY02OAN	Stagecoach	PF52WPW	Go-Ahead
LX60DWD	Go-Ahead	LY02OAP	Stagecoach	PF52WPX	Go-Ahead
LX60DWE	Go-Ahead	LY02OAU	Stagecoach	PF52WPY	Go-Ahead
LX60DWF	Go-Ahead	LY02OAV	Stagecoach	PF52WPZ	Go-Ahead
LX60DWG	Go-Ahead	LY02OAW	Stagecoach	PF52WRA	Go-Ahead
LX60DWJ	Go-Ahead	LY02OAZ	Stagecoach	PF52WRC	Go-Ahead
LX60DWK	Go-Ahead	LY02OBB	Stagecoach	PF52WRD	Go-Ahead
LX60DWL	Go-Ahead	LY02OBC	Stagecoach	PF52WRE	Go-Ahead
LX60DWM	Go-Ahead	LY02OBD	Stagecoach	PF52WRG	Go-Ahead
LX60DWN	Go-Ahead	LY02OBE	Stagecoach	PG04WGN	RATP - London
LX60DWO	Go-Ahead	LY02OBF	Stagecoach	PG04WGP	RATP - London
LX60DWP	Go-Ahead	LY02OBG	Stagecoach	PG04WGU	RATP - London
LX60DWU	Go-Ahead	LY02OBH	Stagecoach	PG04WGV	RATP - London
LX60DWV	Go-Ahead	LY02OBJ	Stagecoach	PG04WGW	RATP - London
LX60DWW	Go-Ahead	LY02OBL	Stagecoach	PG04WGX	RATP - London
LX60DWY	Go-Ahead	LY02OBM	Stagecoach	PG04WGY	RATP - London
LX60DWZ	Go-Ahead	LY52ZDX	Stagecoach	PG04WHA	RATP - London
LX60DXA	Go-Ahead	LY52ZDZ	Stagecoach	PG04WHB	RATP - London
LX60DXB	Go-Ahead	LY52ZFA	Stagecoach	PG04WHC	RATP - London
LX60DXC	Go-Ahead	LY52ZFB	Stagecoach	PG04WHD	RATP - London
LX60DXD	Go-Ahead	LY52ZFC	Stagecoach	PG04WHE	RATP - London
LX60DXE	Go-Ahead	LY52ZFD	Stagecoach	PG04WHF	RATP - London
LX60DXF	Go-Ahead	LY52ZFE	Stagecoach	PG04WHH	RATP - London
LX60DXG	Go-Ahead	LY52ZFF	Stagecoach	PG04WHJ	RATP - London
LX60DXH	Go-Ahead	LY52ZFG	Stagecoach	PG04WHK	RATP - London
LX60DXJ	Go-Ahead	LY52ZFH	Stagecoach	PG04WHL	RATP - London
LX60DXK	Go-Ahead	M507VJO	Metrobus	PG04WHM	RATP - London
LX60DXM	Go-Ahead	M516VJO	Metrobus	PG04WHN	RATP - London
LX60DXO	Go-Ahead	MX10DXR	HCT - CT Plus	PG04WHP	RATP - London
LX60DXP	Go-Ahead	MX56HYR	Abellio	PG04WHR	RATP - London
LX60DXR	Go-Ahead	MX56HYS	Abellio	PG04WHS	RATP - London
LX60DXS	Go-Ahead	MXT179	Original Tour	PG04WHT	RATP - London
LX60DXT	Go-Ahead	N137YRW	RATP - London	PG04WHU	RATP - London
LX61DAA	Stagecoach	N137YRW	Transdev	PG04WHV	RATP - London
LX61DAO	Stagecoach	N138YRW	RATP - London	PG04WHW	RATP - London
LX61DAU	Stagecoach	N139YRW	RATP - London	PG04WHX	RATP - London
LX61DBO	Stagecoach	N140YRW	RATP - London	PG04WHZ	RATP - London
LX61DBU	Stagecoach	N232TPK	Metrobus	PG04WHZ	RATP - London
LX61DBV	Stagecoach	NKJ785	Original Tour	PG04WJA	RATP - London
LX61DBY	Stagecoach	P274FPK	Metrobus	PJ02RBO	Go-Ahead
LX61DBZ	Stagecoach	P278FPK	Metrobus	PJ02RBZ	Go-Ahead
LX61DCO	Stagecoach	P283FPK	Metrobus	PJ02RCF	Go-Ahead
LX61DCU	Stagecoach	P285FPK	Metrobus	PJ02RCO	Go-Ahead
LX61DCV	Stagecoach	P380FPK	Metrobus	PJ02RCU	Go-Ahead
LX61DCY	Stagecoach	P508RYM	HCT - CT Plus	PJ02RCV	Go-Ahead
LX61DCZ	Stagecoach	PA04CYC	RATP - London	PJ02RCX	Go-Ahead
LX61DDA	Stagecoach	PA04CYE	RATP - London	PJ02RCY	Go-Ahead
LX61DDE	Stagecoach	PA04CYF	RATP - London	PJ02RCZ	Go-Ahead
LX61DDF	Stagecoach	PA04CYJ	RATP - London	PJ02RDO	Go-Ahead
LX61DDJ	Stagecoach	PA04CYK	Transdev	PJ02RDU	Go-Ahead
LX61DDK	Stagecoach	PA04CYL	Transdev	PJ02RDV	Go-Ahead
LX61DDL	Stagecoach	PA04CYP	Transdev	PJ02RDX	Go-Ahead
LX61DDN	Stagecoach	PA04CYS	Transdev	PJ02RDY	Go-Ahead
LX61DDO	Stagecoach	PA04CYT	Transdev	PJ02RDZ	Go-Ahead
LX61DDU	Stagecoach	PE56UFH	RATP - Quality Line	PJ02REU	Go-Ahead
LX61DDV	Stagecoach	PE56UFJ	RATP - Quality Line	PJ02RFE	Go-Ahead

Reg	Operator	Reg	Operator	Reg	Operator
PJ02RFF	Go-Ahead	PJ53SOH	Go-Ahead	PN09EOE	Big Bus Company
PJ02RFK	Go-Ahead	PJ53SOU	Go-Ahead	PN09EOF	Big Bus Company
PJ02RFL	Go-Ahead	PJ53SPU	Go-Ahead	PN09EOH	Big Bus Company
PJ02RFN	Go-Ahead	PJ53SPV	Go-Ahead	PN09EOJ	Big Bus Company
PJ02RFO	Go-Ahead	PJ53SPX	Go-Ahead	PN09EOK	Big Bus Company
PJ02RFX	Go-Ahead	PJ53SPZ	Go-Ahead	PN10FOC	Big Bus Company
PJ02RFY	Go-Ahead	PJ53SRO	Go-Ahead	PN10FOD	Big Bus Company
PJ02RFZ	Go-Ahead	PJ53SRU	Go-Ahead	PN10FOF	Big Bus Company
PJ02RGO	Go-Ahead	PL03AGZ	Go-Ahead	PN10FOH	Big Bus Company
PJ02RGU	Go-Ahead	PL05PLN	RATP - Quality Line	PN10FOJ	Big Bus Company
PJ02RGV	Go-Ahead	PL05PLO	RATP - Quality Line	PN10FOK	Big Bus Company
PJ02TVN	Go-Ahead	PL05PLU	RATP - Quality Line	PO54ABZ	Transdev
PJ02TVO	Go-Ahead	PL05PLV	RATP - Quality Line	PO54ACF	Transdev
PJ02TVP	Go-Ahead	PL05PLX	RATP - Quality Line	PO54ACJ	Transdev
PJ02TVT	Go-Ahead	PN02XBL	Go-Ahead	PO54ACU	Transdev
PJ02TVU	Go-Ahead	PN02XBM	Go-Ahead	PO54ACV	Transdev
PJ52LVP	Go-Ahead	PN02XBO	Go-Ahead	PO54ACX	Transdev
PJ52LVR	Go-Ahead	PN02XBW	Go-Ahead	PO54ACY	Transdev
PJ52LVS	Go-Ahead	PN03ULY	HCT - CT Plus	PO54ACZ	Transdev
PJ52LVT	Go-Ahead	PN03UMB	HCT - CT Plus	PO56JEU	Metrobus
PJ52LVU	Go-Ahead	PN03UMK	HCT - CT Plus	PO56JFA	Metrobus
PJ52LVV	Go-Ahead	PN06UYL	Metrobus	PO56JFE	Metrobus
PJ52LVW	Go-Ahead	PN06UYM	Metrobus	PO56JFF	Metrobus
PJ52LVX	Go-Ahead	PN06UYO	Metrobus	PO56JFG	Metrobus
PJ52LVY	Go-Ahead	PN06UYP	Metrobus	PO56JFJ	Metrobus
PJ52LVZ	Go-Ahead	PN06UYR	Metrobus	PO56JFK	Metrobus
PJ52LWA	Go-Ahead	PN06UYS	Metrobus	PO56JFN	Metrobus
PJ52LWC	Go-Ahead	PN06UYT	Metrobus	PO56JFU	Metrobus
PJ52LWD	Go-Ahead	PN06UYU	Metrobus	PO59KFW	Metrobus
PJ52LWE	Go-Ahead	PN06UYV	Metrobus	PO59KFX	Metrobus
PJ52LWF	Go-Ahead	PN06UYW	Metrobus	PO59KFY	Metrobus
PJ52LWG	Go-Ahead	PN06UYX	Metrobus	PO59KFZ	Metrobus
PJ52LWH	Go-Ahead	PN06UYY	Metrobus	PO59KGA	Metrobus
PJ52LWK	Go-Ahead	PN07KPY	HCT - CT Plus	PO59KGE	Metrobus
PJ52LWL	Go-Ahead	PN07KPZ	HCT - CT Plus	PR52TFX	HCT - CT Plus
PJ52LWM	Go-Ahead	PN07KRD	HCT - CT Plus	PR52TGZ	HCT - CT Plus
PJ52LWN	Go-Ahead	PN07KRE	HCT - CT Plus	R370LGH	Go-Ahead
PJ52LWO	Go-Ahead	PN07KRF	HCT - CT Plus	R371LGH	Go-Ahead
PJ52LWP	Go-Ahead	PN07KRG	HCT - CT Plus	R741BMY	Metrobus
PJ52LWR	Go-Ahead	PN07KRK	Metrobus	R744BMY	Metrobus
PJ52LWS	Go-Ahead	PN07KRO	Metrobus	R747FGX	Metrobus
PJ52LWT	Go-Ahead	PN07KRU	Metrobus	R946YOV	RATP - London
PJ52LWU	Go-Ahead	PN07KRV	Metrobus	R948YOV	RATP - London
PJ52LWV	Go-Ahead	PN07KRX	Metrobus	R949YOV	RATP - London
PJ52LWW	Go-Ahead	PN07KRZ	RATP - Quality Line	R950YOV	RATP - London
PJ52LWX	Go-Ahead	PN07KSE	RATP - Quality Line	R951YOV	RATP - London
PJ53NKG	Go-Ahead	PN08SWJ	HCT - CT Plus	R952YOV	RATP - London
PJ53NKH	Go-Ahead	PN09EKR	Metrobus	R953YOV	RATP - London
PJ53NKK	Go-Ahead	PN09EKT	Metrobus	R954YOV	RATP - London
PJ53NKL	Go-Ahead	PN09EKU	Metrobus	RA51KVS	Abellio
PJ53NKM	Go-Ahead	PN09EKV	Metrobus	RD02BJK	Abellio
PJ53NKN	Go-Ahead	PN09EKW	Metrobus	RD02BJO	Abellio
PJ53NKO	Go-Ahead	PN09EKX	Metrobus	RD02BJU	Abellio
PJ53NKP	Go-Ahead	PN09EKY	Metrobus	RD02BJV	Abellio
PJ53NKR	Go-Ahead	PN09ELO	Metrobus	RD02BJX	Abellio
PJ53NKT	Go-Ahead	PN09ELU	Metrobus	RD02BJZ	Abellio
PJ53NKU	Go-Ahead	PN09ELV	Metrobus	RL02FOT	Abellio
PJ53NKW	Go-Ahead	PN09ELW	Metrobus	RL02FOU	Abellio
PJ53NKX	Go-Ahead	PN09ELX	Metrobus	RL02FVM	Abellio
PJ53NKZ	Go-Ahead	PN09EMF	Metrobus	RL02FVN	Abellio
PJ53NLA	Go-Ahead	PN09EMK	Metrobus	RL02ZTB	Abellio
PJ53NLC	Go-Ahead	PN09EMV	Metrobus	RL02ZTC	Abellio
PJ53NLD	Go-Ahead	PN09EMX	Metrobus	RL51DNU	Metroline
PJ53NLE	Go-Ahead	PN09ENC	Metrobus	RL51DNX	Metroline
PJ53NLF	Go-Ahead	PN09ENE	Metrobus	RL51DNY	Metroline
PJ53OUN	Transdev	PN09ENF	Metrobus	RL51DOA	Metroline
PJ53OUO	Transdev	PN09ENH	Metrobus	RL51DOH	Metroline
PJ53OUP	Transdev	PN09ENK	Metrobus	RL51DOJ	Metroline
PJ53OUU	Transdev	PN09ENL	Metrobus	RL51DOU	Metroline
PJ53OUV	Transdev	PN09ENM	Metrobus	RN52EYK	Abellio
PJ53OUW	Transdev	PN09ENO	Metrobus	RN52EYL	Abellio
PJ53OUX	Transdev	PN09ENY	Big Bus Company	RN52FPA	Abellio
PJ53OUY	Transdev	PN09EOA	Big Bus Company	RN52FPC	Abellio
PJ53OVA	Transdev	PN09EOB	Big Bus Company	RN52FRD	Abellio
PJ53OVB	Transdev	PN09EOC	Big Bus Company	RN52FRF	Abellio
PJ53SOE	Go-Ahead	PN09EOD	Big Bus Company	RN52FVR	Abellio

Reg	Operator	Reg	Operator	Reg	Operator
RN52FVS	Abellio	SK07DYX	RATP - London	SN03LFE	RATP - London
RN52FXD	Abellio	SK07DYY	RATP - London	SN03LFF	RATP - London
RN52FYO	Abellio	SK07DZA	RATP - Quality Line	SN03LFG	RATP - London
RN52FZA	Abellio	SK07DZB	RATP - Quality Line	SN03LFH	RATP - London
RX51FGM	Abellio	SK07DZC	RATP - Quality Line	SN03LFJ	RATP - London
RX51FGN	Abellio	SK07DZD	RATP - Quality Line	SN03LFK	RATP - London
S301MKH	RATP - London	SK07DZE	RATP - Quality Line	SN03LFL	RATP - London
S307MKH	RATP - London	SK07DZF	RATP - Quality Line	SN03LFM	RATP - London
S310MKH	RATP - London	SK07DZG	RATP - Quality Line	SN03LFP	RATP - London
S311MKH	RATP - London	SK07DZH	RATP - Quality Line	SN03LFR	RATP - London
S315JUA	Arriva The Shires	SK07DZJ	RATP - Quality Line	SN03LFS	RATP - London
S317JUA	Arriva The Shires	SK07DZL	RATP - Quality Line	SN03LFT	RATP - London
S318JUA	Arriva The Shires	SK07DZM	Go-Ahead	SN03WKU	Metrobus
S876BYJ	Abellio	SK07DZN	Go-Ahead	SN03WKY	Metrobus
S877BYJ	Abellio	SK07DZO	Go-Ahead	SN03WLA	Metrobus
S878BYJ	Abellio	SK07HLM	RATP - London	SN03WLE	Metrobus
S881BYJ	Abellio	SK07HLN	RATP - London	SN03WLF	Metrobus
SK02TZN	Abellio	SK07HLO	RATP - London	SN03WLH	Metrobus
SK02TZO	Abellio	SK07HLP	RATP - London	SN03WLL	Metrobus
SK02TZP	Abellio	SK07HLR	RATP - London	SN03WLP	Metrobus
SK02TZR	Abellio	SK07HLU	RATP - London	SN03WLU	Metrobus
SK02TZS	Abellio	SK07HLV	RATP - London	SN03WLX	Metrobus
SK02TZT	Abellio	SK52MLU	Go-Ahead	SN03WLZ	Metrobus
SK02TZU	Abellio	SK52MLV	Go-Ahead	SN03WMC	Metrobus
SK02TZV	Abellio	SK52MLX	Go-Ahead	SN03WMF	Metrobus
SK02TZW	Abellio	SK52MLY	Go-Ahead	SN03WMG	Metrobus
SK02TZX	Abellio	SK52MLZ	Go-Ahead	SN03WMK	Metrobus
SK02XGT	RATP - London	SK52MMA	Go-Ahead	SN03WMP	Metrobus
SK02XGU	RATP - London	SK52MME	Go-Ahead	SN03WMT	Metrobus
SK02XGV	RATP - London	SK52MMU	Go-Ahead	SN03WMV	Metrobus
SK02XGW	Transdev	SK52MMV	Go-Ahead	SN03WMY	Metrobus
SK02XGX	Transdev	SK52MMX	Go-Ahead	SN03YBA	Metrobus
SK02XHD	Transdev	SK52MOA	Go-Ahead	SN03YBB	Metrobus
SK02XHE	Transdev	SK52MOF	Go-Ahead	SN03YBC	Metrobus
SK02XHG	Transdev	SK52MOU	Go-Ahead	SN03YBG	Metrobus
SK02XHH	Transdev	SK52MOV	Go-Ahead	SN03YBH	Metrobus
SK02XHJ	Transdev	SK52MPE	Go-Ahead	SN03YBK	Metrobus
SK02XHL	Transdev	SK52MPF	Go-Ahead	SN03YBR	Metrobus
SK02XHM	Transdev	SK52MPO	Go-Ahead	SN03YBS	Metrobus
SK02XHN	Transdev	SN03DZJ	RATP - London	SN03YBT	Metrobus
SK02XHO	Transdev	SN03DZK	RATP - London	SN03YBX	Metrobus
SK02XHP	Transdev	SN03DZM	RATP - London	SN03YBY	Metrobus
SK02XHR	Transdev	SN03DZP	RATP - London	SN03YBZ	Metrobus
SK07DXE	RATP - London	SN03DZR	RATP - London	SN03YCD	Metrobus
SK07DXF	RATP - London	SN03DZS	RATP - London	SN03YCE	Metrobus
SK07DXG	RATP - London	SN03DZT	RATP - London	SN03YCF	Metrobus
SK07DXH	RATP - London	SN03DZV	RATP - London	SN03YCK	Metrobus
SK07DXJ	RATP - London	SN03DZW	RATP - London	SN03YCL	Metrobus
SK07DXL	RATP - London	SN03DZX	RATP - London	SN03YCM	Metrobus
SK07DXM	RATP - London	SN03EAA	RATP - London	SN03YCT	Metrobus
SK07DXO	RATP - London	SN03EAC	RATP - London	SN04EFJ	Abellio
SK07DXP	RATP - London	SN03EAE	RATP - London	SN04EGD	Abellio
SK07DXR	RATP - London	SN03EAF	RATP - London	SN06BNA	Go-Ahead
SK07DXS	RATP - London	SN03EAG	RATP - London	SN06BNB	Go-Ahead
SK07DXT	RATP - London	SN03EAJ	RATP - London	SN06BND	Go-Ahead
SK07DXU	RATP - London	SN03EAM	RATP - London	SN06BNE	Go-Ahead
SK07DXV	RATP - London	SN03EAP	RATP - London	SN06BNF	Go-Ahead
SK07DXW	RATP - London	SN03EAW	RATP - London	SN06BNJ	Go-Ahead
SK07DXX	RATP - London	SN03EAX	RATP - London	SN06BNK	Go-Ahead
SK07DXY	RATP - London	SN03EBA	RATP - London	SN06BNL	Go-Ahead
SK07DXZ	RATP - London	SN03EBC	RATP - London	SN06BNO	Go-Ahead
SK07DYC	RATP - London	SN03EBD	RATP - London	SN06BNU	Go-Ahead
SK07DYD	RATP - London	SN03EBF	RATP - London	SN06BNV	Go-Ahead
SK07DYF	RATP - London	SN03EBG	RATP - London	SN06BNX	Go-Ahead
SK07DYG	RATP - London	SN03EBJ	RATP - London	SN06BNY	Go-Ahead
SK07DYH	RATP - London	SN03EBK	RATP - London	SN06BNZ	Go-Ahead
SK07DYJ	RATP - London	SN03EBL	RATP - London	SN06BOF	Go-Ahead
SK07DYM	RATP - London	SN03EBM	RATP - London	SN06BPE	Arriva
SK07DYN	RATP - London	SN03LDY	RATP - London	SN06BPF	Arriva
SK07DYO	RATP - London	SN03LDZ	RATP - London	SN06BPK	Arriva
SK07DYP	RATP - London	SN03LEF	RATP - London	SN06BPU	Arriva
SK07DYS	RATP - London	SN03LEJ	RATP - London	SN06BPV	Arriva
SK07DYT	RATP - London	SN03LEU	RATP - London	SN06BPX	Arriva
SK07DYU	RATP - London	SN03LFA	RATP - London	SN06BPY	Arriva
SK07DYV	RATP - London	SN03LFB	RATP - London	SN06BPZ	Arriva
SK07DYW	RATP - London	SN03LFD	RATP - London	SN06BRF	Arriva

SN06JPV	RATP - London	SN11BNV	Tower Transit	SN12AOU	Abellio
SN06JPX	RATP - London	SN11BNX	Tower Transit	SN12AOV	Abellio
SN08AAE	Arriva The Shires	SN11BNY	Tower Transit	SN12AOW	Abellio
SN08AAO	Metroline	SN11BNZ	Tower Transit	SN12AOX	Abellio
SN09CDU	Metroline	SN11BOF	Tower Transit	SN12AOY	Abellio
SN09CDV	Metroline	SN11BOH	Tower Transit	SN12AOZ	Abellio
SN09CDX	Metroline	SN11BOJ	Tower Transit	SN12APF	Abellio
SN09CDY	Metroline	SN11BOU	Tower Transit	SN12APK	Abellio
SN09CDZ	Metroline	SN11BOV	Tower Transit	SN12APO	Abellio
SN09CEA	Metroline	SN11BPE	Tower Transit	SN12APU	Abellio
SN09CEF	Metroline	SN11BPF	Tower Transit	SN12APV	Abellio
SN09CEJ	Metroline	SN11BPK	Tower Transit	SN12APX	Abellio
SN09CEK	Metroline	SN11BPO	Tower Transit	SN12APY	Tower Transit
SN09CEO	Metroline	SN11BPU	Tower Transit	SN12APZ	Tower Transit
SN09CEU	Metroline	SN11BPV	Tower Transit	SN12ARF	Tower Transit
SN09CEV	Metroline	SN11BPX	Tower Transit	SN12ARO	Tower Transit
SN09CEX	Metroline	SN11BPY	Tower Transit	SN12ARU	Tower Transit
SN09CEY	Metroline	SN11BPZ	Tower Transit	SN12ARX	Tower Transit
SN09CFA	Metroline	SN11BRF	Tower Transit	SN12ARZ	Tower Transit
SN09CFD	Metroline	SN11BRV	Tower Transit	SN12ASO	Tower Transit
SN09CFE	Metroline	SN11BRZ	Tower Transit	SN12ASU	Tower Transit
SN09CFF	Metroline	SN11BSO	Tower Transit	SN12ASV	Tower Transit
SN09CFG	Metroline	SN11BSU	Tower Transit	SN12ASX	Tower Transit
SN09CFJ	Metroline	SN11BSV	Tower Transit	SN12ASZ	Tower Transit
SN09CFK	Metroline	SN11BSX	Tower Transit	SN12ATF	Tower Transit
SN09CFL	Metroline	SN11BSY	Tower Transit	SN12ATK	Tower Transit
SN09CFM	Metroline	SN11BSZ	Tower Transit	SN12ATO	Tower Transit
SN09CFO	Metroline	SN11BTE	Tower Transit	SN12ATU	Tower Transit
SN09CFP	Metroline	SN11BTO	Tower Transit	SN12ATV	Tower Transit
SN09CFU	Metroline	SN11BTU	Tower Transit	SN12ATX	Tower Transit
SN09CFV	Metroline	SN11BTY	Go-Ahead	SN12ATY	Tower Transit
SN09CFX	Metroline	SN11BTZ	Go-Ahead	SN12ATZ	Tower Transit
SN09CFY	Metroline	SN11BUA	Go-Ahead	SN12AUA	Tower Transit
SN09CFZ	Metroline	SN11BUE	Go-Ahead	SN12AUC	Tower Transit
SN09CGE	Metroline	SN11BUF	Go-Ahead	SN12AUE	Abellio
SN09CGF	Metroline	SN11BUH	Go-Ahead	SN12AUF	Abellio
SN09CGG	Metroline	SN11BUJ	Go-Ahead	SN12AUH	Abellio
SN09CGK	Metroline	SN11BUO	Go-Ahead	SN12AUJ	Abellio
SN09CGO	Metroline	SN11BUP	Go-Ahead	SN12AUK	Abellio
SN09CGU	Metroline	SN11BUU	Go-Ahead	SN12AUL	Abellio
SN09CGV	Metroline	SN11BUV	Go-Ahead	SN12AUM	Go-Ahead
SN09CHC	RATP - London	SN11BUW	Go-Ahead	SN12AUO	Abellio
SN09CHD	RATP - London	SN11BVG	RATP - Quality Line	SN12AUO	Go-Ahead
SN09CHF	RATP - London	SN11BVH	RATP - Quality Line	SN12AUP	Go-Ahead
SN09CHG	RATP - London	SN11FFZ	Go-Ahead	SN12AUR	Go-Ahead
SN09CHH	RATP - London	SN11FGA	Go-Ahead	SN12AUT	Go-Ahead
SN10CAV	RATP - London	SN11FGC	Go-Ahead	SN12AUU	Go-Ahead
SN10CAX	RATP - London	SN11FGD	Go-Ahead	SN12AUV	Go-Ahead
SN10CBF	RATP - London	SN12AAE	Metrobus	SN12AUW	Go-Ahead
SN10CBO	RATP - London	SN12AAF	Metrobus	SN12AUX	Go-Ahead
SN10CBU	RATP - London	SN12AAJ	Metrobus	SN12AUY	Go-Ahead
SN10CBV	RATP - London	SN12AAK	Metrobus	SN12AVB	Go-Ahead
SN10CBX	RATP - London	SN12AAO	Metrobus	SN12AVC	Go-Ahead
SN10CBY	RATP - London	SN12AAU	Metrobus	SN12AVD	Go-Ahead
SN10CCA	RATP - London	SN12AAV	Abellio	SN12AVE	Go-Ahead
SN10CCD	RATP - London	SN12AAX	Abellio	SN12AVF	Go-Ahead
SN10CCE	RATP - London	SN12AAY	Abellio	SN12AVG	Go-Ahead
SN10CCF	RATP - London	SN12AAZ	Abellio	SN12AVJ	Go-Ahead
SN10CCJ	RATP - London	SN12ABF	Abellio	SN12AVK	Go-Ahead
SN10CCK	RATP - London	SN12ABK	Abellio	SN12AVL	Go-Ahead
SN10CCO	RATP - London	SN12ABO	Abellio	SN12AVR	Tower Transit
SN10CCU	RATP - London	SN12ABU	Abellio	SN12AVT	Tower Transit
SN11BMU	Tower Transit	SN12ABV	Abellio	SN12AVU	Tower Transit
SN11BMV	Tower Transit	SN12ABX	Abellio	SN12AVV	Tower Transit
SN11BMY	Tower Transit	SN12ABZ	Abellio	SN12AVW	Tower Transit
SN11BMZ	Tower Transit	SN12ACF	Abellio	SN12AVX	Tower Transit
SN11BNA	Tower Transit	SN12ACJ	Abellio	SN12AVY	Tower Transit
SN11BNB	Tower Transit	SN12ACO	Abellio	SN12AVZ	Tower Transit
SN11BND	Tower Transit	SN12ACU	Abellio	SN12AWA	Tower Transit
SN11BNE	Tower Transit	SN12ACV	Abellio	SN12AWC	Tower Transit
SN11BNF	Tower Transit	SN12ACX	Abellio	SN12EGY	Metroline
SN11BNJ	Tower Transit	SN12ACY	Abellio	SN12EGZ	Metroline
SN11BNK	Tower Transit	SN12ACZ	Abellio	SN12EHB	Tower Transit
SN11BNL	Tower Transit	SN12ADO	Abellio	SN12EHC	Tower Transit
SN11BNO	Tower Transit	SN12AOS	Abellio	SN12EHD	Metroline
SN11BNU	Tower Transit	SN12AOT	Abellio	SN12EHE	Metroline

Reg	Operator	Reg	Operator	Reg	Operator
SN12EHF	Metroline	SN51UAJ	Go-Ahead	SN55HKW	RATP - London
SN12EHG	Metroline	SN51UAK	Go-Ahead	SN55HKX	RATP - London
SN12EHH	Metroline	SN51UAL	Go-Ahead	SN55HKY	RATP - London
SN12EHJ	Metroline	SN51UAM	Go-Ahead	SN55HKZ	RATP - London
SN12EHK	Metroline	SN51UAO	Go-Ahead	SN55HLA	RATP - London
SN12EHP	Metroline	SN51UAP	Go-Ahead	SN55HLC	RATP - London
SN12EHR	Metroline	SN51UAR	Go-Ahead	SN55HSD	RATP - London
SN12EHS	Metroline	SN51UAS	Go-Ahead	SN55HSE	RATP - London
SN12EHT	Metroline	SN51UAT	Go-Ahead	SN56AXG	Arriva The Shires
SN12EHU	Metroline	SN51UAU	Go-Ahead	SN56AXH	Arriva The Shires
SN12EHV	Metroline	SN51UAV	Go-Ahead	SN56AYC	Go-Ahead
SN12EHW	Metroline	SN51UAW	Go-Ahead	SN56AYD	Go-Ahead
SN13CGY	Tower Transit	SN51UAX	Go-Ahead	SN57DWE	HCT - CT Plus
SN13CGZ	Tower Transit	SN51UAY	Go-Ahead	SN57DWF	HCT - CT Plus
SN13CHC	Tower Transit	SN51UAZ	Go-Ahead	SN57DWG	Go-Ahead
SN13CHD	Tower Transit	SN53EUD	HCT - CT Plus	SN57DWJ	Go-Ahead
SN13CHF	Tower Transit	SN53EUF	RATP - London	SN57DWK	Go-Ahead
SN13CHG	Tower Transit	SN53EUH	RATP - London	SN57DWL	Go-Ahead
SN13CHH	Tower Transit	SN53EUJ	RATP - London	SN57DWM	Go-Ahead
SN13CHJ	Tower Transit	SN53EUK	RATP - London	SN57DWN	Go-Ahead
SN13CHK	Tower Transit	SN53EUL	RATP - London	SN57DWP	Go-Ahead
SN13CHL	Tower Transit	SN53EUM	RATP - London	SN57DWU	Go-Ahead
SN13CJE	Go-Ahead	SN53EUO	RATP - London	SN57DWV	Go-Ahead
SN13CJF	Go-Ahead	SN53EUP	RATP - London	SN57DWW	Go-Ahead
SN13CJJ	Go-Ahead	SN53KHR	RATP - London	SN57DWX	Go-Ahead
SN13CJO	Go-Ahead	SN53KHT	RATP - London	SN57DWY	Go-Ahead
SN13CJU	Go-Ahead	SN53KHU	RATP - London	SN57DWZ	Go-Ahead
SN51SHJ	RATP - London	SN53KHV	RATP - London	SN57DXA	Go-Ahead
SN51SXG	RATP - London	SN53KHW	RATP - London	SN57DXB	Go-Ahead
SN51SXH	RATP - London	SN53KHX	RATP - London	SN58CDY	Go-Ahead
SN51SXK	Abellio	SN53KHY	RATP - London	SN58CDZ	Go-Ahead
SN51SYA	RATP - London	SN53KHZ	RATP - London	SN58CEA	Go-Ahead
SN51SYC	RATP - London	SN53KJA	RATP - London	SN58CEF	Go-Ahead
SN51SYE	RATP - London	SN53KJE	RATP - London	SN58CEJ	Go-Ahead
SN51SYF	RATP - London	SN53KJF	RATP - London	SN58CEK	Go-Ahead
SN51SYG	RATP - London	SN53KJK	RATP - London	SN58CEO	Go-Ahead
SN51SYH	RATP - London	SN53KJO	RATP - London	SN58CEU	Go-Ahead
SN51SYJ	RATP - London	SN53KKF	Go-Ahead	SN58CEV	Go-Ahead
SN51SYO	RATP - London	SN53KKG	Go-Ahead	SN58CEX	Go-Ahead
SN51SYR	RATP - London	SN53KKH	Go-Ahead	SN58CEY	Go-Ahead
SN51SYS	RATP - London	SN53KKJ	Go-Ahead	SN58CFA	Go-Ahead
SN51SYT	RATP - London	SN53KKL	Go-Ahead	SN58CFD	Go-Ahead
SN51SYU	RATP - London	SN53KKM	Go-Ahead	SN58CFE	Go-Ahead
SN51SYV	RATP - London	SN53KKO	Go-Ahead	SN58CFF	Go-Ahead
SN51SYW	RATP - London	SN53KKP	Go-Ahead	SN58CFG	Go-Ahead
SN51SYX	RATP - London	SN53KKR	Go-Ahead	SN58CFJ	Go-Ahead
SN51SYY	RATP - London	SN53KKT	Go-Ahead	SN58EOR	RATP - London
SN51SYZ	RATP - London	SN53KKU	Go-Ahead	SN58EOS	RATP - London
SN51SZC	RATP - London	SN53KKV	Go-Ahead	SN59AVR	Abellio
SN51SZD	RATP - London	SN53KKW	Go-Ahead	SN59AVT	Abellio
SN51SZE	RATP - London	SN53KKX	Go-Ahead	SN59AVU	Abellio
SN51SZF	Abellio	SN54GPV	Metrobus	SN59AVV	Abellio
SN51SZT	RATP - London	SN54GPX	Metrobus	SN59AVW	Abellio
SN51SZU	RATP - London	SN54GPY	Metrobus	SN59AVX	Abellio
SN51TAU	RATP - London	SN54GPZ	Metrobus	SN59AVY	Abellio
SN51TAV	RATP - London	SN54GRF	Metrobus	SN59AVZ	Abellio
SN51TBO	RATP - London	SN54GRK	Metrobus	SN59AWA	Abellio
SN51TBU	RATP - London	SN55DVR	RATP - London	SN59AWC	Abellio
SN51TBV	RATP - London	SN55DVT	RATP - London	SN59AWF	Abellio
SN51TBX	Transdev	SN55DVU	RATP - London	SN59AWG	Abellio
SN51TBY	RATP - London	SN55DVV	RATP - London	SN59AWH	Abellio
SN51TBZ	RATP - London	SN55DVW	RATP - London	SN59AWJ	Abellio
SN51TCJ	RATP - London	SN55HKD	RATP - London	SN59AWM	Abellio
SN51TCK	RATP - London	SN55HKE	RATP - London	SN59AWO	Abellio
SN51TCO	RATP - London	SN55HKF	RATP - London	SN59AWP	Abellio
SN51TCV	RATP - London	SN55HKG	RATP - London	SN59AWR	Abellio
SN51TCX	RATP - London	SN55HKH	RATP - London	SN59AWU	Abellio
SN51TCY	RATP - London	SN55HKJ	RATP - London	SN60BXX	RATP - London
SN51TDV	RATP - London	SN55HKK	RATP - London	SN60BXY	RATP - London
SN51TDX	RATP - London	SN55HKL	RATP - London	SN60BXZ	RATP - London
SN51TDZ	RATP - London	SN55HKM	RATP - London	SN60BYA	RATP - London
SN51UAD	Go-Ahead	SN55HKO	RATP - London	SN60BYB	RATP - London
SN51UAE	Go-Ahead	SN55HKP	RATP - London	SN60BYC	RATP - London
SN51UAF	Go-Ahead	SN55HKT	RATP - London	SN60BYD	RATP - London
SN51UAG	Go-Ahead	SN55HKU	RATP - London	SN60BYF	RATP - London
SN51UAH	Go-Ahead	SN55HKV	RATP - London	SN60BYG	RATP - London

SN60BYH	RATP - London	SN61BHU	Go-Ahead	SN61DDU	Go-Ahead
SN60BYJ	RATP - London	SN61BHV	Go-Ahead	SN61DDV	Go-Ahead
SN60BYK	RATP - London	SN61BHW	Go-Ahead	SN61DDX	Go-Ahead
SN60BYL	RATP - London	SN61BHX	Go-Ahead	SN61DDY	Go-Ahead
SN60BYM	RATP - London	SN61BHY	Go-Ahead	SN61DDZ	Go-Ahead
SN60BYO	RATP - London	SN61BHZ	Go-Ahead	SN61DEU	Go-Ahead
SN60BYP	RATP - London	SN61BJE	Go-Ahead	SN61DFA	Go-Ahead
SN60BYR	RATP - London	SN61BJF	Go-Ahead	SN61DFC	Go-Ahead
SN60BYS	RATP - London	SN61BJJ	Go-Ahead	SN61DFD	Go-Ahead
SN60BYT	RATP - London	SN61BJK	Go-Ahead	SN61DFE	Go-Ahead
SN60BYU	RATP - London	SN61BJO	Go-Ahead	SN61DFF	Go-Ahead
SN60BZA	Go-Ahead	SN61BJU	Go-Ahead	SN61DFG	Go-Ahead
SN60BZB	Go-Ahead	SN61BJV	Go-Ahead	SN61DFJ	Go-Ahead
SN60BZC	Go-Ahead	SN61BJX	Go-Ahead	SN61DFL	Abellio
SN60BZD	Go-Ahead	SN61BJY	Go-Ahead	SN61DFO	Abellio
SN60BZE	Go-Ahead	SN61BJZ	Go-Ahead	SN61DFP	Abellio
SN60BZF	Go-Ahead	SN61BKA	Go-Ahead	SN61DFU	Abellio
SN60BZG	Go-Ahead	SN61BKD	Go-Ahead	SN61DFV	Abellio
SN60BZH	Go-Ahead	SN61BKE	Go-Ahead	SN61DFX	Abellio
SN60BZJ	Go-Ahead	SN61BKF	Go-Ahead	SN61DFY	Abellio
SN60BZK	Go-Ahead	SN61BKG	Go-Ahead	SN61DFZ	Abellio
SN60BZL	Go-Ahead	SN61BKJ	Go-Ahead	SN61DGE	Abellio
SN60BZM	Go-Ahead	SN61BKK	Go-Ahead	SN61DGF	Abellio
SN60BZO	Go-Ahead	SN61BKL	Go-Ahead	SN61DGO	Abellio
SN60BZP	Go-Ahead	SN61BKO	Go-Ahead	SN61DGU	Abellio
SN60BZR	Go-Ahead	SN61BKU	Go-Ahead	SN61DGV	Abellio
SN60BZS	Go-Ahead	SN61BKV	Go-Ahead	SN61DGX	Abellio
SN60BZT	Go-Ahead	SN61BKX	Go-Ahead	SN61DGY	Abellio
SN60BZU	Go-Ahead	SN61BKY	Go-Ahead	SN61DGZ	Abellio
SN60BZV	Go-Ahead	SN61BKZ	Go-Ahead	SN61DHA	Abellio
SN60BZW	Go-Ahead	SN61BLJ	Go-Ahead	SN62AAF	Metroline
SN60BZX	Go-Ahead	SN61BLK	Go-Ahead	SN62AAK	Metroline
SN60BZY	Go-Ahead	SN61BLV	Go-Ahead	SN62AAO	Metroline
SN60EAX	RATP - London	SN61CXX	Abellio	SN62AAV	Metroline
SN60EAY	RATP - London	SN61CXY	Abellio	SN62DDE	Go-Ahead
SN60EBA	RATP - London	SN61CXZ	Abellio	SN62DDO	Go-Ahead
SN60EBC	RATP - London	SN61CYA	Abellio	SN62DDX	Go-Ahead
SN60EBD	RATP - London	SN61CYC	Abellio	SN62DFL	Go-Ahead
SN60EBF	RATP - London	SN61CYE	Abellio	SN62DFX	Go-Ahead
SN60EBG	RATP - London	SN61CYF	Abellio	SN62DGF	Go-Ahead
SN60EBJ	RATP - London	SN61CYG	Abellio	SN62DGU	Go-Ahead
SN60EBK	RATP - London	SN61CYH	Abellio	SN62DHA	Go-Ahead
SN60EBL	RATP - London	SN61CYJ	Abellio	SN62DHX	Go-Ahead
SN60EBM	RATP - London	SN61CYK	Abellio	SN62DHZ	Go-Ahead
SN60EBO	RATP - London	SN61CYL	Abellio	SN62DJO	Go-Ahead
SN60EBP	RATP - London	SN61CYO	Abellio	SN62DKJ	Go-Ahead
SN60EBU	RATP - London	SN61CYP	Abellio	SN62DLY	Go-Ahead
SN60EBV	RATP - London	SN61CYS	Abellio	SN62DLZ	Go-Ahead
SN60EBX	RATP - London	SN61CYT	Abellio	SN62DMV	Go-Ahead
SN60EBZ	RATP - London	SN61CYU	Abellio	SN62DND	HCT - CT Plus
SN60ECA	RATP - London	SN61CYV	Abellio	SN63JVM	Stagecoach
SN60ECC	RATP - London	SN61CYW	Abellio	SN63JVO	Stagecoach
SN60ECD	RATP - London	SN61CYX	Abellio	SN63JVP	Stagecoach
SN60ECE	RATP - London	SN61DAA	Go-Ahead	SN63JVR	Stagecoach
SN60ECF	RATP - London	SN61DAO	Go-Ahead	SN63JVT	Stagecoach
SN60ECJ	RATP - London	SN61DAU	Go-Ahead	SN63JVU	Stagecoach
SN60ECT	RATP - London	SN61DBO	Go-Ahead	SN63JVV	Stagecoach
SN60ECV	RATP - London	SN61DBU	Go-Ahead	SN63JVW	Stagecoach
SN61BGE	Go-Ahead	SN61DBV	Go-Ahead	SN63JVX	Stagecoach
SN61BGF	Go-Ahead	SN61DBX	Go-Ahead	SN63JVY	Stagecoach
SN61BGK	Go-Ahead	SN61DBY	Go-Ahead	SN63JVZ	Stagecoach
SN61BGO	Go-Ahead	SN61DBZ	Go-Ahead	SN63JWA	Stagecoach
SN61BGU	Go-Ahead	SN61DCE	Go-Ahead	SN63JWC	Stagecoach
SN61BGV	Go-Ahead	SN61DCO	Go-Ahead	SN63JWD	Stagecoach
SN61BGX	Go-Ahead	SN61DCU	Go-Ahead	SN63JWE	Stagecoach
SN61BGY	Go-Ahead	SN61DCV	Go-Ahead	SN63JWF	Stagecoach
SN61BGZ	Go-Ahead	SN61DCX	Go-Ahead	SN63JWG	Stagecoach
SN61BHA	Go-Ahead	SN61DCY	Go-Ahead	SN63JWJ	Stagecoach
SN61BHD	Go-Ahead	SN61DCZ	Go-Ahead	SN63JWK	Stagecoach
SN61BHE	Go-Ahead	SN61DDA	Go-Ahead	SN63JWL	Stagecoach
SN61BHF	Go-Ahead	SN61DDE	Go-Ahead	T202XBV	Original Tour
SN61BHJ	Go-Ahead	SN61DDF	Go-Ahead	T203XBV	Original Tour
SN61BHK	Go-Ahead	SN61DDJ	Go-Ahead	T204XBV	Original Tour
SN61BHL	Go-Ahead	SN61DDK	Go-Ahead	T205XBV	Original Tour
SN61BHO	Go-Ahead	SN61DDL	Go-Ahead	T206XBV	Original Tour
SN61BHP	Go-Ahead	SN61DDO	Go-Ahead	T207XBV	Original Tour

Reg	Operator	Reg	Operator	Reg	Operator
T208XBV	Original Tour	VLT60	Go-Ahead	W492WGH	Go-Ahead
T209XBV	Original Tour	VLT173	Arriva	W494WGH	Go-Ahead
T210XBV	Original Tour	VLT295	Arriva	W495WGH	Go-Ahead
T211XBV	Original Tour	VX10EBN	Arriva Southern Cs	W496WGH	Go-Ahead
T212XBV	Original Tour	VX10EBO	Arriva Southern Cs	W497WGH	Go-Ahead
T213XBV	Original Tour	VX10EBP	Arriva Southern Cs	W512WGH	Go-Ahead
T214XBV	Original Tour	VX10EBU	Arriva Southern Cs	W513WGH	Go-Ahead
T215XBV	Original Tour	VX10EBV	Arriva Southern Cs	W523WGH	Go-Ahead
T216XBV	Original Tour	VX10EBZ	Arriva Southern Cs	W529WGH	Go-Ahead
T217XBV	Original Tour	W116EON	RATP - London	W531WGH	Go-Ahead
T218XBV	Original Tour	W117EON	RATP - London	W532WGH	Go-Ahead
T219XBV	Original Tour	W122EON	RATP - London	W533WGH	Go-Ahead
T220XBV	Original Tour	W124EON	RATP - London	W534WGH	Go-Ahead
T310SMV	Metrobus	W126EON	RATP - London	W536WGH	Go-Ahead
T311SMV	Metrobus	W137EON	RATP - London	W537WGH	Go-Ahead
UAR247Y	Original Tour	W138EON	RATP - London	W538WGH	Go-Ahead
UAR776Y	Original Tour	W139EON	RATP - London	W539WGH	Go-Ahead
V177OOE	RATP - London	W141EON	RATP - London	W541WGH	Go-Ahead
V178OOE	RATP - London	W334VGX	Metrobus	W542WGH	Go-Ahead
V179OOE	RATP - London	W373WGJ	Arriva	W543WGH	Go-Ahead
V180OOE	RATP - London	W374WGJ	Arriva	W578DGU	Go-Ahead
V187OOE	RATP - London	W376WGJ	Arriva	W603UGM	Abellio
V188OOE	RATP - London	W377WGJ	Arriva	W996WGH	Go-Ahead
V190OOE	RATP - London	W378WGJ	Arriva	WLT324	Stagecoach
V194OOE	RATP - London	W379WGJ	Arriva	WLT348	Arriva
V203OOE	RATP - London	W381WGJ	Arriva	WLT372	Arriva
V204OOE	RATP - London	W382WGJ	Arriva	WLT385	Arriva
V205OOE	RATP - London	W383WGJ	Arriva	WLT461	Stagecoach
V206OOE	RATP - London	W384WGJ	Arriva	WLT554	Arriva
V207OOE	RATP - London	W385WGJ	Arriva	WLT652	Stagecoach
V208OOE	RATP - London	W386WGJ	Arriva	WLT664	Arriva
V258HBH	Arriva The Shires	W387WGJ	Arriva	WLT676	Arriva
V260HBH	Arriva The Shires	W388WGJ	Arriva	WLT719	Arriva
V301MDP	Abellio	W389WGJ	Arriva	WLT751	Arriva
V302MDP	Abellio	W399WGJ	Arriva	WLT807	Arriva
V305KGW	Abellio	W401WGH	Go-Ahead	WLT871	Stagecoach
V306MDP	Abellio	W402WGH	Go-Ahead	WLT888	Arriva
V307MDP	Abellio	W403WGH	Go-Ahead	WLT892	Arriva
V309KGW	Abellio	W404WGH	Go-Ahead	WLT895	Arriva
V309MDP	Abellio	W407WGJ	Arriva	WLT970	Arriva
V315KGW	Abellio	W408WGH	Go-Ahead	WLT997	Arriva
V325KGW	Abellio	W408WGJ	Arriva	X149FBB	Go-Ahead
V326DGT	Arriva	W409WGJ	Arriva	X151FBB	Go-Ahead
V327DGT	Arriva	W411WGJ	Arriva	X152FBB	Go-Ahead
V329DGT	Arriva	W412WGJ	Arriva	X153FBB	Go-Ahead
V329KGW	Abellio	W413WGJ	Arriva	X154FBB	Go-Ahead
V330DGT	Arriva	W414WGJ	Arriva	X157FBB	Go-Ahead
V331DGT	Arriva	W415WGH	Go-Ahead	X158FBB	Go-Ahead
V332DGT	Arriva	W432WGJ	Arriva	X159FBB	Go-Ahead
V335DGT	Arriva	W433WGJ	Arriva	X161FBB	Go-Ahead
V337DGT	Arriva	W435WGH	Go-Ahead	X162FBB	Go-Ahead
V338DGT	Arriva	W436WGJ	Arriva	X163FBB	Go-Ahead
V339DGT	Arriva	W437WGJ	Arriva	X164FBB	Go-Ahead
V341DGT	Arriva	W438WGJ	Arriva	X165FBB	Go-Ahead
V346DGT	Arriva	W448BCW	RATP - London	X166FBB	Go-Ahead
V347DGT	Arriva	W449BCW	RATP - London	X167FBB	Go-Ahead
V351DGT	Arriva	W451BCW	RATP - London	X168FBB	Go-Ahead
V352DGT	Arriva	W452BCW	RATP - London	X169FBB	Go-Ahead
V353DGT	Arriva	W453BCW	RATP - London	X311KRX	Abellio
V354DGT	Arriva	W454BCW	RATP - London	X313KRX	Abellio
V355DGT	Arriva	W457BCW	RATP - London	X314KRX	Abellio
V356DGT	Arriva	W459WGH	Go-Ahead	X322KRX	Abellio
V357DGT	Arriva	W461WGH	Go-Ahead	X342NNO	Stagecoach
V358DGT	Arriva	W462WGH	Go-Ahead	X344YGU	Metrobus
V359DGT	Arriva	W464WGH	Go-Ahead	X367NNO	Stagecoach
V361DGT	Arriva	W466WGH	Go-Ahead	X415FGP	Arriva
V362DGT	Arriva	W467WGH	Go-Ahead	X416FGP	Arriva
V363DGT	Arriva	W468WGH	Go-Ahead	X417FGP	Arriva
V364DGT	Arriva	W469WGH	Go-Ahead	X418FGP	Arriva
V365DGT	Arriva	W475WGH	Go-Ahead	X419FGP	Arriva
V628LGC	Arriva	W476WGH	Go-Ahead	X421FGP	Arriva
V633LGC	Arriva	W479WGH	Go-Ahead	X422FGP	Arriva
V640LGC	Arriva	W482WGH	Go-Ahead	X423FGP	Arriva
V650LGC	Arriva	W483WGH	Go-Ahead	X424FGP	Arriva
V660LGC	Arriva	W485WGH	Go-Ahead	X425FGP	Arriva
VLT32	Arriva	W486WGH	Go-Ahead	X426FGP	Arriva

Reg	Operator	Reg	Operator	Reg	Operator
X427FGP	Arriva	Y235HWF	Abellio	Y519UGC	Arriva
X428FGP	Arriva	Y235NLK	Metroline	Y522NHK	Stagecoach
X429FGP	Arriva	Y236NLK	Metroline	Y522UGC	Arriva
X431FGP	Arriva	Y238NLK	Metroline	Y523UGC	Arriva
X433FGP	Arriva	Y293TKJ	Arriva Southern Cs	Y524NHK	Stagecoach
X435FGP	Arriva	Y296TKJ	Arriva Southern Cs	Y529NHK	Stagecoach
X442FGP	Arriva	Y298TKJ	Arriva Southern Cs	Y529UGC	Arriva
X443FGP	Arriva	Y299TKJ	Arriva The Shires	Y532UGC	Original Tour
X445FGP	Arriva	Y301TKJ	Arriva The Shires	Y533UGC	Original Tour
X451FGP	Arriva	Y302TKJ	Arriva Southern Cs	Y541UGC	Original Tour
X452FGP	Arriva	Y359HMY	Metrobus	Y542UGC	Original Tour
X453FGP	Arriva	Y361HMY	Metrobus	Y543UGC	Original Tour
X454FGP	Arriva	Y362HMY	Metrobus	Y544UGC	Original Tour
X501GGO	Arriva	Y363HMY	Metrobus	Y546UGC	Original Tour
X503EGK	Go-Ahead	Y363NHK	Stagecoach	Y547UGC	Original Tour
X503GGO	Arriva	Y364HMY	Metrobus	Y548UGC	Original Tour
X504EGK	Go-Ahead	Y364NHK	Stagecoach	Y549UGC	Original Tour
X506EGK	Go-Ahead	Y365HMY	Metrobus	Y703TGH	Go-Ahead
X506GGO	Arriva	Y366HMY	Metrobus	Y729TGH	Go-Ahead
X507EGK	Go-Ahead	Y367HMY	Metrobus	Y731TGH	Go-Ahead
X507GGO	Arriva	Y368HMY	Metrobus	Y732TGH	Go-Ahead
X508GGO	Arriva	Y368NHK	Stagecoach	Y733TGH	Go-Ahead
X509EGK	Go-Ahead	Y369HMY	Metrobus	Y734TGH	Go-Ahead
X546EGK	Go-Ahead	Y36HWB	Abellio	Y735TGH	Go-Ahead
X547EGK	Go-Ahead	Y371HMY	Metrobus	Y736TGH	Go-Ahead
X548EGK	Go-Ahead	Y372HMY	Metrobus	Y737TGH	Go-Ahead
X549EGK	Go-Ahead	Y373HMY	Metrobus	Y738TGH	Go-Ahead
X551EGK	Go-Ahead	Y374HMY	Metrobus	Y744TGH	Go-Ahead
X552EGK	Go-Ahead	Y376HMY	Metrobus	Y745TGH	Go-Ahead
X553EGK	Go-Ahead	Y377HMY	Metrobus	Y748TGH	Go-Ahead
X554EGK	Go-Ahead	Y378HMY	Metrobus	Y801DGT	Arriva
X559EGK	Go-Ahead	Y379HMY	Metrobus	Y802DGT	Arriva
X561EGK	Go-Ahead	Y37HWB	Abellio	Y802TGH	Go-Ahead
X562EGK	Go-Ahead	Y38YVV	Abellio	Y803DGT	Arriva
X563EGK	Go-Ahead	Y395NHK	Stagecoach	Y804DGT	Arriva
X564EGK	Go-Ahead	Y397NHK	Stagecoach	Y805DGT	Arriva
X566EGK	Go-Ahead	Y398NHK	Stagecoach	Y806DGT	Arriva
X567EGK	Go-Ahead	Y401NHK	Stagecoach	Y809TGH	Go-Ahead
X569EGK	Go-Ahead	Y404NHK	Stagecoach	Y814TGH	Go-Ahead
X584ORV	HCT - CT Plus	Y407NHK	Stagecoach	Y815TGH	Go-Ahead
X585ORV	HCT - CT Plus	Y409NHK	Stagecoach	Y816TGH	Go-Ahead
X586ORV	HCT - CT Plus	Y434NHK	Stagecoach	Y817TGH	Go-Ahead
X587ORV	HCT - CT Plus	Y441NHK	Stagecoach	Y818TGH	Go-Ahead
X588ORV	HCT - CT Plus	Y445NHK	Stagecoach	Y819TGH	Go-Ahead
X589EGK	Go-Ahead	Y447NHK	Stagecoach	Y821TGH	Go-Ahead
X589ORV	HCT - CT Plus	Y448NHK	Stagecoach	Y822TGH	Go-Ahead
X591ORV	HCT - CT Plus	Y449NHK	Stagecoach	Y823TGH	Go-Ahead
X592ORV	HCT - CT Plus	Y452NHK	Stagecoach	Y824TGH	Go-Ahead
X593ORV	HCT - CT Plus	Y452UGC	Arriva	Y825TGH	Go-Ahead
X594ORV	HCT - CT Plus	Y453NHK	Stagecoach	Y826TGH	Go-Ahead
X595ORV	HCT - CT Plus	Y454NHK	Stagecoach	Y851TGH	Go-Ahead
X599EGK	Go-Ahead	Y471UGC	Arriva	Y864KTF	Abellio
X615EGK	Go-Ahead	Y473UGC	Arriva	Y983TGH	Go-Ahead
X616EGK	Go-Ahead	Y474UGC	Arriva	Y986TGH	Go-Ahead
X656EGK	Go-Ahead	Y475UGC	Arriva	Y987TGH	Go-Ahead
X657LLX	Metroline	Y477UGC	Arriva	YE06HNT	Arriva The Shires
X705EGK	Go-Ahead	Y478UGC	Arriva	YE06HNU	Arriva The Shires
X707EGK	Go-Ahead	Y481UGC	Arriva	YE06HPA	Arriva The Shires
X745EGK	Go-Ahead	Y483UGC	Arriva	YE06HPC	Arriva The Shires
Y133HWB	Abellio	Y486UGC	Arriva	YE06HPF	Arriva The Shires
Y134HWB	Abellio	Y487UGC	Arriva	YE06HPJ	Arriva The Shires
Y143NLK	Metroline	Y489UGC	Arriva	YE06HPK	Arriva The Shires
Y146NLK	Metroline	Y491UGC	Arriva	YE06HPL	Arriva The Shires
Y149NLK	Metroline	Y493UGC	Arriva	YE06HPN	Arriva The Shires
Y169NLK	Metroline	Y494UGC	Arriva	YE06HPO	Arriva The Shires
Y184NLK	Metroline	Y495UGC	Arriva	YE06HPP	Arriva The Shires
Y185NLK	Metroline	Y497UGC	Arriva	YE06HPU	Arriva The Shires
Y186NLK	Metroline	Y498UGC	Arriva	YE06HPX	Arriva Southern Cs
Y191NLK	Metroline	Y499UGC	Arriva	YE06HPY	Arriva Southern Cs
Y195NLK	Metroline	Y511UGC	Arriva	YE06HPZ	Arriva Southern Cs
Y201NLK	Metroline	Y512UGC	Arriva	YE06HRA	Arriva The Shires
Y203NLK	Metroline	Y513UGC	Arriva	YE06HRC	Arriva The Shires
Y207NLK	Metroline	Y514UGC	Arriva	YE06HRD	Arriva The Shires
Y232NLK	Metroline	Y516UGC	Arriva	YE06HRF	Arriva The Shires
Y233NLK	Metroline	Y517UGC	Arriva	YE06HRG	Arriva The Shires
Y234NLK	Metroline	Y518UGC	Arriva	YE06HRJ	Arriva The Shires

Reg	Operator	Reg	Operator	Reg	Operator
YE52FGU	RATP - Quality Line	YJ11TVP	Original Tour	YJ60PFO	HCT - CT Plus
YE52FHL	RATP - Quality Line	YJ11TVT	Original Tour	YJ61MKA	HCT - CT Plus
YE52FHM	RATP - Quality Line	YJ11TVU	Original Tour	YJ62FUD	RATP - Quality Line
YE52FHN	RATP - Quality Line	YJ11TVV	Original Tour	YJ62FUG	RATP - Quality Line
YE52FHO	RATP - Quality Line	YJ11TVW	Original Tour	YJ62FVN	RATP - Quality Line
YE52FHP	RATP - Quality Line	YJ11TVX	Original Tour	YJ62FVT	RATP - Quality Line
YE52FHR	RATP - Quality Line	YJ12GVR	HCT - CT Plus	YJ62FWB	RATP - Quality Line
YE52FHS	RATP - Quality Line	YJ12GVT	HCT - CT Plus	YJ62FXA	RATP - Quality Line
YJ06LDK	Arriva The Shires	YJ12GVU	HCT - CT Plus	YJ62FXG	RATP - Quality Line
YJ06LFE	Arriva The Shires	YJ12GVV	HCT - CT Plus	YJ62FXK	RATP - Quality Line
YJ06LFF	Arriva The Shires	YJ12GVW	HCT - CT Plus	YK10AVV	HCT - CT Plus
YJ06LFG	Arriva The Shires	YJ12GVX	HCT - CT Plus	YM55SWU	Metrobus
YJ06LFH	Arriva The Shires	YJ12GVY	HCT - CT Plus	YM55SWV	Metrobus
YJ06LFK	Arriva The Shires	YJ12GVZ	HCT - CT Plus	YM55SWX	Metrobus
YJ06LFL	Arriva The Shires	YJ12PKV	RATP - Quality Line	YM55SWY	Metrobus
YJ06YRP	Arriva The Shires	YJ12PKX	RATP - Quality Line	YM55SXA	Metrobus
YJ06YRR	Arriva The Shires	YJ12PKY	RATP - Quality Line	YM55SXB	Metrobus
YJ06YRS	Arriva The Shires	YJ12PKZ	RATP - Quality Line	YM55SXC	Metrobus
YJ06YRT	Arriva The Shires	YJ12PLF	RATP - Quality Line	YM55SXD	Metrobus
YJ06YRU	Arriva The Shires	YJ13HJN	RATP - Quality Line	YM55SXE	Metrobus
YJ08PGO	Stagecoach	YJ54CFG	Arriva The Shires	YM55SXF	Metrobus
YJ09EYT	RATP - London	YJ55WOA	Arriva The Shires	YM55SXH	Metrobus
YJ09EYU	RATP - London	YJ55WOB	Arriva The Shires	YM55SXO	Metrobus
YJ09EYV	RATP - London	YJ55WOC	Arriva The Shires	YM55SXP	Metrobus
YJ09EYW	RATP - London	YJ55WOD	Arriva The Shires	YM55SXR	Metrobus
YJ09EYX	RATP - London	YJ55WOH	Arriva The Shires	YN03DFA	Metrobus
YJ09EYY	RATP - London	YJ55WOM	Arriva The Shires	YN03DFC	Metrobus
YJ09EYZ	RATP - London	YJ55WOR	Arriva The Shires	YN03DFD	Metrobus
YJ09EZA	RATP - London	YJ55WOU	Arriva The Shires	YN03DFE	Metrobus
YJ09EZB	RATP - London	YJ55WOV	Arriva The Shires	YN03DFG	Metrobus
YJ09EZC	RATP - London	YJ55WOX	Arriva The Shires	YN03DFJ	Metrobus
YJ09EZD	RATP - London	YJ55WPO	Arriva The Shires	YN03DFK	Metrobus
YJ09EZE	RATP - London	YJ56WVF	Metrobus	YN03DFU	Metrobus
YJ09EZF	RATP - London	YJ56WVG	Metrobus	YN03DFV	Metrobus
YJ09MHK	RATP - Quality Line	YJ58PHY	RATP - London	YN03DFX	Metrobus
YJ09MHL	RATP - Quality Line	YJ58PHZ	RATP - London	YN03DFY	Metrobus
YJ09MHM	RATP - Quality Line	YJ58PJO	RATP - London	YN03UWU	Metrobus
YJ09MHN	RATP - Quality Line	YJ58PJU	RATP - London	YN03UWY	Metrobus
YJ09MHO	RATP - Quality Line	YJ58VBA	RATP - London	YN03WPM	Metrobus
YJ09MHU	RATP - Quality Line	YJ58VBB	RATP - London	YN03WPP	Metrobus
YJ09MHV	RATP - Quality Line	YJ58VBC	RATP - London	YN03WPR	Metrobus
YJ09MHX	RATP - Quality Line	YJ58VBD	RATP - London	YN03ZXF	RATP - Quality Line
YJ10EYF	HCT - CT Plus	YJ58VBE	RATP - London	YN05HCA	Metrobus
YJ10EYG	HCT - CT Plus	YJ58VBF	RATP - London	YN05HCC	Metrobus
YJ10EYH	HCT - CT Plus	YJ58VBG	RATP - London	YN05HCD	Metrobus
YJ10EYK	HCT - CT Plus	YJ58VBK	RATP - London	YN05HCE	Metrobus
YJ10EYL	HCT - CT Plus	YJ58VBL	RATP - London	YN05HCF	Metrobus
YJ11EHG	RATP - London	YJ58VBM	RATP - London	YN05HCG	Metrobus
YJ11EHH	RATP - London	YJ58VBN	RATP - London	YN06JXR	Metrobus
YJ11EHK	RATP - London	YJ58VBO	RATP - London	YN06JXS	Metrobus
YJ11EHL	RATP - London	YJ58VBP	RATP - London	YN06JXT	Metrobus
YJ11EHM	RATP - London	YJ58VBT	RATP - London	YN06JXU	Metrobus
YJ11EHN	RATP - London	YJ58VBU	RATP - London	YN06JXV	Metrobus
YJ11EHO	RATP - London	YJ58VBV	RATP - London	YN06JXW	Metrobus
YJ11EHP	RATP - London	YJ58VBX	RATP - London	YN06JXX	Metrobus
YJ11EHR	RATP - London	YJ58VBY	RATP - London	YN06JXY	Metrobus
YJ11EHS	RATP - London	YJ58VBZ	RATP - London	YN06JXZ	Metrobus
YJ11EHT	RATP - London	YJ59NRN	HCT - CT Plus	YN06JYB	Metrobus
YJ11EHU	RATP - London	YJ59NRO	HCT - CT Plus	YN06JYC	Metrobus
YJ11EHV	RATP - London	YJ60KGA	RATP - Quality Line	YN06JYD	Metrobus
YJ11EHW	RATP - London	YJ60KGE	RATP - Quality Line	YN06JYE	Metrobus
YJ11EHX	RATP - London	YJ60KGF	RATP - Quality Line	YN06JYF	Metrobus
YJ11EHZ	RATP - London	YJ60KGG	RATP - Quality Line	YN06JYG	Metrobus
YJ11EJA	RATP - Quality Line	YJ60KGK	RATP - Quality Line	YN06JYH	Metrobus
YJ11EJC	RATP - Quality Line	YJ60KGN	RATP - Quality Line	YN06JYJ	Metrobus
YJ11EJD	RATP - Quality Line	YJ60KGO	RATP - Quality Line	YN06JYK	Metrobus
YJ11TVA	Original Tour	YJ60KGP	RATP - Quality Line	YN06JYL	Metrobus
YJ11TVC	Original Tour	YJ60LRX	HCT - CT Plus	YN06JYO	Metrobus
YJ11TVD	Original Tour	YJ60LRY	HCT - CT Plus	YN07EXF	Metrobus
YJ11TVE	Original Tour	YJ60PFA	HCT - CT Plus	YN07EXG	Metrobus
YJ11TVF	Original Tour	YJ60PFD	HCT - CT Plus	YN07EXH	Metrobus
YJ11TVK	Original Tour	YJ60PFE	HCT - CT Plus	YN07EXK	Metrobus
YJ11TVL	Original Tour	YJ60PFF	HCT - CT Plus	YN07EXM	Metrobus
YJ11TVM	Original Tour	YJ60PFG	HCT - CT Plus	YN07EXO	Metrobus
YJ11TVN	Original Tour	YJ60PFK	HCT - CT Plus	YN07LKF	Metrobus
YJ11TVO	Original Tour	YJ60PFN	HCT - CT Plus	YN07LKG	Metrobus

Reg	Operator	Reg	Operator	Reg	Operator	Reg	Operator
YN08DEU	RATP - London	YN53RXT		Metrobus	YN55NKT	RATP - London
YN08DFJ	Metrobus	YN53RXU		Metrobus	YN55NKU	RATP - London
YN08DFK	Metrobus	YN53RXV		Metrobus	YN55NKW	RATP - London
YN08DFL	Metrobus	YN53RXW		Metrobus	YN55NKX	RATP - London
YN08DFO	Metrobus	YN53RXX		Metrobus	YN55NLA	RATP - London
YN08DFP	Metrobus	YN53RXY		Metrobus	YN55NLC	RATP - London
YN08DFU	Metrobus	YN53RXZ		Metrobus	YN55NLD	RATP - London
YN08DFV	Metrobus	YN53RYA		Metrobus	YN55NLE	RATP - London
YN08DFX	Metrobus	YN53RYB		Metrobus	YN55NLG	RATP - London
YN08DFY	Metrobus	YN53RYC		Metrobus	YN55NLJ	RATP - London
YN08DFZ	Metrobus	YN53RYD		Metrobus	YN55NLK	RATP - London
YN08DHA	RATP - London	YN53RYF		Metrobus	YN55NLL	RATP - London
YN08DHC	RATP - London	YN53RYH		Metrobus	YN55NLM	RATP - London
YN08DHD	RATP - London	YN53RYK		Metrobus	YN55NLO	RATP - London
YN08DHE	RATP - London	YN53RYM		Metrobus	YN55NLP	RATP - London
YN08DHF	RATP - London	YN53RYP		Metrobus	YN55NLR	RATP - London
YN08DHG	RATP - London	YN53RYR		Metrobus	YN55PWJ	Metrobus
YN08DHJ	RATP - London	YN53RYT		Metrobus	YN55PWK	Metrobus
YN08DHK	RATP - London	YN53RYV		Metrobus	YN55PWL	Metrobus
YN08DHL	RATP - London	YN53RYW		Metrobus	YN55PWO	Metrobus
YN08DHM	RATP - London	YN53RYX		Metrobus	YN55PWU	Metrobus
YN08DHO	RATP - London	YN53RYY		Metrobus	YN55PWV	Metrobus
YN08DHP	RATP - London	YN53RYZ		Metrobus	YN55PWX	Metrobus
YN08DHU	RATP - London	YN53RZA		Metrobus	YN55PZC	Metrobus
YN08DHV	RATP - London	YN53RZB		Metrobus	YN55PZD	Metrobus
YN08DHX	RATP - London	YN53RZC		Metrobus	YN55PZE	Metrobus
YN08DHY	RATP - London	YN53RZD		Metrobus	YN55PZF	Metrobus
YN08DHZ	RATP - London	YN53RZE		Metrobus	YN55PZG	Metrobus
YN08DMV	RATP - Quality Line	YN53RZF		Metrobus	YN55PZH	Metrobus
YN08DMX	RATP - Quality Line	YN53SUF	RATP - Quality Line	YN55PZJ	Metrobus
YN08DMY	Go-Ahead	YN53SVK	RATP - Quality Line	YN55PZL	Metrobus
YN08MRV	RATP - London	YN53SVL	RATP - Quality Line	YN55PZM	Metrobus
YN08MRX	RATP - London	YN53SVO	RATP - Quality Line	YN55PZO	Metrobus
YN08MRY	RATP - London	YN53SVP	RATP - Quality Line	YN55PZP	Metrobus
YN08MTU	RATP - London	YN53SVR	RATP - Quality Line	YN55PZR	Metrobus
YN08OAS	Metrobus	YN53SWF	RATP - Quality Line	YN55PZU	Metrobus
YN08OAV	Metrobus	YN53USG		Metrobus	YN55PZV	Metrobus
YN08OAW	Metrobus	YN53ZXA	RATP - Quality Line	YN55PZW	Metrobus
YN08OAX	Metrobus	YN53ZXB	RATP - Quality Line	YN55PZX	Metrobus
YN08OAY	Metrobus	YN54AJU		Metrobus	YN56FBA	RATP - London
YN08OAZ	Metrobus	YN54AJV		Metrobus	YN56FBB	RATP - London
YN08OBP	Metrobus	YN54AJX		Metrobus	YN56FBO	RATP - London
YN08OBR	Metrobus	YN54AJY		Metrobus	YN56FBU	RATP - London
YN51KUU	Abellio	YN54OAA		Transdev	YN56FBW	RATP - London
YN51KUV	Abellio	YN54OAB		Transdev	YN56FBX	RATP - London
YN51KUW	Abellio	YN54OAC		Transdev	YN56FBY	RATP - London
YN51KVA	Abellio	YN54OAE		Transdev	YN56FBZ	RATP - London
YN51KVD	Abellio	YN54OAG		Transdev	YN56FCA	RATP - London
YN51KVG	Abellio	YN54OAH		Transdev	YN56FCB	RATP - London
YN51KVH	Abellio	YN55NHT		Transdev	YN56FCD	RATP - London
YN51KVK	Abellio	YN55NHU		Transdev	YN56FCE	RATP - London
YN51KVL	Abellio	YN55NHV		Transdev	YN56FCF	RATP - London
YN51KVO	Abellio	YN55NHX		Transdev	YN56FCG	RATP - London
YN51KVP	Abellio	YN55NHY		Transdev	YN56FCJ	RATP - London
YN51KVS	Abellio	YN55NHZ		Transdev	YN56FDA	Metrobus
YN51KVU	Abellio	YN55NJE		Transdev	YN56FDC	Metrobus
YN51KVW	Abellio	YN55NJF		Transdev	YN56FDD	Metrobus
YN51KVX	Abellio	YN55NJK		Transdev	YN56FDE	Metrobus
YN51KVZ	Abellio	YN55NJU		Transdev	YN56FDF	Metrobus
YN51KWA	Abellio	YN55NJV		Transdev	YN56FDG	Metrobus
YN51KWB	Abellio	YN55NKA		Transdev	YN56FDJ	Metrobus
YN51KWC	Abellio	YN55NKC		Transdev	YN56FDK	Metrobus
YN51KWD	Abellio	YN55NKD		Transdev	YN56FDL	Metrobus
YN51KWE	Abellio	YN55NKE		Transdev	YN56FDM	Metrobus
YN51KWF	Abellio	YN55NKF		Transdev	YN56FDO	Metrobus
YN51KWG	Abellio	YN55NKG		Transdev	YN56FDP	Metrobus
YN53RXF	Metrobus	YN55NKH		Transdev	YN56FDU	Metrobus
YN53RXG	Metrobus	YN55NKJ		Transdev	YN56FDV	Metrobus
YN53RXH	Metrobus	YN55NKK		Transdev	YN56FDX	Metrobus
YN53RXJ	Metrobus	YN55NKL		Transdev	YN56FDY	Metrobus
YN53RXK	Metrobus	YN55NKM	RATP - London	YN56FDZ	Metrobus
YN53RXL	Metrobus	YN55NKM		Transdev	YN56FEF	Metrobus
YN53RXM	Metrobus	YN55NKO	RATP - London	YN56FEG	Metrobus
YN53RXO	Metrobus	YN55NKP	RATP - London	YN58BNA	Metrobus
YN53RXP	Metrobus	YN55NKR	RATP - London	YN62CLF	Metrobus
YN53RXR	Metrobus	YN55NKS	RATP - London	YP02LCC	Abellio

Reg	Operator	Reg	Operator	Reg	Operator
YP02LCF	Abellio	YR59FZC	RATP - London	YT09BMZ	RATP - London
YP52CTO	Metrobus	YR59FZD	RATP - London	YT09BNA	RATP - London
YP58ACF	RATP - London	YR59FZE	RATP - London	YT09BNB	RATP - London
YP58ACJ	RATP - London	YR59FZF	RATP - London	YT09BND	RATP - London
YP58ACO	RATP - London	YR59FZG	RATP - London	YT09BNE	RATP - London
YP58UFV	Metrobus	YR59NPA	HCT - CT Plus	YT09BNF	RATP - London
YP59ODS	RATP - London	YR59NPC	HCT - CT Plus	YT09BNJ	RATP - London
YP59ODT	RATP - London	YR59NPD	HCT - CT Plus	YT09BNK	RATP - London
YP59ODU	RATP - London	YR59NPE	HCT - CT Plus	YT09BNL	RATP - London
YP59ODV	RATP - London	YR59NPF	HCT - CT Plus	YT09BNN	RATP - London
YP59ODW	RATP - London	YR59NPG	HCT - CT Plus	YT09ZCA	RATP - London
YP59ODX	RATP - London	YR59NPJ	HCT - CT Plus	YT09ZCE	RATP - London
YP59OEA	RATP - London	YR59NPK	HCT - CT Plus	YT09ZCF	RATP - London
YP59OEB	RATP - London	YR59NPN	HCT - CT Plus	YT09ZCJ	RATP - London
YP59OEC	RATP - London	YR59NPO	HCT - CT Plus	YT09ZCK	RATP - London
YP59OED	RATP - London	YR61RPU	Metroline	YT09ZCL	RATP - London
YP59OEE	RATP - London	YR61RPV	Metroline	YT09ZCN	RATP - London
YP59OEF	RATP - London	YR61RPX	Metroline	YT09ZCO	RATP - London
YP59OEG	RATP - London	YR61RPY	Metroline	YT09ZCU	RATP - London
YP59OEH	RATP - London	YR61RPZ	Metroline	YT10UWA	RATP - London
YP59OEJ	RATP - London	YR61RRO	Metroline	YT10UWB	RATP - London
YP59OEK	RATP - London	YR61RRU	Metroline	YT10UWD	RATP - London
YP59OEL	RATP - London	YR61RRV	Metroline	YT10UWF	RATP - London
YP59OEM	RATP - London	YR61RRX	Metroline	YT10UWG	RATP - London
YP59OEN	RATP - London	YR61RRY	Metroline	YT10UWH	RATP - London
YP59OEO	RATP - London	YR61RRZ	Metroline	YT10XBU	RATP - London
YP59OER	RATP - London	YR61RSO	Metroline	YT10XBV	RATP - London
YP59OES	RATP - London	YR61RSU	Metroline	YT10XBW	RATP - London
YP59OET	RATP - London	YR61RSV	Metroline	YT10XBX	RATP - London
YP59OEU	RATP - London	YR61RSX	Metroline	YT10XBY	RATP - London
YP59OEV	RATP - London	YR61RSY	Metroline	YT10XBZ	RATP - London
YP59OEW	RATP - London	YR61RSZ	Metroline	YT10XCA	RATP - London
YP59OEX	RATP - London	YR61RTO	Metroline	YT10XCB	RATP - London
YP59OEY	RATP - London	YR61RTU	Metroline	YT10XCC	RATP - London
YP59OEZ	RATP - London	YR61RTV	Metroline	YT10XCD	RATP - London
YR10BCE	Metrobus	YR61RTX	Metroline	YT10XCE	RATP - London
YR10BCF	Metrobus	YR61RTZ	Metroline	YT10XCF	RATP - London
YR10BCK	Metrobus	YR61RUA	Metroline	YT10XCG	RATP - London
YR10BCO	Metrobus	YR61RUC	Metroline	YT10XCH	RATP - London
YR10BCU	Metrobus	YR61RUH	Metroline	YT10XCJ	RATP - London
YR10FFW	RATP - London	YR61RUJ	Metroline	YT10XCK	RATP - London
YR10FFX	RATP - London	YR61RUO	Metroline	YT10XCL	RATP - London
YR10FFY	RATP - London	YR61RUU	Metroline	YT10XCM	RATP - London
YR10FFZ	RATP - London	YR61RUV	Metroline	YT10XCN	RATP - London
YR10FGA	RATP - London	YR61RUW	Metroline	YT10XCO	RATP - London
YR10FGC	RATP - London	YR61RUY	Metroline	YT59DXY	RATP - London
YR10FGD	RATP - London	YR61RVA	Metroline	YT59DXZ	RATP - London
YR10FGE	RATP - London	YR61RVC	Metroline	YT59DYA	Metrobus
YR10FGF	RATP - London	YR61RVE	Metroline	YT59DYB	Metrobus
YR10FGG	RATP - London	YR61RVF	Metroline	YT59DYC	Metrobus
YR10FGJ	RATP - London	YR61RVJ	Metroline	YT59DYD	Metrobus
YR10FGK	RATP - London	YR61RVK	Metroline	YT59DYF	Metrobus
YR10FGM	RATP - London	YR61RVL	Metroline	YT59DYG	Metrobus
YR10FGN	RATP - London	YR61RVM	Metroline	YT59DYH	Metrobus
YR10FGO	RATP - London	YT09BJU	RATP - London	YT59DYJ	Metrobus
YR10FGP	RATP - London	YT09BJV	RATP - London	YT59DYM	Metrobus
YR52VFH	Go-Ahead	YT09BJX	RATP - London	YT59DYN	Metrobus
YR52VFJ	Go-Ahead	YT09BJY	RATP - London	YT59DYO	Metrobus
YR52VFK	Go-Ahead	YT09BKA	RATP - London	YT59DYP	Metrobus
YR52VFL	Go-Ahead	YT09BKD	Metrobus	YT59DYS	Metrobus
YR52VFM	Go-Ahead	YT09BKE	Metrobus	YT59DYU	Metrobus
YR52VFN	Go-Ahead	YT09BKF	Metrobus	YT59DYV	Metrobus
YR58SNY	Metrobus	YT09BKG	Metrobus	YT59DYW	Metrobus
YR58SNZ	Metrobus	YT09BKJ	Metrobus	YT59DYX	RATP - London
YR59FYO	RATP - London	YT09BKK	Metrobus	YT59DYY	RATP - London
YR59FYP	RATP - London	YT09BKL	Metrobus	YT59PBF	RATP - London
YR59FYS	RATP - London	YT09BKN	Metrobus	YT59PBO	RATP - London
YR59FYT	RATP - London	YT09BKO	Metrobus	YT59PBU	RATP - London
YR59FYU	RATP - London	YT09BKU	Metrobus	YT59PBV	RATP - London
YR59FYV	RATP - London	YT09BKV	Metrobus	YT59PBX	RATP - London
YR59FYW	RATP - London	YT09BKX	Metrobus	YT59PBY	RATP - London
YR59FYX	RATP - London	YT09BKY	Metrobus	YT59PBZ	RATP - London
YR59FYY	RATP - London	YT09BKZ	Metrobus	YT59PCF	RATP - London
YR59FYZ	RATP - London	YT09BMO	RATP - London	YT59PCO	RATP - London
YR59FZA	RATP - London	YT09BMU	RATP - London	YT59PCU	RATP - London
YR59FZB	RATP - London	YT09BMY	RATP - London	YT59RXR	Transdev

YT59RXS	Transdev	YX08FKT	Dial-a-Ride	YX09EUF	Dial-a-Ride
YT59RXU	Transdev	YX08FKU	Dial-a-Ride	YX09EUH	Dial-a-Ride
YT59RXV	Transdev	YX08FKV	Dial-a-Ride	YX09EUJ	Dial-a-Ride
YT59RXW	Transdev	YX08FKW	Dial-a-Ride	YX09EUK	Dial-a-Ride
YT59RXX	Transdev	YX08FKZ	Dial-a-Ride	YX09EUL	Dial-a-Ride
YT59RXY	Transdev	YX08GVT	Dial-a-Ride	YX09EUP	Dial-a-Ride
YT59RXZ	Transdev	YX08GVU	Dial-a-Ride	YX09EUR	Dial-a-Ride
YT59RYA	Transdev	YX08GVV	Dial-a-Ride	YX09EUT	Dial-a-Ride
YT59RYB	Transdev	YX08GVW	Dial-a-Ride	YX09EUW	Dial-a-Ride
YT59RYC	Transdev	YX08GVY	Dial-a-Ride	YX09EUY	Dial-a-Ride
YT59RYD	Transdev	YX08GVZ	Dial-a-Ride	YX09EUZ	Dial-a-Ride
YT59RYF	Transdev	YX08GWA	Dial-a-Ride	YX09EVB	Dial-a-Ride
YT59RYG	Transdev	YX08GWC	Dial-a-Ride	YX09EVC	Dial-a-Ride
YT59RYH	Transdev	YX08GWF	Dial-a-Ride	YX09EVF	Dial-a-Ride
YT59RYJ	Transdev	YX08GWG	Dial-a-Ride	YX09EVK	Dial-a-Ride
YT59RYK	Transdev	YX08KXJ	Dial-a-Ride	YX09FKS	Metroline
YT59RYM	Transdev	YX08KXK	Dial-a-Ride	YX09FKT	Metroline
YT59RYN	Transdev	YX08KXL	Dial-a-Ride	YX09FKU	Metroline
YT59RYO	Transdev	YX08KXM	Dial-a-Ride	YX09FKV	Metroline
YT59SFF	RATP - London	YX08KXN	Dial-a-Ride	YX09FKW	Metroline
YT59SFK	RATP - London	YX08KXP	Dial-a-Ride	YX09FKY	Metroline
YT59SFN	RATP - London	YX08KXR	Dial-a-Ride	YX09FLA	Metroline
YT59SFO	RATP - London	YX08KXT	Dial-a-Ride	YX09FLB	Metroline
YT59SFU	RATP - London	YX08KXW	Dial-a-Ride	YX09FLC	Metroline
YT59SFV	RATP - London	YX08MDV	RATP - London	YX09FLD	Metroline
YT59SFX	RATP - London	YX08MDY	RATP - London	YX09FLE	Metroline
YT59SFY	RATP - London	YX08MDZ	RATP - London	YX09FLF	Metroline
YT59SFZ	RATP - London	YX08MEU	RATP - London	YX09FLG	Metroline
YT59SGO	RATP - London	YX08MEV	RATP - London	YX09FLH	Metroline
YT59SGU	RATP - London	YX08MFA	RATP - London	YX09FLJ	Metroline
YT59SGV	RATP - London	YX08MFK	RATP - London	YX09FLK	Metroline
YT59SGX	RATP - London	YX08MFN	RATP - London	YX09FLL	Metroline
YT59SGY	RATP - London	YX08MFO	RATP - London	YX09FLM	Metroline
YT59SGZ	RATP - London	YX08MHM	RATP - London	YX09FLN	Metroline
YT59SHJ	RATP - London	YX09AEA	Metroline	YX09FLP	Metroline
YT59SHV	RATP - London	YX09AEB	Metroline	YX09FLR	Metroline
YU02GHA	Go-Ahead	YX09AEC	Metroline	YX09FLV	Metroline
YU02GHD	Go-Ahead	YX09AED	Metroline	YX09FLW	Metroline
YU02GHG	Go-Ahead	YX09AEE	Metroline	YX09FLZ	Metroline
YU02GHH	Go-Ahead	YX09AEF	Metroline	YX09FMA	Metroline
YU02GHJ	Go-Ahead	YX09AEG	Metroline	YX09FMC	Metroline
YU02GHK	Go-Ahead	YX09AEJ	Metroline	YX09FMD	Metroline
YU02GHN	Go-Ahead	YX09AEK	Metroline	YX09FME	Metroline
YU02GHO	Go-Ahead	YX09AEL	Metroline	YX09FMF	Metroline
YU52XVK	Metrobus	YX09AEM	Metroline	YX09FMG	Metroline
YU52XVR	Metrobus	YX09AEN	Metroline	YX09FMJ	Metroline
YV03PZE	Metrobus	YX09AEO	Metroline	YX09FMK	Metroline
YV03PZF	Metrobus	YX09AEP	Metroline	YX09FML	Metroline
YV03PZG	Metrobus	YX09AET	Metroline	YX09FMM	Metroline
YV03PZH	Metrobus	YX09AEU	Metroline	YX09FMO	Metroline
YV03PZJ	Metrobus	YX09AEV	Metroline	YX09FMP	Metroline
YV03PZK	Metrobus	YX09AEW	Metroline	YX09FMU	Metroline
YV03PZL	Metrobus	YX09AEY	Metroline	YX09FMV	Metroline
YV03PZM	Metrobus	YX09AEZ	Metroline	YX09FNJ	Metroline
YV03PZW	Metrobus	YX09AFA	Metroline	YX09FNK	Metroline
YV03PZX	Metrobus	YX09AFE	Metroline	YX09HJJ	RATP - London
YV03PZY	Metrobus	YX09AFF	Metroline	YX09HJK	RATP - London
YV03PZZ	Metrobus	YX09AFJ	Metroline	YX09HJN	RATP - London
YV03RAU	Metrobus	YX09AFK	Metroline	YX09HJO	RATP - London
YV03RAX	Metrobus	YX09ESY	Dial-a-Ride	YX09HJU	RATP - London
YV03RBF	Metrobus	YX09ETA	Dial-a-Ride	YX09HJV	RATP - London
YV03RBU	Metrobus	YX09ETD	Dial-a-Ride	YX09HJY	RATP - London
YV03RBX	Metrobus	YX09ETE	Dial-a-Ride	YX09HJZ	RATP - London
YV03RCY	Metrobus	YX09ETF	Dial-a-Ride	YX09HKA	RATP - London
YV03RCZ	Metrobus	YX09ETJ	Dial-a-Ride	YX09HKB	RATP - London
YX08FKE	Dial-a-Ride	YX09ETK	Dial-a-Ride	YX09HKC	RATP - London
YX08FKF	Dial-a-Ride	YX09ETL	Dial-a-Ride	YX09HKD	RATP - London
YX08FKG	Dial-a-Ride	YX09ETO	Dial-a-Ride	YX09HKE	RATP - London
YX08FKJ	Dial-a-Ride	YX09ETR	Dial-a-Ride	YX09HKF	RATP - London
YX08FKK	Dial-a-Ride	YX09ETU	Dial-a-Ride	YX09HKG	RATP - London
YX08FKL	Dial-a-Ride	YX09ETV	Dial-a-Ride	YX09HKH	RATP - London
YX08FKM	Dial-a-Ride	YX09ETY	Dial-a-Ride	YX09HKJ	RATP - London
YX08FKO	Dial-a-Ride	YX09ETZ	Dial-a-Ride	YX09HKK	RATP - London
YX08FKP	Dial-a-Ride	YX09EUA	Dial-a-Ride	YX09HKL	RATP - London
YX08FKR	Dial-a-Ride	YX09EUB	Dial-a-Ride	YX09HKM	RATP - London
YX08FKS	Dial-a-Ride	YX09EUC	Dial-a-Ride	YX09HKN	RATP - London

Reg	Operator	Reg	Operator	Reg	Operator
YX09HKO	RATP - London	YX10FFJ	Abellio	YX11CPZ	Go-Ahead
YX09HKP	RATP - London	YX10FFK	Abellio	YX11CTE	Metrobus
YX09HKT	RATP - London	YX10FFL	Abellio	YX11CTF	Metrobus
YX09HKU	RATP - London	YX10FFM	Abellio	YX11CTK	Metrobus
YX09HKV	RATP - London	YX10FFN	Abellio	YX11CVC	Dial-a-Ride
YX09HKZ	RATP - London	YX10FFW	HCT - CT Plus	YX11CVD	Dial-a-Ride
YX09HLA	RATP - London	YX10FFY	Dial-a-Ride	YX11CVE	Dial-a-Ride
YX09HRL	Dial-a-Ride	YX10FFZ	Dial-a-Ride	YX11CVF	Dial-a-Ride
YX09HRM	Dial-a-Ride	YX10FGA	Dial-a-Ride	YX11CVG	Dial-a-Ride
YX09HRN	Dial-a-Ride	YX10FGC	Dial-a-Ride	YX11CVV	Dial-a-Ride
YX09HRO	Dial-a-Ride	YX10FGD	Dial-a-Ride	YX11CVW	Dial-a-Ride
YX10AYD	HCT - CT Plus	YX10FGE	Dial-a-Ride	YX11CVY	Dial-a-Ride
YX10AYF	HCT - CT Plus	YX10FGF	Dial-a-Ride	YX11CVZ	Dial-a-Ride
YX10BCU	Metroline	YX10FGG	Dial-a-Ride	YX11EVG	Dial-a-Ride
YX10BCV	Metroline	YX11AEA	Abellio	YX11FSF	Dial-a-Ride
YX10BCY	Metroline	YX11AEB	Abellio	YX11FSG	Dial-a-Ride
YX10BCZ	Metroline	YX11AED	Abellio	YX11FSJ	Dial-a-Ride
YX10BDE	Metroline	YX11AEE	Abellio	YX11FSK	Dial-a-Ride
YX10BDF	Metroline	YX11AEF	Abellio	YX11FSL	Dial-a-Ride
YX10BDO	Metroline	YX11AEG	Abellio	YX11FSN	Dial-a-Ride
YX10BDU	Metroline	YX11AEJ	Abellio	YX11FSO	Dial-a-Ride
YX10BDV	Metroline	YX11AEK	Abellio	YX11FSP	Dial-a-Ride
YX10BDY	Metroline	YX11AEL	Abellio	YX11FSS	Dial-a-Ride
YX10BDZ	Metroline	YX11AEM	Abellio	YX11FSU	Dial-a-Ride
YX10BEJ	Metroline	YX11AEN	Abellio	YX11FSV	Dial-a-Ride
YX10BEO	Metroline	YX11AEO	Abellio	YX11FSY	Dial-a-Ride
YX10BEU	Metroline	YX11AEP	Abellio	YX11FSZ	Dial-a-Ride
YX10BEY	Metroline	YX11AET	Abellio	YX11FTA	Dial-a-Ride
YX10BFA	Metroline	YX11AEU	Metroline	YX11FYS	Go-Ahead
YX10BFE	Metroline	YX11AEV	Metroline	YX11FYT	Go-Ahead
YX10BFF	Metroline	YX11AEW	Metroline	YX11FYU	Go-Ahead
YX10BFJ	Metroline	YX11AEY	Metroline	YX11FYV	Go-Ahead
YX10BFK	Metroline	YX11AEZ	Metroline	YX11FYW	Go-Ahead
YX10BFL	Metroline	YX11AFA	Metroline	YX11FYY	Go-Ahead
YX10BFM	Metroline	YX11AFE	Metroline	YX11FYZ	Go-Ahead
YX10BFN	Metroline	YX11AFF	Metroline	YX11FZA	Transdev
YX10BFO	Metroline	YX11AFJ	Metroline	YX11FZB	Transdev
YX10BFP	Metroline	YX11AFK	Tower Transit	YX11FZC	Transdev
YX10BFU	Metroline	YX11AFN	Tower Transit	YX11FZD	Transdev
YX10BFV	Metroline	YX11AFO	Tower Transit	YX11FZE	Transdev
YX10BFY	Metroline	YX11AFU	Tower Transit	YX11FZF	Transdev
YX10BFZ	Metroline	YX11AFV	Tower Transit	YX11FZG	Transdev
YX10BGE	Metroline	YX11AFY	Tower Transit	YX11FZH	Transdev
YX10BGF	Metroline	YX11AFZ	Tower Transit	YX11FZJ	Transdev
YX10BGK	Metroline	YX11AGO	Tower Transit	YX11FZK	Transdev
YX10BGO	Metroline	YX11AGU	Go-Ahead	YX11FZL	Transdev
YX10BGU	Metroline	YX11AHA	Abellio	YX11FZM	Transdev
YX10BGV	Tower Transit	YX11AHC	Abellio	YX11FZN	Transdev
YX10BGY	Tower Transit	YX11AHD	Abellio	YX11FZO	Transdev
YX10EBA	Abellio	YX11AHE	Abellio	YX11FZP	Transdev
YX10EBC	Abellio	YX11AHF	Abellio	YX11FZR	Transdev
YX10EBD	Abellio	YX11AHG	Abellio	YX11FZS	Transdev
YX10EBF	Abellio	YX11AHJ	Abellio	YX11FZT	Transdev
YX10EBG	Abellio	YX11AHK	Abellio	YX11FZU	Transdev
YX10EBJ	Abellio	YX11AHL	Abellio	YX11FZV	Transdev
YX10EBK	Abellio	YX11AHN	Abellio	YX11FZW	Transdev
YX10EBL	Abellio	YX11AHO	Abellio	YX11FZY	Transdev
YX10EBM	Abellio	YX11AHP	Abellio	YX11FZZ	Transdev
YX10FEF	Abellio	YX11AHU	Abellio	YX11GBE	Transdev
YX10FEG	Abellio	YX11CNJ	Transdev	YX11GBF	Transdev
YX10FEH	Abellio	YX11CNK	Metroline	YX11GBO	Transdev
YX10FEJ	Abellio	YX11CNN	Metroline	YX11GBU	Transdev
YX10FEK	Abellio	YX11CNO	Metroline	YX11GBV	Transdev
YX10FEM	Abellio	YX11CNU	Metroline	YX11GBY	Transdev
YX10FEO	Abellio	YX11CNV	Metroline	YX11GBZ	Transdev
YX10FEP	Abellio	YX11CNY	Metroline	YX11GCF	Transdev
YX10FET	Abellio	YX11COH	Transdev	YX11GCK	Transdev
YX10FEU	Abellio	YX11COJ	Transdev	YX11GCO	Transdev
YX10FEV	Abellio	YX11CPE	Go-Ahead	YX11GCU	Transdev
YX10FFA	Abellio	YX11CPF	Go-Ahead	YX11GCV	Transdev
YX10FFB	Abellio	YX11CPK	Go-Ahead	YX11GCY	Transdev
YX10FFC	Abellio	YX11CPN	Go-Ahead	YX11GCZ	Transdev
YX10FFD	Abellio	YX11CPO	Go-Ahead	YX11GDA	Transdev
YX10FFE	Abellio	YX11CPU	Go-Ahead	YX11GDE	Transdev
YX10FFG	Abellio	YX11CPV	Go-Ahead	YX11GDF	Transdev
YX10FFH	Abellio	YX11CPY	Go-Ahead	YX11HOA	Abellio

YX11HPA	Abellio	YX12DKV	Metroline	YX13AGY	Metrobus
YX11HPC	Abellio	YX12DKY	Metroline	YX13AGZ	Metrobus
YX11HPE	Abellio	YX12DLD	Abellio	YX13AHA	Metrobus
YX11HPF	Abellio	YX12DLE	Abellio	YX13AHC	Metrobus
YX11HPJ	Abellio	YX12DLF	Abellio	YX13AHD	Metrobus
YX11HPL	Abellio	YX12DLJ	Abellio	YX13AHE	Metrobus
YX11HPN	Abellio	YX12DLK	Abellio	YX13AHF	Metrobus
YX12AAJ	Tower Transit	YX12DLN	Abellio	YX13AHG	Metrobus
YX12ABF	Tower Transit	YX12DLO	Abellio	YX13AHJ	Metrobus
YX12ABK	Tower Transit	YX12DLU	Abellio	YX13AHK	Metrobus
YX12AEA	Tower Transit	YX12DLV	Abellio	YX13AHL	Metrobus
YX12AED	Tower Transit	YX12DLY	Abellio	YX13AJO	Metrobus
YX12AEF	Tower Transit	YX12DLZ	Abellio	YX13AJU	Metrobus
YX12AEO	Tower Transit	YX12FNG	RATP - London	YX13AJV	Metrobus
YX12AEP	Tower Transit	YX12FNH	RATP - London	YX13AJY	Metrobus
YX12AEU	Tower Transit	YX12FNJ	RATP - London	YX13BJE	Go-Ahead
YX12AEW	Tower Transit	YX12FNK	RATP - London	YX13BJF	Go-Ahead
YX12AEY	Tower Transit	YX12FNL	RATP - London	YX13BJJ	Go-Ahead
YX12AFK	Metroline	YX12FNM	RATP - London	YX13BJK	Go-Ahead
YX12AFO	Metroline	YX12FNN	RATP - London	YX13BJO	Go-Ahead
YX12AFU	Metroline	YX12FNO	RATP - London	YX13BJU	Go-Ahead
YX12AFV	Tower Transit	YX12FNP	RATP - London	YX13BJV	Go-Ahead
YX12AFZ	Tower Transit	YX12FNR	RATP - London	YX13BJY	Go-Ahead
YX12AGY	Tower Transit	YX12FNS	RATP - London	YX13BJZ	Go-Ahead
YX12AGZ	Tower Transit	YX12FNT	RATP - London	YX13BKA	Go-Ahead
YX12AHJ	Tower Transit	YX12FNU	RATP - London	YX13BKD	Go-Ahead
YX12AHK	Tower Transit	YX12FNV	RATP - London	YX13BKE	Go-Ahead
YX12AJY	Tower Transit	YX12FNW	RATP - London	YX13BKF	Go-Ahead
YX12AKK	Tower Transit	YX12FNY	RATP - London	YX13BKG	Go-Ahead
YX12AKN	Tower Transit	YX12FNZ	RATP - London	YX13BKJ	Go-Ahead
YX12AKP	Tower Transit	YX12FOA	RATP - London	YX13BKK	Go-Ahead
YX12AKU	Tower Transit	YX12FOC	RATP - London	YX13BKL	Go-Ahead
YX12AKV	Tower Transit	YX12FOD	RATP - London	YX13BKN	Go-Ahead
YX12AKY	Tower Transit	YX12FOF	RATP - London	YX13EFM	Abellio
YX12AKZ	Tower Transit	YX12FOH	RATP - London	YX13EFN	Abellio
YX12AMK	Tower Transit	YX12FOJ	RATP - London	YX13EFO	Abellio
YX12AOF	Tower Transit	YX12FON	RATP - London	YX13EFP	Abellio
YX12AON	Tower Transit	YX12FOP	RATP - London	YX13EFR	Abellio
YX12AOS	Metroline	YX12FPA	Go-Ahead	YX13EFS	Abellio
YX12AOT	Metroline	YX12FPC	Go-Ahead	YX13EFT	Abellio
YX12APK	Metroline	YX12FPD	Go-Ahead	YX13EFU	Abellio
YX12ARZ	Tower Transit	YX12FPE	Go-Ahead	YX13EFV	Abellio
YX12ATF	Metroline	YX12FPF	Go-Ahead	YX13EFW	Abellio
YX12ATN	Metroline	YX12FPG	Go-Ahead	YX13EFY	Abellio
YX12AUA	Tower Transit	YX12FPJ	Go-Ahead	YX13EFZ	Abellio
YX12AVJ	Tower Transit	YX12FPK	Go-Ahead	YX13EHE	Abellio
YX12AVT	Metroline	YX12FPL	Go-Ahead	YX13EHF	Abellio
YX12AWU	Tower Transit	YX12FPN	Go-Ahead	YX13EHG	Abellio
YX12AXU	Tower Transit	YX12FPO	Go-Ahead	YX13EHH	Abellio
YX12AXV	Tower Transit	YX12FPP	Go-Ahead	YX13EHJ	Abellio
YX12AYF	Tower Transit	YX12FPT	Go-Ahead	YX13EHK	Abellio
YX12AYK	Metroline	YX12FPU	Go-Ahead	YX13EHL	Abellio
YX12AYZ	Tower Transit	YX12FPV	Go-Ahead	YX13EHM	Abellio
YX12AZA	Tower Transit	YX12GHA	Abellio	YX13EHN	Abellio
YX12AZG	Metroline	YX12GHB	Abellio	YX13EHO	Abellio
YX12AZN	Tower Transit	YX12GHD	Abellio	YX57HBZ	Dial-a-Ride
YX12AZW	Tower Transit	YX12GHF	Abellio	YX58DTV	Abellio
YX12CGE	Dial-a-Ride	YX12GHG	Abellio	YX58DTY	Abellio
YX12CGF	Dial-a-Ride	YX12GHH	Abellio	YX58DTZ	Abellio
YX12CGG	Dial-a-Ride	YX12GHJ	RATP - London	YX58DUA	Metroline
YX12CGK	Dial-a-Ride	YX12GHK	RATP - London	YX58DUH	Metroline
YX12CGO	Dial-a-Ride	YX12GHN	RATP - London	YX58DUJ	Metroline
YX12CGU	Dial-a-Ride	YX12GHO	RATP - London	YX58DUU	Metroline
YX12DHZ	Tower Transit	YX12GHU	RATP - London	YX58DUV	RATP - London
YX12DJD	Tower Transit	YX13AFF	Metrobus	YX58DUY	RATP - London
YX12DJE	Tower Transit	YX13AFJ	Metrobus	YX58DVA	RATP - London
YX12DKA	Metroline	YX13AFK	Metrobus	YX58DVB	RATP - London
YX12DKD	Metroline	YX13AFN	Metrobus	YX58DVC	RATP - London
YX12DKE	Metroline	YX13AFO	Metrobus	YX58DVF	RATP - London
YX12DKF	Metroline	YX13AFU	Metrobus	YX58DVG	RATP - London
YX12DKJ	Metroline	YX13AFV	Metrobus	YX58DVH	RATP - London
YX12DKK	Metroline	YX13AFY	Metrobus	YX58DVJ	RATP - London
YX12DKL	Metroline	YX13AFZ	Metrobus	YX58DVK	RATP - London
YX12DKN	Metroline	YX13AGO	Metrobus	YX58DVL	RATP - London
YX12DKO	Metroline	YX13AGU	Metrobus	YX58DVM	RATP - London
YX12DKU	Metroline	YX13AGV	Metrobus	YX58DVN	RATP - London

YX58DVO	RATP - London	YX58FPT	Metroline	YX60CBY	RATP - London
YX58DVP	RATP - London	YX58FPU	Metroline	YX60CCA	RATP - London
YX58DVS	RATP - London	YX58FPV	Metroline	YX60CCD	RATP - London
YX58DVT	RATP - London	YX58FPY	Metroline	YX60CCE	RATP - London
YX58DVU	RATP - London	YX58FRC	Metroline	YX60CCF	RATP - London
YX58DVV	RATP - London	YX58FRD	Metroline	YX60CCJ	RATP - London
YX58DVW	RATP - London	YX58GSO	Dial-a-Ride	YX60CCK	RATP - London
YX58DVY	Metroline	YX58GSY	Dial-a-Ride	YX60CCN	RATP - London
YX58DVZ	Metroline	YX58GSZ	Dial-a-Ride	YX60CCO	RATP - London
YX58DWA	Metroline	YX58GTF	Dial-a-Ride	YX60CJE	Dial-a-Ride
YX58DWC	Metroline	YX58GTU	Dial-a-Ride	YX60CJF	Dial-a-Ride
YX58DWD	Metroline	YX58GTY	Dial-a-Ride	YX60CJJ	Dial-a-Ride
YX58DWE	Metroline	YX58GTZ	Dial-a-Ride	YX60CJO	Dial-a-Ride
YX58DWF	Metroline	YX58HVA	Metroline	YX60CJU	Dial-a-Ride
YX58DWG	Metroline	YX58HVB	Metroline	YX60CJV	Dial-a-Ride
YX58DWJ	Metroline	YX58HVC	Tower Transit	YX60CJY	Dial-a-Ride
YX58DWK	RATP - London	YX58HVD	Tower Transit	YX60CKG	Dial-a-Ride
YX58DWL	Metroline	YX58HVE	Tower Transit	YX60CKJ	Dial-a-Ride
YX58DWM	Metroline	YX58HVM	Metroline	YX60CKK	Dial-a-Ride
YX58DWN	Metroline	YX59AAO	Dial-a-Ride	YX60CKU	Dial-a-Ride
YX58DWO	Metroline	YX59ABN	Dial-a-Ride	YX60CKV	Dial-a-Ride
YX58DWP	Metroline	YX59ABU	Dial-a-Ride	YX60CLV	Dial-a-Ride
YX58DWU	Metroline	YX59ABV	Dial-a-Ride	YX60CLY	Dial-a-Ride
YX58DWV	Metroline	YX59ABZ	Dial-a-Ride	YX60DXL	Tower Transit
YX58DWY	Metroline	YX59ACF	Dial-a-Ride	YX60DXM	Tower Transit
YX58DWZ	Metroline	YX59ACJ	Dial-a-Ride	YX60DXO	Tower Transit
YX58DXA	RATP - London	YX59ACO	Dial-a-Ride	YX60DXP	Tower Transit
YX58DXB	Metrobus	YX59ACU	Dial-a-Ride	YX60DXT	Go-Ahead
YX58DXC	Metrobus	YX59ACV	Dial-a-Ride	YX60DXU	Go-Ahead
YX58DXD	Metrobus	YX59ACY	Dial-a-Ride	YX60DXW	Go-Ahead
YX58EET	Dial-a-Ride	YX59ADO	Dial-a-Ride	YX60DYN	Dial-a-Ride
YX58EEU	Dial-a-Ride	YX59ADU	Dial-a-Ride	YX60DYO	Dial-a-Ride
YX58EEV	Dial-a-Ride	YX59ADV	Dial-a-Ride	YX60DYP	Dial-a-Ride
YX58EEW	Dial-a-Ride	YX59ADZ	Dial-a-Ride	YX60DYS	Dial-a-Ride
YX58EEY	Dial-a-Ride	YX59AEA	Dial-a-Ride	YX60DYT	Dial-a-Ride
YX58EEZ	Dial-a-Ride	YX59AEB	Dial-a-Ride	YX60DYU	Dial-a-Ride
YX58EFA	Dial-a-Ride	YX59BYA	Transdev	YX60DYY	Dial-a-Ride
YX58EFC	Dial-a-Ride	YX59BYB	Transdev	YX60DZA	Dial-a-Ride
YX58EFD	Dial-a-Ride	YX59BYC	Transdev	YX60DZF	Dial-a-Ride
YX58EFE	Dial-a-Ride	YX59BYD	Transdev	YX60DZG	Dial-a-Ride
YX58EFF	Dial-a-Ride	YX59BYF	Transdev	YX60DZJ	Dial-a-Ride
YX58EFN	Dial-a-Ride	YX59BYG	Transdev	YX60DZL	Dial-a-Ride
YX58EFO	Dial-a-Ride	YX59BYH	Transdev	YX60EOE	Go-Ahead
YX58EGD	Dial-a-Ride	YX59BYJ	Abellio	YX60EOF	Go-Ahead
YX58EGE	Dial-a-Ride	YX59BYK	Abellio	YX60EOG	Go-Ahead
YX58EGF	Dial-a-Ride	YX59BYL	Abellio	YX60EOH	Go-Ahead
YX58EGJ	Dial-a-Ride	YX59BYM	Abellio	YX60EOJ	Go-Ahead
YX58EGZ	Dial-a-Ride	YX59BYN	Abellio	YX60EOK	Go-Ahead
YX58EHB	Dial-a-Ride	YX59BYO	Abellio	YX60EOL	Go-Ahead
YX58EHG	Dial-a-Ride	YX59BYP	Abellio	YX60EOO	Go-Ahead
YX58EHH	Dial-a-Ride	YX59BYR	Abellio	YX60EOP	Go-Ahead
YX58EHJ	Dial-a-Ride	YX59BYS	Abellio	YX60EPO	Go-Ahead
YX58EHK	Dial-a-Ride	YX59BYT	Abellio	YX60EPP	Go-Ahead
YX58EHL	Dial-a-Ride	YX59BYU	Abellio	YX60EPU	Go-Ahead
YX58EHR	Dial-a-Ride	YX59BYV	Abellio	YX60EVR	Dial-a-Ride
YX58FOF	Metroline	YX59BYW	Abellio	YX60FBU	Go-Ahead
YX58FOH	Metroline	YX60BZA	Transdev	YX60FBY	Go-Ahead
YX58FOJ	Metroline	YX60BZB	Transdev	YX60FBZ	Go-Ahead
YX58FOK	Metroline	YX60BZC	Transdev	YX60FCA	Go-Ahead
YX58FOM	Metroline	YX60BZD	Transdev	YX60FCC	Go-Ahead
YX58FON	Metroline	YX60BZE	Transdev	YX60FCD	Go-Ahead
YX58FOP	Metroline	YX60BZF	Transdev	YX60FCE	Go-Ahead
YX58FOT	Metroline	YX60BZG	Transdev	YX60FCF	Go-Ahead
YX58FOU	Metroline	YX60BZH	RATP - London	YX60FCG	Go-Ahead
YX58FOV	Metroline	YX60BZJ	RATP - London	YX60FCL	Go-Ahead
YX58FPA	Metroline	YX60BZN	Metroline	YX60FCM	Go-Ahead
YX58FPC	Metroline	YX60BZO	Metroline	YX60FCO	Go-Ahead
YX58FPD	Metroline	YX60CAA	RATP - London	YX60FCP	Go-Ahead
YX58FPE	Metroline	YX60CAE	RATP - London	YX60FCU	Go-Ahead
YX58FPF	Metroline	YX60CAO	RATP - London	YX60FCV	Go-Ahead
YX58FPG	Metroline	YX60CAU	RATP - London	YX60FCY	Go-Ahead
YX58FPJ	Metroline	YX60CAV	RATP - London	YX60FCZ	Go-Ahead
YX58FPK	Metroline	YX60CBF	RATP - London	YX60FDA	Go-Ahead
YX58FPL	Metroline	YX60CBO	RATP - London	YX60FSN	Go-Ahead
YX58FPN	Metroline	YX60CBU	RATP - London	YX60FSO	Go-Ahead
YX58FPO	Metroline	YX60CBV	RATP - London	YX60FSP	Go-Ahead